THE HERAKLES THEME

THE HERAKLES THEME

The Adaptations of the Hero in Literature from Homer to the Twentieth Century

G. KARL GALINSKY

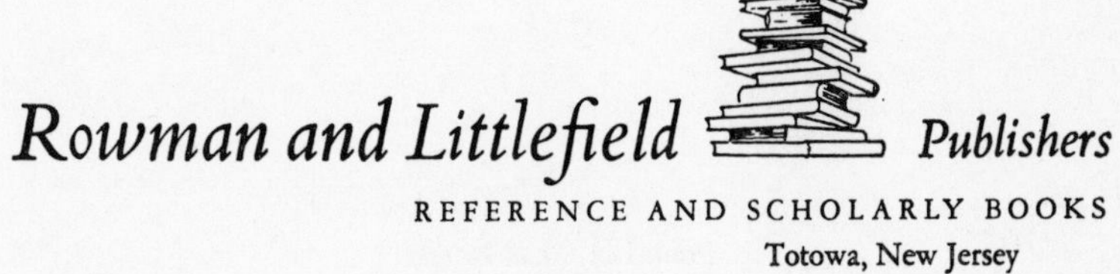

REFERENCE AND SCHOLARLY BOOKS
Totowa, New Jersey

Published in the United States in 1972 by Rowman and Littlefield

The Harvard University Press and the Loeb Classical Library have granted permission to quote short passages from *Hesiod*, trans. by H. E. G. White; *Isocrates*, trans. by G. B. Norlin and L. R. Van Hook; *Diodorus of Sicily*, trans. by C. H. Oldfather; *Seneca's Tragedies*, trans. by F. J. Miller; Epictetus, *The Discourses*, trans. by W. A. Oldfather; and *Valerius Flaccus*, trans. by J. H. Mozley.

The quotation from T. S. Eliot on page 269 is from 'Little Gidding' in *Four Quartets*, copyright 1943 by T. S. Eliot; reprinted by permission of Harcourt, Brace, Jovanovich, Inc., and of Faber and Faber, Ltd.

ISBN: 0–87471–113–4

Printed in Great Britain

FOR MARIANNE

Contents

Foreword

Every generation needs heroes and symbolic figures to embody its ideals and emotions. In the first half of the nineteenth century Prometheus, the indomitable opponent of tyrannous power, was the exemplar that geniuses like Beethoven and Shelley chose. Then a contemporary figure, Byron, captured the admiration of free spirits and held it until Tennyson's Lancelot, or Melville's Captain Ahab, or Conan Doyle's Sherlock Holmes, or some other new hero—or heroine: Florence Nightingale, Queen Victoria—superseded him. Our own century has seen the saturnine ascendancy of Oedipus, the revival of Ulysses, and a strange incursion of Buddha. On the other hand Don Juan, with his concern for etiquette and intrigue as well as for erotics, has retired for a while from a world that prefers less subtle carnality; and the era of nuclear power seems to have forgotten Faust, and the age of democracy finds Don Quixote too aristocratic to be acceptable. Christmases at present are less Pickwickian or Scroogian: air-pilots prefer not to remember Icarus. In matters of religion St. Augustine has yielded to St. Francis, St. Peter to St. John, Torquemada to John Wesley. Yet, though fashions change, some emblematic figures of this kind always remain part of the mind of our western civilization, encouraging us and warning us, affecting our inner yearnings and controlling the unconscious sources of our decisions, whether we like them or not. By understanding them, and our predecessors' attitudes to them, better, we understand ourselves better.

Herakles—as philhellenes like to call Hercules now, to rescue him from latinization—is undoubtedly one of these master-heroes. But, as usual, his popularity has varied greatly from epoch to epoch. At times he has been remembered merely as a personification of enormous strength—the prototype of the 'muscle-man'. When regarded in that light, he is apt to be dismissed by conventional-minded people who assume that brawn always precludes brain, as stupid and uninteresting. This is entirely wrong. As Dr. Galinsky's book clearly shows, many great writers and artists have found Herakles a fascinating subject for creative interpretation.

Yet, surprisingly, this is the first full survey in English of the triumphs and agonies of the Herculean man since he first appeared in early Greek literature and art; and previous studies in other languages have not been numerous. Perhaps scholars have been influenced by the ancient bias of the Athenians and Ionians against this typically Doric hero. Or perhaps the neglect was due to the fact that academic writers naturally prefer to study men of thought rather than men of action. Happily, however, both for scholars and for the general reader Dr. Galinsky has not been deterred by any such prejudice from giving us this much needed study. Under his guidance we can sympathetically follow the fortunes of Herakles, tragic and comic, pitiable and enviable, through the whole course of European literature. In reading it we are doing much more than trace the vagaries of creative mythology. We are also exploring the ideals, hopes and fears of a man faced with the arduous task of protecting and preserving human society from its natural enemies such as writers have seen Herakles for over two thousand years. If this should help to replace the era of Oedipus with an era of admiration for the hero who laboured to rid the world of monsters, so much the better.

Trinity College, Dublin W. B. STANFORD
January, 1972

Preface

This book is a study of the tradition of Herakles in western literature from Homer to our time. It is not a *catalogue raisonné* of all references to Herakles in literature, nor does it pretend to be literary criticism. Its aim is to survey, in both descriptive and interpretive terms, the most significant adaptations of Herakles. I have tried to emphasize throughout the more original and creative portraits of the hero; my discussion of Euripides and Hölderlin, for instance, thus is far more extensive than my discussion of Silius Italicus or Rotrou. In the same vein, Chapter 9, with the exception of Le Fèvre, is largely a survey of a good many authors, whereas Chapter 11 is a more detailed interpretation and even *explication de texte* of a few, but very remarkable adaptations of the theme.

The need for a literary study of Herakles, even in Greek and Roman literature, requires no lengthy explanation. Most studies concerning the hero in ancient times have been written by scholars of mythology, religion, or art, who have tended to analyse his role in a given poem or play merely in terms of the evidence they present for certain cult practices, local legends, or myths. In spite of the deplorable lack of a comprehensive mythological study of the hero—the compilations in the mythological handbooks cannot be regarded as such—this approach has led to a considerable neglect of Herakles as a literary figure and of the question why an author, to suit his purposes, would stress and develop certain traits of the hero. The Greek period was summarily surveyed in the thesis of a French scholar one hundred years ago. There are many scattered articles and monographs on select phases and authors of the classical and vernacular traditions. But this is the first time the development has been traced continuously from ancient to modern times.

As for the classical period, I have not tried to present a synthesis of scholarly or critical opinion on the various works and authors. Anyone who knows classical scholars also knows that such syntheses are hard to come by, and in fact would tend to obscure and dull rather than enlighten and stimulate. In some cases I have adopted a point of view that seemed most cogent to me, although I recognize the merits of the opposite point of view; my discussion of Sophocles' *Trachiniae* is one example. In others—my discussion of Herakles in Apollonius' *Argonautica*, for instance—my treatment is more of a dialogue with a recent, critical discussion of the same theme. Often I have, of course, continued and built on the arguments of earlier critics. Lastly, I am immodest enough to claim some originality in discussing the adaptations, e.g. of Vergil and Ovid, and even Euripides' *Alcestis*. Merely by placing specific adaptations of Herakles in the context of his literary tradition I hope to have contributed some new perspectives and points of view. My treatment of the modern tradition is mostly that of an inquisitive amateur—an ideal highly prized in fifth-century Athens—and I can only apologize for omitting, either through ignorance or misjudgement, any major modern variations on the classical theme. Compression and reduction of the manuscript have led to the elimination of additional documentation especially in the footnotes.

The illustrations I have chosen are not meant to reflect the whole range of Herakles' many roles. In their selection I have purposely emphasized the comic aspect of Herakles, because it has been largely forgotten that, in literature, the Greeks knew him best and loved him most in his comic role. The many fragments from Greek comedy cannot speak as eloquently as the paintings and statuettes.

I am profoundly grateful to many friends, and colleagues, and to my wife in particular, for help in collecting material and preparing this work for publication. Professors Helen H. Bacon, E. V. George, and J. P. Sullivan read earlier drafts or individual chapters, and Professor W. B. Stanford commented on the entire manuscript. My debt to his *Ulysses Theme* is obvious. For assistance on special problems thanks are due to Mrs. Ann Hanson, and to Professors Emmett C. Bennett, Jr., Julius S. Held, and Michael Jameson. For help in securing the illustrations I am indebted particularly to Dr. Hellmut Sichtermann, and also to M. Bieber, R. A. G. Carson, M. Chuzeville, F. F. Jones, R. Noll, and A. Mayer-Meintschl.

It is my pleasure to thank the American Council of Learned Societies for awarding me a fellowship in 1968–9, and the University of Texas for granting me a leave of absence during that period. I am very grateful to the Principessa Margherita Rospigliosi for her gracious hospitality and to her, Professor Frank Brown, Mr. Jay Deiss, and Mrs. Inez Longobardi for letting me use the facilities of the American Academy in Rome. Thanks are also due to the Vatican Library, the German Archaeological Institute in Rome, the Marciana in Venice, and the Universitätsbibliothek in Basle for granting me ready assistance. I also acknowledge with gratitude the generous manner in which the Research Institute of the University of Texas has aided this project at most of its stages. Finally, I should like to thank Sir Basil Blackwell for his encouragement and interest in publishing this book.

Austin, August, 1971

List of Illustrations

Introduction

The figure of Herakles in literature is the opposite of what many of his representations in art might lead us to believe.[1] A hero whose only function seemingly is to exude unbending and all-conquering strength appears destined for the grandeur and lifelessness of a majestic monolith and for ready fossilization in proverb or symbol. Yet Herakles met with a kindlier fate in the literary tradition. There he appears in a surprising variety of roles and his myth has been revived many times. While he might not have matched the Apostle Paul or a modern political candidate in being all things to all men, he has proved to be, in the course of more than two and one-half millennia, surprisingly many things to surprisingly many men.

The adaptability of a mythological character, as is well known, is directly dependent on the diversity and latitude of characteristics with which he is endowed in the mythological tradition. A creative writer, of course, will not consider himself rigidly bound by the tradition and will propose certain modifications as he adapts the theme.[2] On the other hand, unless he is willing to risk great controversy and be rejected by most of his audience, he will be careful not to present too many radical and innovative additions to the traditional characterization. Some mythological figures, therefore, can be reborn only under a favourable psychological or historical constellation on the firmament of literary history. Oedipus is such a figure, and he would lose his identity if he appeared in one century as the great, tragic sufferer, in another as the paragon of superhuman physical prowess and bravado, in another as the ideal nobleman and courtier, in another as the incarnation of rhetoric and intelligence and wisdom, in another as the divine mediator and a model of that way of life whose reward can only be heavenly, in another as a metaphysical struggler, and in yet another as a comic, lecherous, gluttonous monster or as a romantic lover, and in still another as the exemplar of virtue. Herakles, even in the same century, could assume all of these roles which are heterogeneous but not out of character. The traditional range of his qualities was varied and complex enough to be susceptible to ever new interpretations and thus to assure the hero survival and popularity. A writer did not have to break with an accepted tradition to make his Herakles relevant to his society or his own purposes. But since the tradition was uncommonly varied and ambivalent, a writer had to choose those aspects that he wanted to emphasize and develop. Even Euripides, who initiated the most far-reaching re-evaluation of Herakles by internalizing his struggles and labours and viewing him in purely human terms, did not have to add much to the mythological foundation.

This adaptable conception of the archetypal Herakles was not the result of one writer's work or genius. The first author who mentions him, Homer, does so only in passing and clearly presumes that his reader or listener is quite familiar with the hero's life and exploits. Nor do later writers, except for the mythographers and historians, bother greatly with spelling out the facts. This, in part, accounted for Herakles' attractiveness, at least in antiquity, for the common knowledge of the 'factual' material about him freed the writer to set out immediately on his interpretive and creative task. The reason is that Herakles was by far the most popular hero of the Greeks. His origins belong to the folktale, the *Märchen*, where he initially seems to have been no more than the type of strong boy who recurs, with a different *ethnikon*, as Jack the Giant-killer, *der starke Hans*, Juan de l'Os or Giovanni Benforte.[3] Unlike his brethren in other lands, however, Herakles did not remain confined to the green pastures and pure fantasies of a dreamworld. The essential change in his historical development came when he entered into myth and cult. When and where this took place has been the subject of much scholarly debate, but things such as *Märchen* are known to be elusive, even for scholars, and the Greeks themselves were rather nonchalant about Herakles' chronology; he is treated, for instance, as belonging to a past age in the *Iliad* whereas he appears as Odysseus' contemporary in the *Odyssey* (21. 13–30). While any efforts to establish a systematic chronology of Greek myth are doomed because such a chronology simply never existed,[4] we can trace the Herakles myth at least to Mycenean times. An eminent scholar of Greek religion, who is humble enough to admit that 'strict, logical proof is not possible', has pointed out that many Greek mythological cycles, among them that of Herakles, are constantly connected with Mycenean sites.[5] Two of the great centres where Herakles was localized were Thebes and Tiryns. Now Tiryns flourished during the Mycenean age, whereas it led a meagre existence after the downfall of Mycenean civilization. It is therefore extremely unlikely that Herakles should have been so strongly associated with Tiryns only *après le déluge*, and thus his localization there—and elsewhere—more reasonably belongs to Mycenean times. Tiryns was a vassal town of Mycenae; Herakles thus became the vassal of Eurystheus who was the legendary King of Mycenae.

The Herakles of the folktale had belonged to all of Greece, and the mythical Herakles was the one true Panhellenic hero. He was not merely the property of the Dorians, into whose genealogy he was fitted rather indirectly, but his cult and shrines were distributed all over Greece, Attica being a splendid example.[6] As a mythological and cultic hero, Herakles replaced, in many towns, local heroes whose exploits promptly were absorbed into his mythological baggage train. Because he was the national hero of Greece, all kinds of characteristics were attributed or transferred to him, and Herakles' capacity to absorb these is matched only by his ability to complete even the most difficult labours. From this confluence and diversity of traditions a hero arose who, in one word, was composite.

If we try to explain this development, as much as it can be explained, we can take as its starting point his prodigious strength, which set him apart from and elevated him above his fellow men. Purely materially, this meant that no feat was impossible for him, which all by itself gives a story-teller or poet some latitude. Moreover, like most human qualities, physical strength is ambivalent. It can be used for a bad purpose, with terrifying results; this is the Herakles who kills a host in rage, who ransacks a house to heap up a pyre for his own children, who kills his wife in a frenzy or deflowers and impregnates fifty girls in one night. But if Herakles' strength and prowess were superhuman so were his weaknesses, and because he carried everything to the excess, he could also become the most moving symbol of the human condition.

This tendency of the hero to push everything to an extreme and his very abnormality were other reasons why many writers were attracted to him. A hero who is far out of the ordinary is, in many respects, easier to treat and more appealing than, to take but one example, the bourgeois protagonist or average citizen of domestic drama. The variegated nature of Herakles' traditional qualities prevented him from being frozen in a schematized role. Most writers, to be sure, in both the classical and post-classical tradition chose to emphasize but one of the many aspects of Herakles, but cumulatively, they never forgot the diversity of the hero's roles and, as Goethe sadly realized, an integrated portrait of this most complex of all mythological figures was near impossible. One particular characterization of Herakles might hold sway during a certain period, as did the exemplar of virtue in the Renaissance and the Baroque, but none was strong enough to obliterate his other traits and no one portrait of Herakles established itself as the definitive one. While taken together, then, the majority of writers kept up the memory of the hero's heterogeneous traits, others provided a further creative impetus by exploiting the tensions which naturally arose from these diverse characteristics. Once more, the result was anything but a monolithic tradition.

To return to Herakles' uses of his strength: while some authors developed its negative implications, the other and predominant part of the tradition emphasized Herakles' use of his strength for his personal or, more frequently, the common good. This had its basis in cult; all over Greece Herakles was worshipped as Ἀλεξίκακος, the averter of evil, which was understood in its broadest sense—war, death, ghosts, sickness, and the trials and tribulations of life in general. Against all these the common man called upon him as a trusty and invincible divine helper. His role as the boon companion in Euripides' *Alcestis* originates from there and so, somewhat more removed from the level of folklore, does the conception of him as the divine mediator, dispenser of God's blessings, and rival of Christ especially at the time of the Roman empire. The view of Herakles as a culture hero, which profoundly influenced the post-classical tradition, also has its roots here; in ancient Greece he already appears as the educational patron of the

Ephebes. Even then the range of his activities was not limited to Greece; he extended Greek influence around the Mediterranean countries, becoming the only common hero they have ever known.

The toiling Herakles, whose good deeds finally ensure his divinity, was not regarded merely as an external bringer of aid, but served as a positive example of human aspirations that called for emulation. Once more, the hero did not impose himself, and different attitudes to his achievement were possible.[7] One could view Herakles as a god, direct one's thoughts to heaven, and forget about one's earthly life. His cult then could serve as a vehicle of escapism, as religions do at times. In literature, this view of the myth found its greatest resonance in the works of Seneca, Hölderlin, and Browning. Or one could stay in this world, as he had done, and focus on his labours and struggles—in short, his heroism—by which he had gained final acceptance into heaven. The two attitudes are combined perhaps most explicitly at the end of Sophocles' *Philoctetes*, where Herakles appears as the *deus ex machina* to bring a solution that is entirely dependent on human effort, toil, and co-operation. Many writers, especially in classical times, would take this view and emphasize this aspect of Herakles. Pindar became the earliest prophet of this Herakles *ethicus*, and the Stoics and Cynics continued the tradition by making Herakles the paragon of their moral and ethical ideals.

This flexibility of Herakles again was no purely literary or philosophical invention. His cult in Greece was unique in that it was dual: he was worshipped as both a god and a hero—ἥρως θεός, as Pindar calls him (*Nem.* 3. 22).[8] Even if the line between hero and god was not always sharply drawn especially in Greek literature, the basic distinction between the two was well known. In contrast to the god, the hero was originally a man who came to enjoy divine honours after his death. The literary evidence overwhelmingly supports the view that Herakles first was a man, then a hero, and then also became a god.[9] To invert this evolutionary process would be going against all plausibility: where, for instance, does a god shed his divinity to become the strong-man of the *Märchen*? The essence of Herakles, then, has been summed up succinctly by one scholar: 'He was born man, became god; suffered labours and gained heaven.'[10] This was a dynamic ideal, which corresponded to one of man's deepest longings: immortality. It was a timeless ideal which, since it was profoundly personal and individual, had to be constantly revised, and the frequency of Herakles' appearance in literature comes in great part from this font.

This Herculean ideal, however, did not become the preserve of paeans on the *kallinikos* and of philosophical eulogies, but offered opportunities for dramatic development. The self-sufficiency of Herakles also contained the roots of *hybris*. Although he rarely became a Promethean figure in the sense that he defied the gods, he was too vital even at the beginning of his literary development to be absorbed into the codified system of Homeric ethic, 'summed up in the word *aidos*, which exhorted all to keep their stations and show respect to those above them—the young to the old, slaves to masters, men to gods'.[11] Herakles was the hero with the inherent capacity to break out of an established pattern and to have a choice open to him, as Prodicus well recognized. This side of Herakles thus was sublimated, added greatly to man's ability to identify with him, and initiated an important development in the literature and also the artistic tradition of the hero.

More intensely, it was the contrast between Herakles the man and Herakles the god that was to determine many of his literary fortunes once the Greeks had ceased, after Aeschylus and Pindar, to look at the world and man with a profound sense of religiosity. It is perhaps the greatest testimony to Herakles' mythopoeic power that after the scepticism and agnosticism of fifth-century Athens had been brought to bear on him and denied him his otherworldly reward, he did not revert to the *Märchen* world but came to claim his place as the noblest incarnation of man's ideals. To Euripides, whose view was followed especially by modern authors, Herakles' greatness was not 'to have been born man and become god', but to have remained man and achieved heroic greatness in purely human terms. So Herakles became the living example of the indomitable human spirit and of a humanity engaged in the never-ending struggle to rise above its own limitations. The man who had become a god in early Greece thus became a man again, without, however, losing his force as an ideal and an inspiration. It was a secular, man-oriented ideal, but it was the basic reason why Herakles retained his momentum and dynamism in secular and man-oriented times and did not become merely a mythological fixture useful for little else than 'to point a moral or adorn a tale'.

The many heterogeneous aspects of this composite personality were held together by the one constant trait which is common to the Herakles' of all periods: more than human strength and endurance. Especially for the trained scholar, who often is *a priori* expected to think in terms of theses, there is always the temptation to perceive and impose an underlying pattern on however original and diverse a topic, and his success in so doing is often taken as an indication of his acumen. But we have to resist this temptation and treat the occurrences of Herakles in literature on their own, individual merits. There are, as we just have outlined, some constant components which make it possible for us to use the term 'tradition' in spite of many diverse ways in which he was adapted. And although Herakles has borne preconceived conclusions—such as that he was primarily the incarnation of Doric manhood—as patiently as his labours, we must not take advantage of his endurance. What needs to be studied is the variety of his manifestations in literature and the many reasons—personal, historical, social and moral, and the reasons of genre—which conditioned an author's response to him. This response has lasted over twenty-seven centuries and we now must turn to its beginning.

NOTES TO THE INTRODUCTION

1. Even as sensitive and well-read an observer as Winckelmann was captivated primarily by Herakles' strength, which had brought him immortality; see his 'Beschreibung des Torso im Belvedere zu Rom', in J. Lessing, ed., *Johann Joachim Winckelmanns Geschichte der Kunst des Alterthums* (Berlin, 1870) 350–3. This is not to say that artists, sculptors in particular, did not try to present a spiritualized Herakles—witness the Herakles Farnese (Plate 1), and the evidence discussed by Susan Woodford, *Exemplum Virtutis: A Study of Heracles in Athens in the Second Half of the Fifth Centruy B.C.* (Columbia Univ. Diss., 1966)—but even there Herakles tends towards the dourly imposing rather than the dynamic.
2. Stanford has some useful remarks on the causes of these variations. See especially his first chapter on 'The Adaptability of Mythical Figures'.
3. The most detailed discussion of this aspect of Herakles is found in Schweitzer

184–240, although it is marred by the ethnographic attempt of seeing in Herakles the representative of the 'Nordic soul' (p. 240). For ancient sources and modern discussions of Herakles' oriental and Asiatic connections see J. E. Fontenrose, *Python* (Berkeley and Los Angeles, 1959) 323 n. 2, and on the relation between myth and folktale, M. Eliade, *Myth and Reality* (New York and Evanston, 1963) 195–202 and G. S. Kirk, *Myth* (Cambridge, 1970) 31–41.

4. So L. Radermacher, *Mythos und Sage bei den Griechen* (Vienna and Leipzig, 1938) 79.
5. M. P. Nilsson, *The Mycenaean Origin of Greek Mythology* (Berkeley and Los Angeles, 1932) 187ff.; cf. T. B. L. Webster, *From Mycenae to Homer* (New York, 1964) 57–8. No name capable of being construed as meaning 'Herakles' has been found on Mycenean tablets so far.
6. The immense evidence is discussed well and concisely by Farnell 94–145 and Preller-Robert 471–765. Only one of the three Dorian tribes, the Hylloi, claimed one of Herakles' sons, Hyllos, as their eponymous hero; see, e.g. Hdt. 9. 26; Schol. Pind. *Ol.* 10. 79; Apollod. 2. 171.
7. Cf. Wilamowitz 37.
8. See, e.g. Paus. 2. 10. 1 (Sicyon) and M. Launey, *Le sanctuaire et le culte d'Héraklès à Thasos* (Paris, 1944). P. Maas' emendation (*MH* 11 [1954] 199) of the Pindaric phrase to ἥρως θεός is therefore unwarranted.
9. The only dissenter is Herodotus (2. 43–4) who postulated an Egyptian origin for Herakles; his account has righly been rejected.
10. Wilamowitz 38: 'Mensch gewesen, Gott geworden; Mühen erduldet, Himmel erworben'.
11. W. K. C. Guthrie, *The Greeks and their Gods* (London, 1950) 241.

CHAPTER I
The Archaic Hero

Homer wrote his epics about the Trojan War and its heroes, and not about Herakles, Greece's most popular hero. The reasons for this are hardly external. Many towns craved association with Herakles, many noble families claimed descent from him, his exploits were on the lips of all people, and there is good reason for assuming the existence of oral and, later, written Herakles epics.[1] But although he refers to him frequently, Homer found Herakles basically unsuitable for his aims, and the preference of the Trojan cycle to Herakles continued in Greek drama which drew far more topics from the former than from the latter.

The reason is that the heroic ideal and code of behaviour of Homer's protagonists could be reconciled only with the greatest of difficulties to what Herakles stood for. The Iliadic hero is constantly striving for glory and honour,[2] which are manifested materially by a prize or trophy, and he is trying to outdo his peers at every turn. He is keenly aware, however, that he is a part of a community of heroes and he badly needs their recognition and applause, for without them, the glory of his deeds, *klea andrōn*, would not survive. Homer does not extol the ideal of lonely splendour and of a lifelong struggle to achieve equality with the gods by one's own works rather than divine grace. The saviour ideal of Herakles is a world apart from chivalrous assistance in combat. The Iliadic hero is not a fiercely independent individualist but almost makes a cult of proper procedure (*themis*) and of paying proper respect (*aidōs*) to whomever proper respect is due.

The *Iliad* may be a poem of force, as it has been called by a recent writer,[3] but such force is accepted only so long as it operates within a well-defined and circumscribed code. Even the most blood-thirsty acts, such as Agamemnon's slaying of Hippolochos (*Il.* 11. 145–7), are carried out not because of love of violence or battle *per se*, but because they bring the hero honour in form of a trophy—the slain man's armour—however foolish this might be from a military point of view. But 'there could be no honour without public proclamation, and there could be no publicity without the evidence of a trophy'.[4]

The *Iliad*, of course, has heroes who transgress beyond the proper limit, and here Herakles suggested himself as a mythological *paradeigma*. It is in such a role that we encounter him for the first time in the epic. Diomedes has been raging against Aeneas, who is being rescued by Aphrodite. Drunk with victory, the man, Diomedes, presses on against the goddess and wounds her badly (*Il.* 5. 318–62) and he later does the same to Ares. This kind of deed is unparalleled in the *Iliad*. It is a relic of archaic, pre-Homeric times, as the poet does not fail to point out through Dione, Aphrodite's mother (*Il.* 5. 381–404). She mentions three incidents of gods suffering attacks from humans. The first concerns two giants, the other two, Herakles, who struck Hera and Hades, causing them unbearable pain. Such an incredible deed is condemned in the strongest possible terms (403–4):

> That abominable man, the wrong-doer, that godless person who hurt with his arrows the gods who live on Olympus.

It is not so much Dione who condemns Herakles as Homer. After all, Herakles did have to fight against the gods virtually from the very beginning, and Athena was his helper (*Il.* 8. 362–9) just as she helped and abetted Diomedes. Besides, the giants and Herakles were of partially divine parentage whereas Diomedes was not. But Diomedes' wild, unregenerate strong-man behaviour, even though it was caused by Athena, was unacceptable in Homer's idealized picture of the heroic aristocracy.

The discrepancy between the world of Herakles and that of the *Odyssey* was even greater. The *Odyssey* belongs to a more advanced stage of civilization than the *Iliad*; it extols the intellectual achievement of its hero and the virtues of the finishing school—social refinement, polite speech, decorum, courtesy, 'good breeding'—rather than the battlefield. To that world Herakles, at worst, seemed like a barbarous caveman, and the references to him in the *Odyssey* are far fewer than those in the earlier poem. On two occasions he serves as a foil for Odysseus. At the court of Alkinoos, Odysseus is taunted about his presumed lack of athletic prowess by two Phaeacian youngsters. Angered, he proceeds to prove them wrong by hurling the discus farther than any Phaeacian. This is reminiscent of a Herculean feat, but Odysseus pointedly dissociates himself from the hero. First, he modestly says, (*Od.* 8. 223–5), he cannot compete with men of previous generations, such as Herakles. They are superior, and everyone knows it. But then a second reason for Odysseus' refusal to be compared with past heroes becomes obvious: Herakles and Eurytus had dared 'to set themselves against the immortals with the bow'. This is an ambiguous phrase; we know nothing about a contest in archery between Herakles and a god, and perhaps we have here an allusion to the *paradeigma* of Herakles' onslaught on the gods in *Iliad* 5.[5] At any rate, as in his reply to Eurykleia after the slaying of all the suitors (*Od.* 22. 411–18), Odysseus makes it clear that presumption has no place in the time in which he lives.

The purpose of the story about Herakles and Iphitos at the beginning of *Odyssey* 21 (11–41) is even more explicit. The mythological digression is closely related to the events which are about to be described in this book and the next, and it is structured with consummate artistry. Homer tells us first of Odysseus' and Iphitos' meeting in Lakedaimon; Odysseus becomes Iphitos' guest-friend and Iphitos gives him arrows as gifts. Next, in the central and largest section of the story, the poet relates how Iphitos, with twelve beautiful mares, arrived at the house of

> that man called Herakles, privy to great deeds (*μεγάλων ἐπιίστορα ἔργων*),
> who killed him in his household although he was a guest,
> that abominable man, he had no shame before the gods looking on
> nor for the table which he had prepared for him. And after he
> killed him, he himself kept the strong-footed horses in his palace.
> (*Od.* 21. 26–30)

Then Homer resumes the story where it started and describes in more detail the meeting between Odysseus and Iphitos and their exchange of gifts. Their 'kindly friendship' (21. 35) cannot come to fruition, i.e. entertainment in each other's palace, because the son of Zeus killed

Iphitos, 'one like the immortal gods'. The description ends on the note of Odysseus' clearly cherishing Iphitos' gift.

This is one of the most devastating indictments of Herakles in literature, exceeded only by Sophocles and the shrill bias of the church fathers, and most subsequent writers took care to make him a more civil fellow. Whereas earlier in the *Odyssey* Homer had relegated Herakles to the mythological past, he now propels him into Odysseus' own time without softening his stone-age behaviour. Because of this anachronism the clash is all the more violent.[6] The mythological digression underscores the wickedness and arrogance of the suitors, who, like Herakles, disregarded the rules of guest-friendship and tried to kill Odysseus' son. The phrase 'privy to great deeds' is spoken with grim irony and may well be a slur on Herakles' labours or at least parerga, although the cycle of the twelve labours, the *dodekathlos*, in all probability did not evolve until much later.[7]

But Homer, unlike Verhaeren and Wedekind later, was not content merely with viewing Herakles as a misfit. Foreshadowing the long literary tradition of Herakles' adaptation, he attempted in both the *Iliad* and the *Odyssey* to soften or ignore his objectionable aspects and to stress the traits that he and the contemporary heroes had in common. The most obvious such example is found at the end of the eleventh book of the *Odyssey*, which is considered by some to be a later addition. At the conclusion of his journey through the underworld Odysseus sees Minos, Orion, Tityos, Tantalus, Sisyphus, and, at last, Herakles. The author risked considerable clumsiness in making Odysseus and Herakles meet. The real Herakles of course was in heaven and thus Odysseus can meet only his shadow which has been invented for the occasion.[8] The result, however, must have seemed worth the awkwardness, and it is. Odysseus, who has endured so many afflictions and wanderings, meets that paragon of labours and wandering

> powerful Herakles. (601)
>
> Around him was a din of the dead as of affrighted birds
> fleeing in every direction. But he stood there, like dark night,
> holding his bow uncased, with an arrow laid on the bowstring,
> and he glanced fiercely, as one who was ever ready to shoot.
> (605–8)

The poet has captured the splendid, awesome loneliness of Herakles in a few lines. Nobody else is present; Odysseus alone is worthy to be Herakles' companion.

The description of Herakles' baldric follows. There are chiefly two other such decorations described in Homer, but this ecphrasis is one of the most primeval—'bears and wild boars, and lions with flashing eyes, and conflicts, and battles, and murders and slayings of men' (611–12). The poet concludes the description by expressing the hope that this may be the only belt of the kind the craftsman has made and ever will make. The fierceness of Herakles could not be ignored, but it is transferred to the decoration of his armour.

Herakles' subsequent speech is brief and to the point. From the outset he emphasizes that his fate and Odysseus' are similar. 'Wretched man,' he exclaims, 'you too are leading the sort of miserable destiny I suffered when I was still in the sunlight!' He goes on to say that he was Zeus' child, but none the less his sufferings were without end. This certainly was some solace for Odysseus who had been despairing about the endlessness of his sufferings, and Odysseus was only a man. Herakles continues by explaining what caused him the most grief: he was the bondsman of a man inferior to him. The *Iliad* (15. 639–40) refers to this in passing: Eurystheus was so afraid of Herakles—according to one version he hid in a jar so he could not be seen by the hero—that he never communicated with him directly but sent his henchman Kopreus, 'Dungboy', to carry messages. Herakles' comment in the *Odyssey* thus serves as an implicit corrective to Achilles' remark to Odysseus that he would rather be the lowliest servant of a dirt farmer on earth than the king of the dead. The tribulations on earth can be miserable, and Herakles does not try to make them palatable to Odysseus, except by giving him to understand that his sufferings are not unique and would be even more humiliating if he were descended from a god. But, Herakles concludes, the gods helped him, Hermes and, pointedly at the end of the speech, 'grey-eyed Athena'. She is, of course, Odysseus' patron goddess *par excellence*, and her association with Herakles is already known from the *Iliad* (8. 362–9).

Odysseus does not reply to Herakles. This does not mean that because 'Herakles and Odysseus come from different worlds and ages' Odysseus has 'indeed nothing of interest to say'.[9] Odysseus was not easily at a loss for words, but he also knew when to be quiet, and any reply on his part would have lessened the grandeur of the finale of his visit to Hades. Herakles, the son of Zeus and the most famous and brilliant hero of the Greeks, identifies with Odysseus. Thus strengthened, Odysseus returns to the upper world, to Pallas Athene and, ultimately, to the murder and manslaughter of the suitors that has been prefigured by the representations on Herakles' baldric. Herakles does not yet wear his lion's skin nor does he wield his club

> but he stood there, like dark night,
> holding his bow uncased, with an arrow laid on the bowstring
> and he glanced fiercely, as one who was ever ready to shoot.

This is how Odysseus will appear to the suitors in Book 22.

More briefly Herakles is cited as a parallel to the central hero of the *Iliad*, Achilles. This is entirely appropriate; Achilles is the hero who breaks the noble code of behaviour and truculently refuses to participate in the common undertakings of the Greeks. Even after he finally relents, he does not lose the lonely grandeur which sets him apart from the others.

The reference to Herakles comes at a crucial point in the epic. Nestor has just informed Achilles that Patroclus has fallen, and the Nereids and Thetis have sung their moving lament. Achilles knows that he, too, will die (*Il.* 18. 115–21):

> My death I will then accept, whenever
> Zeus wishes to bring it about, and the other immortal gods.
> For not even powerful Herakles escaped death (κῆρα),
> although he was dearest to lord Zeus, son of Kronos,
> but his fate overcame him, and the troublous anger of Hera.
> So I, too, if the same fate has fallen to me,
> shall lie outstretched, when I have died.

Herakles is the noblest mythological precedent that Achilles can turn to in his awareness of the inescapability of death. There is some poignancy in this also, for Herakles was widely invoked as the averter of the κῆρες, the spirits of death. But Herakles also won eternal glory for himself, and so will Achilles. Herakles is called 'dearest to Zeus', and similarly, Achilles later is called 'dearer to the gods' (*Il.* 20. 334).

Both Achilles and Herakles were the sons of a mortal and a deity; both are untamed and violent but, in the end, accepting.

Herakles stood in a special relation to the Greeks' expedition against Troy. He, too, had destroyed the city, but the references to this exploit are kept brief[10] (*Il.* 5. 640–2; 20. 145). When the episode is developed in greater detail the poet dwells on that part of it which detracts as little as possible from the Greeks' achievement and, at the same time, assimilates Herakles to the human level of Homer's heroes: he is being driven by Hera over the sea to Kos. Like Odysseus, he was pursued by a deity, was alone on the raft for days and landed on the island without any companions (*Il.* 14. 249–56). This assimilating and humanizing tendency characterizes other occurrences of Herakles in the *Iliad*: like a Homeric hero, he weeps and cries to heaven and is rescued by divine intervention (8. 364–5). And he destroys Troy because his trophy, some horses, are withheld from him by Laomedon (5. 650–1).

The briefest summary of Herakles' ambivalent associations is found in the *Homeric Hymn* (15) to Herakles. In this poem of nine lines, Herakles is characterized as one who 'himself did many wicked things, but also endured many'.[11] The poet is not trying to vindicate Herakles, but the idea that a hero should passively endure unbearable acts was largely alien to the early Greeks. Even later, when Sophocles put such a man—Oedipus—on the stage, Aristotle did not believe what he saw and started looking for Oedipus' *hamartia*. In the hymn, Herakles' endurance leads to his acceptance into heaven from where he is asked to bestow *aretē* and *olbos*. The phrase, however conventional, has special relevance in this hymn. *Aretē*, 'excellence', was the quintessential ideal of Greek aristocratic education, and Herakles was widely known as the patron of this manly virtue. This was recognized, for example, by Aristotle who praised Herakles as *Aretē*'s protagonist of his hymn *On Aretē*.[12] One of the best examples in Greek literature of *olbos*, non-material blessings, is in the tale of the brothers Kleobis and Biton, prize-winners (*athlophoroi*) both, who achieved this lasting happiness through an extraordinary physical deed (Hdt. 1. 31). The association of Herakles with this state of blessedness was to continue in Greek poetry.[13]

The gap between Homer's aristocratic bias and the sphere of popular religion, to which Herakles belonged and which Homer studiously ignored, made Herakles an ambiguous figure. By contrast, Hesiod's social and spiritual world was totally different. He was a representative of the small peasantry, and for him Herakles, without any reservations, is the shining white knight who can assume even the trappings of the Homeric hero.

In the *Theogony*, Herakles is mentioned strictly by way of digressions. This underlines his importance rather than detracts from it; if the poem were a tightly-knit and logically proceeding account of the creation of the gods, Herakles' place in it would be minimal. Instead, references to him recur with the frequency of a counterpoint. Hesiod extols Herakles' labours, his life's work that earned him entrance into Olympus (954–5): 'Happy (*olbios*) he! For he finished his great work and lives among the immortal gods, free from misery and old age all his days.' Herakles has gained the very happiness for which he was invoked in the *Homeric Hymn*.

Elsewhere the emphasis is on Herakles as the saviour. He slays monsters such as Geryon (289–94), the Lernaean hydra (313–18), and the lion of Nemea (326–32). He was to suffer from the insatiable anger of Hera (314–15), who is reconciled to him, however, when he becomes a god (fr. 25. 32), and Athena is his helper (318). Most important, Herakles, the *alexikakos* (527), killed the eagle that pained Prometheus (526–34). In the *Theogony*, Zeus' relenting is far less complicated than in Aeschylus' theodicy in the *Prometheus Bound*. Zeus' motive is quite Homeric: he wants the glory (*kleos*) of Herakles 'to be yet greater than it was before over the plenteous earth', and he wants to honour (*tima*) his famous son. The *Theogony* is essentially about the glorification of Zeus, and Herakles' frequent mention is called for because he lives up to the Greek ideal that the father's deeds and fame should live on in his descendants. Like Zeus, Herakles is a beneficent, regulatory force that fights against the disorderly and abnormal forces of a nature which is in the process of being formed.[14] In the *Theogony*, we catch the first glimpse of Herakles as an ethical ideal and culture hero.

Being close to the people as he was, Hesiod also portrayed Herakles as the folksy, jolly good fellow. The few fragments that have been preserved of the *Wedding of Ceyx* give us some indication of this. One of the main subjects of the poem was the wedding-feast of Ceyx and Alcyone at which Herakles intervened. He crashed the party, justifying himself with jovial magnificence: 'Of their own accord good men betake themselves to good men's feasts.'[15] This phrase became so proverbial that it was quoted, among others, by Plato in the *Symposium*.[16] The remark shows that Hesiod attributed to Herakles the quality, which he undoubtedly found in the folktales, of taking himself lightly, and it kept our hero from becoming too lofty and untouchable. Much of the rest of the poem seems to have been concerned with Herakles' prodigious appetite, a theme on which the comic poets were to seize with so much glee. Having stilled his hunger, Herakles entertained the party by proposing several riddles.

The glory and honour which Zeus was eager to let Herakles achieve in the *Theogony* were thoroughly Homeric ideals. The *Shield of Herakles*, which may or may not have been written by Hesiod, is a far more extensive post-Homeric *interpretatio Homerica* of Herakles. This poem of 480 hexameters deals with Herakles' battle against the highwayman Cycnus, Ares' son. Since Cycnus kills pilgrims on their way to Delphi, Apollo enjoins Herakles to fight him. From the violator of *xenia* in the Odyssey, he has developed into its defender. The fight itself is described in the manner of an Iliadic *aristeia*: boastful speeches lead up to it; there are many similes; Herakles uses a chariot, and the fight is carried out with spears. Its outcome is inevitable (416–23):

> But the son of Amphitryon, mighty Herakles, with
> his long spear struck Cycnus violently in the neck
> beneath the chin, where it was unguarded between
> helm and shield. And the deadly spear cut through
> the two sinews; for the hero's full strength
> lighted on his foe. And Cycnus fell as an oak falls
> or a lofty pine that is stricken by the lurid thunderbolt
> of Zeus; even so he fell, and his armour adorned with
> bronze clattered about him.

Ares then tries to attack the 'stout-hearted' Herakles. In a stunning reversal from *Iliad* 5 it is Ares, and not Herakles, who is criticized for transgressing beyond what is proper and ordained (*themis*, 447). Athena deflects the spear of Ares, who has to be rescued. At the end of the poem, Herakles once more proves a nobler fellow than the god: he gives decent burial to Cycnus, but Apollo is so vengeful that he washes out the grave.

Like the *Theogony*, the *Shield* conceives of Herakles as an ethical force. Although he is dressed up like a Homeric knight, he fights against no ordinary opponent, but against a personification of sacrilegious impiety and evil. Zeus does not make Herakles fight for his glory or honour, but it is made clear from the outset that 'he fathered him to be a defender against destruction for gods and bread-eating men' (28–9). Thus Zeus' amorous adventure with Alcmena is given a lofty purpose and Herakles becomes the universal saviour.

The lengthy description of the shield, which forms the main part of the poem, is related to this scheme. In contrast to Achilles' shield in the *Iliad*, bloody battle scenes and destructive monsters predominate. Their preponderance adequately reflects Herakles' fight, for the greater part of his life, against these very demons such as the frightful serpents (111–17). The battle that follows is a specific example of the general point: Herakles does not fight Cycnus to satisfy a bloodthirsty impulse, but the world abounds with inhuman monsters and it must be freed from them. Phobos, Fear, is in the centre of Herakles' shield, and Herakles is shown fighting against him because it is Phobos who later comes to the rescue of Ares (463). The description of the shield thus serves a similar purpose to that of Herakles' baldric in *Odyssey* 11.

The poet, however, took pains not to give too one-sided a picture of Herakles' character. Wrestlers and boxers are represented, too, and Herakles was of course their patron. The athletes' endeavour is skilfully likened to Herakles'. The charioteers, for instance, are said to be 'engaged in an unending toil, and the end with victory came never to them, and the contest was ever unwon' (310–11). The word for contest, *athlos*, is the same as that designating Herakles' labours. Throughout the *Shield*, the poet extols and, implicitly, asks us to emulate Herakles' works on earth, although he does not mention his final reward. Herakles' actions are good *per se*, and not because they open up the gates of heaven. This, then, is the earliest occurrence in literature of the secular conception of Herakles' works. In this poem it is primarily accounted for by the partial assimilation of the hero to a Homeric nobleman, and it is certainly devoid of the opposition between the human Herakles and the divine which was to characterize his adaptation by some later writers. In another scene of the shield there is an ethereal description of Apollo and the Muses on Mount Olympus (201–6). Herakles' fight in behalf of Apollo may have suggested that the latter be included in the decorations of the shield. The detail with the Muses, however, shows an early awareness of Herakles' softer and aesthetic side, which was to continue until it found its most striking expression in the figure of Hercules Musarum or Musagetes, Leader of the Muses, in Hellenistic and Roman times.[17]

Whatever one may think of its poetic merits, the *Shield* has a definite place in the literary tradition of Herakles. Using Homeric form, it discards the negative heritage of the hero and establishes him as the resplendent victor, the *kallinikos*, and as a man of high morality, the saving *alexikakos*. These were his most famous titles in cult, and they called for and found a literary expression.

In the personal lyric poetry of the Greeks, Herakles appears only infrequently. This is not surprising; poets such as Sappho and Alcaeus do not find it necessary to describe their own personal feelings by reference to a mythological precedent. The poet's own personality is enough and it does not have to be enhanced by a mythological *paradeigma*. Even when Archilochus writes a poem about a virtue that was proverbial for Herakles, his endurance (*tlēmosynē*), he addresses his own heart (*thymos*) rather than trying to live by the example of a mythical hero.

One of the most famous Herakles poems that has come to us from that time is therefore rather conventional. Archilochus won the hymn-writing contest to Demeter at Paros, and then celebrated this victory by composing a short hymn to Herakles (120 D) in which he hailed him as the *kallinikos*. This was a private epinikion, but it was impersonal enough soon to become a more general paean on Herakles, and its first words—τήνελλα καλλίνικε ('hail to the victor')—were commonly used to salute victors in the games. We should not forget, however, that Archilochus found it entirely appropriate to sing to Herakles after winning a musical competition. In a similar vein the poet Echembrotus, who had won in song at Delphi, set up a tripod to Herakles at the beginning of the sixth century (Paus. 10. 7. 3). The Muses on Herakles' shield, as we noted earlier, were no mere decorative adornment.

The heroic stature of Herakles was to be paid scant attention in this kind of poetry. One fragment of Ibycus (298 P.) starts out traditionally enough with a reference to Herakles, who is fighting for Zeus (*Diomachos*), but then the poet turns to Athena so he can mention what interests him most: her birth from Zeus' head. Similarly, when Herakles tells how he killed the 'Siamese Twins' Kteatos and Eurytos, Ibycus is more interested in their grotesque anatomy than in their destruction by Herakles, which is a violent exploit in Pindar: 'I slew the white-horsed lads, Molione's children, of the same age, equal-headed, single-bodied, both born in a silver egg.'[18] Whereas Ibycus thus ignored Herakles, the early choral lyricists Alcman and Stesichorus found a way to cut him down to size. At the beginning of his *Partheneion* or *Maidens' Song*, Alcman tells the story of Herakles' slaying Hippocoon and his sons (1 P.). Herakles does not win immediately but is wounded. Likewise, Stesichorus departed from the straightforward account in the Hesiodic *Shield of Herakles* by saying that Herakles preferred discretion to valour when Ares joined forces with Cycnus, but later returned and slew Cycnus. 'Not even Herakles against two' (*οὐδὲ Ἡρακλῆς πρὸς δύο*) thus became a proverb in Greece.[19]

As a western Greek, however, Stesichorus was particularly attracted to Herakles and several of his poems—*Cycnus*, *Geryoneis*, *Scylla*, and *Cerberus*—told of Herakles' exploits. Originally, the Herakles legend in that part of the Mediterranean may have been a reminiscence of Mycenean trade contacts, but at the time of Greek colonization it was revived because Herakles 'was almost the ideal embodiment of the Greek settler, who destroyed aboriginal monsters and gave peace to the regions which he traversed'.[20] Stesichorus had Herakles travel to Geryon's island Erytheia in the west by using the Sun's cup (185 P.) which travelled empty daily from east to west before the Sun used it for the return trip. In order to get the cup, Herakles threatened the Sun with the bow, but desisted upon the Sun's pleading, and because he yielded, the Sun gave him the cup. Herakles again threatened a deity when Ocean rocked the cup on the way, and Ocean was cowed and calmed the waves. In contrast to his behaviour in the works of Hesiod and Homer, Herakles shies away from attacking an Olympian god, whereas the Ocean, a brother of the giants, could be defied more easily. In this respect, Herakles once again is closer to the pre-Homeric world in which men fought against gods than to the Homeric age and

Pindar's (*Ol.* 9. 29ff.) which insisted that this should never happen.[21] Later poets subsequently remodelled the story, eliminating the struggle with the Sun and making Herakles abide by more respectable standards of conduct. Stesichorus' Herakles therefore is a transitional figure, being unheroic and archaically heroic at the same time. For the rest, Stesichorus followed in Hesiod's footsteps by relating the folksy Herakles' drinking bout with the centaur Pholus and the ensuing brawl with the other centaurs (181 P.).

The most remarkable mention of Herakles at the time is found in an epinikion of Simonides for Glaucus of Carystus, who was victorious in the boys' boxing contest at Olympia in 520 B.C. As in the epic and in Pindar's poetry, Herakles is the standard by which a mortal can measure his attainment, but Simonides goes so far as to say that Glaucus in fact was superior to Herakles (508 P.). This is, to be sure, a deliberate exaggeration. At a time, however, when the lyric poets were reacting against the norms of epic and were searching for their own attitude *vis-à-vis* the traditional mythology, it is hardly surprising that the pendulum occasionally should have swung too far to one side before coming to a temporary rest in the middle.

NOTES TO CHAPTER I

1. For the Herakles epics of Stesichorus see pp. 20f. and for Panyassis' *Heraklid*, pp. 24f. For others, see Aristotle, *Poetics* 1451a and Gruppe 1118–19.
2. Summed up in the word κῦδος—our kudos—something which Apollonius' Herakles, for instance, rejects pointedly (*Arg.* 1. 345).
3. Simone Weil, *The Iliad or the Poem of Force* (Wallingford, Pa. n.d.). It is also good to remember that the Homeric gods never reduce decisions to force alone.
4. M. I. Finley, *The World of Odysseus* (London, 1956) 132; cf. Thorstein Veblen, *The Theory of the Leisure Class* (London, 1924) 18. More detailed accounts of Homer's morals and values are found in Finley 119–57; W. Jaeger, *Paideia: The Ideal of Greek Culture* (Oxford, 1939) 1–54; Biehlolavek 22–8. On Herakles in *Iliad* 5 see also H. Erbse, *RhM* 104 (1961) 161–4, 186–9.
5. This was assumed by one scholiast; see Dindorf's edition ad loc. Cf. A. Emerson, *De Hercule Homerico* (Munich, 1881) who lists all the Homeric references to Herakles and discusses possible sources.
6. The same technique is used in Herakles' favour by Dürrenmatt; see pp. 287ff.
7. The most recent discussion is that by Brommer who advocates a third-century B.C. date (*Herakles* 61–2).

8. This was duly satirized by Lucian, *Dialogues of the Dead* 11. On the other hand, neo-Platonic and neo-Pythagorean writers readily accepted the notion of the duality of Herakles' soul; see e.g. Plutarch, *Mor.* 944F and *De Vita et Poesi Homeri* 13; Plotinus, *Enn.* 1. 1. 12; 4. 3. 27, 32; 6. 4. 16.
9. D. L. Page, *The Homeric Odyssey* (Oxford, 1955) 39, following E. Rohde, *Psyche* (London, 1950) 39. On the question of the authorship of the passage see Page, 48–9. To me it seems rather well integrated into the poem; cf. already Ameis-Hentze's commentary ad loc. and Webster, op. cit. (Introduction, note 5) 247.
10. Contrast, for instance, with Isocrates' extensive description and praise of the event (5. 112) to stir Philip, a Greek, to emulate Herakles.
11. *πολλὰ μὲν αὐτὸς ἔρεξεν ἀτάσθαλα, πολλὰ δ' ἀνέτλη*. The etymology of *ἀτάσθαλος* as 'unbearable' (from *α-τλῆναι*) would give added poignancy to this phrase. The *Hymn to Herakles* is *Hymn* 15 in the collection of *Homeric Hymns*.
12. Athenaeus 15. 696b–d; see p. 107. Cf. *IG* 14. 1003: *αὐτὸν ἀλεξητῆρα κακῶν, αὐτόν σε δοτῆρα/παντοίης ἀρετῆς κλήιζομεν, Ἡράκλεες*.
13. For Hesiod, see next paragraph; also, Alcman (fr. 1 P., line 37); Bacchylides 5. 55 Sn., and Pindar, *Nem.* 1. 72, 4. 24; *Isth.* 4. 76.
14. So Des Essarts 19.
15. *αὐτόματοι δ' ἀγαθοὶ ἀγαθῶν ἐπὶ δαῖτας ἴενται* (fr. 155 Rzach=) fr. 264 in R. Merkelbach and M. L. West, *Fragmenta Hesiodea* (Oxford, 1967), where the other fragments from the *Wedding of Ceyx* can be found also (nos. 263–9). The same authors have discussed them in detail in *RhM* 108 (1965) 300–17.
16. 174B; cf. Bacchyl. fr. 4. 21–5 Sn.; Eupolis fr. 289 Kock.
17. See p. 108. The phenomenon of Herakles' association with the Muses needed an explanation by the time of Plutarch who thought that it came about because Herakles taught Evander writing (*Quaest. Rom.* 59).
18. Fr. 285 P. (=D. L. Page, *Poetae Melici Graeci* [Oxford, 1962]). See C. M. Bowra, *Greek Lyric Poetry*, 2nd ed. (Oxford, 1961) 245. My discussion of the lyric poets is much indebted to Bowra's perceptive and more detailed remarks.
19. Fr. 207 P.=Schol. Pind., *Ol.* 10. 19. The incident is different from the heroic prudence Herakles displays in trapping the monster in *Il.* 20. 147–8. The most prominent Greek writer to quote the proverb is Plato (*Phaedo* 89C and *Euthydemus* 297C) and it is mentioned by authors as late as Erasmus (*Adagia* 1. 5. 39) and Rabelais (*Pantagruel* Ch. 29).
20. Bowra 89. It might be more accurate to speak of Herakles as the ideal protector of Greek settlers. The impression one gets from Diodorus and other writers is that Herakles often preceded the Greek settlers and cleared the land. For the Mycenean connections see E. Sjöqvist, 'Herakles in Sicily', *Opusc. Rom.* 4 (1962) 117–23.
21. In his discussion of Stesichorus Bowra also points out many other changes and additions Stesichorus contributed to the traditional stories about Herakles. For C. G. Jung's interpretation of Herakles' journey in the cup see p. 252.

CHAPTER II

Herakles in Transition: Pindar and Bacchylides

The transformations that Herakles underwent in the literature of the fifth century were fundamental for his survival in the subsequent literary tradition. Like many other trends, the response of the fifth century to Herakles was based on the intellectual tendencies that had begun to appear during the sixth. When Herakles became a dominant figure in the poetry of Pindar and Bacchylides during the 470s and 460s the two poets had to take into account the rationalizing influences of the Ionian enlightenment of the sixth century. This rationalism called into question the credibility of many 'factual' details of Herakles' exploits and discouraged a continuation of the uneasy amalgam that Herakles had become in Hesiod's poetry—the shining folk hero with Homeric trappings. Besides, the lyric poetry of the sixth century had signified a turn from the without to the within: a person's inner experience and values were considered to be of more interest than splendid deeds that would lead to such mere externals as fame and glory. The folktale emphasis on Herakles' stunning exploits therefore yielded increasingly to the exploration of Herakles' inner man. The choral lyricists, then, were instrumental in freeing Herakles from his epic and conventionally mythological bonds and in preparing the way for his complete internalization by Euripides and the philosophers.

Because of the fragmentary state of our sources, we can catch only a glimpse of the Ionian critique of the Herakles myth. Hecataeus, who made the first scientific attempt to describe the geography of the earth, rejected the location of Geryon's island Erytheia as being far in the west, beyond the Great Sea. According to him, Geryon was a king on the mainland around Ambracia and Amphilochia. Herakles drove off the oxen from the mainland and that was itself achievement enough. By the way of etymology, Hecataeus also refuted the popular tradition of the grisly monster-dog Cerberus and asserted that Cerberus was merely a serpent, albeit a fiercer one than others.[1] But there also was a constructive side to this scrutiny of the Herakles myth in the sixth century. Foreshadowing what Pindar would do on a far more grandiose scale, there was an attempt in one of the Herakles epics, which was written in that century and is commonly attributed to Pisander of Rhodes, to cleanse the hero of his objectionable aspects. The author realized that if Herakles was to become morally acceptable the violence of some of his deeds, which Homer had criticized so harshly, had to be justified. Pisander therefore called him 'a most just killer' because Herakles committed his slayings 'for purification from evils'.[2] The meaning probably is that Herakles purified the world by ridding it of monsters and harmful men, a view that led to Herakles' traditional title as the earth's 'purifier'. Aristophanes would invoke the hero in that capacity (*Wasps* 1043) and so, in a much more sublime way, would Hölderlin.

Herakles was a hero in search of his character also in that *Heraklid* which was to supersede the previous ones because it assembled all the information about Herakles that later scholars and mythographers found so useful. This epic was written in the early fifth century by Panyassis, an uncle or cousin of Herodotus', and seems to have been a rather prolix work of fourteen books, totalling about 9,000 lines. The Alexandrian scholars esteemed Panyassis highly and even included him in their canon of the five greatest epic poets, and Panyassis in fact anticipated Hellenistic poetic practice by diversifying traditional mythological themes with ingenious and picturesque touches. Whether his epic was truly popular is another question. The few fragments that have been preserved are, of course, a woefully inadequate basis for determining what Panyassis' Herakles was like, but it is fair to say that they do not contain a trace of anything that would point to the spiritualization of the hero, let alone an *Hercule moralisé*. The largest fragments (12–14K.) which, not surprisingly, come from Athenaeus' *Doctors* (or rather more correctly, *Dons*) *at Dinner*, deal with some host's arguments to induce Herakles to drink. Some of them read almost like a parody of traditional Herakles themes: the host proclaims drinking to be an *aretē* and exploits in feasting to be on a par with those in war (fr. 12. 1–6). He goes on to say that the man who does not drink does not deserve to be called 'enduring' (ταλασίφρονος), but 'nitwitted' (ἐνεόφρων); whereas the former epithet is Homeric and very suitable for Herakles, the latter is a new, mock-Homeric formation. The fragment concludes with the host's dictum that wine is a noble defender from evil (*alexikakos*; line 13). The allusion to Herakles *alexikakos* could not be more obvious. The two fragments that follow are full of dire admonitions against excess in drinking, and they would not have had a point if Herakles had not needed such advice.

The closest parallel to all this is the arguments used by Odysseus in Euripides' *Cyclops* to make Polyphemus drink (519–44), but whether Panyassis' Herakles was in fact no more than a muscled yokel cannot be ascertained.[3] Panyassis, however, seems to have revived the violent Herakles who attacks the Olympian gods (fr. 21), although there are conflicting versions as to whether he attacked Helios (fr. 6) or was given Helios' cup by Nereus (fr. 7). On the other hand, Panyassis stressed Herakles' affinity with the gods by enumerating the deities, among them Ares, who had to serve a mortal as Herakles did (fr. 16). But even this parallel is external enough and points to no ideal motivations on the part of Herakles such as we find in Bacchylides and Pindar. The concentration of these poets' interest in Herakles within little more than a decade suggests that they were responding to the appearance of Panyassis' epic. For all we can make out from the fragments—and it is not much—Panyassis' Herakles was the *bonhomme* and *starker Hans redivivus*, and the epic, an attempt, even if humorous, to re-create the Herakles of the folktale in total disregard of a changed intellectual climate. Pindar and Bacchylides reacted by portraying a loftier and more spiritual Herakles, and therefore he was to stay alive in literature.

The most extensive example of Bacchylides' new conception of Herakles is the epinikion (5 Sn.) he wrote for Hiero, tyrant of Syracuse, in 476 B.C. Its introduction, praising Hiero and his brothers, concludes with the following gnome or maxim (50–5): 'Happy (*olbios*) is he to whom the god has granted a portion of honours and life of wealth with enviable fortune: for no man on earth is blessed in all things.' This applied to Hieron, who had been honoured and prosperous but had weak health, and Bacchylides proceeds to illustrate this point by telling, in the largest part of the poem (lines 56–175),[4] the story of Herakles' encounter with Meleager in Hades.

To sharpen the contrast with Herakles' subsequent behaviour, Bacchylides starts off on a very conventional note: parallel to Hieron, Herakles is introduced as the 'sacker of cities', the unconquered son of Zeus who descends into Hades to fetch Cerberus. But the poet is not interested in the execution of that labour, and he deliberately never gets around to telling it. Instead, the bold Herakles is awestruck by the apparition of Meleager. The epic gusto and trimmings are still there, but only to be deflated: Herakles takes up the bow as he did against the gods in the epics, but this time out of fright rather than heroic bravura. Like Aeneas in Book 6 of the *Aeneid* (290–4), he is told that his 'opponent' is only a shade. Once the traditional shell of Herakles has been stripped away, it turns out the hero has some unexpected qualities left. He immediately empathizes with Meleager. The warrior who slew Meleager, he says, surely will soon be sent by Hera to kill him also. Herakles' awareness of death brings tears to Meleager's eyes, who replies with the maxim that 'it is hard for mortal men to turn aside the purpose of the gods' (94–6) and proceeds to expound on it with the account of the Calydonian hunt and his death. It is a moving story, and its epic breadth all the more sets in relief the human simplicity of Herakles' response, which is told with unepic economy. Meleager wept, and tears well up in Herakles' eyes (155–75):

> They say that then, and then alone, tears came to the eyes of Amphitryon's fearless son, as he pitied the fate of that sorrow-enduring man. And answering him he said this: 'For mortals it would be best not to be born nor to look at the light of the sun. But those who grieve about this cannot act, and so one must talk about what can be done. In the palace of the warrior Oeneus is there a girl among his daughters resembling you in form? That one I should like to take as my radiant bride.' And to him spoke the soul of steadfast Meleager: 'I left Deianeira at home, in the fresh bloom of youth, a stranger still to golden Aphrodite the enchantress.'

With this the myth ends rather unexpectedly, and Bacchylides returns to singing the praises of Hieron.

Bacchylides has suffered, somewhat unjustly, from the general condescension among scholars towards his supposedly traditional and conventional way of saying things, especially when contrasted with Pindar. But it is in Bacchylides' *Ode*, and not in Pindar's poetry, that we find a first intimation of the complex figure which Herakles was to become soon and which he remained throughout the tradition. Whereas Pindar's Herakles is a powerful, but simple character, there are several aspects of Bacchylides' portrait of the hero all of which were developed more fully by later writers.

The end of the mythological digression—the kind of suggestive open end which de Heredia also found suitable for some of his Herakles poems many centuries later—exemplifies and reinforces Bacchylides' view of the hero. Herakles will marry Deianeira[5] and seal his own doom. A woman, and not a warrior hero as Herakles had thought, killed Meleager and a woman will destroy Herakles. By choosing this emphasis and revealing the futility of Herakles' heroic pose—his attack on Meleager—Bacchylides continued the deflation of the heroism of Herakles that had been begun by some of his lyric predecessors.

Unlike them, however, Bacchylides was able to put something in the place of the old heroic Herakles ideal, and this poem therefore is a turning point in the literary tradition of Herakles. Not satisfied with completely eliminating Herakles' violent aspects, Bacchylides created a truly human and humane Herakles. His Herakles has compassion; his tears of grief and sympathy anticipate those of the Vergilian Aeneas and have nothing in common with the whining of Homer's protagonists. While the narrative owes much to the epic style, Bacchylides purposely drew on one of the oldest and pre-epic versions of the Meleager story.[6] Most importantly, Bacchylides' treatment of the myth is dramatic and contains the seeds for the tragedies of both Euripides, who was to exploit the contrast between the *kallinikos* and the human Herakles much more than Bacchylides, and Sophocles' *Women of Trachis*. The rosy vision of the ingénue Deianeira at the end once more underlines the contrast with the grisly events that she will conjure up. The chivalrous motif of one hero's defending the female survivors of another is inverted with tragic irony. And true to the maxim that no man is blessed in all things, Herakles serves as a *paradeigma* of tragic acceptance.

But while humanizing Herakles and deflating his external heroism,

Bacchylides took pains not to make him into an unheroic figure. In his attitude towards heroic standards Herakles is differentiated clearly and deliberately from Meleager. Meleager has surrendered to complete resignation and despair, and the world of action has lost its meaning for him. Herakles, by contrast, is the unceasingly active hero, a trait that remained constant in the entire tradition and has been re-emphasized especially in our century. The human condition is pitiful, says Herakles, but since we are born to it, we must act and cannot go on grievously contemplating our lot. 'One must talk about what can be done.' This is not a return to the blindfolded heroism of the warrior epic, but the heroism of Herakles is his indomitable spirit and his call to renewed action and purpose even after personal loss and despair. This is essentially the heroism of such 'anti-heroes' as Odysseus and Aeneas. Therefore it was not restricted to epic conventions, and Euripides was to expand greatly the characterization of Herakles which Bacchylides only adumbrates here.

Still, there is an important difference in point of view. Although Bacchylides' portrait of Herakles is far more secular than Pindar's, the meaning of the myth transcends the purely human dimension. The suffering of Meleager and Herakles, in Meleager's own words (95), is the result of the gods' *noos*. In the sense of 'rational thinking' this word played an important part in the lyric poetry of the sixth century, the ancient age of reason. Rejecting the Homeric notion that the gods were made in man's image, Xenophanes had stressed *noos* as the essential quality of the one God.[7] Herakles therefore can be humane and does not have to fight against the gods, because there is some purpose in what is happening to him. In this, the philosophers would gladly follow Bacchylides whereas Sophocles and Euripides had their doubts.

Eschewing the length of epic narrative, Bacchylides returned to the dramatic treatment of the Deianeira story in a dithyramb (16 Sn.). The story is sketched in barely twice as many lines—twenty-three—as are taken up by the invocation to Dionysus (lines 1–11). As he had in *Ode* 5, Herakles at first appears as the triumphant victor, who is preparing to consummate his victory by a magnificent sacrifice to Zeus. Unlike in the earlier poem, however, Herakles remains fixed in this tableau because this suited Bacchylides' penchant for stark contrasts. The poet then shifts the scene to Deianeira, but the reader has already been forewarned. For Herakles was introduced as 'leaving Oichalia to be devoured by fire' (Οἰχαλίαν πυρὶ δαπτομέναν), not knowing that exactly the same fate will soon be his. This fate is nothing external: to Bacchylides, following Heracleitus, it is Deianeira's unconquerable character—ἄμαχος δαίμων (23)—which Herakles has offended by sending Iole, his bride, to his wife's home. Deianeira now weaves the destructive design for Herakles just as the veil Nessos had given her had been woven earlier (32–3). At the end of the poem, the literal meaning fuses with the metaphor: Nessos' robe, by which Deianeira's revenge will be effected, is called 'a fateful gift of wondrous power' (δαιμόνιον τέρας). This Deianeira, full of passionate jealousy, has nothing in common with the innocent girl Deianeira in the epinikion, and it was left to Sophocles to combine the two. In sum, with its brilliant contrasts and the purposeful placing of its metaphors, Bacchylides' dithyramb is a drama *in nuce*.

In another epinikion (I Sn.) Bacchylides strikes a more Pindaric note. The first part of the poem has been lost, and the remainder begins in the middle of a prophecy about Herakles. Continuing the transformation of the morally objectionable strong-man into an ethical ideal, Bacchylides has the speaker, perhaps Athena, extol him as the antagonist of arrogant violence, the *hybris* against which Herakles himself was warned in Panyassis' *Heraklid*. Herakles fights for justice, *dikē* (45), as he did in Pisander's epic. More specifically, Herakles is the model of the athletes, who will 'strive in the strenuous toil of the pankration' just as he wrestled with the Nemean lion (56–7). That Bacchylides, following Pisander, was anxious to portray Herakles as just is also evident from his version of the hero's address to Ceyx (fr. 4. 23–5 Sn.): 'Of their own accord the just'—and not 'noble-born' as in Hesiod—'come to the plenteous banquets of the good.'

Although he probably was seriously concerned about the justice of Herakles, Bacchylides injected this concern into a rather light context—the hero's jocose arrival at the banquet of Ceyx—and this is indicative of the difference between his and Pindar's attitude to the Herakles theme. Whereas Bacchylides uses the clear and well-modulated voice of the dramatic tenor *con brio*, Pindar's brass and percussion orchestration is a relentless *fortissimo*. Uncompromising in the severity of his ethical assertions, Pindar turned to the world of myth to impress upon the winners in the athletic contests the permanence of those values in which they had come to share by their victories. This solemn religious ideal admitted of no hero who was beset by human frailties and imperfections. In the true sense of the word, this idol, held up for emulation and inspiration, had to be superhuman. Thus Pindar chose Herakles, and once he had cast him in the ideal image, he lost no opportunity to glorify him wherever possible throughout his poetry.[8] Even more that Ajax, Herakles meant to Pindar all that was good and noble and necessary to be saved from the onslaught of the incipient democracy and its non-values. Herakles was the ideal of aristocratic ethics, and once he had chosen his hero-god (*N.* 3. 22), Pindar became his ardent prophet. But before he could elevate Herakles to the summit of high morality, Pindar had to face the same problem that had bedevilled Homer, Hesiod, Pisander, and Bacchylides—Herakles' violence. Pindar felt even less constrained than other poets by the existing mythological versions, whether they concerned Herakles or others, and he decided to cleanse Herakles of any ambiguities in the most direct manner. In so doing, he used both the pruning hook and the scalpel.

In the *Ninth Olympian Ode*, Pindar states that he is cultivating the garden of the Muses—the traditional guarantors of truth—and proceeds to the aphorism that 'good and wise men have become so by divine dispensation'. This thought, that we are given all virtues by the gods, is dear to Pindar's heart, and he elaborates it by fiercely rejecting the myth according to which Herakles attacked Poseidon, Apollo, and Hades, and came off successfully (30–9):

For how could it be true[9] that Herakles wielded the club against the trident?
when Poseidon, who stood in Pylos' defence, pressed him hard,
and when Apollo pressed him hard, fighting with his silver bow,
nor did Hades keep his rod unmoved,
with which he leads mortal bodies down to the hollow way of the dying.
Cast away this tale with contempt, my lips!

for to blaspheme the gods is a hateful skill,
and loud, untimely boasting sounds in unison with mad ravings.

For several reasons, this is a remarkable myth. It is synthetic in that Pindar combines the separate battles of Herakles against the three gods into one such 'historical' encounter. In so doing, he already undermines the credibility of myths that pit a hero against a god—they are not to be taken seriously, on principle. Besides, because Herakles is god's son, he shares more in the divine dispensation than ordinary mortals, and therefore it stands to reason that he is also more of a wise and good man than others. Of course he would not turn against the very dispensers of these qualities. Instead of rationalizing the mythology, however, Pindar, true to his religious mission, condemns it in terms of sacrilege and impiety.

Delight in battle, then, is totally absent from Pindar's Herakles. Pindar himself condemned force[10] and Herakles tries to avoid it. He takes the diplomatic route and, 'with reasoned speech' (πείσαις . . . λόγῳ) persuades the Hyperboreans to give him the olive (*Ol.* 3. 16). Herakles as a coaxing Peitho—all for the sake of the Olympic games! Noble manners, of course, result from noble motivations, in this case filial piety and the desire to set a monument to the *aretē* of the future competitors. Later in the poem (28) Pindar states that it was 'necessity imposed by his father' (ἀνάγκα πατρόθεν) that sent Herakles on his labours.

Yet this was not enough. It left Herakles open to the charge, which the sophists would eventually level at him, that the end justified the means, and even the end might often have seemed confused and ignoble enough. Whenever he dwelt on Herakles' forceful exploits, therefore, Pindar left no doubt that the hero was pitted against opponents who made a mockery of human and divine law, and that by dispatching these enemies he did a service to mankind. The *Tenth Olympian Ode* provides a good example of Pindar's aims in this respect. It was written long after the event, for a man from Locri in Magna Graecia, and as the Locrians had no particular mythology of their own, Pindar relates another version of the foundation of the Olympic games by Herakles. Throughout the poem, Pindar's interest focuses on this civilizatory achievement. When Herakles is introduced, therefore, his warlike aspects are toned down considerably (15–16): 'Cycnus' onset turned back Herakles the over-strong (ὑπέρβιον Ἡρακλέα).' This is a chivalrous compliment to the Locrians, who prided themselves on their worship of Ares (15), and it is relevant to the Ode's addressee who had won only after a hard fight: Cycnus was almost too much even for Herakles. In contrast to the Hesiodic *Shield*, nothing is said of Cycnus' monstrosity: all that matters is his valour in battle. After the customary praise of *aretē* (20), Pindar states the maxim (22–3):

> But without hard toil, few have won the kind of victory that sheds a light upon their lifetime for all the deeds they accomplished.

For elucidation, Pindar does not cite one of Herakles' famous twelve labours, but a parergon, his expedition against king Augias who had refused to pay Herakles his due after the latter had cleaned out the stables. Augias is clearly in the wrong. He is called ὑπέρβιον (29) which now has moral connotations and means 'overbearing', and like Laomedon, he is 'one who cheats guests' (ξεναπάτας 34). As he did in Hesiod's *Shield of Herakles*, the hero here fights for the hallowed custom of guest-friendship. Augias' city therefore falls into 'the deep channel of Atē'—this channel is a mocking echo of the one with which Herakles had effected the cleaning of the stables. The Moliones, Augias' nephews, support their uncle in this unworthy cause. They too are arrogant[11] and at first manage to destroy Herakles' army. Herakles returns and prepares an ambush. In contrast to other versions, however, he does not slay them deceitfully but in open combat on the road, which at least in Attic law at Demosthenes' time was considered 'just murder' (Dem. 23. 53). According to a considerable part of our tradition, the Moliones at the time were on their way to the Isthmian games as the ambassadors of the Epeians and as such, they were inviolable.[12] If this version existed at Pindar's time, as seems likely, we would have one of the most startling examples of his turning a myth inside out *ad maiorem Herculis gloriam*, for Herakles proceeds to found the Olympic games. To make his intent clearer yet, Pindar appends another moralistic maxim (40): 'It is impossible to fend aside the quarrel with stronger men.' Read in context, this sentiment is closer to Aeschylus than to Machiavelli. Herakles' cause was just, but fighting against mighty opponents he needed more might to subdue them. His opponents' use of force is further characterized by lack of wisdom (ἀβουλία 41); by implication—and not to the surprise of the reader familiar with the 'wise' Herakles of *Olympian* 9—this is not true of Herakles. Victory in the cause of justice does not come easy, but it is this kind of deed, rather than others, that sheds lustre over Herakles' life.

Once he had found this true note and realizing its importance, Pindar was to return to this theme time and again. It therefore is more than regrettable that so little of his poetry outside of the epinikia has survived and we depend on fragments from papyri, however large they may be. In one of these poems (fr. 140a) the train of thought is quite similar to that in *Olympian* 10. Driven by a sea storm from Troy, Herakles lands on the island of Paros. Two of his companions disembark and—in flagrant violation of the law of *xenia*—are slain by the sons of the king. In characterizing the crime, the poet chooses his words in such a way that there is only one thing Herakles can do. The deed was wicked; the Greek word for it (ἀτασθαλία) is the same term that Homer used in the *Odyssey* proem to describe the actions of Odysseus' companions which led to their ruin. Herakles is rightly incensed about it (57) and so would be anyone else. To emphasize the cruelty of the crime Pindar coined a new word for its perpetrator—'one who cleaves asunder guests' (ξενοδαΐκτα 56)—and, significantly enough, Euripides later applied this term to Cycnus (*HF* 391). The crime does not cry for punishment, it shrieks, and Herakles, 'with overwhelming strength' (ὑπέρβιος 54), lays siege to the city. Pindar tells nothing more of this military effort—Apollodorus (2. 59) mentions that Herakles did not kill anyone, but exacted two of king Minos' nephews to replace his slain comrades—but turns to Herakles' building an altar in honour of Zeus and Apollo. This act of piety, so different from Herakles' reception on Paros, is more important than the details of the war, even though the war is waged in just retribution.

The most ringing affirmation of the justice of Herakles' use of force comes from a poem of which only the beginning was known until recently.[13] The poem (fr. 169 Sn.) is about the justification of Herakles, and its lively, graphic narrative is quite different from Pindar's epinician style. The maxim, which the rest of the poem is to illustrate, **is** stated at the outset. '*Nomos*,' Pindar says, 'king of all, mortals and immortals, leads, chastising [or: bringing to justice] whatever is most violent, with highest hand.' Thereupon, with emphatic uniqueness, Pindar links the *gnomē* to the myth: 'I judge from the deeds of Herakles.' Then, in no more than three lines, he mentions Herakles' driving away the cattle of Geryon before relating in detail the taming of the mares of Diomedes.

Why does Pindar single out these two events? The Hesiodic influence on Pindar's thought explains the brevity of the allusion to Geryon. In the *Theogony*, Geryon is one of the baneful monsters begotten by Chrysaor. The earth has to be rid of these monsters and to make the point, Hesiod told Herakles' feat—the slaying of Geryon—not once, but twice (289, 982), both times stressing the force Herakles had to use (βίη Ἡρακλείη). Or course Herakles cannot be blamed for not buying the oxen from such a monster. Just the opposite: Pindar's godfearing contemporary Aeschylus explicitly called Geryon and his herdsmen 'unjust' (fr. 74N.). As for Diomedes, he had taught his horses to eat men—to transgress the *nomos* (παρανομεῖν) as Diodorus put it (4. 15. 3). Whereas Geryon was inhuman by birth, Diomedes, a son of Ares like Cycnus, was inhuman by his own, impious design. Like in the reference to Cycnus, however, in *Olympian* 10. 15, Pindar refrains from dwelling on Diomedes' *hybris*. He is a valorous opponent who chooses to fight for his horses rather than give them away, but his *aretē*[14] is inferior to that of Herakles and he succumbs. This emphasis on Diomedes' bravery adds to Herakles' stature rather than detracts from it; there is no glory in overcoming a foe who will not fight or fights poorly, and only the best man can overcome the better one. The point, however, is not that Diomedes fights bravely, but that he fights for an unjust cause. Lest the reader forget this, Pindar paints at length the blood-dripping picture of Diomedes' horses munching on one of the grooms (23–32):

> Forthwith a noise cracked through the shattered white bones. He [Herakles] thereupon tore off, from underneath the animals' tables, the entwined bronze, fastened to links along the stable, and stung the mares with his club by the root of the neck, while one was carrying off a leg, one a forearm, and another in her teeth the head.

Diomedes may fight nobly in his last bout, but he unleashed the forces of violence by turning them over to unthinking animals, and violence has gone berserk, incapable, it seems, of ever being brought under human control again. If Diomedes fights for this perversion of nature, he cannot be a good and just man. After impressing this gory picture on the reader, Pindar returns to Diomedes and describes how he was awakened. Diomedes now is characterized as ζαμενής, which originally means 'very strong', but then carries the bad connotations of rage and violence. Be this as it may, Diomedes' demise is told very briefly, in three or four lines that have not been preserved. Again the battle as such does not matter, but the spirit behind it does. In the second strophe we find Herakles, faithful to the behests of Hera and Eurystheus, setting out for a new labour, 'without any allies' (46). Shortly thereafter the poem breaks off, but it appears that its main theme, the celebration of Herakles' deeds, continued.

The exact meaning of *nomos* has been the subject of much sophistic debate in ancient[15] as well as modern times, but from the literary context of the poem and the whole tradition of Herakles' justification it can be seen what Pindar had in mind. He combines a particular with a general principle. The immediate cause for Herakles' fighting is the decree of his father Zeus—the 'Necessity imposed by his father' of *Ol.* 3. 28—which is represented as a king sitting by the side of Zeus. Justification, however, is not necessarily the same thing as justice, and here Pindar faced the same question as Aeschylus: was Zeus just? The answer is an unqualified yes. Herakles fights against enemies who flout a general, universal 'order' or 'law', which has become the generally accepted norm or way of life for both men and gods. Both Hesiod and Heracleitus conceived of this *nomos* as god-given.[16] Pindar thus gave theological substance to Herakles' role as the saviour and deliverer, and he extolled Herakles' role as a divine agent who metes out punishment for crimes committed against gods and men. In the end the Cynics completely identified the idea of an ethical, kingly *nomos* with Herakles, and he became the very model of the ideal king.

Having removed all obstacles to the ethical interpretation of Herakles' deeds, Pindar sang of the hero's high ethos with compelling straightforwardness. 'That man is a fool who does not unfold Herakles in the song of his lips' (*Pyth.* 9. 87), he states bluntly. The *First Nemean* contains Pindar's most inspired expression of his faith in Herakles. The poet affirms his personal creed that he wants to use all his resources to serve his friends (32), for 'the hopes of men that labour long have some community' (32–3). This theme of unselfish help in the tribulations of life leads to another personal confession: 'But for myself, I readily cleave to Herakles, among the lofty places of his deeds of *aretē*', and Pindar then describes the first such deed, the infant Herakles' strangling the snakes. The selection of this story is more purposeful than is commonly thought. It exemplifies Herakles' φυή, his inborn qualities and prowess. One of Pindar's favourite doctrines, reflecting his aristocratic outlook, was the superiority of the φυή or *ethos* to any training or teaching, and he alludes to this in the *First Nemean* shortly before turning to the myth. Besides, in order to win acclaim for his portrait of Herakles, Pindar had to draw on the popular rather than the epic tradition, and the story of the Herakles child certainly belonged to the realm of the folktale. Awestruck Amphitryon summons Teiresias, who prophesies Herakles' future: he will slay lawless, brutish beasts of the sea and 'that most hateful man who, treacherously, is insolent to men'; the latter is not identified but seems to be generic. Herakles will also help the gods fight the giants and then, attaining peace and rest as his reward in 'the halls of happiness' (ὀλβίοις ἐν δώμασι) he will marry Hebe, and feasting beside Zeus, will praise that holy *nomos* (72).

Throughout the epinikia, Pindar's ethical portrayal of Herakles is simple and unequivocal. To this end, as we have already seen, Pindar would freely adapt the mythological material he had to work with. Another, quite startling example of this procedure is found in *Isthmian* 4. In order to liken its addressee, Melissus, to Herakles, Pindar makes Herakles a man 'short of stature' (53). Like Melissus, however, he is untiring of spirit and therefore is able to overcome godless opponents, such as the giant Antaeus, who may physically be superior to him. It is not his genealogy that ennobles Herakles but his ethics.[17] He is the deliverer who 'made the straits kindly to the seafarer' (57), and Herakles' journey to the far west, where he set down the famous pillars, becomes for Pindar a symbol of the farthest limit, which should not be transgressed, of human capacity.[18] Ever so far from depicting merely a shining and always victorious *kallinikos*, Pindar stresses

Herakles' suffering and temporary setbacks in the pursuit of his goals: 'It is fitting that the man who is active should also suffer' (*N.* 4. 32).

Pindar therefore frequently associates Herakles with that other hero who was dear to his heart, the straightforward, toiling Ajax. In *Nemean* 7 he juxtaposes the latter, misjudged and overcome, with the victorious Herakles to whom Pindar addresses a prayer, because Herakles can give strength and deliverance from life's helplessness (*amēchania*). The faith in this power of Herakles is Pindar's answer to Archilochus' acceptance of his *amēchania* (67a D.).

The *Sixth Isthmian Ode* is yet more optimistic. Reflecting the joy which Pindar celebrates, Herakles arrives at the happy banquet of Telamon.[19] In the *First Nemean* Teiresias made a prophecy about Herakles; now Herakles asks Zeus to give Telamon a son so he can be Herakles' guest-friend, a son 'whose spirit shall match his strength' (49). Zeus immediately hears the prayers of his son and sends an eagle (*aietos*), foretelling the birth of Ajax. The whole picture is drawn vividly and impressively—Herakles in the lion's skin, welcomed by the royal house of Aigina, standing before the banqueters, holding up the goblet 'bristling around with gold', lifting to the sky his invincible arms, and praying for someone else, and not himself. It is the sort of tableau which Seneca and de Heredia would cherish, and it served Pindar to catch up the monumental and spiritual permanence of his Herakles into one unforgettable moment.

Like Pindar himself, Pindar's Herakles belonged to an age of transition. The poet chose as the incarnation of his ideals a hero who had held a time-honoured place in the epic and mythological tradition. Into this mythical form Pindar breathed new life by spiritualizing and sublimating the hero. While Pindar's Herakles lacks the dramatic suppleness of Bacchylides', Pindar confronted the same problem that preoccupied the dramatists of the fifth century: the reinterpretation and the making relevant of myth. His Herakles is a swan song for all that was noble and aristocratic in archaic Greece. At the same time, his Herakles *ethicus* became the basis for the hero's literary respectability and survival and for the philosophers' eager choice of the hero as an ideal. The ultimate reason that his adaptation of Herakles bore fruit and inspired writers as diverse as Ronsard, Hölderlin, Leconte de Lisle, and Browning is that Pindar imparted to him his own essential qualities—sincerity, straightforwardness, and burning faith in the nobility of man.

NOTES TO CHAPTER II

1. Geryon: *FGH* 1 F 26 (=Arrian 2. 16. 5); Cerberus: *FGH* 1 F 27 (=Paus. 3. 25. 5–6). Pausanias' paraphrase has been confirmed by the papyrus find of a passage from the Commentary of Antimachus of Colophon, where Hecataeus is quoted directly; see G. Nenci, *PP* 10 (1955) 130–6. For a complete survey of the references to Herakles in the epic cycle and in historiography from Hellanicus to Xenophon see Des Essarts 33–44 and 127–36, respectively. *The Sack of Oichalia* by the epic poet Creophylus of Samos is frequently mentioned as a source for Sophocles' *Trachiniae*, but we know nothing about Creophylus' characterization of Herakles.
2. ἐπὶ καθάρσει τῶν κακῶν (fr. 10 K.). The fragments of the epic writers are quoted from the edition of G. Kinkel, *Epicorum Graecorum Fragmenta* (Leipzig, 1877).
3. The opinion of F. Stoessl, 'Panyassis', *RE* (1949) 893 that he was is based on a rather forced interpretation of the few extant fragments and of the many passages in later writers which, according to Stoessl, were influenced by Panyassis. Stoessl, however, greatly exaggerates their number. On Panyassis see also G. L. Huxley, *Greek Epic Poetry from Eumelos to Panyassis* (Cambridge, Mass., 1969) 177–88.
4. 'Il culmine etico e poetico del carme', as B. Gentili, *Bacchilide* (Urbino, 1956) 16 put it so aptly.
5. According to a scholion on *Iliad* 21. 194 (fr. 249a Sn.) Pindar also wrote a poem on Herakles' encounter with Meleager in Hades and it was Meleager who asked Herakles to marry Deianeira. It has been argued that 'the version followed by Pindar is in truer and finer harmony with the myth' (R. C. Jebb, *Bacchylides* [Cambridge, 1905] 472), but it is questionable why this version would be superior; cf. M. R. Lefkowitz, 'Bacchylides' Ode 5', *HSPC* 73 (1969) 86 n. 50. In his freedom of handling myth Bacchylides anticipates the dramatists and it is indicative of his dramatic intentions that he shifts the cause of the fateful marriage to an impulse originating in the mind of Herakles himself; cf. Jebb, loc. cit.
6. Gentili, op. cit. (note 4, above) 45. This view is sounder than the ascription to an unknown epic source (H. Preuss, *De fabulis apud Bacchylidem* [Regensburg, 1902] 28) or to Stesichorus (M. Croiset in *Mélanges Henri Weil* [Paris, 1898] 67–72). The most extensive discussion of the poem, abundant with biblio-

graphical references, is Mary Lefkowitz' article (note 5, above) 45–96, which at times lapses into over-interpretation. I cannot agree with her view of Herakles as a traditional hero, and she overlooks what to my and Gentili's mind is a very important aspect of Bacchylides' adaptation of the myth, i.e. its dramatization. On the latter, see also E. Romagnoli, *Bacchilide* (Rome, 1898) 7–15.

7. Frgs. 19–21 D.; cf. Simonides fr. 48 D.; Anaxagoras frgs. 12–14 (Diels-Kranz, 6th ed.). For comment, see H. Fränkel, *Dichtung und Philosophie des frühen Griechentumes* (Munich, 1951) 395–6, 427–9.
8. Full details in C. M. Bowra, *Pindar* (Oxford, 1964) 45–8.
9. For this translation of ἐπεὶ πῶς ἄν see the important discussion of L. R. Farnell, *The Works of Pindar* 2 (Oxford, 1932) ad loc.
10. *N.* 7. 66–7: 'Also among my folk at home I have a sunny glance for all/ keeping from all excess and withdrawing all violence from my path' (βίαια πάντ' ἐκ ποδὸς ἐρύσαις). Shortly thereafter (86ff.) Pindar addresses a prayer to Herakles; see below.
11. ὑπερφίαλοι (line 34). This adjective may have been formed from ὑπέρβιος; see *LSJ*.
12. D.S. 4. 33. 3; Apollod. 2. 7. 2; Paus. 5. 2. 1; Plutarch, *Pyth. Orac.* 400E; Scholia Plato, *Phaid.* 89C.
13. The most thorough and perceptive discussion is that of Carlo Pavese, 'The New Heracles Poem of Pindar', *HSCP* 72 (1967) 47–88. Pavese takes the poem as his starting point but does not relate it to the literary tradition of Herakles and only in passing to Pindar's concept of Herakles as seen in the other poems. Valuable also is M. Gigante's article in *Atti dell' XI Congresso Internazionale di Papirologia* (Milan, 1966) 286–311.
14. I follow the traditional view that line 15 (οὐ κό]ρῳ ἀλλ' ἀρετᾷ) refers to Diomedes, although Pavese (pp. 67–9) argues that it could refer to Herakles. The 'way of violence' (ὅδον βίας) which Herakles is said to have found (line 19) must be interpreted locally as 'the way where violent deeds took place'. Herakles has entered the outer stable (line 18) and finds the way or path that leads to the manger; this way seems to have had no name of its own, but Xenophon, *Hipp.* 4. 4 likens it to a ὅδος. The traces of the mares' former repasts were visible all around the manger; see Eur., *HF* 382–6 and *Alc.* 496–8.
15. For the ancient sources see A. Turyn, *Pindari carmina cum fragmentis* (Oxford, 1952) 350–2.
16. Hesiod, *Works and Days* 276–80; Heracleitus fr. 114 (Diels-Kranz, 6th ed.).
17. Dio Chrysostom (*Or.* 2. 78 and 69. 1) and Epictetus (2. 16. 44) combined the two concepts and asserted that Herakles was the son of Zeus because of his *aretē*. Cf. Archilochus' description of a man 'short of stature' (fr. 60D.).
18. Line 13; *Ol.* 3. 43–4; *N.* 3. 19–23. Cf. E. Bundy, *Studia Pindarica. Univ. Cal. Public. Class. Phil.* 18. 2 (1962) 43–4.
19. Cf. J. H. Finley, *Pindar and Aeschylus* (Cambridge, Mass., 1955) 143.

CHAPTER III

The Tragic Hero

The appearance of Herakles in the plays of the three great Greek tragedians reflects two important developments in his literary tradition. The first evidently is the entry of the Herakles myth into drama and this raises the question to what extent his portrayal was influenced by the particular exigencies of that genre. Did Herakles take on any new dimensions in Greek tragedy, did these changes leave an impact on the subsequent tradition, and can they be attributed to the intentions of the playwright rather than being the result of the new medium? Before we turn to these questions, a brief word must be said about Herakles' association with Athens, which found its literary fulfilment in the plays of both the tragic and the comic writers. The authors we have discussed so far were from Ionia, Boeotia, and Sicily, and local patriotism influenced the views on Herakles, for instance, of Stesichorus and Pindar. For the next century, from Aeschylus to Antisthenes, Herakles was entrusted to Athenian writers and the Athenian public. Were they in any way predisposed to him?

They were, and favourably so. Herakles did not belong to the earliest stratum of Attic religion and mythology and therefore his cult was not localized on the Acropolis, Athens' oldest cult centre.[1] He was, however, ardently worshipped in the suburbs, the Attic countryside, and, certainly by the fifth century, throughout the city. This latter situation prompted the question why Herakles was so widely recognized in cult and Theseus, Athens' national hero, so little. Euripides made a valiant attempt to explain it by saying that all precincts sacred to Herakles in the city formerly had belonged to Theseus, who gave them to Herakles out of gratitude for Herakles' saving him.[2] The truth of the matter was, of course, that Herakles was an older hero than Theseus, and through the whole tradition of Theseus there runs the constant endeavour to model Theseus' feats and exploits on those of Herakles. In the second half of the sixth century Herakles was officially adopted as an Athenian citizen so he could be initiated into the Eleusinian mysteries.[3] The Athenians' esteem for him is further reflected by their claim that they were the first to make him a god (D.S. 4. 39. 1).

Considering this popularity of the hero it may, at first sight, seem disappointing that his appearances in Greek tragedy are not more frequent. To explain his relative absence from the tragic stage, various suggestions have been offered. The most widely held view is that the Herakles myth did not lend itself to dramatic staging because of Herakles' frequent fights against monsters,[4] and what nowadays represents a cinematic attraction has been considered a handicap for the staging techniques of fifth-century Athens. This hypothesis, however, is immediately contradicted by Herakles' abundant appearance on the comic stage, most of the time in knockabout roles in which his physical exploits against assorted beasts and ogres figure prominently. If one takes tragedy, comedy, and satyr play together, Herakles appears with a frequency that reflects his great popularity with the Athenians.

The obstacles to Herakles' representation on the tragic stage lay in the nature of Greek tragedy rather than its technical exigencies. Greek tragic drama is not a spectacle that revolves around the 'factual' development of the plot, nor are the plot's various turns and twists designed to create surprise.[5] Either through the prologue or other plentiful hints in advance, the audience knows from the very start whither the plot will evolve. Rid of the obligation to focus their interest on the events, playwright and spectator can concentrate on their interpretation. Greek tragedy thus is basically a theatre of ideas and this explains why Herakles, whose physical, external associations still far outweighed any others, *a priori* was not an ideal protagonist. He had to be adapted to the genre and this means that the tragic poets continued and greatly intensified the process of internalization that had been heralded by the choral lyricists. Seen against this background, the fact that Herakles plays a major role in several plays of each of the great tragic poets, including four—Sophocles' *Trachinian Women* and *Philoctetes*, and Euripides' *Alcestis* and *Herakles*—that have been fully preserved, is a remarkable testimony both to the imaginative power of the Greek tragedians and to the hero's own inherent flexibility.

Herakles played a significant part in Aeschylus' *Prometheia*. Only one play is extant, the *Prometheus Bound*, and scholarly controversy has raged over the question whether it was the first play in the trilogy, followed by the *Prometheus Unbound* and *Prometheus the Firebearer*, or whether it was the second play, with the *Prometheus Unbound* as a sequel.[6] At any rate, by its very nature the *Prometheus Unbound* resolved much of the conflict that takes place between Prometheus and Zeus in *Prometheus Bound*, even if the consummation and details of this reconciliation were reserved for a third play, the *Firebearer*. It is predicted in the *Prometheus Bound* that Herakles, a descendant of Io, will free Prometheus after shooting the eagle Zeus sent to torment him (771–5, 870–2). Furthermore, we have several fragments from the *Prometheus Unbound* in which Prometheus addresses Herakles (frs. 195–201 N.). Hesiod had outlined the myth in the *Theogony* (526–34) where, as we saw earlier, Zeus' motive was to aggrandize Herakles' glory. Aeschylus discarded this conventionally heroic concept and made Herakles' function far more profound and meaningful.

To Aeschylus, Herakles represented a more advanced and enlightened kind of culture hero than did Prometheus. The dramatic conflict in the *Prometheus Bound* is between the stubborn righteousness and intractability of Prometheus, and Zeus' brutal, tyrannical use of his superior authority, might, and force. It is the personifications of the latter two, Kratos and Bia, who chain Prometheus to his rock. At the end of the *Prometheus Unbound*, a reconciliation came about and its fitting instrument became Herakles who, in the course of the previous literary tradition, had changed from the arbitrary perpetrator of excessive force to an ideally motivated and awesome advocate of justice. This is exactly the change that overcomes Zeus in the *Prometheus Unbound*. It was in the nature of its theme that much of the action of the *Prometheus Unbound* was parallel to that in the preceding play, although it is, as is so often the case in Aeschylean drama, a parallelism of inversion. In the *Prometheus Bound*, Prometheus' resentment climaxes with the appearance of Io. She is persecuted by Zeus as is Prometheus; the sight of the unjustly suffering creature prompts Prometheus' most bitter outburst against Zeus and his prediction of Zeus' fall. He then goes on to prophesy at length the wanderings of Io to the eastern and southern limits of the world. In the *Prometheus Unbound*, Prometheus is not yet reconciled to Zeus when Herakles appears, because he greets the latter as 'the most welcome child of a hateful father' (fr. 201 N.).[7] Then he goes on to issue to Herakles the prophecy—the formal counterpart to Io's—about the hero's wanderings to the north and the west. The wanderings of Io and Herakles, extending over the whole surface of the earth, manifest the worldwide power of Zeus. Whereas Io's wanderings were caused by injustice, Herakles', as Pindar had proclaimed, served a just purpose. In contrast to Io, Herakles will suffer his tribulations under the aegis of a compassionate Zeus. Prometheus makes this clear when he foretells Herakles' fight against the Ligurians on his return from his fight against Geryon (fr. 199 N.). The Ligurians will attack in great numbers, forcing Herakles to shoot off all his arrows:

> But then you shall not be able to take any stone from the earth there, because the whole place there is soft. And seeing you in your helplessness, Zeus will take pity on you. He will hold a cloud over you with a shower of round rocks (πέτρων) and will cast a shade over the place. And using these rocks as your weapons you will easily dispel the Ligurian army.

Prometheus, whom Kratos and Bia chained to high-towering rocks (πέτραις) at the outset of the *Prometheus Bound* (line 4)[8] at Zeus' request, now predicts, while he is still chained to the stone, that Zeus will deliver Herakles by means of rocks. From a later source (Hyg., *Astr.* 2. 6) we know that Prometheus went on to foretell that Herakles, who had been forced to his knees during this fight, would be set after his death among the stars in that image. Prometheus' prophecy therefore probably concluded with an allusion to Herakles' final reward for all his labours—his ascent to heaven. As the prediction to Io concluded with his birth, so the prediction to Herakles is likely to have concluded with his deification,[9] a theme, as we have seen, about which the Athenians felt some local pride.

Most importantly, Prometheus himself admits in this prophecy that Zeus is capable of compassion. His prediction that Zeus will have regard for Herakles, 'seeing his helplessness' (*amēchania*), is applicable to Prometheus himself. At the beginning of the *Prometheus Bound* Kratos spoke of Prometheus' formidable ability to find a way even out of a helpless situation (*κἀξ ἀμηχάνων*; 59). Prometheus has found none, but Zeus has found one for him by means of Herakles, whom Pindar had invoked as the defender against helplessness (*N.* 7. 97). Since Prometheus is still hostile to Zeus at Herakles' approach, but is reconciled to him at the end of the *Prometheus Unbound*, the change of Prometheus' attitude must have come about as a result of his prediction to Herakles. Formally, this is suggested by the reversal of the stone image and the parallel, but reversed function of Prometheus' lengthy prophecies in the two plays: as his prediction to Io marked the culmination of his unbending resentment in the *Prometheus Bound*, so his prediction to Herakles marks his willingness to be reconciled with Zeus in the *Prometheus Unbound*. Prometheus now is aware—and Herakles may have pointed this out to him—that Zeus is a good and just god, for Aeschylus began to portray Zeus as such in the *Prometheus Unbound*.

So far from being the accidental instrument of the reconciliation, Herakles was so well suited for this task that he may have effected the reconciliation himself. He appears, of course, in the role of the *alexikakos*, and as such he will engage in all the tasks that Prometheus is predicting to him. These deeds will be done for the benefit of man—in other words, Herakles will continue where Prometheus left off. The spirit, however, in which Herakles will pursue Prometheus' work is very different. Prometheus defied the gods, Herakles is subservient to them; Prometheus was proud and impatient, Herakles is humble and enduring; Prometheus did good from unreasonable and imperious impulse, Herakles' actions are caused by the gods and aimed at establishing the *nomos*. Herakles is a universal culture hero like Prometheus, but he is a more mature culture hero because he works more unselfishly, more effectively, and with more discipline for the common good than Prometheus was able and willing to do.

And, we might add, because he is—literally—more human than Prometheus. Ever since the Romantic period we are accustomed to see in Prometheus 'the symbol of Man as opposed to God';[10] Goethe's Prometheus, to cite but one example, is made by the poet in man's image and then makes men in his. In ancient Greece, however, Prometheus the Titan was not the most obvious incarnation of humanity, whereas Herakles, the man who became god through his own efforts, was a more realistic and less symbolic model of the aspirations of mankind. Aeschylus therefore refrained from decking out his Herakles with the superhuman trappings of Hesiod's and balanced the divine causation of the *alexikakos* with that of Herakles' very human frailty. For Herakles had accidentally wounded the centaur Chiron, who was immortal, with a poisoned arrow. The wound caused Chiron such intolerable pain that he wanted to die and he therefore agreed that Herakles should offer him to Zeus as a substitute for Prometheus.[11] By supplying this motive, Aeschylus accomplished a twofold purpose. First, instead of gaining the heroic sheen of great glory, as in the *Theogony*, Herakles frees Prometheus in order to redeem himself for a previous lapse. Herakles' action is the result of his imperfection. In that sense, Herakles clearly belongs to the human race which Prometheus saved, thereby perpetuating all its weaknesses and imperfections, whereas Zeus wanted to create another, perfect race of men. Secondly, Prometheus now accepts the substitution of Chiron's undeserved punishment for his merited punishment. This signifies Prometheus' submission and acknowledgement of his guilt, which is underlined by his doing the voluntary penance of wearing a wreath of osier as a reminder of his fetters, and of enjoining mankind to wear the same wreath for all times to come.[12] In sum, Aeschylus strikes an exquisite balance between the human and near-divine aspects of Herakles, whereas much of the subsequent tradition would exploit their polarity.

Aeschylus' treatment of Herakles in other plays need not detain us long. We have already quoted a fragment from the *Herakleidae* in which the chorus sang of Herakles' fight against Geryon and his 'unjust herdsmen'.[13] Taking his cue from Pindar and Hesiod, Aeschylus tendentiously wrote his account of this exploit in favour of Herakles. This is also consistent with his reference to Herakles in the *Agamemnon*. Clytemestra is trying to bully Cassandra into submitting to her slave's lot by sneeringly citing the precedent of Herakles (*Ag.* 1040–1):[14]

> They say that even Alcmena's son once was sold in bondage and endured to touch the bread of servitude.

Otherwise, Clytemestra says, she will use force and as Cassandra does not reply, Clytemestra parts on the note of threatening her with violence. The process of de-emphasizing Herakles' violence has reached its culmination here: he is cited as a *paradeigma* for patiently enduring the injustice of a vile master. The passage also contains an allusion to Herakles' big appetite, a favourite theme in the Satyric drama, and we know that Aeschylus wrote a Satyr play about Herakles, the *Heralds*, in which the hero strutted about in the lion's skin (frgs. 108–13 N.).

Sophocles was frequently inspired by episodes from the life of Herakles. Among the titles that have survived we find an *Amphitryon*, a satyr play called *Herakles at Taenarus*—the legendary entrance to the underworld through which Herakles descended to fetch Cerberus—and another tragedy, *Athamas.*[15] Its central incident was Herakles' rescue of Athamas who was about to be sacrificed by his people because he had killed his own children. The parallels to Euripides' *Herakles* are interesting because Athamas, too, was victimized by Hera and struck with delusion that led to the murder, but the few fragments of the play amount to nothing more conclusive. The biographers have it that Sophocles built a shrine to Herakles. We would be ill-advised, however, to let this guide our interpretation of the *Trachinian Women* and the *Philoctetes*, for the dramatic treatment of Herakles in the two plays is radically different.

To understand the intent of the *Trachinian Women*[16]—and the same holds good of any play dealing with Herakles—we must start from the changes that Sophocles made in handling his mythological material. The genre, of course, restricted the action to one or two places and a few days, and this purely technical reason ruled out the dramatization of various labours. But Sophocles went further than that. The scene is Trachis, where Deianeira has been waiting, for fifteen months, to hear from or about Herakles. What occupies the spectator from the outset—Deianeira's prologue—is not the labours of Herakles, for they are complete, but the anguish Herakles has caused Deianeira by his frequent absences, which more often than not had nothing to do with his labours. Sophocles dwells in the most explicit way on the reverse of Herakles' adventures: the fears, the pangs, and the agony of his incredibly understanding and patient wife. Not once does she criticize him, for he delivered her from her suitor, the monstrous river god Achelous.

It was a fierce fight, and Zeus ordained well by having Herakles win—if he indeed ordained well (27), because Deianeira has been unhappy and fearful, on Herakles' account, ever since. It was a dubious sort of deliverance. In the course of the play it becomes increasingly clear that Herakles does not care about Deianeira except for satisfying with her—among many others—his prodigious appetite for sex. His fight against Achelous simply pitted one monstrous creature mad with lust against another.

This characterization of Herakles is reinforced when Lichas, the messenger, appears. As in Deianeira's account of the battle, Sophocles again starts out with a quick, clichéed sketch of the Herakles *kallinikos* which rapidly yields to a grim and quite different reality. Resplendent with victorious exploits, the hero is about to offer a huge sacrifice to Zeus at Ceneum as he had done in Bacchylides' sixteenth *Dithyramb.* A brilliant pageant is to wipe out the seedy memories of the past fifteen months. What had happened since Herakles left home? First, he got drunk at the court of Eurytus, king of Oichalia, and was thrown out of the banquet hall. Then, to avenge his hurt, he seized Iphitus, Eurytus' son, and dashed him to death from a tower. This is the same story that we found in the *Odyssey*, but Sophocles has accomplished the seemingly impossible by outdoing Homer in incriminating Herakles. If anything, the motive for the murder has become more petty and vindictive; Iphitus now does not even have any horses whose theft, though not justifiable, at least had some significance in the agricultural society of Homer's heroes. Moreover, the deceit with which Herakles prepared his crime is too much even for Zeus, his own father. If Herakles had wreaked his vengeance openly, Sophocles says (278–9), Zeus would have forgiven him as one who acted with justice,[17] but Herakles has become guilty of *hybris* (280), the cardinal 'sin' in Greek drama. So Herakles is given in bondage to Omphale for one year. After that, Herakles, with the logic of a brute, blames Eurytus for the whole trouble and sacks Oichalia. But the validity even of this motive crumbles quickly. Lichas has not told Deianeira the full story, but another messenger does, and every word in his account is emphatic and well chosen. Neither his servitude to Omphale nor the death of Iphitus made Herakles do this, but Eros—his love for Iole.

What follows is the story, so familiar to the Athenians and us from Thucydides' Melian dialogue, of the stronger man overpowering the weaker (359–64):

> Well, when he would not persuade (ἔπειθε) the father to give him the girl so she might be his mistress, he devised some petty complaint as a pretext, made war upon her land—the land in which, as Lichas said, Eurytus was king—and he slew the prince, her father, and sacked the city.

It is as if Sophocles were answering Pindar here. A boor does not have the faculty of persuasion, no matter how hard Pindar had tried to impute it to him (*Ol.* 3. 16). But Herakles has read his Thucydides, even if only the preface: he comes up with a *casus belli* to justify archaic savagery and a slaughter of epic proportions.

What is Deianeira's reaction? What should be the reaction, as Kitto has put it so aptly,[18] of the lady of the house who one morning at her doorstep finds a beautiful young girl who from now on will occupy the front bedroom? Not too kindly, as the Athenians knew, but at least Agamemnon had been so considerate as to come along and explain the situation to his loving wife. Sophocles has taken pains to make Deianeira the total opposite of Clytemestra. Seeing the sad cortege—in a horror-stricken sadness that once more deflates the splendour of Herakles' actions—she gently addresses Iole. The reason for the latter's presence, one suspects, is quite clear to Deianeira. Once she has learned Iole's identity from the messenger, she insists that Lichas also tell her the truth. And when the truth is known, Deianeira's attitude is truly remarkable (457–69):

> And if you are afraid your fear is mistaken. Not to learn the truth—that indeed would pain me; but to know it—what is there terrible in that? Has not Herakles loved others before—more, alas, than any man alive—and no one of them has had a harsh word or taunt from me; nor shall this girl, although her whole being should be absorbed in her passion; for indeed I felt a profound pity when I beheld her, because her beauty has wrecked her life, and she, hapless one, all innocent, has brought her fatherland to ruin and to bondage.
>
> Well, those things must go with wind and stream.—To you I say: deceive whom you will, but ever speak the truth to me.

Several things stand out here. Deianeira is compassionate, and she empathizes with Iole. This is not particularly surprising: virtually all critics are agreed that Sophocles, throughout the play, portrays Deianeira in the most favourable way. She is meant to have our sympathy, and she has our attention in the first part of the play, which is three times longer than the part that centres on the appearance of Herakles. The point needs no labouring. But Sophocles also characterizes Herakles and Deianeira by contrasting them. When Deianeira hears the truth, she thinks of someone else, Iole; when Herakles hears it—Deianeira's innocence—he has no word for Deianeira but can think only of himself. Whereas Herakles makes no effort to learn the truth and Hyllos is barely able to get in a word, Deianeira unwaveringly searches for it, no matter how grievous it may be for her. In this resoluteness she anticipates Oedipus.[19] Sophocles, then, has changed the myth not only by presenting Deianeira as a mature, loving woman, who is a far cry from the rosy, bedroom-picture-like ingénue of Bacchylides, but also by making her courageous and undeterred. She sends off Lichas with the admonition to be truthful; the next time we hear about Lichas[20] Herakles has smitten him, who was completely blameless (773), against the rocks (781–2):

> He made the white brain ooze from the hair, as the skull was dashed to splinters, and blood scattered therewith.

Once before we witnessed a scene like this: when Pindar described the cruel perversion of the horses of Diomedes whom Herakles punished for ignoring the holy *nomos*. The point is symptomatic of Sophocles' treatment of the myth: he has turned it inside out. The saviour, the benefactor, is turned into the opposite, 'into a man who follows his own nature and desires without restraint, commits outrageous misdeeds, and thus becomes a danger and menace to other people. . . . The tales about the monsters he slew are almost forgotten, and his strength, his terrifying greatness have turned against other fellow-beings.'[21]

Are we too harsh on Herakles? Scholars, who are uncomfortable with the notion that the easygoing (εὔκολος; Arist., *Frogs* 82) Sophocles —of whom we have all of seven out of 120 plays—might have been more Euripidean than Euripides in treating the Herakles theme, have objected that a great hero has to be outside the norm. As a result, these scholars argue, Herakles is bound to be misunderstood by the more domestic characters who have to live with him, and that is the whole point of the *Trachiniae*.

External and internal reasons contradict this view. The intellectual life of Sophoclean Athens was dominated by the sophists, one of whom, Protagoras, loudly proclaimed that man was the measure of all things. Herakles, who was strong enough to be a *nomos* unto himself, was cited in these sophistic discussions.[22] The Athenian audience would not merely look at Herakles, but they would judge him. So does Sophocles. He concludes the play by saying that 'there is nothing in all this that is not Zeus'. This is not a pious platitude, but Sophocles makes it quite clear in the play[23] that Zeus punishes Herakles for the killing of Iphitus. Herakles is not a law unto himself because he has violated *dikē*, Justice.

Before Herakles appears on the stage and the spectator will be able to see what the man is like, Sophocles adds one more touch to his characterization. At the beginning of Lichas' speech, which is permeated by Sophocles' proverbial irony,[24] Herakles is introduced as a man 'unburdened by disease' (235). Soon, however, Deianeira three separate times refers to Herakles' passion as a disease (445, 491, 544). She is not angry with him for it but Hyllus, in his passionate account of his father's agony, uses the theme of disease again so that one suspects that Herakles' new illness is merely a continuation of the old one.[25] Finally, Herakles himself describes its symptoms. He mentions the convulsions of which Hyllus had spoken earlier, with one important difference: the *spasmos* is a cause and, not, like in other writers, an effect.[26] The sickness is internal, not external, and it causes the *atē* (1082) which Herakles blames soon thereafter for destroying him (1104). This *atē* is his own work since he is guilty of *hybris* just as he was in the slaying of Iphitus. Sophocles changed the myth again by pointing out that the sickness which befalls Herakles from Nessus' robe is merely a manifestation of his own inward disease. This is the logical inversion of the Greek ideal that the beautiful body is an expression of a good and beautiful mind, and Herakles at the time was of course the ideal of that Greek incarnation of the *kaloskagathos*, the athlete.

Herakles' egomania, his most pronounced quality in the final part of the play, works against any sympathy one might have with him and strongly suggests the limitations of his achievements. It is Herakles who tells of his labours and not the chorus as in Euripides' *Herakles*. Therefore his labours, which Euripides glorifies as labours in the *Herakles*, are reduced to mere individual achievements in Sophocles' play.[27] Hyllus eventually succeeds in telling Herakles that Deianeira is dead, but Herakles wastes no word on Deianeira, with whom the audience has suffered and sympathized during the entire play. Instead, he commands Hyllus to kill him by burning him on the pyre on Mount Oeta and to marry his father's most recent concubine, Iole. Hyllus protests vigorously against these impositions, the proposed match with Iole in particular. Herakles can persuade his son as little as he was able to persuade Eurytus. When Hyllus yields, he makes it clear that he yields only because Herakles is sick (1230). He is sick because he is maddened by avenging fiends (1235): the Erinys that Hyllus had misguidedly wished upon his mother (809) now is vexing his father. Herakles, however, looks at it differently: to him his command to Hyllus is holy and sanctified by the gods (1248). Hyllus, in turn, proceeds to indict these very gods for their cruelty (1267–8). He curses the gods who beget children (1268), for he and others are suffering from the monstrous deeds which god's own child has inflicted on them.

Finally, in making Herakles tell of the preparations for his burial on Mount Oeta, Sophocles changed the myth again. He knew that the audience—which has been followed in this by many modern scholars—would be prone to associate Mount Oeta with Herakles' apotheosis. But not only does Sophocles, unlike Pindar, make no mention of it, but he also does his best to counteract any implications. According to the legend, Herakles did not die but rose from the flames to the gods. By contrast, Sophocles, by putting the words in Herakles' own mouth, insists on the finality of the man's death. Herakles realizes that this is the meaning of the oracles he received from Zeus' oak at Dodona (1169–73):

> It [the oak] said that, at the time which liveth and now is, my release from the toils laid upon me should be accomplished. And I looked for good fortune; but the meaning of it was only that I should die; for toil comes no more to the dead.

'I looked for good fortune'—this again is a cruelly mocking echo of Lichas' introduction of Herakles as 'a man of good fortune' (230–1). As Herakles was pronounced to be free from sickness and turned out to be thoroughly diseased, so his presumed good fortune has turned into its exact opposite. The rest from his troubles is not transfiguration, but death—'this is the end, the last end of Herakles' (1256). Throughout the play, Herakles has not been able to rise above his own nature, superman-like—in a negative way—as it is, and there is nothing that would justify his becoming a god. With the hope for a glorious existence in the other world gone, Herakles, like Dido, can concentrate only on a grandiose and splendid death.

The exact date of the *Trachiniae* has been subject to many a learned argument,[28] but the *Philoctetes* was doubtless written later (about 409 B.C.). The portrayal of Herakles is radically different here. He actually appears on the stage only shortly—much less even than in the *Trachiniae* —at the end of the drama. His 'ideal presence',[29] however, permeates the play. Herakles represents the ideal standard to which Neoptolemus and Philoctetes are trying to live up and against which they are constantly measured. The *deus ex machina* appears not to rescue a plot that has run amuck, but because he has been in and behind this play from the very outset. Sophocles makes this quite explicit, again by working freely with the mythological tradition.

According to the myth, Apollo gave Herakles the bow because of Herakles' *aretē* (D.S. 3. 4. 14). It was in this spirit that Herakles passed the bow on to Philoctetes who lit his pyre on Mount Oeta. 'It was by a good deed that I myself won it', says Philoctetes (670), not realizing that the bow was an obligation for further deeds of *aretē*. Sophocles saw the starting point for his drama here. In contrast to Aeschylus' and Euripides' *Philoctetes*,[30] Herakles appears only in Sophocles' and his bow is kept before our eyes and referred to throughout the entire drama. Whereas the other two dramatists, following the myth, treated Herakles' bow merely as the necessary instrument for the conquest of Troy, Sophocles was concerned with its spiritual implications. The bow, divine in origin, was the weapon of the culture hero Herakles. With it, 'he freed Prometheus, father of the arts, he slew the centaurs, wild monsters who refused their birthright to become men. This bow symbolized man's intelligence brought into action, to guarantee man's domination of the earth.'[31] The bow is Herakles' legacy and a symbol of the man's achievement. He gave it to Philoctetes, the man whom he thought most able to carry on his work. Philoctetes in turn gives it to Neoptolemus. Both presume to be like Herakles, and each winds up as a Herakles *manqué*.

To make his intent clear, Sophocles again altered the mythological tradition by changing Philoctetes' homeland from the Megarian peninsula to the gulf of Malia, a country closely associated with Herakles. Odysseus emphatically introduces Philoctetes as the Malian, and only then does he give the name of the father, Poias—a highly unusual procedure (4–5). Furthermore, Philoctetes assents only once to his descent from Poias (263)—but only *after* he has stated that he is the owner of Herakles' arms. From then on, he persistently creates some ambiguity about the identity of his father and insinuates that his father is Herakles rather than Poias.[32] When he laments the loss of his bow, he becomes quite explicit about this by calling himself 'a miserable Heraklid' (1131–2). Since Neoptolemus keeps addressing Philoctetes mostly as 'son of Poias' the audience would keep Philoctetes' claims in perspective.

True, however, to his vision of himself as a Heraklid, Philoctetes tries to make Neoptolemus assume to him the same attitude as Philoctetes has been assuming *vis-à-vis* Herakles. Outwardly, Philoctetes has much in common with Herakles. He, too, suffers afflictions (πόνον 637; πολύπον' 777) from unjust persecution. In several passages that describe Philoctetes, Sophocles imitates the sleeping Herakles of the *Trachiniae*—in the similarity of Philoctetes' affliction to his (*Tr.* 980–1, 1010), the similar appeal for death (*Tr.* 1004–6, 1040–2), the similar warning not to wake the sufferer (*Tr.* 974–82, 988–91).[33] The services Philoctetes wants from Neoptolemus can be regarded as similar to those Philoctetes rendered to Herakles on Mount Oeta. 'By setting fire to Herakles' pyre, Philoctetes both saves Herakles from his suffering and "sends him home" to the gods.'[34] Philoctetes was a benefactor to Herakles (670) and expects Neoptolemus in the same way to be a benefactor to him. Moreover, just as Philoctetes attempts to picture himself as Herakles' son, so he acts towards Neoptolemus as if Neoptolemus were his own son. The lineage Herakles—Philoctetes—Neoptolemus is explicitly established in three passages that come within

150 lines of each other and appear at the very heart of the play. First, Philoctetes allows Neoptolemus to touch the bow of Herakles (667–70). He is given this privilege because of his *aretē* (669). Philoctetes defines *aretē* in the narrow personal sense we have just discussed, i.e. he was given the bow because he was Herakles' benefactor, and Neoptolemus is to follow suit. A little later, Neoptolemus receives the bow from Philoctetes and thus becomes its temporary possessor (776–8):

> There it is, my son, and pray to the jealous gods that it may not bring you troubles (πολύπον'), such as it brought to me and to him who was its lord before me.

At this very moment, however, Neoptolemus is more the son of Odysseus than the son of Herakles, for he received the bow by lying.

Finally, when he is racked by his agony, Philoctetes begs Neoptolemus to burn him just as Philoctetes once burned Herakles, and Neoptolemus is asked to keep the bow which Philoctetes once received from Herakles. The great symbolic acts that link Herakles and Philoctetes—the handing over of the bow and the lighting of the pyre—are purposely extended by Sophocles to include Neoptolemus.

Herakles' appearance at the end of the play, which takes up all the important themes and problems, sets an end to Philoctetes' and, to a lesser extent, Neoptolemus' pretensions to being Herakles' successors. He pointedly addresses Philoctetes as 'son of Poias' (1410), thus settling all the ambiguity Philoctetes has been trying to create about his descent. Then he holds out before Philoctetes his own labours (πονήσας . . . πόνους, 1419) and sharply sets apart his own goal from that of Philoctetes' labours: whereas Philoctetes' will bring him only fame (εὐκλεᾶ βίον, 1422) Herakles' labours brought him immortal *aretē*. This fame was something Philoctetes had craved throughout the play. In this respect, Philoctetes is the typical Homeric hero and Sophocles has been careful to portray him as such. Philoctetes' first bitterness comes when he hears that nobody knows about him (254–6). The appeal to this desire of Philoctetes is Neoptolemus' most powerful argument in trying to prevail on the man. After telling him of Herakles' oracle, Neoptolemus tells Philoctetes that if he goes to Troy he will be singled out as the *aristos* of the Greeks and win matchless fame (κλέος ὑπέρτατον; 1347). Neoptolemus fails because he had earlier lied to

Philoctetes and because Philoctetes is too recalcitrant to make up his quarrel with the Atreidae—almost like Achilles, the greatest of Homer's heroes.

Herakles repeats Neoptolemus' arguments in virtually the same words. Philoctetes will get his *kleos*, he will receive the trophies (*aristeia* 1429), and the army will single him out as being first in *aretē* (1429; cf. 1344–7). Yet this is not the less selfish, ethical *aretē* of Herakles, who endured all his sufferings and even turned them *pro bono publico*. It is the old-fashioned, self-centred *aretē* of the Homeric hero, and the contrast between these two forms of heroism and *aretē* is central to the play. Then Herakles makes it clear that Neoptolemus has no kinship with him either. He is Achilles' son (1433) and therefore, ironically, there remains some truth in Philoctetes' treating him as if he were his own son, because Philoctetes is more akin to Achilles than to Herakles. Having thus dissociated himself completely from his unworthy followers, Herakles sends them off to Troy. The duality Sophocles uses here (1436) emphasizes that Philoctetes and Neoptolemus have much in common, and their inability to be true successors of Herakles is one of these bonds. They will take Troy and reap all the outward glory a Herakles can ever get. Measured, however, against the more mature standards of another time, as represented by the Herakles *ethicus*, they go off as failures, because unlike Herakles, they were not able to grow beyond themselves and their human limitations. And this, of course, had been exactly the trouble with Herakles in the *Trachiniae*.

Why did Sophocles choose to portray Herakles as an ethical ideal in the *Philoctetes*? Part of the answer lies in the dramatic themes of the play. One is, as we have seen, the contrast between an archaic kind of *aretē* and a more advanced *aretē*, and the projection of anachronisms into the present can make for powerful drama. The other theme, very topical at the time, is the contrast between *physis*, nature, and *technē*, training.[35] The sophists proclaimed that everything could be taught whereas Sophocles, in this play, is firmly on Pindar's side. The machinations of Odysseus, who is the embodiment of the sophistic movement's vilest side, cannot overcome Neoptolemus' *physis*. Nor can Philoctetes and Neoptolemus claim to have changed their *physis* for the better by a mere technical device, i.e. the possession of Herakles' bow.

Here some training would be necessary, but not in the sophistic sense.

The chronological sequence of Herakles' negative and favourable portraits should not be over-interpreted. But there is no question that Sophocles found the tendencies at the close of the fifth century more congenial for a favourable characterization of Herakles than the earlier decades. Prodicus' moral view of Herakles' choosing a philosophy of life had made a strong impression. He was followed in this by Antisthenes, the 'founder' of the Cynic school.[36] At the same time, the rationalizing approach to the legend of Herakles, which had been begun by Hecataeus, was continued to the point of allegorical interpretation by the logographer and sophist Herodorus of Heraklea. He wrote the story of Herakles in seventeen volumes and can be considered the creator of the philosophical Herakles allegories, even though his *Herakles* was not organized from this point of view. While Herodorus mostly discussed the motley collection of Herakles myths from the rationalizing approach of ethnography and Ionian scientific inquiry, one fragment in particular[37] shows the allegorization of the myth, which launched a mighty tradition in European literature:

> They write that he is wearing a lion's skin and carrying a club and holding three apples in his hand. They tell as a myth that he took away these very three apples when he killed the dragon with the club, that is to say when he conquered the manifold calculations of stinging desire by the club of philosophy, having noble reason as a garb like a lion's skin. And he took away the three apples, that is to say three virtues (*aretās*): of not getting angry, of not loving money, of not being fond of pleasure. By the club of the strong soul (*psychē*) he overcame the earthly struggle of vile desire, living like a philosopher until his death.

Thus Herakles' life was viewed as a model worthy of being followed. That, and the failure of Philoctetes and Neoptolemus to do so, is much of what the *Philoctetes* is about.

Still, this ideal was little more than a kind of *noblesse oblige*. It was Euripides who created the most meaningful and thoroughgoing idealization of Herakles for his time and, we might add, for ours. He completed a development whose most eloquent spokesman had been Pindar, and against which Sophocles had rebelled in the *Trachin-*

iae—the purification of Herakles. Euripides went beyond Pindar, however, in his definition of Herakles' heroism. Pindar showed Herakles as being free from wantonness and violence, and as fighting assiduously *pro bono publico*. That was enough in the first part of the fifth century to justify reverence for the hero–god. It did not, however, make Herakles particularly relevant to the last part of the same century when the Olympian religion had become little more than formal and was not what we would call a living faith. To be sure, in Periclean Athens with its magnificent temples we find all the paraphernalia and outward splendour a traditional religion can provide. The only thing this religion was unable to supply any longer was inspiration and a deeper meaning for guiding people's lives. Euripides was keenly aware of this and took every opportunity to castigate the gods for the lack of these very qualities and for their obstruction of the effort of humans to work out their own destiny.

In dramatizing an event from Herakles' life, Euripides was at the crossroads himself. He had the choice to treat Herakles as a god or almost that, and thus put him into the pillory or, really, on to the shelf with the other Olympians. The alternative was to portray him in more human terms. Pindar, of course, had also concentrated on the earthly struggle of Herakles, but in his poetry Herakles is a divine agent and the hero's heavenly reward always looms just around the corner. This, after all, had been the traditional religious and ethical inspiration behind the Herakles myth: all human aspirations and exertions were finally crowned with divine reward and attainment of divinity itself. Whereas Sophocles, in the *Trachiniae*, debunked this meaning of the Herakles myth by denying Herakles his deification, Euripides chose to humanize it. In Euripides' play, Herakles does not become a god either, because that would have been a meaningless and merely external achievement. Rather, to Euripides, Herakles' accomplishment was something purely internal and human and therefore vastly more enduring and valuable. The *Herakles* is a reinterpretation of the meaning of the Herakles myth in those terms. This is made dramatically explicit by the division of the play into two parts. The first, in many respects, is the standard, deliberately run-of-the-mill drama about Herakles, the great doer of deeds, *kallinikos*, saviour, and all the rest of the conventional trappings. The second action is the total opposite of the first, whose values it undercuts and revaluates. The *Herakles* is a purposeful *tour de force* whose two actions are related as point is to counterpoint.[38]

The humanization of the theme determined the changes Euripides made in his mythical material. Traditionally, Hera inflicted the labours on Herakles as penance for the murder of his children. In this play he murders them and his wife, Megara, after the completion of his labours, at the pinnacle of his outward success. The new motive for his labours is not divine retribution, but human, filial piety: he undertakes the labours to win back the country from which his father Amphitryon had been exiled for the murder of Elektryon (lines 17–20). The humane enlightenment of the Athenian citizenry, as exemplified by Theseus, takes the place of the burial on Mount Oeta; Herakles will receive honour and burial at Athens. The argument between the two divine minions, Madness (Lyssa) and Iris, which is the interlude in heaven between the actions, has the same purpose as had the argument between Kratos and Bia in Aeschylus' *Prometheus Bound*. It points up the profoundly unjust and cruel nature of the gods' repugnant treatment of the noble Herakles.[39] Unlike in the *Trachiniae*, Herakles' madness comes from without, and not from within the man: he is a tragic hero without having the Aristotelian 'tragic flaw'. Instead of the purposeful, Pindaric 'Necessity imposed by the father' Necessity is wantonly forced on Herakles in this play. A fourth change in the mythology, the invention of the tyrant Lycus who persecutes Herakles' family, serves to underscore Herakles' role as a family man and saviour and adds greatly to the tone of the first action.

That tone is melodramatic as Euripides is intentionally overdoing the clichés of Herakles' traditional role. The scene opens with the tableau of innocence oppress'd: the aged Amphitryon, helpless Megara, and her two infant sons are cowering as suppliants by the altar of Zeus in front of Herakles' palace at Thebes. As in the Herakles plays of Sophocles, the hero is absent but the play still is about him. His task, announces Amphitryon, was to civilize the world through his labours (20). This is conventional enough, but the word used by Euripides for 'civilize'—*ἐξημερῶσαι*—already prepared for Herakles' humanization. It has no Pindaric connotations of superhuman and bloody pacification,[40] but actually means 'to make tame' or 'gentle'. By contrast, the incantation to Herakles as *kallinikos* (49) and noble-born (εὐγενής 50) is purely conventional. So is Amphitryon's conclusion of the prologue on the note of the Heraklids' utter helplessness (*aporia*) that calls for salvation. The theme of Herakles the deliverer from *aporia* was familiar enough from Pindar (*Nem.* 7. 96–7).

Megara's lament, which follows, adds some more touches to the hero's portrait. She wistfully reminisces about her early life of happiness (*olbos*), the very quality for which Herakles was invoked in the *Homeric Hymn*, and by Pindar and Bacchylides. To insure that no eye is left dry in the audience, Euripides then resorts to the most proven of all sentimental devices, the childrens' lachrymose questions about their father. Once more, however, the poet is careful to strike up certain notes that may seem quite trite in their soap-operatic context, but will be invested with greater meaning in the second action. Amphitryon does not give up his love of life and its hopes. Nothing is constant in human life, he says; if fate is good to you today (εὐτυχοῦντες 103), it will not be good to you in the end. To make the relevance to Herakles clearer yet, Euripides has Amphitryon sum up his sentiments with this phrase (105–6):

> He is the best (ἄριστος) man who always trusts in what hope he has.
> The bad man is the one who gives up.

Only a few moments later, Lycus sneeringly refers to Herakles as 'the best of men' (ἀρίστου 150), and his ability to overcome *aporia* was, as we have seen, traditional. It is not outward success, which is at the mercy of fate, that makes a man outstanding, but his internal courage and willingness to persist even in adversity.

After a brief choral interlude Lycus comes on stage. He is the villain in the melodramatic part of the play, but again, Euripides makes him into something more than that. Besides being the bully, Lycus uses the arguments of an Ionian logographer. The story of Zeus' paternity, he reasons, was concocted by Amphitryon—an empty boast, no more. As for the labours (151–4):

> What was your husband's awe-inspiring feat?
> To have killed a hydra in the marsh?
> Or the Nemean beast? That one he snared with nets,
> but he brags he choked him with his arms.

This is the sort of reinterpretation of the Herakles myth for which Euripides has scant sympathy. It amounts to little more than scholarly quibbling about what to Euripides were peripheral aspects of the Herakles myth. At the same time, he was aware of the frequency of this kind of criticism, and this confirmed him in his decision to make Herakles impervious to it by emphasizing that the hero's glory was based on internal achievement rather than external deeds.

As so very often, Euripides could not resist the temptation to beat the rationalizers at their own game. The result—as in so many other of his plays—is a full-blown rhetorical debate between Lycus and Amphitryon about the courage of a man who uses the bow, rather than the spear, for his weapon. Lycus denounces it as a coward's weapon, because it is not designed for the one and only martial encounter of true men, combat at close quarters. The argument would have troubled Pindar, who insisted that his man fought openly, but not Euripides. Amphitryon defends the use of the archaic weapon with the arguments of an Athenian sophist. In an age of individualism, dependence on your comrades in the ranks of the spearsmen would be foolishly anachronistic. The most profitable strategy in war is to protect yourself and hurt your foe, and therefore it is good to remain concealed. This alone is worthy of a wise man (*sophos* 189). The image of Herakles fighting with a primitive weapon is converted into that of the self-reliant individualist who is using his head rather than his brawn. Thus Herakles, an anachronistic warrior in Homer's epics, now is brilliantly adapted even in this respect to Euripides' time, and it is his turn to make the Homeric heroes look anachronistic.

Little more need be said of the melodrama's grinding to its seemingly inexorable end except that we must briefly focus on the attitudes of Megara and Amphitryon. They are facing extreme adversity, and so will Herakles later. He thus is characterized by contrast as well as by direct action.

Megara lapses into pious resignation. It would be folly to wrestle with necessity, she says (282–3). To be sure, the reputation of her husband demands that his sons and wife die a better death, but one cannot fight necessity, even if necessity brings disgrace. Accordingly, Megara concludes that (309–11):

> The man who struggles out of fate inflicted by the gods
> shows zeal, but his zeal is foolish.
> No man can set aside the decree of fate.

With this, Megara becomes almost a foil for Herakles. It is clear that what she says is relevant to him. This relevance is made most explicit, on a verbal level, by her choice of the word 'to struggle out of' (ἐκμοχθέω) that had characterized his labours, of which the greatest is yet to come, from the outset.[41]

Amphitryon does not reply directly to Megara's argument that resistance to necessity is futile. Instead he lives up to his earlier maxim (105–6) by deciding to persevere and trust in whatever faint hope there is of saving Herakles' sons. He is fully aware that this is hoping against hope: 'I am in love, it seems, with what cannot be' (318). This lonely courage makes him, a mortal, superior in *aretē* to the god, Zeus (342), whom he angrily denounces as callous and unjust.

This suffices for anticipating the second action and Euripides quickly returns the first action to its conventional mould. The subsequent stasimon of the chorus is the longest preserved praise of Herakles' deeds in Greek poetry and combines several of his labours proper with some of the parerga such as slaying the centaurs and Cycnus. The hero's civilizing mission of ridding the world from monsters is the leitmotif. When Herakles unexpectedly appears, he is quick to reject this traditional role of the culture hero and the *kallinikos*. We learned at the beginning of the play that his labours were motivated by filial piety, and he emphatically reaffirms that this should be the only consideration (574–82):

> For whom should I defend more than my wife and sons
> and my aged father? Farewell, my labours!
> Vainly I wrought them, and did not help these.
> I should die defending these, if they die
> for their father. Or shall we call this a noble deed
> to have done battle with the lion and the hydra
> at Eurystheus' behest, and not to avert
> death from my sons? I shall be called no more,
> as in olden times, 'Herakles, the *kallinikos*'.

Because Herakles has already divested himself of his outward greatness, his life will not lose its meaning when the gods try to humiliate him. Before he leaves the stage, he is characterized as the completely domestic and loving family man, who in this respect is at least the equal of Sophocles' Deianeira.[42] He goes into the palace to thank the household gods for his safe return from Hades (607–9). He sets aside his bow and club so he can take his children by their hands (cf. Plate 2) and lead them in his wake 'like a ship that tows its little boats behind'. All men are equal in the love of their children, he says, and on this tender note the scene ends. Its visual impact has been carefully impressed upon the spectator and contrasts savagely with the next description we hear of Herakles—the messenger's terrifyingly vivid account of the hero's slaughter of his children and wife.

To add to the contrast, the chorus continues with the conventional praise of Herakles and attributes his return to the justice of the gods (813–14). Hardly have they finished these words when their living contradiction[43] comes on the stage in the persons of Madness and Iris. Madness resists at first by citing the achievement of Herakles' labours: he fought for the honour of the gods when it was trampled under by evil men. It is an impassioned paraphrase of the Pindaric concept of Herakles as the protagonist of the *nomos*, but it has no effect. Iris curtly rejects Lyssa's—the goddess of Madness!—appeal to the time-honoured Greek virtue of *sōphrosynē* and Herakles is struck mad. The deflation of the external aspects of his labours now becomes visual as he re-enacts during his fit some of the most typical scenes from his struggles. As he rages through the palace, he fancies himself riding on his chariot, attacking cities. and wrestling with an opponent—

> then he wrestled with no one
> and proclaimed himself the victor (*kallinikos*)
> to the shouts of no one (960–2).

The messenger sums up the story by saying that he knows of no man 'more miserable than Herakles'. Besides intending a reversal—one of the many reversals in this play—of the traditional phrase 'Herakles, the best of men', Euripides pointedly expresses 'more miserable' with the word *athliōteros* which is derived from *athla*, labours.

The next scene, in which the sleeping Herakles is brought upon the stage, is reminiscent of the corresponding scene in the *Trachiniae* and points up the contrast between Euripides' and Sophocles' view of Herakles. In the earlier play, Herakles rants and raves and protests; here he comes slowly to his senses, asks for the truth, and learns it. His fame and reputation ruined, he is ready to take the conventional heroic way out by committing suicide. Here Euripides' redirecting of the myth is of course most evident. Theseus, whom Herakles had just saved from the underworld, appears, ready to give aid to Amphitryon. As in the *Oedipus at Colonus*, this Theseus is the noblest personification of enlightened, compassionate Athenian humanism. He tells Herakles that Herakles' misfortunes are no reflection of his quality. The inner man is what matters. Euripides makes this shift to internalization explicit by having Theseus define what a noble man really is: one who bears unflinchingly what heaven sends (1227–8). The word for 'noble' (εὐγενής) is the same which Megara (292) and the chorus (696) had used for praising Herakles' noble descent. Nobility of lineage now is replaced by nobility of spirit,[44] a spirit of perseverance.

The winning over of Herakles to this realization is the principal theme of the second action. To make this conversion of Herakles believable, the playwright has him struggle against it with the traditional attitudes for which Herakles was known. Thus even the old Homeric Herakles, the defiant fighter against the gods, makes his brief reappearance here. Herakles' misery towers to heaven, therefore he will strike heaven. And with even greater apodictic force he continues; 'Heaven has a will of its own. And so do I' (1243). When Theseus castigates him for being presumptuous, Herakles' mood changes abruptly: once more, he wishes to die. But now Theseus is not deceived by the 'heroic' veneer of such an action; rather, he calls Herakles' words those of an ordinary man. Herakles, who endured so much, has the obligation to endure this new trial also, even though it is of a different nature. Mankind's greatest benefactor and friend owes it to Hellas not to die foolishly.

Theseus' appeal to the duty of internal heroism incumbent on a great hero[45] goads Herakles into delivering a speech of magnificent bitterness. He discards his labours, because they were futile. Whereas he earlier put them second in importance to his family, they now are even more odious to him because he views the murder of his family as their culmination. Actually, his last labour had been his descent to Hades, but now hell is within Herakles: 'I am like Ixion, bound for ever to a wheel' (1297–8). Once more, the force of traditional attitudes seems to oppress Herakles. He is accursed—similar to Oedipus—and is afraid that no one will receive him. Still, Theseus' arguments have left their mark. At the end of his lament, Herakles calls himself the first man of Hellas and Hellas' benefactor. Theseus therefore repeats his appeal to Herakles' obligation to persevere (1313–14). And he succeeds. Herakles now admits that even in his abject misery he asked himself whether suicide would not be the act of a coward (1347–8). He now realizes that it takes more courage to endure under the blows of fate than to fight against an enemy (1349–51):

> The man who cannot bear up under the blows of fate
> would flinch even from the weapons of a man.
> I shall await death steadfastly.

This new heroism is not without connection to his earlier life. Stripped of their external qualities, the hero's labours constitute a spiritual legacy to which Herakles must continue to live up (1353–7):

> For countless are the labours of which I have experience;
> never have I shrunk from any, never yet
> have I wept, nor had I ever thought
> that I should come to this: to shed tears from my eyes.
> But now, it seems, I must serve necessity.

Now that the labours are an example of internal fortitude and spiritual strength rather then external success, he remembers their noble purpose and quality even though the remembrance is mingled with the earlier bitterness about their tragic outcome (1368–70). For this reason, he also decides to retain the weapons with which he accomplished his labours, even though they remind him of the slaughter of his family. Re-emphasizing the pivotal theme of the play, Euripides has Herakles waver once more in his resolution. And again, Theseus reminds him of his labours, of the strength he mustered for them, and of the resulting fame. It takes no courage, Herakles agrees, to dispatch oneself to the literal Hades (1415); it takes real courage to bear one's own hell in this life. Strengthened by Theseus' unfailing friendship,

Herakles leaves the stage just as his children left the stage in the first action—'towed in Theseus' wake like some little boat'. His last words are an affirmation of the superiority of spiritual values, such as friendship, over externals:

> The man who would rather have wealth or strength
> than good friends thinks like a fool.

'To think', 'to have understanding' is Herakles' last word (1426), reminiscent of the debate between Lycus and Amphitryon about Herakles' reasoning.[46] Because his great deeds have been matched by and ultimately are based on this spiritual endurance, the chorus characterizes him, in the play's last line, not as the greatest of all men, as before, but as the greatest of all friends. Herakles has truly become a member of the human community.

We noted earlier that the humanization of Herakles was necessary to keep him from becoming divinely irrelevant. Whereas the gods, Hera in particular, act capriciously and compel Herakles and men to suffer without cause, it is the men who aspire to a standard which the gods do not care to attain. In the first action, this is exemplified by Amphitryon who rightly considers himself better in *aretē*—which we may translate in this context with 'moral force'—than Zeus. By persevering against the power that ruins him Herakles is the even more perfect son of his father. Euripides takes pains to stress that this father is the mortal Amphitryon and not, as in the legend and the tradition-inspired praise of the chorus, the god Zeus (1264–5).

In the history of the adaptation of Herakles in literature, Euripides' treatment of the theme marks a true turning point. On the one hand, it is the culmination of all the efforts to purge Herakles of his objectionable qualities and deeds. Characteristically, Euripides met the problem head on. He chose the most odious episode of Herakles' life and converted its consequences into the hero's greatest achievement. This had been so, of course, in the traditional myth, where the labours followed upon the murder. True to converting Herakles' outward achievement into an inward one, Euripides turned the myth inside out and reversed the order of events. The result is that Herakles' internal heroism literally takes the place of the external one. More importantly, by humanizing the hero's struggles and grandeur, Euripides gave him a new dimension which went far beyond his ethical idealization by Pindar and others. Instead of the *kallinikos*, no matter how nobly inspired he may have been, we from now on will see Herakles cast more and more often in the almost archetypal role of the suffering and toiling hero. For Euripides and his contemporaries glorified, heroic humanism was enough of a reward; man, in a sense, was the measure of all things after all.[47] Euripides' basically optimistic humanization of the Herakles myth reflects, above all, the enlightened spirit of his time. His own, bold contribution was to make Herakles the dramatic symbol of that spirit.

But even if this play is the single most important and influential treatment of the Herakles theme whose tone has been much imitated especially in the last century and ours, it did not discourage survivals of the earlier tradition. To a scholar like Apollonius, Herakles still was the primeval, archaic hero *par excellence* and Goethe, at least in his youth, was more impressed with the physical qualities of Herakles than the spiritual ones. On the other hand, the Stoics, while emphasizing Herakles' incessant toil, found divine reward more compatible with human greatness, and Herakles would be rewarded once more for his toils like Doctor Faustus—*wer immer strebend sich bemüht, den können wir erlösen.* Finally, playwrights such as Seneca, Wedekind, and MacLeish would not be content with Euripides' optimistic humanization of Herakles' achievement but used the hero's labours for expressing their doubts about the validity of any human accomplishment. Being a product of fifth-century Athens, Euripides could believe in the greatness of man, whereas these writers and others could not. Whenever this happened, Herakles would be in search of his true character once more.

Several years before the *Herakles*, in 438 B.C., Euripides wrote the *Alcestis*, his earliest surviving drama. It was produced as the last play of a tetralogy, a place which was commonly held by a satyr play. The only complete satyr play that has survived is Euripides' *Cyclops*, and the *Alcestis* is far removed from the latter's burlesque humour and buffoonery. Without being a tragedy outright, the *Alcestis* is a play about tragic themes even though they are treated with a light touch. The tragedy is about Admetus rather than Alcestis. In the folktale, from which the material for this play was drawn, the young man accepts his wife's sacrifice and since nothing more is heard of him, he can be expected to have lived happily ever after. By contrast, the starting point of Euripides' drama is not Alcestis' action itself, but its consequences for Admetus. Euripides' basic intent was to show what happens when the ideal, wishful world of a folktale is transposed into reality.[48]

For this reason alone, it was entirely suitable for Euripides to introduce Herakles into the story.[49] Herakles belonged to both worlds; traditionally the *Märchen* hero, he had been made relevant to real life especially by Pindar and Sophocles. Euripides' own *Herakles* was the culmination of the latter process, and we will shortly see that Herakles is associated in the *Alcestis* with the same themes that are treated as profoundly tragic in the *Herakles*. Furthermore, the introduction of Herakles made possible the psychological and ethical emphasis on the role of Admetus. Herakles is Admetus' foil and, throughout the play, his good-natured antagonist. Both by contrast and by direct confrontation with Herakles, Admetus' limitations become all the more obvious. In the first scene in which he appears, Herakles is characterized at the outset as willingly accepting what has been imposed on him. Euripides develops this theme at length in the dialogue between Herakles and the chorus. Herakles is on his way to capture the horses of Diomedes. The chorus repeatedly warns him of the danger; a fight will be necessary and Herakles may lose his life. Herakles' only answer is that he cannot refuse his labours even if this means death (489). Euripides is concerned only marginally with justifying Herakles' actions; what he wants is to impress upon the spectator that Herakles is not a shirker like Admetus.

Admetus then comes on the stage and prevails on Herakles to stay at the palace in spite of Herakles' protestations that it is not proper to banquet in the house of a mourning friend. Admetus' defence of his action to the chorus re-emphasizes his greatest limitation: he is a prisoner of convention. 'What else should I have done?' is the gist of his plea to the citizens of Pherae. 'You would have blamed me even more if I had sent the man away, who is my greatest guest-friend, and thus had given my house an inhospitable reputation.' And then he reveals that the motive for his *xenia* is not altruistic, but a scrupulous concern to live up to the principle of *do ut des* (559–60):

> For this man happens to be my best host
> whenever I go to Argos, which is a thirsty place.

'All good and true,' replies the chorus, 'but if this man really is your best friend, he will understand.' Admetus, however, reiterates his obsession with a social convention. Herakles has to be hosted properly; the death of Alcestis and the mourning are secondary.

So far from being his greatest virtue and saving grace, Admetus' excessive *xenia* is his most serious shortcoming. He is so preoccupied with its external aspects that he completely ignores that it is no more than a means to the end of establishing a genuine trust and friendship between two persons. This is what *xenia* at its best meant in Homer, and the ideal continued to be relevant in the fifth century. Looked upon merely as a formality, it could become meaningless and be abused as, for instance, by the suitors in the *Odyssey*. This is precisely Admetus' mistake and it makes him a timeless character; the king of ancient Pherae today would be well reincarnated as the Organization Man. He is so obsessed with social conventions, the approval of his peers, with 'doing the right thing' and doing things 'properly' that he incapacitates himself for reacting spontaneously, on the basis of human and humane feeling and instincts. T. S. Eliot summed this up perfectly when he has Harcourt-Reilly, the Herakles of the *Cocktail Party*,[50] say to Edward:

> You are nothing but a set
> Of obsolete responses.

It is in this respect that Euripides contrasts Admetus most expressly with Herakles. The lengthy complaint of the servant (747–72) serves only one purpose: to show that Herakles has violated every rule in the Golden Book of etiquette. But the moment Herakles finds out that it was Alcestis who died, he reacts with spontaneous grief, and without Admetus' hesitation, selfishness, and ambiguity. His first reaction, of course, is to ask incredulously whether all this was going on while he was being hosted. The servant attempts to lead Herakles on to praising Admetus' *xenia* (823):

> He could not bear to turn you from his palace

but Herakles' first concern—as Admetus' should have been—is Alcestis:

> Wretched Admetus, what a wife and companion you have lost!

Now it is the servant who follows Herakles' lead and admits, even if by overstatement, what Admetus did not want to admit to himself—

'we all have perished, not only she'. Herakles proceeds to blame himself for listening to Admetus in spite of his premonitions, and for turning his own, traditional *bia* against himself. Then he decides to save Alcestis, and only in the end does he praise Admetus for his great guest-friendship.

We can see now why Euripides chose Herakles as a foil for Admetus. Herakles was the archetypal 'man of nature'—a concept that Goethe was to express so eloquently—who would not be inhibited by conventions. Homer had stressed the bad aspects of this by pillorying Herakles for his gross violation of *xenia* in killing his guest-friend Iphitus. Pindar, as we saw earlier, cleared away this image of Herakles by depicting him as the protector of *xenia*, and Euripides went even further: Admetus imposes *xenia* on an unwilling Herakles.[51] More importantly, however, Herakles' traditional, relaxed attitude to social conventions shows up here in a most positive light. Herakles abides by them, but is not dominated by them. He therefore preserves his natural impulses and vital humanity. His values are not warped as are Admetus': to him people come first and social niceties second.

Euripides' *Alcestis*, then, and Herakles in particular are that playwright's reaction against the trend to over-civilization which made itself felt in the highly refined and complex society of fifth-century Athens. It was a theme to which Euripides remained faithful to the end of his life for he treated it, far more grandiosely, in his last play, the *Bacchae*. One need only look at Plato's and others' descriptions of a symposium to see that even these occasions for convivial relaxation and gaiety had in many respects become a very stylized affair, which followed strict rules. This is a far cry from the unspoiled vitality with which Herakles bursts on the scene and which he—like Dionysus later in the *Bacchae*—represents throughout the *Alcestis*. The same desire for a simple and less shackled life force led the Cynics to adopt Herakles as their hero, even if in a more austere manner.

Before discussing Herakles' drunken speech, which so many later authors and critics have found objectionable, let us turn to the play's final scene in which Herakles prevails on Admetus to accept the veiled woman that is Alcestis. This scene is an inversion of the first Herakles–Admetus scene. Now Herakles lies to Admetus and tries to persuade him although Admetus resists and protests. By subtly inverting the former situation, Herakles is able to play on and mock the conventions which for his host have become the essence of life. This alone shows the quality of Herakles' humour. It is that of the *homo ludens*, who is delighted with playing his game. There is nothing crude and distasteful in Herakles' teasing. Superior as it is, his humour is good-natured, sophisticated, and urbane.[52] For a moment, even his traditional role as the enduring and suffering hero is reversed. The chorus piously counsels Admetus to 'endure what the god gives' (1071), and Herakles says wistfully he would like to be strong enough to bring Alcestis back (1075–8):

> Adm.: I know that this was your desire. But how can this be done?
> The dead cannot return.
> Her.: Don't overdo it, then, but bear it as is fit.
> Adm.: Easier to exhort than to suffer and endure.

Throughout the scene Admetus tries to show that he is a decent man who is worthy of Alcestis. But he is not, because the concern for the proper and socially acceptable thing to do still is uppermost in his mind. Just before Herakles returns, Admetus recognizes his own wretched situation, but he does not change. He says virtually nothing about Alcestis except that she has her glory and is free from much trouble now that she is dead (938). Admetus spends infinitely more time commiserating with himself. He does not feel miserable because of grief for Alcestis, but because he is terrified by the prospect of what other people might say about him. Our other-directed king is greatly worried that society might reject him. Herakles' first words therefore are designed to meet the peculiar requirements which Admetus' mentality imposes on anyone who wishes to communicate with him. Herakles cannot allow himself a sincere, spirited expression of sorrow as he did in his dialogue with the chorus. Rather, since he deals with Admetus, he first addresses him with a lecture on manners, chastising him for the misguided social favours that Admetus had bestowed on him. After thus establishing a rapport with Admetus, he asks him for the favour of keeping the girl in his absence.

When Admetus states his two objections, he predictably mentions first the blame he might incur from his countrymen, and only then the reproaches of his dead wife. Before thinking even of these possibilities

Admetus has discussed the technicalities of putting the girl into someone else's house and dismissed this solution on equally technical grounds.[53] After these external arguments have been dealt with, Herakles begins to lead Admetus to the heart of the matter. For once, Admetus rises to the moral occasion. He refuses Herakles' appeals to his loneliness and even his habits of hospitality, although Herakles is at his coaxing best, far surpassing the Pindaric precedent in subtlety.[54] Admetus promised Alcestis celibacy, and he will honour that promise even if it means death (1096). At the very moment, however, when it appears that Admetus has finally overcome himself, he suddenly reverts to his more familiar character. He is afraid that Herakles, his friend, might be angry with him if he keeps refusing (1106). Herakles does not answer to that, but hints that something unknown to Admetus makes him so insistent, and Admetus obeys. His concern not to incur the displeasure of a friend wins out as it did in the first Herakles–Admetus scene. Admetus cannot shake off his self-imposed habit of paying excessive respect to social obligations.

By contrast, Herakles states his own philosophy of life in the drunken scene which later writers, who adapted the theme, considered so embarrassing and incongruent that they either eliminated it or rewrote it.[55] Herakles' first remarks again are designed to set in relief the difference between him and Admetus. Death, he says, is an obligation which we all must pay (782). His acceptance of death had been the keynote of his first appearance. Now, however, Herakles goes on providing a reason for it. He does so in a tipsy and jolly mood—one might think of Sir Toby Belch talking to Malvolio—but the implications are serious and Euripides was to develop their tragic nature in the *Herakles*. Our lives, says Herakles, are at the mercy of Tychē, Necessity (785–6):

> The ways of Tychē are out of our sight.
> We cannot learn the ways, nor can we make them ours by craft.

In the *Herakles*, Amphitryon would point out that the man who has good Tychē today stands not to have it for the rest of his life. The advice Herakles gives the sour-looking servant is based on the same realization (787–9):

> Now that you have heard me and have learned from me, make merry, drink, reckon the life you live today your own, but only that—the rest belongs to Tychē.

A girl and a few drinks are the best remedy against the present necessities (*tychas* 796).[56] There is no point worrying constantly about Tychē because life, in that case, would not be life, but a disaster (802). To live in the face of ever-threatening Tychē is our human condition (799). Herakles' joyful acceptance of this condition is a far cry from shallow hedonism and, as is clear from the contrast with the other personages in the play, shows real strength of character. In the *Herakles*, only the accent is different as it shifts to tragic human heroism. In the *Alcestis*, Herakles professes to teach wisdom by expounding on this view of life. In the *Herakles*, there is even more emphasis on the use of his mind and his wisdom.

To suit his dramatic purpose, however, Euripides has Herakles in the *Herakles* gradually come to the realization of which he is already cognizant in the *Alcestis*. His situation in the *Herakles* therefore is analogous, in some important respects, to that of Admetus. Both are responsible for the death of their wives.[57] In the *Herakles*, Herakles also is intensely preoccupied with what society will think of him and do to him. Like Admetus, he expresses doubts about the usefulness of continuing his life and argues in favour of an accepted convention, suicide. The difference is of course that Herakles, who was so superior to Admetus in the *Alcestis*, proves his superiority when he is tragically confronted with the same problem as Admetus. Admetus' nobility[58] remains external; Herakles' does not.

Sublime and moving as the *Herakles* is, we should note that Euripides' portrait of Herakles in one respect is a regression from the *Alcestis*. In the *Alcestis*, Euripides made the eminently successful attempt to put on the stage an integrated Herakles. Herakles had his comic and his serious sides, and they are combined in the *Alcestis*. Herakles here is the boon companion and good-natured helper of the folktale tradition, but his portrayal nowhere degenerates into gross caricature or buffoonery. His view of life is serious and his standards are superior to those of his host, but there is no heavy-handed moralizing and the tragic situation is handled with wit and ease. The peculiar form of the drama—

a mixture between tragic and comic which defies ultimate definition—is consistent with Euripides' view of Herakles' character. From then on, most writers would stress only one aspect of Herakles' complex personality. To some extent this was the result of the tradition, which made Herakles an increasingly more composite and complex character. In Euripides' day it was less difficult to create an integrated portrait of the hero, whereas later poets who harboured this ideal—notably Ronsard, Goethe, and Spitteler—had to give up in despair.

Whatever the specific reasons, the one-sided view of Herakles took its toll on the most important adaptations of the *Alcestis*.[59] In Wieland's and Alfieri's versions he becomes the epitome of non-alcoholic virtue, and the drunken scene disappears. In Hofmannsthal's *Alcestis* Herakles still is quite drunk when he comes on stage, but sobers up completely and gives a long, melancholy speech on the relation between death and drunkenness. This romantic, presumed sublimation impoverishes the Euripidean concept of the tragic Herakles as it takes the place of Herakles' remarks on Tychē. We are finally left with an attenuated bumpkin rather than an idealized Herakles. Browning's Balaustion, in turn, rids Herakles of his humanity and spends scores of lines, which are not even suggested by Euripides' *Alcestis*, on glowing depictions of the heavenly, magnificent, shining, and victorious aspects of Herakles, who is cast as a superhuman demi-god. The hapless servant, who dares to criticize Herakles' drunken behaviour, comes in for a merciless tongue-lashing from the romantic author. He is denounced as a court bureaucrat, who suffers from all the concomitant spiritual limitations:

> Stupid? Nay, but sagacious in a sort:
> Learned, life-long, i' the first outside of things,
> Though bat for blindness to what lies beneath,
> And needs a nail-scratch ere 'tis laid you bare.
>
> (*Balaustion's Adventure* 1626–9)

This antithesis may have been suggested to Browning by the long tradition of the sensitive, perceptive Herakles whose earliest proponents were Euripides and Isocrates. In a long tirade, Browning-Balaustion then goes on castigating the servant for not volunteering his life for

Alcestis. Nor is this all. Balaustion rallies to Herakles' defence with yet another argument:

Herakles
Had flung into the presence, frank and free,
Out from the labour into the repose,
Ere out again and over head and ears
Is the heart of labour, all for the love of men:
Making the most o' the minute, that the soul
And body, strained to height a minute since,
Might lie relaxed in joy, this breathing-space,
For man's sake more than ever; till the bow,
Restrung o' the sudden, at first cry for help,
Should send some unimaginable shaft
True to the aim and shatteringly through
The plate-mail of a monster, save man so.
(1722–34)

Browning thus continued the literary tradition of Herakles' justification in his own high-blown, romantic manner.

Most characteristic of the difference between Euripides' and Browning's Herakles is, as we already noted, Browning's conception of him as the divine, glorious son of Zeus. His setting out for the rescue of Alcestis is put in terms of almost cosmic significance. Herakles' deed suggests the eternal cycle of birth, death, and rebirth, and this cycle in turn takes place within Herakles himself:

So, one look upward, as if Zeus might laugh
Approved of his human progeny,—
One summons of the whole magnific frame,
Each sinew to its service,—up he caught,
And over the shoulder cast, the lion-shag,
Let the club go,—for had he not those hands?
And so went striding off, on that straight way
Leads to Larissa and the suburb tomb.
Gladness with thee, Helper of our world!
I think this is the authentic sign and seal
Of godship, that it ever waxes glad,

And more glad, until gladness blossoms, bursts
Into a rage of suffer for mankind,
And recommence at sorrow; drops like seed
After the blossom, ultimate of all.
Say, does the seed scorn earth, and seek the sun?
Surely it has no other end and aim
Than to drop, once more to die into the ground,
Taste cold and darkness and oblivion there:
And thence rise, tree-like grow through pain to joy,
More joy and most joy,—do man good again.
(1909–27)

With this, Herakles stalks off in monolithic splendour. Browning's characterization of him has been of one piece throughout, and the time-honoured clichés of the saviour and the helper have been rapturously blown up to the point of bursting. But as rhetoric and bombast have grown, so the fullness of Herakles' role has declined. Whereas his characterization in Euripides' *Alcestis* was a finely balanced whole of the hero's many traits, Herakles becomes a monolinear and simplistic figure in the poetry of the adaptors. The romantic tendency, which still is so influential in the criticism of classical literature, and the 'scientific' method of lingering nineteenth-century classical scholarship with its insistence on 'logical', consistent character delineation have led to the same result by imposing an equally one-sided interpretation on this Euripidean Herakles. In fact, however, the *Alcestis* presents one of the few complete portraits of the hero that was ever attempted in creative literature. With so many-sided a hero, detailed filigree was impossible, and Euripides therefore contented himself with sketching Herakles' portrait with a few, vigorous strokes of the brush.[60]

NOTES TO CHAPTER III

1. For details, see Farnell 107–10.
2. Euripides, *HF* 1328–31; see also Philochorus *FGH* 328 F 18 (=Plut. *Theseus* 35. 2) and Jacoby's commentary ad loc.
3. Plutarch, *Theseus* 33. 2. H. Lloyd-Jones, 'Heracles at Eleusis: POxy 2622

and P.S.I. 1391', *Maia* 19 (1967) 206–29 discusses some papyrus fragments which make reference to this initiation; the author may have been Pindar.

4. So, e.g. Conradie 134 and Léon Parmentier, *Euripide* 3 (Paris, 1965) 4.
5. In Coleridge's terms, this would be the superiority of expectation to surprise (*Essays and Lectures on Shakespeare* [Everyman ed., 1907] 52–3).
6. A good summary of the basic arguments is found in N. Wecklein, *The Prometheus Bound of Aeschylus*, trans. by F. D. Allen (Boston, 1891) 13–22. Cf. C. J. Herington, *The Author of the 'Prometheus Bound'* (Austin, 1970) 123–6.
7. This rules out the possibility that Ge effects the reconciliation because, parallel to Okeanos in *Prometheus Bound*, she appears prior to Herakles in *Prometheus Unbound.*
8. Various forms of πέτρα recur in lines 31, 56, 242, 269, 447, 760, 970; cf. 300, 561, 1021. It is a motif that is well established in the *Prometheus Bound* and this is pertinent to the use of the word in the *Prometheus Unbound.*
9. See G. Thomson, *Aeschylus and Athens* (London, 1946) 335. Thomson believes that the *Prometheus Unbound* was the second play of the trilogy, but he overshoots the mark by postulating that the plot of the third play was concerned with the future of Herakles and Herakles' continuation of Prometheus' work.
10. So David Grene in the introduction of his translation of the *Prometheus Bound* in D. Grene and R. Lattimore, eds., *Aeschylus* 2 (Chicago, 1956) 134.
11. See *Prometheus Bound* 1026–9, supplemented by Apollodorus 2. 5. 4 and 2. 5. 11.
12. Wecklein (note 6, above) 13, with reference to Athen. 15. 674d and 15. 672e.
13. Fr. 74 N.; see p. 34.
14. *Pace* Fraenkel, I do not believe that Clytemestra's remark is well-intentioned.
15. The fragments and a commentary on the lost plays are found most conveniently in R. C. Jebb and A. C. Pearson, *The Fragments of Sophocles* I–III (Cambridge, 1917).
16. Sophocles has captured the attention of twentieth-century critics more than the other two tragedians. I have benefited from consulting the relevant chapters in K. Reinhardt, *Sophokles*, 3rd ed. (Frankfurt, 1947); C. M. Bowra, *Sophoclean Tragedy* (Oxford, 1945); A. J. A. Waldock, *Sophocles the Dramatist* (Cambridge, 1951); C. Whitman, *Sophocles. A Study of Heroic Humanism* (Cambridge, Mass., 1951); S. M. Adams, *Sophocles the Playwright* (Toronto, 1957); G. M. Kirkwood, *A Study of Sophoclean Drama* (Ithaca, 1958); Stoessl 39–57; Pohlenz 198–208. I have built mostly, however, on Gilbert Murray's essay, 'Herakles, the Best of Men', *Greek Studies* (Oxford, 1946) 106–26; V. Ehrenberg, 'Tragic Herakles', *Aspects of the Ancient World* (Oxford, 1946) 144–57; H. D. F. Kitto, *Poiesis* (Berkeley and Los Angeles, 1966) 154–99 and, of course, Sophocles' *Trachiniae* as edited by R. C. Jebb (Cambridge, 1908). For the opposite view of the one presented here see especially Bowra and Adams, followed by Waith 20–6.

17. Contrast this with Pindar, *Ol.* 10. 30 as discussed on p. 32.
18. Kitto (note 16, above) 168.
19. This has rightly been stressed by A. Beck, *Hermes* 72 (1953) 19.
20. The deliberate contrast between Herakles' and Deianeira's treatment of Lichas again could not be more extreme. For further examples of Sophocles' technique of contrast see especially Kirkwood (note 16, above) 110ff.
21. Ehrenberg 154.
22. For a favourable view of Herakles by sophists see Plato, *Symp.* 177B, for its opposite, *Gorgias* 484B–C. Prodicus' parable related by Xenophon, *Mem.* 2. 1. 21ff. is discussed on pp. 101ff.
23. Especially by developing, on no fewer than three occasions, the implications of Herakles' sacrifice to Zeus; see Kitto 175ff.
24. Aside from the examples mentioned here, consider the very beginning of it (229–31): 'We are happy in our return, and happy in our greeting, lady, which befits the deed achieved; for when a man has good fortune, he by necessity must win good welcome.' There is an echo here of line 57 where the Nurse enjoins Deianeira to send Hyllus to find out about Herakles' 'good fortune'. The pious *a priori* assumption that Herakles' fortune always turns out well is completely destroyed in this play.
25. So Whitman (note 16, above) 116.
26. *Trach.* 1082: ἔθαλψε μ'ἄτης σπασμὸς' ἀρτίως ὅδ' αὖ. See A. A. Long, *Language and Thought in Sophocles* (London, 1968) 134–5.
27. H. D. F. Kitto, *Greek Tragedy* (Garden City, N.Y., 1961) 314.
28. See, most recently, E. R. Schwinge, *Die Stellung der Trachinierinnen im Werk des Sophokles* (Göttingen, 1962) and S. G. Kapsomenos, *Sophokles' Trachinierinnen und ihr Vorbild* (Athens, 1963). Many details of my interpretation of the *Philoctetes* are based on H. C. Avery, 'Heracles, Neoptolemus, Philoctetes', *Hermes* 93 (1965) 279–97. Also helpful are A. Spira, *Untersuchungen zum deus ex machina bei Sophokles und Euripides* (Kallmünz, 1960) 12–30 and P. W. Harsh, 'The Role of the Bow in the *Philoctetes* of Sophocles', *AJP* 81 (1960) 408–14.
29. This is Reinhardt's phrase (note 16, above) 200.
30. These plays, along with Sophocles', are summarized, even if sketchily, by Dio Chrysostom (*Or.* 52). The artistic and other literary evidence about Euripides' *Philoctetes* has been compiled by T. B. L. Webster, *The Tragedies of Euripides* (London, 1967) 57–61.
31. Harsh (note 28, above) 412.
32. Especially by references to his Oetan homeland or father: 453, 479, 490–9, 664, 721–9.
33. This has been noticed by D. M. Jones, *CR* 63 (1949) 85 who comments: 'By such reminiscent touches is built up the importance of Herakles as an ideal in Philoctetes' mind and as a power behind the action of the play, while preparation is made for his epiphany at the end.'
34. Avery (note 28, above) 290.

35. Cf. Spira (note 28, above) 16. Philoctetes thus calls Odysseus 'the most hateful *technēma* of clever villainy' (928).
36. See pp. 106f. The popularity of the Herakles myth at the end of the fifth century is attested, among others, by Socrates' comparison of his search for the true meaning of the Delphic oracle to Herakles' laborious wanderings (*Apol.* 22a), and by the references to prestigious descent from Herakles in Plato's *Thaetetus* 175A and *Lysis* 205C.
37. *FGH* 31 F 14. More details on Herodorus, whose *floruit* usually is given as 400 B.C., can be found in Jacoby's commentary ad loc. and in his article 'Herodorus' in *RE* 8. 980–7. Another allegorical interpretation of one of Herakles' labours—his fight against the Hydra—is found in Plato, *Euthyd.* 297C; this particular allegory found a great echo in the Renaissance (see pp. 193 and 195).
38. For this basic division of the play see already Wilamowitz 113ff. For good, literary interpretations of the *Herakles* see especially W. A. Arrowsmith's introduction in D. Grene and R. Lattimore, eds., *The Complete Greek Tragedies* 3 (Chicago, 1959) 266–80; D. J. Conacher, *Euripidean Drama* (Toronto, 1967) 78–90; Conradie 50–8, 83–94, 113–33; and the introduction by L. Parmentier to the Budé text (note 5, above) 4–19. Cf. Ehrenberg (note 16, above) 158–66, and Kitto (note 27, above) 248–61.
39. For the dramatic effect of this scene compare also the argument between the two murderers in Shakespeare's *Richard* III, I. 4 and Tyrrel's description of the murderers' feelings in IV. 3.
40. Pindar uses the term in *Isth.* 4. 75 (ναυτίλιαισί τε πορθμὸν ἡμερώσαις), but the connotations are clear from *Nem.* 3. 23–6.
41. 22: ἐξεμόχθησεν πόνους; 1369: ἐκμοχθῶν βίου εὐκλείαν.
42. The domestic aspect of Herakles is re-emphasized in the second action where the hero pays glowing tribute to his faithful wife and her many vigils in his absence (1371–3).
43. The inversion is underscored by the verbal echo of τὸ δικαῖον (813) in Iris' phrase μὴ δόντος δίκην (842).
44. Both are combined in Amphitryon's referring to Herakles as 'my noble child' (50), which is the first occurrence of *eugenēs* in the play.
45. Conacher (note 38, above) 86.
46. Compare also Theseus' injunction that Herakles should not die through folly (*amathia* 1254).
47. Cf. Ehrenberg 164.
48. So von Fritz 320. Von Fritz' essay is by far the most stimulating discussion of the play and its modern adaptations. Valuable also are the introduction in A. M. Dale's edition of the play (Oxford, 1954) and J. R. Wilson, ed., *Twentieth-Century Interpretations of Euripides' Alcestis* (Englewood Cliffs, 1968). The folktale background has been explored comprehensively by A. Lesky, *Alkestis: Der Mythus und das Drama. Sitzungsber. Akad. Wien* (Phil.—Hist. Klasse) 203. 2 (1925) 1–86.
49. The great probability that Euripides introduced Herakles into the story is

supported, with different arguments, by H. L. Ebeling, *TAPA* 29 (1898) 65–85, esp. 74–7, and Conacher (note 38, above) 332–3. The contention that Herakles did not appear in Phrynichus' earlier Alcestis drama is more than an *argumentum ex silentio*.

50. Since this book is about Herakles, and not Herculean characters, a discussion of this interesting play is beyond our scope. Suffice it to say that the contrast between convention and uninhibited vitality recurs in *The Cocktail Party*, even if in a different manner; for a recent, sensible discussion see K. J. Reckford in *Comp. Lit.* 16 (1964) 1–18, esp. 4, 8–10. In Thornton Wilder's *Alcestiad* (see pp. 218ff.) Herakles blames Admetus for failing to realize that guest-friendship is for guests, but not for brothers and friends.
51. A passage in the *Odyssey* (15. 68–74; cf. 195–201, 209–14) provides a definite indication that, in the courtly tradition, it was not proper for the host to overstep the limits of generosity in such a way as to encumber the guest. Menelaus tells Telemachus: 'I should blame even another man who, as host, loves too much or hates too much; everything is better in moderation' (69–71). This is very relevant to Admetus' behaviour, although Euripides takes it one step further and blames Admetus chiefly for the motive that leads him to excess. The *Odyssey* passage has been discussed by H. L. Levy in *TAPA* 94 (1963) 150; most modern interpretations of the *Alcestis* are flawed by the assumption that Admetus' excessive concern for *xenia* is his saving virtue. Nor does it follow that Herakles would otherwise not have rescued Alcestis.
52. Cf. Kitto (note 26, above) 327: 'Needless to say, in the urbane and sophisticated *Alcestis* there is not a trace of the satyric.'
53. For Admetus' inadequacies in the final scene see the spirited discussion by A. W. Verrall, *Euripides the Rationalist* (Cambridge, 1913) 69. Verrall, however, overlooks that Admetus temporarily gains new strength of character, which has been emphasized by W. D. Smith in *Phoenix* 14 (1960) 144–5.
54. *Ol.* 3. 16; see p. 31.
55. See Chapters 9, 10, and 11 for detailed comments on the versions of Wieland, Alfieri, von Hofmannsthal, and Browning. Voltaire's reaction sums it up well enough: 'Il ne faut pas disputer des goûts; mais il est sûr que de telles scènes ne seraient pas souffertes chez nous à la foire' (*Dictionnaire philosophique* 1, s.v. 'Anciens et Modernes'). But no such uproar has accompanied Shakespeare's *Romeo and Juliet* IV. 4, where Peter jests with the musicians while Juliet lies dead in the next room.
56. The emphasis on Tychē is one of the leitmotifs of the *Alcestis*; cf. 213 (setting the tone for the choral ode), 240, 695, 889 (where Tychē is termed 'hard to wrestle against'—an obvious reference to Herakles' wrestling match with Death), 926.
57. Pheres says explicitly that Admetus killed Alcestis (696) because he overstepped his *tychē* (695).

58. *To eugenes* (600); with this compare the references to Herakles' *eugeneia* in the *Herakles* as discussed above.
59. Cf. note 55, above. For a listing of other adaptations, in music and literature, see H. Hunger, *Lexikon der griechischen und römischen Mythologie*, 2nd ed. (Vienna, 1954) 20. To it should be added the poem of Theodore Morrison, *The Dream of Alcestis* (1950), on which see pp. 285f.
60. Aside from the *Herakleidae*, which contains various conventional descriptions of Herakles, Euripides' *Alcmena* and *Auge* are drawn from the Herakles cycle. The fragments from the *Auge* show a surprising number of parallels with the *Herakles*. The hero again is a family man who loves his children and prefers them to his labours (frs. 264, 272 Nauck); he bursts out against tyrants (fr. 275 N.) as he and Amphitryon do against Lycus; and someone remarks on the reversals of Fortune (fr. 273 N.). For Herakles' treatment in the minor Greek tragedians see Des Essarts 104–6, and in Euripides' *Licymnius*, p. 106.

CHAPTER IV

The Comic Hero

The length of our discussion of the tragic Herakles may satisfy our desire, which is assiduously instilled into the student of the classics in both secondary school and college, to see something very profound and meaningful in every extant piece of classical literature. It is completely disproportionate, however, to the frequency of his appearance on the comic stage.[1] The number of serious dramas in which he has a part is a small trickle compared to the torrent of satyr plays, farces, and comedies in which Herakles kept entertaining his audiences, and their delight with him does not seem to have known a saturation point. It was in this role that he was known best to the Greeks of both the mainland and the western colonies, and seen in this light, his philosophical and tragic manifestations seems all the more remarkable. The reasons the latter are generally dealt with in more detail are easy to see. Humour, especially when it is not of the subtle kind, does not become funnier when it is being discussed, and ancient comedy was never meant to be pored over and dissected by scholars. Furthermore, only a very few of the comedies in which Herakles appeared are fully preserved. The numerous fragments and titles of plays, however, give us a good, if somewhat monotonous, idea of Herakles' comical qualities. They are fortunately supplemented by a host of artistic evidence, mostly in the form of vase paintings.

From these it appears that Herakles was the most popular character of the satyr play.[2] The satyrs of course were the followers of Dionysus, and Herakles' association with Dionysus may have contributed to the importance of his role in this genre. According to legend, both Herakles and Dionysus were sons of Zeus and mortal women, both were persecuted by Hera, and both were known as great, warring civilizers,

Dionysus in the east and Herakles chiefly in the west. On a vase in Oxford, the two are shown at a banquet (Plate 2).[3] Whereas Dionysus still holds his attributes—a horn and the thyrsus—Herakles has given up his and is clutching an outsized drinking cup, while looking intensely at the god of wine. Preference for good food and drink rather than his labours was a stock characteristic of the comic Herakles. In another vase painting Herakles participates with Dionysus and Hermes in a Dionysiac revel, a *kōmos* (Plate 3).[4] On a third vase, Dionysus has disappeared, and only Herakles is left at the banquet and is waited upon by a satyr (Plate 3).[5] A lekythos in Vienna finally shows him staging his own *kōmos* (Plate 4).[6] He has put down his club and is playing the flute as he is marching along. A garlanded satyr is cavorting behind him and another, in front. The latter deferentially points to a huge emptied wine jar that is lying on the ground. Rubens' painting 'The Drunkenness of Hercules' seems to have been inspired by this tradition as Herakles is accompanied by cavorting Maenads and satyrs, who point to a cluster of grapes (Plate 5). The satyrs did not stop there but played their pranks on Herakles. When Herakles is helpless as he is holding the earth for Atlas, satyrs approach and steal his bow, quiver, and club, and the thief of the club gaily waves him good-bye.[7] Clad in the lion's skin and brandishing Herakles' club, a satyr then attacks the serpent which is guarding the tree of the Hesperides. The fruits of that tree are wine jars rather than apples (Plate 6).[8] Fittingly enough, this painting adorned such a wine jar, an oinochoe.

The last two illustrations reflect the choice of plot in the satyric drama and the principal reason Herakles became that genre's favourite protagonist. 'The plot represented those parts of ancient legends which were grotesque in themselves or which could be made so by burlesquing them.'[9] And what legends were more suitable for that purpose than those of Herakles, who pushed everything—both good and bad—to superhuman excess and fought against the strangest creatures that could be imagined?

Of the known satyr plays, Sophocles' *Herakles at Taenarus*, which we mentioned earlier,[10] perhaps conformed most readily to this pattern. Herakles' fight with the hellhound Cerberus doubtless was its high point, and the comic anguish of the Hostess in Aristophanes' *Frogs* about this incident may be an echo of its satyric treatment by Sophocles.

There was some literary parody in Sophocles' play also, for Herakles proudly quotes (fr. 209 N.) what Pindar had said about him: 'It is fitting that the man who is active should suffer.'[11] The fight against another fearsome monster may have provided most of the entertainment in the satyr play *Hesione*. Its author is unknown, but a composite scene from it is shown on the so-called Pronomos vase in Naples.[12] In its centre is the god of the theatre, Dionysus, with his bride Ariadne. A vine is sprouting next to Dionysus, and the personification of the plays, Paidia, is sitting at the other end of the couch. Next to her is standing an actor with the mask and costume of Herakles while another actor, in oriental dress and holding the mask of an oriental king, is standing by the vine. He is generally identified with Laomedon, the legendary king of Troy who failed to keep his promise to give his daughter Hesione in marriage to Herakles after the hero had killed the sea monster that threatened Troy. Herakles punished the king by making war on Troy and sacking it.[13]

In several of the known satyr plays he appears in this role of taking revenge on an unjust ruler. In Euripides' *Syleus*, Herakles pretends to be a slave so that Hermes, with much fast sales talk, can pass him on to Syleus, a cruel, barbaric tyrant. The roles of master and servant are reversed soon enough as Herakles helps himself generously to Syleus' food and best wine, using the house door as a table for his repast. He then begins to boss Syleus around before flooding the place as he flooded the stables of Augias, and thus drowning him. Most characteristic of the tone of these dramas is perhaps Herakles' bombastic provocation of Syleus (fr. 687 N.):

> Burn, baby, burn my flesh and get your fill
> drinking my black blood. The stars will be
> below the earth, and the earth will go up to the heaven
> before you hear some flattering speeches from me.

This is the voice—Ercles' vein—of the primeval bully, but the tradition of justifying Herakles was not to be denied even in the satyr play. The hero himself affirmed that he was 'a just fellow for the just but the greatest enemy of all evil-doers on earth' (fr. 692 N.). If a man is depraved, as Syleus is, he deserves to be treated in kind. This is the timeless morality of comedy, and it is closer to the *ius talionis* than to the

Pindaric *nomos*. Accordingly, Herakles drags off Syleus' daughter Xenodike to violate her, but not before he tells her what is about to happen: 'Come on inside, and let's go to bed. And just wipe your tears off' (fr. 694 N.).

In the *Syleus* we find all the characteristic traits for which Herakles was known on the comic stage: he is a gross monster, a brute, a glutton, and a libertine. But even apart from his justification, it is more than doubtful that the joke was on Herakles in those satyr plays in which he was pitted against a despot, who usually happened to be a barbarian. In the many vase paintings, for instance, which show Herakles killing the Egyptian king Busiris and his priests, the barbarians are caricatured tendentiously. The scene on a hydria in Munich is typical in this regard (Plate 6).[14] A tall Herakles, whose head projects into the meander decoration, towers over the grotesquely contorted Negro-Egyptians. Three priests, one of them lying on the ground, scratch their heads in desperation and fright, whereas a fourth, whom Herakles has seized by the throat and who is bleeding all over, grovels for mercy and drops his sacrificial basket. It stands to reason that in Euripides' *Busiris* it was the Egyptians who were ridiculed and not Herakles, especially as he once again was cast in the role of the avenger of *xenia*. That Herakles' fight against some barbarian despot was a prevailing theme in satyric drama is further evident from a Hellenistic satyr play, the *Lityerses* of Sositheos (frs. 2–3 N.). Sositheos seems to have conformed to the standard treatment of the theme. Lityerses, a Phrygian tyrant, perverted the law of *xenia* by hosting guests sumptuously, then making them harvest with him, and finally beheading the unwary with his sickle. Herakles inflicted the same fate on him and threw the corpse into the Meander river. By so doing he saved Daphnis who was about to be killed by Lityerses.[15] Euripides apparently preceded Sositheos in writing the satyr play the *Harvesters* about the same story.

The frequent choice of this kind of theme in the fifth century can be attributed to the Greek dislike of tyrants and barbarian kings. When Herakles gave them their whacks, amid all the concomitant horseplay, he merely continued *sub specie ludi* his role as the purifier, saviour, and bringer of justice and Greek standards to oriental lands. It is quite consistent with this basic outlook that he should speak in his defence on occasional Pindaric *gnomē*, such as that a man's *physis* is far more important than his being a legitimate child.[16] The fragments of other satyr plays, however, more definitely anticipate comedy in their almost one-sided emphasis on Herakles as a glutton. A particularly graphic example is found in Ion's *Omphale* where Herakles, 'in ravenous hunger, gulped down even the fire logs and coals'.[17]

The popularity of Herakles in Greek comedy has often been considered in connection with the origins of that genre. Both Attic comedy and the phlyakes, the farcical drama of the Greeks in southern Italy, have been regarded as being indebted to the Peloponnesian farce, and Herakles was of course the great Doric hero. This is, however, an argument from no evidence. We cannot date the Doric farce earlier than the earliest Attic comedy, nor can Herakles be shown to have appeared in the Peloponnesian folk drama in the fifth century or earlier.[18] Rather than stereotype Herakles as the archetypal Dorian, we must take into account that he was the popular hero of Greeks anywhere, and he entered on the comic stage in all parts of the Greek world independently of any central influence.

The earliest writer of comic Herakles plays was the Sicilian Epicharmus, who flourished perhaps as early as around the turn of the sixth century.[19] His dramas were sufficiently coherent to be called comedies, although they were probably more farcical and mimic than Attic comedy. Most of his plays were mythological travesties. Herakles appears in more titles—five—than any other mythological figure. The wedding feast of Herakles and Hebe was the subject of the *Marriage of Hebe*, and the fragments amount to over fifty lines, all cataloguing fish and other food in trochaic tetrameters. Similarly, in the *Busiris* Herakles let first things be first and wolfed down a meal before killing Busiris. A frightened messenger relates the spectacle to the king (fr. 21 K.): 'First, if you would see him eating, you'd die. His throat roars within, his jaws gnash, his molars bang, his dog-tooth squeaks, he hisses through his nostrils, and he waggles his ears.' Another play, *Herakles with Pholus*, presented Herakles drinking with the centaur Pholus and the violent fight with the other centaurs who sniffed the wine and tried to join the party. Herakles was on his way to one of his labours—catching the Erymanthian boar—and he was human enough to prefer Pholus' gay hospitality to his labours (fr. 78 K.):

But of necessity (*anankē*) I do all these things.
I believe no one of his own free will suffers labours or disaster.

This is not blasphemy, as Wilamowitz thought,[20] but already Pindar had stressed Herakles' 'necessity imposed by the father' (*Ol.* 3. 28), and Euripides was to give this *anankē* a new dimension. This attitude kept the hero humanly believable and relevant. The fragments and titles of Epicharmus' remaining Herakles dramas—his fight against the giant Alcyoneus in the *Alcyoneus* and *Herakles' Voyage to the Sword-Belt of Hippolyte*—yield no further information, except that the audience liked to see Herakles brawl.

Aristophanes knew full well the comic effects to which Herakles could be put. By his time, they were not those of thoughtful, sophisticated comedy but rather designed to produce a roar. Occasionally, Aristophanes sneers at this low-level approach to comic writing. In the parabasis of the *Peace* he has the Chorus proudly announce about himself (741–3):[21]

It was he that indignantly swept from the stage that paltry, ignoble device
of a Herakles needy and seedy and greedy, a vagabond sturdy and stout
now baking his bread, now swindling instead, now beaten and battered about.

Similarly, in the 'preface' to the *Wasps* he declares that cheap tricks such as 'Herakles cheated out of his supper' are strictly beneath him (60).

All this is tongue in cheek, to be sure. The ancient commentator on the *Peace* hastened to point out that in the *Birds* and the *Sicon as Aeolus*, of which only a few fragments have been preserved, Aristophanes put exactly such a Herakles on the stage. In the *Birds*, Herakles is one of the three ambassadors sent by Zeus to prevail on Pisthetaerus and his bird state to lift their embargo on sacrifices, which has led the gods to the brink of starvation. The other two envoys are Poseidon, who turns out to be a rather incompetent diplomat, and a Triballian god. The latter is a representative of the barbarian gods who had reached Olympus in the age of participatory democracy but whose knowledge of Greek remained limited to a few grunts and gurgles. Before this grotesque trio reaches Cloudcuckooland, they try to decide on their strategy. Herakles is the Texas-sized strong-man who is throwing his weight around (1574–8):

> *Herakles:* You have heard
> what I propose; I'd throttle the man off hand
> whoever he is, that dares blockade the gods.
> *Poseidon:* My dear good fellow, you forget we are sent
> to treat for peace.
> *Herakles:* I'd throttle him all the more.

The moment, however, they are within smelling distance of Pisthetaerus, who is roasting a few renegade birds, Herakles' attitude changes abruptly. This is all the more so as Pisthetaerus promises that he will let the ambassadors share his meal if they are willing to bargain Zeus' dominion away. Whereas Poseidon ponderously seeks to explain that the treaty should be made on the basis of equality, Herakles is ready to sell out at once. He thus draws Poseidon's ire who calls him a glutton and a fool. Poseidon proceeds to have a lengthy argument with Pisthetaerus which Herakles interrupts impatiently by saying that he is voting to give all the power to the birds. To insure a majority, he intimidates the Triballian god, whose gibberish he blandly interprets as an affirmative vote. Encouraged by this, Pisthetaerus raises the price of the settlement: he now wants to marry Basileia, the personification of Zeus' rule. Poseidon is ready to break off; Pisthetaerus stirs the gravy, and Herakles drags Poseidon back. 'What a foolish thing,' he says, 'to fight about one woman' (1639). What to others was worth the launching of a thousand ships Herakles would gladly give away for a meal.

At this point, Poseidon castigates Herakles once more for his stupidity and tries to convince him that if Zeus loses power, Herakles, Zeus' son, will inherit nothing. Pisthetaerus' answer is to quote verbatim Solon's law of inheritance, which bars bastards from inheriting anything. He promises Herakles to install him as the *tyrannos* of the birds and feed him for the rest of his immortal life. This appeal carries the day. Herakles, the traditional defender of justice, announces that Pisthetaerus' claim to the girl strikes him as just and that he himself will secure her for him. Poseidon votes the other way; the Triballian jabbers something which Herakles once more claims as supporting his position, and Poseidon gives up in despair. Herakles invites Pisthetaerus to join the three back on their way to heaven, but when Pisthetaerus mentions the preparations for the wedding feast, Herakles quickly changes his mind and offers to roast the meat while the others are on their way. Poseidon blasts him for his uninhibited gluttony and leads the wistful Herakles from the scene.

The fun is all derived from the exaggeration. Herakles is a monstrous glutton, bully, and nitwit, but it is just because of this exaggeration that he comes off as good-natured rather than terrifying.[22] There is no malice in Aristophanes' portrayal of Herakles and certainly none of the excremental, humiliating humour with which Aeschylus, for instance, had treated Odysseus.[23] Aristophanes could use both as, for example, against the Athenian demagogue Cleon, his favourite butt and political opponent. But when he describes his fight against Cleon, he views himself as another Herakles. His comic braggadocio is merely a veneer to temper the edge of his fundamental seriousness (*Peace* 752–60):

> No, he at the mightiest quarry of all with the soul of Herakles flew,
> And he braved the vile scent of the tan pit, and went through foul-mouthed revilings for you.
> And I at the outset came down in the lists with the jagged-fanged monster to fight,
> Whose eyeballs were lurid and glaring with flames of Kynna's detestable light;
> And his smell was the smell of a seal, and his voice was a brawling tempestuous river,
> and his hinder parts like a furnace appeared, and a goblin's uncleansable liver.
> But I reckoned not the least for the look of the beast; I never desponded or quailed,
> And I fought for the safety of you and the Isles; I gallantly fought and prevailed.

In the parabasis of the *Wasps*, where these lines are repeated with only minor variations, Aristophanes goes on to call himself the *alexikakos* and 'the purifier of this land' (1043).

This is the earliest example of a writer's identification of himself with the hero.[24] It is a remarkable personal reaction which would have been impossible if Herakles, even in the context of comedy, had been considered merely as a burlesque figure. It may be this self-realization under the positive aspect of the traditional Herakles that kept Aristophanes from making Herakles the central character of any of his plays,[25] quite in contrast, apparently, to his contemporaries Eupolis and Cratinus, and certainly to many of his successors. To that extent, Aristophanes' claim, which comes immediately before his identification with the hero, to have driven the rollicking Herakles from the stage is certainly justified. While we cannot go so far as to suggest that Aristophanes would have eliminated Herakles from his comedies completely, the subordinate role he assigned to Herakles is hardly more than a minimal concession to the force of a comic tradition.

In the *Frogs*, Herakles is cast in the most favourable role comedy can provide for one of its protagonists—as the mocker of the pretensions of others. Dionysus, who is on his way to the underworld, has clad himself in the lion's skin and is wielding the club because he hopes to make a big impression on the inhabitants of Hades, who knew Herakles from his previous trip there. To find out about the best route, Dionysus and his slave Xanthias stop at Herakles' house on the way. When Herakles sees Dionysus' costume, he bursts into a fit of, well, Homeric laughter (45–7):

> I vow I can't help laughing, I can't help it.
> A lion's hide upon a yellow silk,
> A club and a buskin! What is it all about?

The audience would laugh with him. Because Herakles at first stood in amazement at the unbelievable sight of effeminacy decked out with Herculean attributes, Dionysus thought he had scared him. Now he finds that he causes laughter which, by Kant's famous definition, arises from 'the sudden transformation of a strained expectation into nothing'.[26] After this disappointment, however, Dionysus begins to communicate effectively with Herakles. To make Herakles understand his desire for Euripides, Dionysus likens it to Herakles' craving for bean soup. Down to earth as he is, Herakles has only contempt for Euripides' style of writing—'miserable stuff'—and Dionysus, breaking off the literary discussion, finally comes to the point of his visit. He asks Herakles to tell him about

> the havens, bread shops,
> brothels, rest rooms, bypaths, fountains, roads,
> towns, lodgings, and hostesses with whom were found
> the fewest bugs.

Herakles does not oblige but keeps Dionysus on tenterhooks. In great detail he tells him about the three quickest ways to go to hell—all are different kinds of suicide. Dionysus finally implores him to let him know the way he himself took. 'That', Herakles retorts as he sizes up Dionysus, 'is some undertaking.' Savouring Dionysus' agony, Herakles launches into a mock-epic description of the horrors of Hades and wishes good health to his guest, whose knees have started wobbling.

It soon becomes even more obvious that Dionysus, in this comedy, is as little a worthy follower of Herakles as Neoptolemus and Philoctetes were in Sophocles' *Philoctetes*. When Dionysus is afraid to knock on the door of Pluto's hall, Xanthias eggs him on (463): 'You've got, remember, the lion hide and pride of Herakles.' Dionysus, however, is more than anxious to divest himself of both when Aeacus, the doorkeeper, bursts into a tirade of threats and swears to avenge Herakles' maltreatment of Cerberus. First goes the pride, as Dionysus relieves himself, and then the hide and the club, which Xanthias assumes. No sooner has Xanthias done so, than he, as Herakles, receives the warmest welcome from Persephone's maid. Mindful of the hero's proverbial voracity, she invites him to a sumptuous dinner. Providing for the hero's other appetites, dancing girls will be there—'young budding virgins, freshly tired and trimmed'. That is enough for Dionysus who greedily takes on the attire of Herakles once more. But again, things take a turn for the worse. The two hostesses promptly take him for the real Herakles and curse him for the gross voracity from which they suffered on his last visit (556–63):

> O, you thought,
> I shouldn't know you with your buskins on!
> Ah, and I've not yet mentioned all that fish
> No, nor the new-made cheese: he gulped it down,

Baskets and all, unlucky that we were.
And when I just alluded to the price,
He looked so fierce, and bellowed like a bull.
Xanthias: Yes, that's his way, that's what he always does.

This is the same greediness that had led Herakles to devour the firewood and coals in Ion's satyr play *Omphale.*[27]

What follows is a parody of the mad Herakles (564–8):

First Hostess: O, and he drew his sword and seemed quite mad.
Second Hostess: O, that he did.
First Hostess: And terrified us so
We sprang up to the cockloft, she and I
Then out he hurled, decamping with the rugs.
Xanthias: That's his way too; but something must be done.

To get the better of Herakles-Dionysus, the hostesses call for Cleon so that with his help they can tear out Herakles' œsophagus. Again Dionysus is terrified and surrenders the hero's attributes to Xanthias, this time for keeps.

As can be seen, it is Dionysus, and not Herakles, who is held up to ridicule. Aristophanes deflates Dionysus' Herculean pretensions for the duration of Dionysus' posturing as Herakles.[28] Unlike Herakles-Aristophanes, this false, unworthy Herakles is frightened by the mere threat of Cleon's arrival.

The multitude of pertinent fragments from the entire range of Greek comedy, Old, Middle, and New, associate Herakles with seemingly endless gluttony. The tradition begins with Cratinus' *Busiris* and ends with Menander. There are countless variations on the stock theme of Herakles the glutton. As he had in Epicharmus' play, he appears in Archippus' *Wedding of Herakles* as the groom and drools at the catalogue of morsels (fr. 11 Edm.):

And here's what is more,
Piglets' trotters galore,
Veal steaks young and tender
And long ribs of boar.

By contrast, Nicochares entitled his comedy *Herakles as the Bride* because Omphale dominated Herakles. In the *Afflictions of Zeus* by the comedian Plato, a contemporary of Aristophanes, Herakles combined wenching with eating while he was playing the popular dice game of cottabus with a few harlots. These qualities took the place of Herakles' preoccupation with his labours.

> Stay in to drink, if happy; brawls and bothers (πόνος)
> May well be left by happy men to others

says a character, perhaps Herakles himself, in the *Omphale* of Cratinus the Younger (fr. 4 Edm.). Eubulus, another Middle Comedy poet, tried to give Herakles' insatiable appetite a mythological basis. When Herakles wrestled with Achelous for Deianeira's possession, he broke off one of Achelous' horns, which he later gave back to the river god in return for the horn of Amalthea. It was a fitting gift because this horn, according to legend, had the power of supplying in abundance any food or drink for which a man would pray to it. Blessed with this culinary cornucopia, Herakles refuses to settle for some lowly vegetables and pronounces meat, whether hot, cold, or 'medium', as being much more valuable than the conquest of Troy (fr. 7 Edm.). This last phrase is lifted from Euripides' *Andromache*,[29] and the procedure is typical of the spirit of Middle Comedy. A significant part of it was concerned with the travesty of myth. Since the myths then were known chiefly by the treatment in tragedy, Middle Comedy often parodied tragedy rather than the myths themselves.[30]

When one looks over the titles of Herakles plays during that period, the trend towards the more exotic and spectacular themes is unmistakable. Besides the *Busiris* we now find a *Geryon*, *Antaeus*, and the *Kerkopes*.[31] The last was the subject of one of the oldest epics, which some even ascribed to Homer, and dealt with Herakles' conquest of two mischievous, monkey-like fiends. Representations of this motif are found in archaic art, as for instance on a metope from the sixth-century temple of Hera by the Sele river in Italy (Plate 7).[32] According to Apollodorus (2. 6. 3), Herakles caught the Kerkopes while he was in the service of Omphale. On a vase from the fourth century, however, he brings them back to an obviously pleased Eurystheus.[33] Herakles uses the fearsome club as a walking stick and carries the reed cages with the Kerkopes at the ends of his bow. In a fragment of Eubulus' *Kerkopes*, Herakles is, needless to say, again associated with eating (fr. 53 Edm.). In comedy, this foible was getting the upper hand even over Herakles' traditional, lofty role as the saviour. In Alexis' *Hesione*, for instance, the girl whom Herakles boldly rescued from the sea monster complains (fr. 86 Edm.):

> When he saw two serving-men bring in the tray
> With motley side-dishes abounding gay,
> He had no eyes for me.

Alexis' *Linus* is about a more domestic theme and thus foreshadows New Comedy, in which such subjects were to predominate. Linus was Herakles' teacher whom Herakles, unable to repress his anti-authoritarian feelings, finally slew in a fit of anger. Before that, Alexis drew heavily on the stereotyped contrast between the ethereal teacher, who revels in the world of the great authors, and his boorish student (fr. 135 Edm.) for the following, more peaceful exchange:

> *Linus*: Any book you need
> Go up and take from it and sit down and read;
> The titles, look, will tell you there it is—
> Orpheus, Hesiod, Homer, tragedies,
> Epicharmus, Choerilus, any prose-work you please;
> It'll tell me what you've been on.
> *Herakles:* I'll take this.
> *Linus:* What have you got? Before you start, show me.
> *Herakles:* The title says The Art of Cookery.
> *Linus:* You've learnt a thing or two, it's manifest,
> Preferring Simus' textbook to all the rest
>
> * * *
>
> *Herakles* (looking up): Call me what you will;
> Please understand I want to eat my fill.

Accordingly, Herakles' mask in Old and Middle Comedy featured an enormous mouth and goggling eyes, complemented by a shortish beard, a squat nose, and a paunch (Plate 8).[34]

Herakles preserved his popularity in the Hellenistic New Comedy, which generally eschewed mythological themes. As late as the first century A.D., when New Comedy still delighted the Greek world, Dio Chrysostom would write the *Alexandrians* (32. 94): 'Just as in comedies and theatrical performances they do not arouse much laughter by bringing on a drunken (cook) Carion or (slave) Davus, yet when a drunken Herakles staggers about in the customary yellow coat the audience think it really funny.' In New Comedy, the humanization of Herakles found yet another expression. Alexander and his successors identified themselves with the hero by wearing the lion's skin, and one Nikostratos of Argos even dressed with club and lion's skin for battle (D.S. 16. 44). What was good for the kings was good enough for that perennial stock character, the braggart soldier. Such a fellow was the subject of Menander's *Sham Herakles* (frs. 517A–525 Edm.). Plutarch (*Mor.* 59C) tells us that this impostor came on not even with a solid club like Herakles', but with a hollow, fake club which, naturally, was much lighter. The fragments are about the usual Herculean predilections—food, wine, and girls—and the play's hero also let it be known that he had no 'natural affection' for the austere life.

This is not to claim that this particular adaptation of Herakles was the creation of New Comedy. Already Aristophanes' rival Pherecrates wrote a *Sham Herakles* (fr. 154 Edm.), but it is impossible to say whether he caricatured the same kind of person. If Miss Bieber's ingenious argument is correct, we have such a braggart sham Herakles in a terracotta statuette—it happens to be yellow, too—which dates towards the end of the Middle Comedy period (Plate 8).[35] She points out that

> This is not the ordinary type of Herakles found in statuettes of old comedy, where he stands with his legs crossed, leaning on his club as a walking stick, holding his bow in his hand. This lion's skin is drawn over his head so that the ears stand out at the top and the claws are knotted on his breast. In the New York statuette there are really two lions' skins, or at least lions' heads. One is made into a cap for the hero's head, the other hangs down next to the bow and beside a claw on the left side. This is a two-fold Herakles, and may be parallel to Dionysus dressed up as Herakles in the *Frogs* of Aristophanes. . . . Here the joke may be that some braggart

> soldier has dressed as Herakles. . . . The false Herakles is not thinking of fighting, but of some good meal. He is hungry. That is why he puts his finger in his mouth.

It is doubtful that the physical appearance of the sham Herakles in New Comedy was much different from that of the somewhat earlier terracotta statuette. In this form, as the braggart warrior, Herakles could easily enter into the domestic drama of everyday characters.

Throughout the fourth century, Herakles celebrated his most raucous triumphs in the phlyakes, the popular comedy of the Greeks in southern Italy. These farces were not given literary form until the very end of that century by Rhinthon of Syracuse,[36] and the genre then was called hilarious tragedy (*hilarotragodia*). Titles such as *Iphigenia at Aulis*, *Iphigenia among the Taurians*, *Medea*, *Telephus*, and *Orestes* indicate that phlyakes and hilarious tragedy derived much of the fun from spoofing Euripides' tragedies in particular. Among these was the *Herakles*. Rhinthon parodied it, and the famous vase of the Paestum painter Assteas provides a somewhat earlier example (*c.* 350 B.C.) of the same kind of play.[37] The mad Herakles, whose helmet is crested with two gigantic plumes, is throwing his child into a hastily arranged pyre, which consists in part of noncombustible metal articles. Instead of rescuing the child, Megara makes the grand gestures of tearing her hair and beating her breast as she runs off to the right. Looking down upon the scene from a kind of gallery are, from left to right, the goddess of Madness, who also beats her breast; Herakles' trusty companion Iolaus, who arily waves at the whole commotion; and Herakles' wrinkled mother Alcmena, who gazes at him in dumb amazement.

An actual phlyakes vase gives us an even better impression of the horseplay and rigmarole supplied by Herakles in these farces (Plate 9).[38] It is a parody of his arrival at Delphi where he went to expiate the murder of Linus. When Apollo refused to purify him, Herakles wrested the tripod away from the god, and Zeus or Athena finally had to reconcile the two. This episode was often represented in serious art, as for instance in the pediment of the Siphnian Treasury at Delphi (Plate 9) where both Zeus and Athena try to restrain the two combatants.[39] In the farce it is all different. Herakles has jumped on the holy tripod, which is in his undisputed possession. He has threatened Apollo with his club, and the god has fled to the edge of the temple's roof. While greedily looking at the basket of fruits and cake that Herakles is temptingly holding out to him, Apollo is carefully keeping his attributes, the bow and the laurel, away from Herakles. Inevitably, Apollo will give in to his baser desires and reach for the gifts, and Herakles will swat him with the club, causing Apollo to fall into the basin of holy water beneath him. While he is splashing and shivering in it, Iolaus will snatch the laurel and the bow and the audience will duly howl with laughter. Although Herakles and Apollo are personalities in their own right, they anticipate here stock types which became so very popular in the Roman farce and the *commedia dell'arte*: the clever hunchback and the greedy blockhead.

For once, Herakles here is not represented as the glutton. He makes up for it, however, in a visit to a shrine of Zeus which is depicted on another phlyakes vase (Plate 10).[40] While his companion, probably Iolaus, piously is pouring a libation on the altar, Herakles gobbles up the sacrificial offerings right under the nose of a smallish Zeus, who tries to kick him in anger and brandishes his diminutive thunderbolt. Elsewhere Herakles is shown pounding with this club on a door,[41] a device with which Aristophanes had already associated our strongman ('he broke the front door in, doorposts and all' [fr. 287 Edm.]) and which, although dissociated from Herakles, was to cause so much merriment in Roman comedy. The door on which he knocks seems to be that of a shrine. As soon as Herakles is inside, he once more shows little respect for the holiness of the place and lustily drags off a woman, perhaps Auge, from the altar.[42] An old couple frame the scene and are looking on smirkingly.

The comic Herakles overdid everything, and that was exactly the reason for his great success. To the reader several centuries later the constant emphasis on the hero's voracity for food, wine, and women—in that order—may appear tedious. But exaggeration is exactly the stuff that makes popular comedy work. Max Eastman has observed that in comedy 'it is the *too* much—always and absolutely—and not the *much* that is funny'.[43] This is true both of Herakles' qualities and of their constant repetition in the Greek comic tradition.

One final question remains. To use a favourite character for laughs is one thing; to use a god for it may be another. Thus a profound uneasiness pervades all scholarly discussions of the gods', including Herakles', role in Greek comedy. 'In spite of all the good fun and travesty, the picture of the gods which the comic poets paint reveals a profound and moving disillusionment', writes Victor Ehrenberg.[44] Others have gone further and blamed the decadence and decay of religion directly on the comic poets. And yet, the cult of Herakles flourished, especially in the west, even as he roistered about the comic stage. Could the same people who saw him in the theatre really go to his temple the next day and seriously pray to him to help them in life's perplexities?

There is no divine analogy to this today, to be sure, but it is not quite as incongruous as it sounds. For one thing, Herakles was treated differently from the other gods, and there is no indication that he was ever humiliated by the laughter he aroused. Apollo falls into the water and Dionysus relieves himself on the stage, but when Herakles' faults are displayed, as in the *Birds*, their deliberately gross exaggeration keeps them from being taken seriously.[45] Even in comedy, Herakles could remain the normative figure and champion of justice he had been in serious literature, as is shown, for instance, by Aristophanes' *Frogs*, *Wasps*, and *Peace*, and the many *Busiris* plays. We should also keep in mind that in Middle Comedy and the phlyakes the fun mostly consisted of parodying the tragic treatment of the myths rather than ridiculing the myths themselves. Moreover, we have seen that it was mostly Euripides who was being lampooned in this manner, but this reflected rather than detracted from the popularity of his tragedies and the esteem in which they were held. The same can be said of the characters of his plays. Today, the idiosyncrasies of the President of the United States, for instance, are satirized on television, which often seems to be an unconscious latter-day counterpart of the phlyakes. Rarely, however, is such satire meant to be vindictive, nor does it lessen the respect for the President's office. If he is a serious man, we will again consider him seriously the next day.

It is a commonplace in the theory of comedy that comedy is a release, especially from the things that we take or have to take most seriously. Otherwise they might be too difficult to live with. The 'festive spirit' of comedy—and ancient comedy was performed on festival days—turns the regular order of things upside down.[46] This is 'play' as defined and brilliantly studied by Johan Huizinga.[47] Its essential characteristic is that it is different from every day and strictly limited in time. Every participant realizes that what happens is unreal, and that he is experiencing a temporary anarchy that implies order. Herakles was the most popular figure in the ancient festive comedy exactly because the Greeks took him seriously, more seriously, at any rate than other deities. He was superior to them because he was, in part, a man. Euripides' utterly tragic Herakles and the comic Herakles ultimately are two expressions of the same attitude.

NOTES TO CHAPTER IV

1. The only longer treatments of the comic Herakles are Des Essarts 99–125, and R. Hosek, 'Herakles auf der Bühne der alten Komödie', *ΓΕΡΑΣ Thomson* (Prague, 1963) 118–27. The latter study is restricted to satyr play and Old Comedy. The fragments of the satyr plays are quoted from Nauck, *TGF*, and those of the comedies, from the three-volume edition of J. M. Edmonds, *The Fragments of Attic Comedy* (Leiden, 1957–61). For the artistic evidence in general see Bieber, *History of the Greek and Roman Theater*.
2. So Brommer, *Satyrspiele* 34. In his *Vasenlisten zur griechischen Heldensage*, 2nd ed. (Marburg, 1960) 144–5, the same author lists fifty-nine vases with Herakles and satyrs and satyrs dressed as Herakles.
3. Oxford 1929. 752; *CVA* Oxford 2, pl. 52. 1; *ARV* 451, 2. For an example of the survival of this association, in a serious context, see Spenser's *Faerie Queene* v. i. 2–3. 2 and pp. 208f.
4. Rome, Villa Giulia 8346; *ARV* 290.
5. Princeton 170; Brommer, *Satyrspiele* 75, no. 61b.
6. Kunsthistorisches Museum, Vienna, Antikenabteilung; S. Reinach, *Répertoire des vases peints grecs et étrusques* 2 (Paris, 1900) 221, 2.
7. From a private collection in southern Italy; Bieber 14, fig. 43.
8. British Museum E 539; F. Brommer, *JDAI* 57 (1942) 113, fig. 7.
9. A. Pickard-Cambridge, *Dithyramb, Tragedy, and Comedy*, 2nd ed. by T. B. L. Webster (Oxford, 1962) 62–3.
10. See frs. 205–15 N. and p. 46.
11. *Nemean* 4. 32; see pp. 36f.
12. Naples 3240; *ARV* 1336, 1; see Bieber 10–11 with figs. 31–3 and Brommer, 10–11 with fig. 1.
13. Cf. p. 15.
14. Munich 2428; *CVA* Munich 5, pls. 227. 4, 228. 4; *ARV* 191, 12.

15. Matthew Arnold used the episode for the serious context of his *Thyrsis* (182–5):

> Putting his sickle to the perilous grain
> In the hot cornfield of the Phrygian king,
> For thee the Lityerses-song again
> Young Daphnis with his silver voice doth sing.

16. Euripides, fr. 377 N., from the satyr play *Eurystheus*. In Athens, Herakles was the patron of the gymnasium of the bastards at Kynosarges.
17. Fr. 29 N. For other occurrences of this theme in Greek literature see Athenaeus 10. 411a–412b.
18. For details, see L. Breitholz, *Die dorische Farce im griechischen Mutterland vor dem 5. Jahrhundert. Hypothese oder Realität?* (Stockholm, 1960), esp. 66–71.
19. The most up-to-date and judicious discussion of Epicharmus' life and work that of Webster in Pickard-Cambridge (note 9,above) 230–88; the fragments can be found in G. Kaibel, *Comicorum Graecorum Fragmenta* 1. 1 (Berlin, 1899).
20. *Herakles* 1. 99–100. On the Pindaric passage cf. p. 35.
21. The translations are those of Benjamin Bickley Rogers, with occasional modifications.
22. Cf. Hosek (note 1, above) 123.
23. Frs. 180 (from the *Bone-gatherers*) and 275 N. (from the *Ghost-raisers*). In the former play, a chamber-pot was emptied over Odysseus' head; in the latter, he died of sepsis after a heron had befouled it.
24. Aristophanes' colleagues took him up on this by humorously proclaiming that he was born on the fourth of the month like Herakles, because he took upon himself the burden of writing plays without producing them himself and thus reaping the benefits, i.e. reimbursement by the state. See Aristonymus fr. 4 (Edm.) and Sannyrion fr. 5 (Edm.).
25. *Pace* W. Schmid, *Geschichte der griechischen Literatur* pt. 1, vol. 4. 2, 1 (Munich, 1946) 185, this is true even of the comedy entitled *Plays* or *The Centaur* (frs. 267–77, 287–8 Edm.). The centaur most probably was Pholus, and the name of the play shows that Pholus had the main part, in contrast, e.g. to Epicharmus' *Herakles with Pholus*.
26. Immanuel Kant, *Critique of Judgement*, trans. J. H. Bernard, 2nd ed. (London, 1914) 223.
27. See p. 85.
28. Paul Goodman, *The Structure of Literature* (Chicago, 1954) 82, defines 'deflation' as 'one of the purest comic actions'.
29. *Andromache* 365; the same priority of values had, as we have seen, been espoused by Herakles in the *Birds* (1639).
30. Cf. G. Schiassi, 'Parodia e travestimento mitico nella commedia attica di mezzo,' *RIL* 88 (1955) 99–120, and with particular reference to Herakles, pp. 103–10.

31. *Busiris*: Cratinus the Younger (title only); Ephippus (fr. 2 Edm.); Antiphanes (frs. 65–6 Edm.); Mnesimachus (fr. 2 Edm.). *Geryon*: Ephippus (frs. 3–4 Edm.). *Anteaus*: Antiphanes (fr. 33 Edm.). *Kerkopes*: Eubulus (fr. 53–4 Edm.); Menippus (title only). For the Kerkopes epic see Kinkel (Chapter 2, note 2) 69–70.
32. See P. Zancani Montuoro and U. Zanotti-Bianco, *Heraion alla foce del Sele* 2 (Rome, 1954) 185–95 with pls. 69–71.
33. Museo Civico, Catania; M. Bieber, *Die antiken Denkmäler zum Theaterwesen* (Leipzig and Berlin, 1920) 143, no. 107, fig. 127.
34. British Museum 741; T. B. L. Webster, *Greek Theatre Production* (London, 1956) 181, no. 13 and fig. 17c.
35. Metropolitan Museum of Art, New York, inv. no. 13. 225. 15; discussed by Bieber 46–7. T. B. L. Webster, 'South Italian Vases and Attic Drama', *CQ* 42 (1948) 20, stresses the difficulty of dating such statuettes. According to him, the New York statuettes are as advanced as any and date before 348 B.C. Miss Bieber suggests that the statuette might be an artistic reflection of the *Herakles* of the Middle Comedy poet Anaxandrides, but this is unlikely as Anaxandrides' play (fr. 15 Edm.) seems to have been a travesty of the real Herakles. The *Herakles* of the New Comedy poet Diphilus (fr. 46 Edm.) was so named because Herakles spoke the prologue; see Lesky, *History of Greek Literature* 663.
36. For the fragments and titles see Kaibel (note 19, above) 185–9.
37. Archaeological Museum, Madrid, no. 11094. See A. D. Trendall, *Paestan Pottery* (Rome, 1936) 31–2, pl. 7, and Bieber 130, fig. 479a.
38. Leningrad, Hermitage 1115. Trendall 37–8, fig. 15; Bieber 131, fig. 481.
39. C. Picard and P. de la Coste-Messelière, *Fouilles de Delphes* 4. 2 (Paris, 1928) 153–62; Flacelière-Devambez 93–4, pl. 11; B. S. Ridgway, *AJA* 69 (1965) 1–5.
40. Leningrad, Hermitage 1775; Bieber 132, fig. 482.
41. Berlin 3046; Bieber 133, fig. 487.
42. From Lentini, Palazzo Comunale. See H. Heydemann, 'Die Phlyakendarstellungen auf bemalten Vasen', *JDAI* 1 (1886) 271; Bieber 134, figs. 488a–b; cf. Herakles' characterization in Propertius 4. 9, as discussed on pp. 154f. Heydemann (pp. 260–313) offers a *catalogue raisonné* of phlyakes vases. Herakles is the mythological character who is represented most frequently.
43. *The Enjoyment of Laughter* (New York, 1936) 150.
44. *The People of Aristophanes* (New York, 1962) 266.
45. This is the comic adaptation of Herakles' superhuman aspects; cf. again Eastman (note 43, above) 150: 'It is only when exaggeration goes *beyond some humanly reasonable bounds* that it makes you want to laugh' (italics mine).
46. This has been well demonstrated for Shakespeare by C. L. Barber, *Shakespeare's Festive Comedy* (Cleveland and New York, 1963) and for Plautus, by Erich Segal, *Roman Laughter* (Cambridge, Mass., 1968).
47. *Homo Ludens: A Study of the Play Element in Culture* (Boston, 1950) esp. 9 and 13. For a different explanation of Herakles' comic role see p. 286.

CHAPTER V

Herakles among the Philosophers and Alexandrians

Besides the internalization of Herakles' achievement, another, related development began in the serious literature of the final part of the fifth century, and it was to have considerable significance for the hero's subsequent literary and artistic tradition. This was what might be called his intellectualization. With it, the metamorphosis of the folktale strong-man was complete. The intellectual Herakles, however, superseded the brawny one as little as the tragic hero replaced the buffoon. Rather, intellect was merely added to the hero's already plentiful qualities and provided writers, who adapted the theme, with a new choice. Some authors would gladly avail themselves of it whereas to others, such as Apollonius and the early Goethe, Herakles' vitality remained mostly corporeal.

The writer who firmly established Herakles as using his mind was the sophist Prodicus. It may be that he had some personal admiration for Herakles, for Plato (*Symp*. 177b) numbers Prodicus among those sophists who wrote praises of Herakles. At any rate, the general admiration of Herakles' ethics provided the point of departure for Prodicus' famous parable 'The Choice of Herakles',[1] although, the Renaissance and latter tradition to the contrary, the ethical implications were not the essence of Prodicus' story so far as it concerns Herakles. We saw earlier that Pindar had presented Herakles as an ethical ideal and Herakles' labours and exploits as an implementation of the *nomos* decreed by the gods. His motivation, however, for these labours—*anankē*—was unacceptable to the sophists and philosophers who emphasized that man was free to choose his own destiny. Euripides' tragic view of Herakles marks the midway point between Pindar's pious answer and the philosophers' search for a free-willed Herakles. Even though it is still within the framework of an *anankē* imposed on him, Herakles in Euripides' play makes a choice in favour of a more spiritualized concept of his labours. Prodicus emphasized that the ethical way of life of the *kaloskagathos*, which Herakles chose freely, was conforming to the *nomos* decreed by the gods. The association between Herakles and the divine *nomos* was, as we have seen, known from Pindar and may well have been the primary reason Prodicus was attracted to the myth. Of all the myths, this one could be adapted most easily for making his point and all the more so as the whole tradition of Herakles was very conducive to presenting him as the archetypally simple lad who is endowed only with a good nature, *physis*. This *physis*, which really is the *physis* of every man, has to be perfected; 'it acquires its value as a result of the use made of it by the *nomos* which interprets it'.[2]

To arrive at the *nomos* from his uncultivated state of *physis*, Herakles had to have knowledge of virtue. He had to deliberate and use his mind before making the decision. This is what really mattered to Prodicus. He did not choose Herakles because he was concerned about Herakles, but because the most popular hero of Greece, besides offering a myth that was eminently adaptable for the purpose, most readily suggested himself as Everyman. In that respect the medieval morality plays about Everyman's choice between Vice and Virtue are the direct descendants of Prodicus' allegory. In contrast to them, however, Prodicus was not so much concerned with the alternatives as such, but with man's power to reach a decision with full consciousness of his own freedom of choosing.[3] The process of choosing, which took the place of *anankē*, was an intellectual effort and intelligence thus became one of the hero's attributes.

The story, because of its literary and artistic *Nachleben*, is familiar, involving as it does the argument between Aretē, Virtue, and Kakia, Vice. Consistent with the portrait of Herakles elsewhere, Vice duly emphasizes the pleasures of food, drink, and women. Equally well-chosen is her offer to Herakles that if he follows her, he shall have the fruits of others' toil. It had, of course, been just the other way around in the mythological tradition. The intellectual ambience that led Euripides to internalize the heroism of Herakles also is reflected in Prodicus' story: Vice promises that Herakles will be freed from the labours and anguish of both the body *and* the mind.

Similarly, the appeal of Virtue contains traditional and contemporary themes. Herakles is to be the benefactor (εὐεργέτης) of his friends. He will reap honour if he acts *pro bono publico* and he will be the great liberator. Prodicus is as explicit about Herakles' true strength as Euripides had been, for Virtue stresses that the body must be the servant of the mind. Furthermore, to the crudely materialistic and luxuriating pleasures of Vice, Virtue opposes simpler and more natural pleasures. The hedonistic attraction to this natural way of life is the reaction against artificiality and over-civilization.[4] That was precisely the role in which Herakles appeared in the *Alcestis*. At the same time, Prodicus forcefully continued the humanization of Herakles, which had been propounded by Sophocles and Euripides. There is no heavenly reward or apotheosis, nor is there the grimly human heroism of the *Herakles*. Rather, Herakles' reward will be happiness in this life.

The impact of Prodicus' parable was immediate[5] and left its mark even on the fourth century, when the vogue which Herakles had enjoyed during the entire fifth century in all genres of serious literature—epic, lyric, tragedy, and in the allegorical and rationalistic interpretation of myth—did not continue. Instead of those genres, rhetoric came to the fore. One of Isocrates' followers drew directly on Prodicus' story and contrasted Herakles' *aretē* with Tantalus' *kakia.*[6] The occasion was a discourse on practical ethics, which aimed to give precepts on the proper conduct of life. Almost two thousand years later, Edmund Spenser adapted Prodicus' parable for exactly the same purpose in the similar, albeit more poetic context of his 'courtesy book' *The Faerie Queene*.

Rhetoric's most influential representative, Isocrates, fully recognized Herakles' value as an ideal. Herakles was the Panhellenic hero whose cause had been all of Greece, and not merely one of its provinces. Isocrates therefore presented him as a fitting model for Philip of Macedon, whom he urged to unify Greece. The rhetor even suggested that Philip consider himself a direct-line descendant of Herakles, a claim which Philip's son Alexander gladly took up, but the political uses of the Herakles legend are not our concern here. Isocrates' view of the personal qualities of the hero is far more enlightening, and he presents it at the beginning of a long digression on Herakles (5. 109):

> Coming now to Herakles, all others who praise him harp endlessly on his valour or recount his labours; and not one, either of the poets or the historians, will be found to have commemorated his other excellences—I mean those which pertain to the spirit (*psychē*). I, on the other hand, see here a field set apart and entirely unworked—a field not small or barren, but teeming with many a theme for praise and with glorious deeds, yet demanding a speaker with ability to do them justice. If this subject had claimed my attention when I was younger, I should have found it easy to prove that it was more by his wisdom, his lofty ambition, and his justice than by strength of his body that your ancestor surpassed all who lived before his day. But approaching the subject at my present age, and seeing what a wealth of material there is to discuss, I have felt that my present powers were unequal to the task, and I have also realized that my discourse would run to twice the length of that which is now before you to be read.

In the same century, Xenophon, too, wrote that Herakles was famed more for his *psychē* than his body (*Symp*. 8. 29). Isocrates, however, is more specific and chooses carefully the Greek terms denoting Herakles' qualities of excellence. They are not meant to be complex as they associate him with certain traditional qualities of Greek life, and therefore they do not need detailed analysis. *Phronēsis*, which Isocrates singles out first, originally means 'thought', 'activity of the mind'. It therefore is the antithesis of body, as if exemplified by a passage in Plato's *Republic* (461a). We find the same opposition in Isocrates' passage. Plato also contrasts *phronēsis* with ignorance, *amathia* (*Symp*. 202a). The contrast between *amathia* and prudent action had been central to Theseus' arguments in Euripides' *Herakles*, after Pindar had already differentiated one of Herakles' opponents from the hero by saying that the former lacked judgement (*aboulia*; *Ol*. 10. 41). More specifically, *phronēsis* connoted practical wisdom, a quality that Isocrates and his followers, such as the author of the discourse which we have already cited, prized very highly. Epicurus, who was born soon after the middle of the fourth century, rated *phronēsis* much higher than *philosophia* proper.[7] Unlike some of the Stoics and Cynics, Isocrates did not see in Herakles the ethereal 'wise man' philosopher. Being concerned with the political exigencies of his day, Isocrates extolled Herakles as a man of action whose wisdom was pragmatic rather than speculative.

That it had to be so is illustrated by the next quality, *philotimia.* It means 'ambition' and, as Antony told the Roman people: 'Ambition should be made of sterner stuff'. *Philotimia* was primarily the desire for honour and glory. As such it was the incentive for heroic action in the *Iliad.* 'Ever to be the best and excelling the others'—this is how old Phoinix sums up his ideal of *aretē* to Achilles. It never lost its validity for the Greeks. Jakob Burckhardt rightly saw in this competition—*agōn*—the underlying principle of Greek culture. After the heroic age, the most spendid expression of this competition for excellence was the athletic games. Herakles was the patron of the most famous of these, and Pindar had constantly invoked him as the most perfect embodiment of their spirit.

Similarly, *dikaiosynē*—Justice—was a cardinal virtue. Isocrates' mention of it shows that the assiduous efforts of earlier poets to associate Herakles with this quality had borne fruit. Like *phronēsis* and *philotimia, dikaiosynē,* besides being time-honoured, had contemporary relevance. We need only remind ourselves that the subtitle of Plato's *Republic* was 'On Justice'.

Two circumstances suggest that Isocrates was sincere in his praise of Herakles here. First, he eschews the opportunity for 'proving' (ἐπέδειξε) his intentions in detail. The term he uses for 'prove' suggests what he had in mind: an epideictic speech. This type of speech was known better for rhetorical grandstanding than credibility; Isocrates, in fact, wrote *elogia* of this kind on such unlikely characters as Helen and Busiris and in them even attempted to deprecate Herakles' importance.[8] By contrast, the *Oration to Philip* was intended to be widely read and to be taken most seriously since it expressed Isocrates' heartfelt desire for the unification of Greece. Secondly, at the end of the digression Isocrates singles out Herakles once more for his non-physical qualities. 'I do not mean', he addresses Philip (5. 114), 'that you will be able to imitate Herakles in all his exploits; for even among the gods there are some who could not do that; but in the qualities of the spirit, in devotion to humanity (*philanthropia*), and in the goodwill which he cherished towards the Hellenes, you can come close to his purposes.'

Isocrates, then, remembers Herakles best for his spiritual values, his *ethos*. Among them is *philanthropia*, which Isocrates stresses again when he urges Philip in Herculean terms to become the benefactor (εὐεργέτης) of the Greeks and to adopt towards them a policy of humanity (*philanthropia*). The association of this latter virtue with Herakles can also be traced back to Prodicus' parable where, however, the motive for *philanthropia* is entirely egocentric. If you want your friends to cherish you, do them good, Aretē exhorts Herakles. While Herakles' *philanthropia* played a great role several centuries later when he became paganism's last, desperate choice to head off the appeal of Christianity, it does not appear at all in the early writings of that sect which idealized him, the Cynics.[9] Their influence on the Stoics was considerable and both in turn were a new influence on the Herakles tradition.

The basic emphasis of this influence was clear from the earliest beginnings. Antisthenes pronounced that happiness was based on virtue (*aretē*) and virtue, in turn, on knowledge. The only kind of pleasure that contributed to happiness was the result of toil, *ponos*. None of this is inconsistent with Prodicus' story. In fact, in one of Euripides' earliest dramas, the *Licymnius*, we find a characterization of Herakles which anticipates most of the qualities for which the Cynics lauded him (fr. 473 N.):

> Plain, unadorned, staunch to do great deeds,
> with all his share of wisdom curtailed
> to action, a man not versed in idle talk.

The Cynics definitely did not admire Herakles for his intellectual gifts. They praised his labours and exertions which, true enough, were conceived of as being spiritual rather than bodily. For that reason it is more than likely that Antisthenes continued the Herakles allegories of sophists such as Herodorus and Prodicus. Far from being viewed as an imposition by *anankē*, Herakles' toils were something he had chosen voluntarily for his own good. By following in Herakles' footsteps and taking exertions upon himself, a Cynic or Stoic would arrive at his ideal of being a wise man, far removed from *hoi polloi*. It was an ideal fraught with austere grandeur, which did much to shape Herakles' image in both literature and—until our day—art (Plate 1). It is in this spirit, for instance, that Prometheus addresses Herakles in Antisthenes' version of the story:[10]

> Your conduct is very contemptible as you are striving for worldly things, for you have neglected to care about what is more important. You will not be a perfect man until you have learned what is higher than man, and when you have learned that, you have also learned what humanity is worth. If, however, you learn only earthly things, you are erring like the wild animals.

Affirming his idealization of Herakles, Antisthenes wrote three works about him.[11] In so doing, he was influenced by the popularity of Herakles in the literature of the fifth century. With the exception of Diogenes, none of the Cynics in the fourth century wrote on him. The reason can be attributed to a change of intellectual attitude. Allegorical interpretations, such as those of the sophists and Antisthenes, required certain intellectual powers both in the interpreters and their audience. By contrast, early Cynicism was unabashedly anti-intellectual and regarded such amenities as culture a bother unworthy of the true sage who could live happily in rags, filth, a tub, and self-sufficiency. Accordingly, Diogenes reverted to regarding Herakles as the glorified nature boy who asserted his individual freedom against the accretions of convention, tradition, and social existence. So much we can say about Diogenes' *Herakles* (Diog. Laertius 16. 50), which seems to have been a didactic treatise rather than a tragedy. We might add that this Herakles, in spite of the similarity of purpose, lacked the urbane gaiety with which he was delightfully endowed in the *Alcestis* and that although his toils continued to be interpreted ethically, he was definitely cast in the role of the non-intellectual primitive. At the very same time, the traditional Pindaric praise of Herakles as the embodiment of *aretē* was continued by none less than Aristotle.[12]

Thus, at the beginning of the Hellenistic age, the manifestations of Herakles were more complex and varied than ever before. Prodicus and, more explicitly, Isocrates had started a trend by attributing intellectual powers to Herakles; Diodorus (4. 13. 1) later would characterize Herakles' mental acumen by the word ἀγχινοία, which Homer had associated with Odysseus (*Od.* 13. 332), Servius would refer to a tradition praising the hero for his intellect, and Lucian would present the

Gallic Herakles as the god of inspired eloquence,[13] which left its mark on the Gallic myth of the hero until the eighteenth century. By contrast, the Cynics made a cult of the non-intellectual Herakles, however ethically noble the hero remained. And yet, during the same period the musical and cultural tradition of Herakles found its tangible, outward expression in Rome, where the temple of Hercules of the Muses was built in 189 B.C. . . . It would serve no purpose to be concerned about the apparent contradictions involved here. The Greeks were not concerned about them either because 'the heroes and gods for them were living personages, as complex and multi-form as life itself'.[14] The creative tension that existed between these contrasting portraits of Herakles prevented him from becoming stereotyped and continued to attract writers to adapt the theme.

The director of the great library at Alexandria, Apollonius of Rhodes, was certainly familiar with all facets of the Herakles tradition as he had access to far more of the literature than we do today. Therefore it might at first be surprising that this *poeta doctissimus* presents us with a more consistently archaic Herakles than even Homer had portrayed. The reason is that the genre pure and simple forced Apollonius' hand. The *Argonautica* was his courageous attempt to revive epic, which contemporary critics, notably Callimachus, dismissed as an outmoded type of literature.[15] About the form of epic there was little Apollonius could do besides making it shorter, thus meeting Callimachus' strictures halfway. To save it from being obsolete, however, its hero had to be relevant to Apollonius' time and society. In that regard, the *Argonautica* simply is an account of what happens when a Hellenistic burgher is forced to head a mythical expedition. Jason is the absolute antithesis of the traditional hero. He is always cautious, hesitating, and reluctant. In no other epic are the protagonist and most of his companions afraid so often, and nowhere else is an epic hero continually overwhelmed by resignation and despair in the face of a never-ceasing series of dilemmas. Jason's *amēchania*, helplessness, is a leitmotif in the *Argonautica*. This alone sets him apart from Herakles, the Pindaric defender against *amēchania*. To fulfil a superhuman, heroic task Jason has available only the resources of an ordinary man. Lacking the bravura of a superman or the conventional hero's instinctive self-confidence and zest for initiative and action, he has to become a master in the art of expediency and opportunism in order to be successful. As Euripides rudely transposed the Admetus of the folktale world into the world of reality, so Apollonius transposes a real, ordinary citizen of his time into the world of heroic myth. Euripides used Herakles as a foil, and so, very extensively, does Apollonius.

Apollonius therefore took pains to demonstrate that Herakles' heroism was clearly of the kind that was beyond Jason's reach. Whether it was desirable is another question which we will try to answer later. So Herakles appears among the Hellenistic citizen-heroes of the *Argonautica* like a solitary mastodon left over from the palaeolithic world, like, as Tennyson would later say, 'a grand creation' that inspires awe in proportion to his all too evident anachronism. There might be not much that is interesting about such a character, but since Apollonius' Herakles is the only surviving Greek specimen of *Hercules epicus* he merits some closer study. He is, then, the hero of the old order, the man who relies on brawn because he has got more of it than others. Merely physically, he is so big that he has to be given the mid-ship seat without drawing a lot like everybody else, and when 'his mighty bulk' finally takes his seat he 'made the ship's keel underfoot sink deep into the water' (1. 531–3).[16] Brawn, however, even has purely physical limitations. In a rowing contest, Herakles at first not only outlasts all other Argonauts with ease, but goes on to propel the Argo single-handed against adverse winds 'pulling his hardest with his great arms and sending shudders through the framework of the ship' (1. 1162–3). But before Herakles can row the boat out of contemporary reality, the oar snaps in the middle, and primitive heroic will and strength are defeated. 'Glowering in silence', Herakles sits, a frustrated man. *Seul le silence est grand. . . .*

This picture soon gives way to another. Herakles anxiously sets out for the woods to make himself another oar. He finds a pine tree, loosens it by clubbing it and then, 'trusting in his strength', he tears it out, clods and all, 'deep-rooted as it was'. Thereafter, in yet another graphic scene, Herakles trudges back to the shore, a gigantic, beweaponed apparition, shouldering the tree along with the club, the bow and the arrows, and the lion's skin.

At this point the poet digresses to narrate how Herakles came to possess Hylas. Hylas was the son of Theiodamas, king of the Dryopians, a tribe 'that lived not caring about justice (*dikē*)'. It is quite in keeping with Herakles' traditional role as a civilizer and *defensor iustitiae* that he should make war on such people. All that has to be found is a specific reason to justify such an action. Callimachus, for one, provided it in his version of the story:[17] Herakles, who is carrying his starving boy Hyllus, begs Theiodamas for one of his oxen, but the king laughs cruelly and refuses. This act of inhospitality leads to Theiodamas' swift demise. In that version, Theiodamas is an 'inhuman' king, as Ovid (*Ibis* 487) called him, whereas in the *Argonautica* there is no mention of his inhumanity. Instead, Apollonius says that Herakles asked Theiodamas to give him the ox because Herakles was anxious to find a pretext for attacking the Dryopians, and when Theiodamas refused, Herakles killed him 'ruthlessly'. Unlike Pindar, Apollonius is not concerned about justifying Herakles.

It soon turns out that Herakles' use of force not only is archaic but also can be misguided. This is evident from his reaction to the news of Hylas' disappearance. As before, we first see a physical picture of the hero which is followed by a simile that illustrates his state of mind (1. 1261–72):

> When Herakles heard this, sweat in abundance poured down from his temples and the dark blood boiled within him. In his fury he threw down the pine and rushed off, little caring where his feet were carrying him. Picture a bull stampeding from the water-meadows when he is stung by the gadfly. He tears along and does not care about the herd and herdsmen; and off he goes, sometimes pressing on without a stop, sometimes pausing to raise his mighty neck and bellow in his pain. So Herakles in his frenzy ran at full speed for a while without a break, then paused in his exertions to fill the distance with a ringing cry.

The man is converted into a beast—precisely the kind of fate against which Antisthenes' Herakles had been warned by Prometheus.

It might be objected that reason cannot possibly control Herakles' reaction because Hylas was, after all, his lover. In contrast to Theocritus, however, who dwells on this aspect at length, Apollonius completely ignores it. He says no more than that Herakles has educated Hylas to be an efficient servant (1. 1207–11). This reinforces the point of the Theiodamas episode: Herakles again goes berserk without much reason. The point is hammered home once more when Apollonius stresses that Herakles will take dreadful revenge on Calais and Zetes because they prevailed on the other Argonauts, with the sanction of Zeus himself, not to turn back the Argo in order to search for Herakles. Left alone in the country of the Mysians, Herakles does not stop making his presence felt. He 'threatens to lay waste the land if the people failed to find out for him what had become of Hylas, living or dead'. To appease him, the Mysians give him some of their best young men as hostages. Being a kindly lot, some of the Mysians, Apollonius goes on to say, still inquire after Hylas today. Herakles' grotesque behaviour bred grotesque customs among the descendants of the people on whom he inflicted himself.

With this, Herakles' role in the epic is not exhausted. He continues to be the standard against which the Argonauts measure themselves in a manner reminiscent of Neoptolemus and Philoctetes. After a long, protracted struggle they finally overcome Amycus and his Bebrycians. Like Busiris and Lityerses, Amycus is a barbarous host who challenges every guest to a fatal boxing match. One of the Argonauts sums up their feelings in an epilogue to this incident (2. 146–50): 'Had Herakles been here, the issue would never have been decided by boxing. Straightway with the club he would have made him forget his arrogance and all the rules he came up to proclaim.' The comparison turns out to be very appropriate. The Argonauts soon find out that they are following in Herakles' footsteps because by defeating the Bebrycians, they protect king Lycus and his people as Herakles had formerly done by similar means. Exploits like these were part of Herakles' expedition to fetch the girdle of Hippolyta. That expedition took Herakles into the same regions as the Argonauts and thus forms a contrasting background which is frequently alluded to, to their own expedition. But whereas Herakles won the girdle through ambush and war, Jason will shun any direct confrontation in battle with Aeetes: he states programmatically that it is better to rely on persuasive words than on force (3. 179–81). This, of course, lengthens his task. On another occasion, the timely recall of Herakles' stratagem against the Stymphalian birds helps the Argonauts to cope efficiently with a similar situation (2. 1052–7).

Finally, near the end of Book Two, there is a description of Prometheus and his eagle which brings to mind Herakles' future expedition to free the Titan. In Book Three, where Jason comes into his own, the force of Herakles as a mythical model diminishes and he is mentioned only once. Only Herakles, Apollonius says, would have been able to withstand Aeetes' 'unconquerable spear' (3. 1231–4).

The Herakles *exempla* show why Apollonius had to remove him from the epic's action by the end of the first book. If Herakles had stayed, the Argonauts' labours—and they are consistently referred to as *athloi*[18]—would have been resolved with ease, and Apollonius would have defeated one essential purpose of his epic. This purely technical reason basically accounts for the stereotype of Herakles which emerges in the episodes that we have mentioned so far. There was no psychological reason why Apollonius could not have adapted Herakles to the human level of the other Argonauts. Euripides had shown him to be a man who was exposed to the capriciousness of *Tychē* and assailed by nagging doubts, and he and others had portrayed the hero as a family man who cared more about his children than his labours. Herakles' recourse to persuasion rather than force can be traced as far back as Pindar, and his use of intelligence had been stressed in the fourth century. The stark fact, however, was that Herakles could be humanized only in those episodes of his life that were not a part of his mythic deeds. In contrast to the nineteenth and twentieth centuries, it was unthinkable at Apollonius' time to humanize the basis of Herakles' mythological fame and to present a Herakles who was plagued by human limitations while actually performing his great, heroic achievements. Since time-honoured, heroic deeds make up the action of Apollonius' epic, Herakles had perforce to be relegated to his archaic, traditional role from which many Greek writers had been trying to emancipate him.

Herakles' portrait in the *Argonautica*, then, was primarily the ineluctable result of Apollonius' choice of genre. It narrowly circumscribed Herakles' role but did not prevent the author from adding a few touches that reveal his own attitude to the hero. Herakles' physical feats are simply meant to be looked at in awe. A few times, however, we are invited to admire him outright. This is the case when he magnanimously refuses to become the leader of the expedition, and when he rebukes his young colleagues in a wonderfully ironic speech for interminably succumbing to Hypsipyle and the Lemnian women (1. 865–74):

> My good sirs, are we exiled for manslaughter? Cast out for killing relatives at home? Or have we come here in want of brides, in scorn of our own women there? Are we really content to plough the rich soil of Lemnos? We shall win no crown, I assure you, by tarrying so long with a set of foreign women. And it is no good praying for a miracle. Fleeces do not come to people of their own accord. We might as well return home to our wives, leaving this captain of ours to spend all day in the embrace of Hypsipyle until he has won the admiration of the world by repopulating Lemnos.

Here Herakles combines the shrewdness of the elder statesman with the compassionate wit he showed in the *Alcestis*, and with a rather surprising abstinence.[19] In a situation where Vergil's Aeneas can be impelled only with heavy-handed divine machinery and the ever-present *fatum*, Herakles succeeds with persuasion. 'So he won over the group. Nobody dared to look him in the eye and answer him. With no more said, the meeting broke up and they hurried off to make ready for departure.' The un-Homeric brevity of Herakles' speech makes it all the more admirable.

Other incidents, such as his murder of Theiodamas and the Boreads, might tend to denigrate Herakles. They must be viewed, however, in the context of this epic where they amount to little, compared to the several instances in which Apollonius pillories the sabre-rattling heroism of hotheaded and witless warriors such as Telamon and Idas. More importantly, any attempt[20] to over-interpret Herakles' shortcomings is seriously qualified by Jason's own, 'anti-heroic' course of action. Jason stumbles from dilemma to dilemma, being constantly compelled to choose between two evils.[21] One short-range expedient supplants another and Jason becomes a monstrous opportunist. In the end, the arms of the modern hero—skill, improvisation, and persuasion—fail abysmally. Cornered by Medea's brother Apsyrtus and his army, Jason is ready to buy his way out by giving up the girl to whom he owes his success. Medea rages and protests, blaming Jason for his cruelty (ἀτροπίῃ 4. 387). The same term is later used for king Aeetes and his hordes (4. 1006); the Hellenistic citizen hero Jason is no better than the barbarians who live at the fringe of the world. Terrified by Medea's outburst, Jason readily assents to the scheme she proposes, especially as it is the logical conclusion to the arguments he has been using throughout: 'Evil deeds commit us to exploits as evil as the deeds themselves' (4. 411–12). The trap is laid for Apsyrtus. Under false pretenses of *xenia*,[22] they lure Apsyrtus to the island of Artemis where Jason butchers him right at the goddess' temple. Not to be outdone, Jason immediately engages in the appropriate rites. 'After lopping off the dead man's extremities he licked up some blood three times and three times spat the pollution out, as killers do in the attempt to expiate a treacherous murder.' Jason here is a combination of Herakles, the murderer of Iphitus in the *Odyssey*, the blasphemous Herakles of the *Trachiniae*, and the godless Lycus of Euripides' *Herakles*.

Apollonius' pessimism is unmistakable. It is the pessimism that Horace expressed by lamenting that 'our parents' age, worse than our grandparents', has brought forth us who are less worthy and who will soon yield an offspring yet more depraved'. Herakles was by no means perfect, but his epigones are even less so. For Theiodamas and the Dryopians, Herakles was a harsh servitor of justice. Jason, by contrast, is a harsh servitor of his own interests.[23]

This is not to say that Herakles in Apollonius' epic has the same role as in the *Philoctetes*, although we might modify Reinhardt's statement about Sophocles' play and say that Herakles' presence, though certainly not his ideal presence, permeates the *Argonautica*. This is brought out once more, after the action of the epic is essentially finished, in what may be called the epic's coda.[24] With both force and *aretē*, Herakles' traditional qualities, the Argonauts carry their ship through the Libyan desert (4. 1384). They are called sons of gods as they now undertake a task that is imposed on them by *anankē*. The Herculean reminiscences prepare for the fact that the Argonauts again are following in the hero's footsteps. They find a place where Herakles, only on the previous day, had slain the serpent that guarded the golden apples of the Hesperides. Because of the epitomizing function of the coda, the fetching of the golden apples furnishes an even closer parallel to Jason's expedition than did the story of Hippolyta's girdle. There are the golden apples and the golden fleece, the apple tree and the oak tree, the two serpents that guard the trees, the sacred groves and the women (the Hesperides and Medea) who play their divergent roles in the stories.[25] Although Herakles' and Jason's approaches are different, each leaves a scene of death and misery behind. Aigle, one of the Hesperides, naturally berates Herakles in the strongest possible language. To her, he was a 'merciless' man (4. 1438), which is a patent echo of his 'merciless' slaying of Theiodamas. She regards him as a perpetrator of *hybris* and twice likens him to an animal: he acted like a dog and worse (4. 1433), and after he struck water, he 'fell on his hands and chest and drank greedily from the cleft till, with his head down like a beast in the fields, he had filled his mighty paunch'.

Is this Apollonius' final condemnation of Herakles? Hardly. True enough, Herakles had been compared to a beast before—to a maddened bull, after the loss of Hylas. The Argonauts, however, behave no better than Herakles. Before finding the Hesperides, 'they dashed off, like mad dogs', in search of fresh water (4. 1393–4). The fresh water they find is that which Herakles had tapped the day before. Carping as it is, Aigle's speech begins with the admission that Herakles' exploit is a boon to the Argonauts, even though it brought grief to the Hesperides. The Argonauts' reaction to Aigle's complaint is unmitigated delight. They care about her grief as little as had Herakles, but

> they ran off in happy haste towards the place where Aigle had pointed out the spring. When they had reached it, the whole crowd milled round the cranny in the rock, like a swarm of burrowing ants busily gather around a little hole, or flies lighting upon a drop of honey cluster around with insatiate eagerness.

With the water still dripping from their lips, the Argonauts praise Herakles as their saviour. Physically removed as he is from them now, he has taken his place with the many deities that have continually rescued the Argonauts from their ever-present dilemmas. A search expedition is sent out, but it fails. In a beautiful simile Apollonius expresses the physical and metaphysical distance between Herakles and the modern heroes of the Argo. 'Lynceus thought he saw a lonely figure on the verge of that vast land, as a man, when the month begins, sees or thinks he sees the new moon through the clouds. He went back and told his comrades there was now no chance of overtaking Herakles' (4. 1477–82). The grand exit of the 'grand creation' was not lost on Vergil who adapted the simile for Dido in Hades whom Aeneas was trying to reach in vain (*Aen.* 6. 451–4).

While forcing his hand in portraying Herakles, the mythological tradition did not force on Apollonius this extensive role of Herakles in the *Argonautica.* Aristotle (*Pol.* 3. 8. 3.) and Apollodorus (1. 9. 19) refer to a popular version according to which Herakles volunteered, but could not come along because he was too heavy for the Argo. Apollonius retained Herakles because he needed a reference point for his epic and its hero, just as, later, Vergil would invite deliberate comparison with his predecessors. This was a bare necessity for an ancient writer if he wanted to claim his place in an existing literary tradition. To Apollonius, as we have seen, Herakles in many ways stood for the spirit and style of the old epic. Without the latter as a backdrop, Jason's new kind of 'heroism' would be pointless. In spite of his pessimism, however, Apollonius had no moralistic concern to show that Herakles was a better man than Jason. Rather, the one timeless quality of a hero, whether traditional or contemporary, which Apollonius seems to suggest, is that the hero's strengths also turn out to be his greatest liability.

Whereas his choice of genre forced Apollonius to revive the archaically heroic Herakles, his contemporary Theocritus belongs to the more influential tradition that saw in Herakles a human being rather than a heroic superman. Instead of being a foil for a contemporary hero, Herakles himself now is adapted to the Hellenistic scene. The genre which enabled Theocritus to do so was the epyllion, a Hellenistic creation. It was not only smaller than epic in size but was based on an entirely different premise. Its aim was to be picturesque in the original sense of the word. Unlike Apollonius', Theocritus' portrait of Herakles was not determined by the genre he chose, but he used Herakles to shape a new genre. The popularity of the Hylas theme after Theocritus[26] shows that he had imparted to Herakles what Apollonius' antiquarianism could not give him: new mythopoeic power.

Genealogical considerations played a part in Theocritus' predilection for Herakles, as it would for French writers to the eighteenth century. Like the whole Gallic nation later, the Ptolemies claimed to be descended from Herakles. Besides exalting their common pedigree, this claim served them to demonstrate that they were Alexander's true heirs, for Alexander's emulation of the hero was widely known.[27] In his encomium on Ptolemy Philadelphus Theocritus therefore devotes a lengthy passage (*Id.* 17. 20–33) to describing how his father, Ptolemy Soter, and Alexander are Herakles' immortal associates in heaven, 'for to both of these the mighty son of Herakles was forbear, and both in the end trace back their birth to Herakles'. They escort Herakles and Hebe, Ptolemy bearing the bow and quiver, and Alexander, the club.

None of these connotations are found in *Idyll* 24 where Theocritus treated the subject of Pindar's First *Nemean*, the infant Herakles. The story, which served Pindar to express an ethical creed, has become a charming domestic genre scene. In this piece of Hellenistic Biedermeier, there is no mention even of Herakles' divine birth or Hera's mighty wrath. From the outset, which describes Alcmena's motherly chores, she and Amphitryon appear just like the people next door. Sent by Hera, who has more in common with a witch in Grimm's fairy tales than with the greatest of all the goddesses, the snakes slip into the house amid an eerie glow. Iphicles shrieks, and there is considerable commotion as the servants—who have taken the place of Pindar's Theban chieftains 'with their brazen armour'—drowsily stumble on the scene. Amphitryon arms himself as a suburbanite would when he hears a burglar in the house, and he comes upon his little boy who gaily waves the snakes (Plate 10) and lays them at his father's feet. Whereas Pindar thundered that 'there he [Amphitryon] stood, possessed with rapture overpowering and delightful, for he saw the unusual spirit and power of his son', Theocritus' Amphitryon simply puts the boy to bed and, 'anxious to sleep some more', goes back to bed himself. It is as if they all had been roused to turn a cat out of the house or to shut a window. The next morning Teiresias is summoned and duly predicts the hero's labours and deification. But then, updating his repertoire to suit the taste of his Hellenistic clientele, he goes on to spend just as much time on the mumbo-jumbo of the expiation ritual. The ensuing catalogue of Herakles' teachers, which has its cute touches, does not cast Herakles in a heroic mould either.

Similarly, the only thing that is left of the heroic Herakles in Theocritus' Hylas (*Idyll* 13) is the epithet χαλκεοκάρδιο, 'with the heart of brass'. For the rest of the poem, Herakles 'is a lover and pederast simply'.[28] In order to make Herakles a contemporary, quasi-Alexandrine figure Theocritus, in complete contrast to Apollonius, rids him of all his epic aspects and concentrates on his love for Hylas. Theocritus uses this episode to show the poem's addressee, Nicias, that in love even a great mythical hero is 'just like us'. The beginning of the poem also marks a new stage in Herakles' cultural refinement. Far from being the unruly schoolboy, who slew Linus, or the incipient Cynic sage who was taught by Chiron and Prometheus, Herakles has turned educator himself, for 'he teaches Hylas everything' (line 8). As such he was to appear in Ronsard's *Hylas* which Ronsard addressed to a friend, Jean Passerat, who had been appointed private tutor to the son of a French nobleman. Ronsard's Herakles, like Le Fèvre's, instructs in all skills and virtues:

> Que de grossier habille homme tu fis
> en le forceant et contraignant d'aprendre
> toutes vertues, dès sa jeunesse tendre.

But it is Herakles the lover who engages Theocritus. The rowing contest, the other Argonauts, Herakles' uprooting of the pine tree—all these are not even mentioned. Instead, Theocritus dwells on the natural setting of the incident, a luxuriant *locus amoenus*: 'Soon in a low-lying place he spied a spring, round which grew rushes thick, and dark celandine, green maiden-hair, and wild celery luxuriant, and creeping dog's tooth. . . .' Herakles thus is one of the earliest examples of that literary tradition which contrasts the tormented lover with the bliss of the pastoral surrounding. 'Troubled for the boy' (ταρασσόμενος περὶ παιδί) Herakles goes in search of him. He is the exact opposite of the Stoic or Cynic sage to whom ἀταραξία, freedom from troubles, was the highest good. So the mad Herakles—μαινόμενος is placed emphatically at the beginning of line 71—rages throughout the country. The god that strikes Herakles mad is not Lyssa or Hera, but Eros (72).[29] Like Euripides' Herakles, however, Theocritus' is not concerned about further exploits and great deeds; 'all of Jason's things', as he puts it, 'take second place' to Herakles' love for Hylas (67).

This humanized portrait of Herakles was possible only by isolating him from the context of the performance of his epic and heroic labours and feats. Theocritus thus continued, in a far more concise fashion, what Euripides, for example, had done. When Herakles returns to his heroic context at the end of the Hylas episode, the difficulty is resolved with casual, flippant wit: 'Hence the fair Hylas is numbered among the immortals, but Herakles the heroes mocked for a deserter, because he left the Argo of the thirty thwarts and came on foot to the Colchians and the inhospitable Phasis.' The conclusion purposely epitomizes the inversion of Herakles' role in the *Idyll.* Theocritus had used him at the very beginning of the poem as proof of his contention that immortals in love are only human. Throughout the poem, Herakles appears in this human role, and in the end, it is an immortal Hylas who leaves Herakles behind. This Herakles, as the good-natured teasing of his companions shows, is just one of the boys.

Other writers who treated the same episode tried to resolve in their own way the disparity between the myth which Herakles came from and the modern role that he was made to play. Propertius, André Chenier, and d'Annunzio proceeded most radically by virtually ignoring Herakles. In Propertius' poem (1. 20), which is addressed to Gallus, the episode does not serve to illustrate the power of Eros but of Fortuna, bad luck, which befalls a lover if he is not on his guard. Accordingly, Propertius is not concerned with Herakles' amorous torment but with the details of Hylas' mishap, which include a lengthy description of the pastoral setting. By the eighteenth century, these depictions of bucolic *loci amoeni* had become so hackneyed a theme[30] that E. D. de Parny in his Hylas poem discarded it completely and versified just the bare, few facts of the story. Chénier made a splendid attempt at evoking landscape again, and his poem ends on the note of Hylas' voice dimly reaching Herakles through some reeds:

> Mais Alcide inquiet, que presse un noir augure,
> Va, vient, le cherche, crie; auprès de l'onde pure,
> 'Hylas, Hylas!' il crie mille et mille fois.
> Le jeune enfant de loin croit entendre sa voix,
> et du fond des roseaux, pour le tirer de peine,
> lui repond une voix non entendue et vaine.

This is a brief but beautiful sketch of Herakles' anxiety. Still, the poet only alludes to Herakles' actual love for Hylas by beginning his poem as follows:

> Vous savez, ou bien venez apprendre
> quels doux larcins, d'Hercule insidieux rivaux,
> du jeune et bel Hylas firent un dieu des eaux.

There is some mannerism about this, which Chénier himself admitted,[31] but at least he expressed the idea that Herakles and the nymphs were rivals in love for Hylas. Not all writers, however, would accept the peculiar kind of Herakles' love with equanimity. As early as Hellenistic times the historian Anticlides asserted that Herakles' son Hyllus, and not Hylas, disappeared into the river.[32] The same squeamishness may have been one reason why post-classical authors in particular tended drastically to diminish Herakles' role in the story.

In contrast to the poets whom we have just mentioned, Ronsard, the foremost poet of the French Renaissance, was not content with giving an impressionistic vignette of Herakles. His vast Hellenic erudition commanded him to do otherwise, and his expansive version of the Hylas episode is a combination of the versions of Apollonius and Theocritus, 'with an occasional glance at the *Argonautica* of Valerius Flaccus'.[33] From the start there is no doubt that Herakles is the protagonist once again. The opening lines are a spirited defence of the patron hero of Gaul against the presumed slanders of antiquity:

> Mais de ton temps les Chantres ont menty,
> qui ton bien-fait en blasme ont converty . . .

The epic breadth of the narration, which initially follows Apollonius very closely, is tempered by some amusing touches. Herakles joins Jason because he believes 'un voyage si beau' should not take place without him, and little Hylas hurriedly trips behind him:

> Car, ô bon roy, le moindre de tes pas
> en valloit cinq des petits pieds de Hylas.

When his oar snaps, Herakles at first is angry. Then he decides to make light of the mishap and throws himself lengthwise across the Argo, his feet touching the prow and his head, the stern. It is as if Ronsard were trying to outdo Apollonius in presenting Herakles as the giant from another age. He continues in this vein by describing at length Herakles tearing out the tree. All these tableaux do not bring the hero any closer to the reader, nor was this Ronsard's intention. Even in his mad despair, Herakles is primarily an uncommon apparition at which we can marvel rather than a human being with whom we can empathize. Accordingly, the poem ends on the note of grandeur and elevation when Hylas' shade utters words of noble consolation of a wearied Herakles:

> Mon seul Seigneur, qui fus mon espérance,
> qui les vertus m'apris des mon enfance,
> Afin qu'un jour je peusse devenir
> grand come toy, puis au Ciel parvenir:
> Bien que ton nom j'eusse en vain soupiré
> en t'apellant, mais quoy? la destinée
> avoit ma vie a tel sort terminée,
> pour prendre un jour une mortelle fin,
> hé qui pourroit résister au destin!

Instead of Herakles' love, Hylas remembers Herakles, the Pindaric teacher of virtue, and the stirring maxim about *destin*, *anankē*, is chosen accordingly. The French Pindar, as Ronsard called himself, portrays Herakles as a grand creation all right, but it is a classicistic and not a creative portrait. Perhaps it would be unfair to expect the latter from a representative of the Renaissance, which often was concerned more with the disinterment of the classical authors than with their creative adaptation or their relevance, in the contemporary sense of the word, and we will see later that the classicistic Herakles was granted a long and boring life. Ronsard's attempt, however, sets in relief that of Theocritus. For Theocritus also lived at a time when scholarly preoccupation with the classics prevailed and originality was at a low ebb, as is exemplified by Apollonius' antiquarian Herakles. Theocritus' depiction of Herakles in the Hylas *Idyll* is the exact opposite of these tendencies. Although this new departure was only imperfectly realized by Theocritus' imitators, his example shows that the mythopoeic reinterpretation of a traditional hero is, above all, the work of the individual poet rather than the prevailing spirit of the age.

Nonetheless, in at least one other, if minor, respect the Hellenistic age had its effect on the tradition of Herakles. There were some details in Herakles' life and adventures which to a Ptolemaic courtier would seem rather gross and unseemly. Herakles was accepted as a pederast, but he ought not to get his hands dirty in enterprises such as cleaning the stables of Augias. Over-civilization breeds its own *nostalgie de la boue*, but it is still not the literal kind of filth, let alone dung. The pseudo-Theocritean *Idyll* 25 is a masterpiece of suppressing all the repugnant features of the Augias story.[34] In fact, the author does not even mention 'dung' by name. Since allusiveness alone cannot quite make a 'little epic' work, Herakles' conquest of the Nemean lion eventually takes the place of the more unseemly labour and is told at great length. While fifth- and fourth-century writers had done their best to refine Herakles' soul, it was now time for his body to be ennobled also. Diogenes might emulate Herakles, but the Herakles who was destined to join the ranks of the French chevaliers was not allowed to look like a Diogenes. The Hellenistic concern for the *comme il faut* reinforced the traditional reluctance to denigrate or humiliate Herakles. It rid him of objectionable externals, and he became the proper subject for the court poets to whom his fate would be entrusted.

NOTES TO CHAPTER V

1. *Memorabilia* 2. 1. 21–34. Xenophon's speaker admits that he is giving only an outline of the story, but it is confirmed in all essentials by the scholiast on Aristophanes' *Clouds* 361 (Diels-Kranz, *Fragments of the Pre-Socratic Philosophers* 84 B 1). The best study of the literary aspects of the subject in antiquity is that of Alpers; its artistic and literary reflections especially in the Renaissance have been elucidated by Panofsky.
2. Mario Untersteiner, *The Sophists* (Oxford, 1954) 217.
3. Cf. Untersteiner 220, with further bibliographical references.
4. So Höistad 32.
5. As is evinced by the argument between the Just and the Unjust Way of Life in Aristophanes' *Clouds* (889–1104). It includes a eulogy of Herakles (1048–52) because he is the best of all men in regard to his spirit, *psychē*; for this—rather than his strength—he was also praised by Xenophon and Isocrates, as quoted below. Plato's presenting men with the choice of two ways of life in the *Gorgias* probably was also inspired by Prodicus' parable, although the motif is found already in Hesiod (*Works and Days* 287–92).

6. The speech, *To Demonicus*, is usually numbered as Isocrates' First Oration; the passage we are discussing occurs in paragraph 50.
7. *Ep.* 3 p. 64 (Usener).
8. In *Helen* 23–5, Isocrates contrasts the general usefulness of Theseus' exploits with those of Herakles, which merely secured him personal fame and involved him in many unnecessary dangers; although the point was not to be taken seriously, it may have been made to soothe Athenian inferiority feelings about their own hero in comparison to Herakles (see pp. 40f.), whom the Athenians in the fourth century respectfully conceded to Sparta (see, e.g. Xen. *Hell.* 6. 3. 6). In the *Busiris*, Isocrates speciously tries to disprove Busiris' death at the hands of Herakles because of the chronological difficulties involved.
9. The most useful discussion of Herakles in the writings of the early Cynics is that of Höistad 33–50.
10. A literal translation is impossible because the Greek original has not survived. We have only a Syrian translation, which was translated into German by J. Gildemeister and F. Bücheler (*RhM* 27 [1872] 450–1); our English version, in turn, is based on this German translation. Still, the essence of Prometheus' remarks appears to have been preserved.
11. *Herakles Major* or *On Strength*, *Herakles* or *Midas*, *Herakles* or *On Phronesis* or *On Strength*. All three titles are cited by Diogenes Laertius 6. 16 and 18, who in another place (2. 61) mentions a *Herakles Minor* also, though that may have been yet another title for either of the last two of Antisthenes' works on Herakles. J. B. Tate, *Eranos* 51 (1953) 15 and 18, argues that in the strict sense of the word, Antisthenes did not write allegories about Herakles.
12. Aristotle's *Hymn to Aretē* is quoted in full by Athenaeus 15. 696b–d. See D. Page, *Poetae Melici Graeci* (Oxford, 1962) 444–5.
13. Servius, *ad Aen.* 6. 395: *Hercules a prudentioribus mente magis quam corpore fortis inducitur*. For Lucian and the myth of the Gallic Herakles see pp. 222f., and on the connotations of ἀγχινοία, Stanford 32–3.
14. Flacelière-Devambez, *Héraclès* 13.
15. Although several Hellenistic epics were written; see Lesky, *History of Greek Literature* 736. They included a *Heraklid* in fourteen books by Rhianos of Crete (second half of the third century). For discussions of the peculiar character of the *Argonautica* and its hero see H. Fränkel in *MH* 14 (1957) 1–19 and *MH* 17 (1960) 1–20, and especially G. Lawall, 'Apollonius' *Argonautica*: Jason as Anti-hero', *YCS* 19 (1966) 119–70. Lawall discusses Herakles' role on pp. 124–31, but his interpretation and mine differ in several essential points.
16. This is Apollonius' modification of a traditional version according to which Herakles almost made the Argo sink and therefore was barred from joining the expedition; see below.
17. *Aetia* fr. 24 (Pfeiffer), whereas in the more playful context of the *Hymn to Artemis* (160–1) the same poet referred to the Theiodamas episode as the crowning example of Herakles' gluttony. The poet of *Anth. Graeca* 16. 101

went even further than Apollonius and wrote, facetiously perhaps, that Herakles' murder of the *ox* was wicked.

18. E.g. 1. 877, 3. 1255, 3. 1407 (the note on which that book ends), 4. 8. Jason's acceptance of the task Aeetes imposes on him is couched in terms reminiscent of Herakles' labours: 'I will bear this labour even though it is excessive (*τῷ καὶ ἐγὼ τὸν ἄεθλον ὑπερφίαλόν περ ἐοντα/τλήσομαι* 3. 428–9). Jason then attributes all his toils to *anankē* (430) and Aeetes, in reply, refers to the task as *ponos* (434). All the while, the poet stresses Jason's un-Herculean *amēchania* (423, 432).
19. Flacelière-Devambez, *Héraclès* 51 attribute it to the influence of Prodicus' virtuous portrait of Herakles. But in the dramatic and epic tradition there was no trace of this quality as is evinced, e.g. by Sophocles' *Trachiniae.*
20. Such as Lawall's (note 15, above).
21. Cf. Fränkel, *MH* 14 (1957) 9–10.
22. Jason must be judged by what he said earlier about the barbarian king Aeetes: 'Every man on earth, even the greatest rogue, fears Zeus, the god of hospitality, and keeps his laws' (3. 192–3).
23. It is worth noting that when the Argonauts claim to fight for justice (4. 1057), Apollonius at once points out that their *dikē*, unlike Herakles', does not necessarily coincide with Zeus' (4. 1100).
24. Lawall's term (note 15, above) 128 n. 17.
25. These parallels are noted, but interpreted differently, by Lawall 129.
26. Which is evident from Vergil's rhetorical question *cui non dictus Hylas?* (*Geo.* 3. 6). Unfortunately, the other Hellenistic Hylas poems have not survived.
27. For detailed documentation see A. S. F. Gow, *Theocritus* 2 (Cambridge, 1952) 331 and W. W. Tarn, *Hellenistic Civilization*, 3rd ed., (Cleveland and New York, 1961) 51.
28. B. Otis, *Virgil. A Study in Civilized Poetry* (Oxford, 1963) 14.
29. Herakles overcome by Eros also was represented in Hellenistic art; see *Anth. Graeca* 16. 103 (on a statue by Lysippus—Herakles in Omphale's bondage), and 16. 104.
30. Especially because of the medieval tradition; see E. R. Curtius, *European Literature and the Latin Middle Ages* (New York, 1963) 197–200. For some other aspects of the Hylas poems of Ronsard, Chénier, and also, Leconte de Lisle see P. Moreau, 'Les trois Hylas', *Mélanges de philologie, d'histoire et de littérature offerts à Joseph Vianey* (Paris, 1934) 425–35.
31. He struck out the phrase 'd'Hercule insidieux rivaux' and wrote beside them '*maniéré*'; see G. Scarfe, *André Chénier. His Life and Work* (Oxford, 1965) 187–8.
32. *FGH* 140 F 2.
33. Isidore Silver, *Ronsard and the Hellenistic Renaissance in France.* Vol. 1: *Ronsard and the Greek Epic* (St Louis, 1961) 383. On Valerius Flaccus, see pp. 163f.

34. The story was not quite as proverbial as one is often led to assume. Brommer 28–9 emphasizes that its representations in Greek art are quite rare and relatively late, although they include a statue by Lysippus. For a more detailed analysis of *Idyll* 25 see I. M. Linforth, *TAPA* 78 (1947) 77–87. In the poem *Megara*, which is commonly ascribed to Theocritus or Moschus and in which Megara and Alcmena bewail Herakles' fate, the characterization of the hero is conventional.

CHAPTER VI
Roman Hercules

Long before Romulus laid the foundation of Rome, the everlasting city, Herakles had left his mark on the site. The tradition has it that when he returned from Spain with the cattle of Geryon, they were stolen from him on the pastures that were to be Rome. Herakles recovered the cattle and punished the culprit. In memory of the event king Evander, a Greek exile, or Herakles himself built what was the greatest altar in those regions at the time. The cult of Hercules at the Ara Maxima in the Cattle Market, the Forum Boarium, continued through the entire pagan history of Rome.[1] So far from being a literary figure pure and simple, Hercules in Rome was a religious phenomenon which we must briefly describe before proceeding to its adaptations and reflections in literature.

Besides the cult of Hercules in Italy, the cult of Herakles in Greece continued through the Hellenistic age and the Roman period. But there is a significant difference. Greek religion was vital because it engendered myth and ultimately wound up being myth. While the Greek Herakles appealed to the popular and mythic imagination, his properly religious role—in the sense of his fulfilling a real religious need—progressively declined. Alexander and his contemporaries did not hail Herakles as the giver of strength or helper in adversity, but as the achiever of wondrous deeds and as a fellow-traveller to exotic lands. In passing from Greece to Rome, Herakles took on 'a new seriousness more in keeping with the character of the people that welcomed him'.[2] There he satisfied true, religious aspirations which the ritualistic and rather impersonal state religion could not provide. The essential characteristic of the Roman Hercules cult was exactly its contrast to and freedom from the mortifying interference of the pontifical religion. According to the tradition, a private family, *gens*, originally was in charge of the cult at the Ara Maxima and even after the state priests became its custodians and the feast of Hercules was given a place in the official Roman calendar, the worship remained private and individual. Unlike the traditional gods of the state religion, Herakles was worshipped on individual occasions rather than one day of the year, the people—rather than the priests alone—partook in the sacrificial banquet, and so far from being localized at one, state-supported sanctuary, Herakles' cult was practised in a multitude of smaller shrines and temples, which had been built as tokens of private gratitude. Herakles satisfied the personal cult needs that were left unfulfilled by the state religion and thus came to share in the same religious intensity that was accorded the oriental cults for exactly the same reason. The capacities in which he was invoked ranged from provider of a good birth to silent partner in business deals. Herakles, in short, regained religious functions similar to those he had held in sixth-century Greece: he was once more the ἀλεξίκακος, the patron saint who would help one overcome all imaginable difficulties of life and hence he was called *invictus*, the invincible one. Above all, he was a personal god and worshipped as such by Roman generals from Scipio to Antony.

The absorption of Herakles into Roman religion had two important results for his literary tradition. First, since Roman religion in contrast to the Greek was not mythopoeic, little was added to the Herakles myth in the way of new stories or adventures. The one new event Roman writers treat is his foundation of the Ara Maxima. There are several versions, but they do not spin off into additional or more extensive products of the mythical imagination. Quantitatively, very little is added to the mythological Herakles tradition. Spiritually, however—and this is our second point—the Roman contribution was significant. It consists of the total seriousness with which the hero is now approached. Roman religion and the philosophies, that is mostly Stoicism—and the Romans were Stoics long before Stoicism became a philosophical system—worked hand in hand to shape an image of Herakles whose *gravitas* has been a distinctive trait to our day. From here, for instance, stems the uneasiness of the adaptors of the *Alcestis* about the burlesque Herakles and their zealous obliteration of his unseemly behaviour. There is an occasional humorous note such as in

Propertius, Ovid and in Seneca's *Apocolocyntosis*, but the reasons are anti-Augustanism and literary parody rather than a mockery of the hero himself. His absence, in any comic role, from the Roman stage, is truly remarkable considering the dominant role of the comic Herakles in the Greek theatre. At the time when the Alexandrian audience guffawed about 'the drunken Herakles in his yellow coat' teetering over the stage, Caesar and Seneca were writing tragedies on Herakles, and Cicero, Dio Chrysostom, and Epictetus idealized him as the perfect embodiment of Stoic wisdom and virtue.

Herakles' early popularity in Roman literature is sufficiently attested by the comedies especially of Plautus where references to him abound. *Mehercle!* (by Herakles!) is a stock exclamation and Herakles' labours and other exploits are frequently used as metaphors.[3] For example, a troubled lover, in one of the comparisons typical of Roman comedy, contends that his labours are far greater than Herakles' (*Persa* 1–5), and an uppity *adulescens* warns his tutor that they might play Herakles and Linus (*Bacch.* 155). The brevity of such references, which are not accompanied by any explanations, attests the Romans' thorough familiarity with the stories, but the exploitation of the hero for raucous entertainment is missing entirely. The *Amphitruo*, Plautus' only mythological comedy, is unique because of his exalted treatment of the theme which is a far cry from the farcical, slapstick humour that prevailed, e.g. in Rhinthon's *Amphitryon* or whatever the Greek model happens to have been.[4] Throughout the play, Plautus seems to allude to the pretensions of the Scipionic family and the Elder Scipio in particular. Plautus' dramaturgical emphasis in this play on the divine birth of Herakles agrees well with that purpose. The association of Scipio and Herakles is familiar from later Roman literature—Silius, as we shall see, being the most explicit example—and had its roots in Ennius' attempt to deify Scipio. Herakles, the mortal who became a god by strength of his own *virtus*, was his model, just as the Augustan poets would almost canonically associate Augustus with Herakles for the same reason. *Virtus*, a word related to both *vir* ('man') and *vis* ('energy'), was the counterpart of the Greek *aretē*.

The absence of the comic Herakles from the Roman plays is explained not only by the *pietas* with which 'the masters of the earth, the togaed race' regarded him. He also does not appear in the tragedies of

1. Herakles Farnese, by Glycon of Athens; original attributed to Lysippus (fourth century B.C.)

PLATE I

23. The Triumph of Herakles, by G. B. Tiepolo

the early Roman dramatic poets, thus making impossible the parody of such a tragedy on the part of the comedians. Aside from Herculean subjects, the range of Roman tragedies reflects that of their Greek originals, Euripides in particular, with some more preference being given to the Trojan cycle because of Rome's incipient awareness of her Trojan legend. The failure of the Roman tragedians to write on Herakles reflects the very un-Greek, strict distinction between religion and myth. In Republican Rome, Herakles belonged too much to the former to be a ready subject for the latter. It was only Vergil who absorbed Roman religion into his epic, a fact that accounts for a considerable part of its uniqueness.

Before turning to Vergil's Herakles, who made a strong impression on the Renaissance, we must mention briefly one tendency that left some imprint on the tradition, at least through the Middle Ages, and provides a backdrop for Vergil's and Seneca's portrayal of Herakles as the divine man, *θεῖος ἀνήρ*. That was the anthropological criticism of myth by one Euhemerus, who lived around 300 B.C. Reduced to its simplest terms Euhemerus' theory was that the gods originally were men who had been elevated to divine status through the respect of their descendants.[5] Whereas Euhemerus' contemporaries do not seem to have been impressed with his speculations, Ennius translated his work into Latin in the early second century, and the first writer who openly espoused Euhemerus' principle was the Greek historian Diodorus, a contemporary of Caesar and Augustus. To Diodorus Prometheus, for example, so far from being a martyred Titan, was a governor in Egypt whose province was threatened by an inundation of the Nile which was called 'eagle' because of its destructiveness (I. 19. 1–4). To rescue Prometheus from his predicament, Herakles was therefore cast as a sort of glorified ancient engineer.[6] Similarly, the giant Antaeus, according to Diodorus, was simply another, rebellious governor whom Herakles, a general, brought to bay (I. 21). At the site of Rome Herakles did not meet any governor, but Diodorus' debunking of the story was even more thoroughgoing than in the other episodes. Herakles, as usual, appears merely as a general who is leading an army back from Spain. One should think that the traditional version of the cattle theft and the punishment of Cacus, the thief, would have attracted Diodorus because it supported his basic thesis: Herakles achieved some deed and, as a result, was worshipped as a god at the Ara Maxima. Instead, Diodorus went even further and turned the myth inside out. Herakles is received with great hospitality by Cacius, as Diodorus calls him. Instead of there being a meaningful *raison d'être* for his deification, Herakles simply takes it for granted and offers the Romans a good deal along the lines of *do ut des* (4. 21. 3–4):

> Now Herakles received with favour the good will shown him by the dwellers on the Palatine and foretold to them that, after he had passed into the circle of the gods, it would come to pass that whatever men should make a vow to dedicate to Herakles a tithe of their goods would lead a more happy and prosperous life. And in fact the custom did arise in later times and has persisted to our own day; for many Romans, and not only those of moderate fortunes but some even of great wealth . . . have presented him with a tenth of their possessions, which came to four thousand talents.

The euhemeristic humanization of Herakles at first may strike one as absurd. After all, virtually all writers, with the exception of Herodotus, were in agreement that Herakles had originally been a man. Anticipating the Latin church fathers, however, Diodorus went on to deny that Herakles and others, such as Castor and Pollux, had been transformed into real deities and said that they had simply remained men on whom worship had been falsely bestowed. The euhemeristic concept is quite different from the humanization Herakles underwent at the hands of an author like Euripides. The latter had humanized the divine aspirations of the cultic Herakles into an exalted, if human, spiritual idealism. Herakles was worth emulating not because his life held out the promise of divinity, but because he was a great man. To Euhemerus and his followers, by contrast, Herakles was a man pure and simple, and there was nothing ennobling about him. Thus it is not surprising that Lucretius, who needed some way of belittling the tenets of his Stoic adversaries, offers a critique of Herakles that is entirely euhemeristic in spirit (5. 22–54).

Lucretius pointedly uses Herakles as a foil for happiness' onlie begetter, the Master himself, Epicurus. 'Well,' he says with a patronizing sneer, 'in case you are one of the deluded men who happen to believe that Herakles' famed labours are distinguished, be advised that you are removed even further from the true ground of all reason.' Then Lucretius cavalierly tosses off the names of a few of the monsters against which Herakles fought, and he concludes with a deprecating So what? Would those creatures be of any harm, he asks, if they had remained alive? Of course not, because the earth still swarms with wild beasts and we all survive anyway. All these external dangers are nothing compared to the rending troubles of the mind—desires, cares, agonies, fears, pride, filthy lust, and wanton conduct in general. 'Therefore the man who subdues all these and drives them from his mind—with words, not arms—is it not fitting that this man should be numbered among the gods?' And that man, needless to say, is Epicurus—*deus ille fuit, deus, inclyte Memmi*. For Epicurus was the first to find the philosophy of life that is now called wisdom. . . . Lucretius, it will be noticed, now has it both ways: he uses Euhemerism for debunking Herakles and for deifying Epicurus. He contrives blithely to ignore any spiritual interpretation of Herakles, such as the Stoic one,[7] and presents him as the primitive strongman whose exploits are as meaningless as they are useless. And Lucretius' critique was not to be denied. It was echoed, for instance, by the Epicurean Cotta in Cicero's dialogue *On the Nature of the Gods* (3. 15, 16, 19), by Tiberius in his eulogy of Augustus (Dio 56. 36. 4), and by Varro, the greatest of all Roman scholars, who proceeded to dissect Herakles into forty-three different men of that name, much to the edification of Renaissance authors such as Salutati.[8] Even though Lucretius' view of Herakles was anything but universally accepted by his contemporaries—it certainly was not by Cicero,[9] who may have edited Lucretius' poem—it did reinforce Apollonius' characterization of the hero and reminded writers, such as Vergil, who were sympathetic to Herakles that the hero's ancient, non-spiritual past still could render him vulnerable.

Vergil's *Aeneid* is one of the most complex works of literature, and, accordingly, the reasons for Herakles' role in the *Aeneid* are many. One of them, however, stands out in particular since it is related to one of the central purposes of the epic. *The Aeneid* was an attempt to make Aeneas the truly popular, national hero of all of Italy, to give him precisely the role that Herakles had held in Greece. The Aeneas legend lacked the popular foundation which the Herakles myth had in Greece and even in Italy. Vergil's contemporary Dionysius (*Rom. Antiq.* 1. 40. 5) relates that

> In many other [i.e. outside Rome] places in Italy precincts are dedicated to this god and altars erected to him, both in cities and along highways; and one could scarcely find any place in Italy in which the god is not honoured.

It therefore was by no means impossible that Herakles might have been accepted as the popular ancestor of the Romans and Italians.[10] For even in Rome, Aeneas had been the sole property of a few noble families, among them the Julians, and since Octavian was a member of that family Aeneas was chosen to be the hero of the new epic.

Vergil assimilates Aeneas to Herakles virtually from the very beginning. In its proem, which is a programmatic synopsis of the *Aeneid*, Aeneas is introduced as 'a fugitive by fate' and a man 'persecuted by the relentless wrath of harsh Juno'. The traditional echoes are obvious and intentional. We need only compare what Homer's Achilles, another model of the Vergilian Aeneas, said about Herakles (*Il.* 18. 119): 'But fate subdued him and the troublesome wrath of Hera.' Of all the themes sketched in the seven-line proem, Vergil proceeds to reiterate that of Juno's wrath in the invocation to the Muse. He explicitly impresses upon the reader that of the basic themes in the *Aeneid*, this is the most significant. 'What reason,' asks the poet, 'what hurt drove Juno to make Aeneas undergo so many labours? Is divine wrath so great?' 'Labour' and 'wrath' are placed emphatically at the end of lines 10 and 11. Throughout the epic, Juno is the personal enemy of Aeneas and she acts from petty, personal motives. Both Juno's prominent role and her characterization are Vergilian innovations which are the result of the poet's desire to portray Aeneas as a second Herakles.[11]

The strongest verbal reminder of Aeneas' Herculean role is the persistent use of *labor* to denote Aeneas' task. Aeneas himself uses it many times to characterize himself and his adventures to those whom he meets on the way. The beginning of his programmatic introduction to Venus, whom he at first fails to recognize, is perhaps the most typical example (I. 372–4):

> O dea, si prima repetens ab origine pergam,
> et vacet annalis nostrorum audire laborum,
> ante diem clauso componet Vesper Olympo.

(O goddess, if I should tell you my story from its beginnings, and you had time to listen to the story of my labours, the Evening Star would close Olympus' gates and end the day before I finished.)

Only after Aeneas has stressed his *labores* does he mention the quality for which he was dear to the Romans and to Augustus in particular, his *pietas* (1. 378).

This conception of Aeneas of himself is confirmed by the many oracular and divine agencies who are guiding him through his trials. Venus pleads with Jupiter to grant Aeneas an end to his *labores* (1. 241), and she uses the term again when she asks Vulcan to provide Aeneas' arms (8. 30). After all the oracles in Book III apply the term *labor* to each new trial of Aeneas, Jupiter himself sanctions it in Book IV when he asks Mercury to tell Aeneas to shoulder his burden (*molitur* . . . *laborem* 4. 233). The expression recalls the exertion of Atlas, but Herakles' shouldering of Atlas' starry burden was well remembered in Augustan Rome. Ovid (*Fasti* 1. 565–8) linked it explicitly to Herakles' fight against Cacus which, as we shall see, plays such a significant part in the *Aeneid*. Aeneas' greatest *labor*, foreshadowed by the Herakles–Cacus episode in Book VIII, is his fight against Turnus and the Latins. This is the note on which Anchises ends his prophecy in Book VI (890–92):

> exin bella viro memorat quae deinde gerenda,
> Laurentisque docet populos urbemque Latini,
> et quo quemque modo fugiatque feratque laborem.

(He tells him of the wars which he has to wage and of the Laurentian peoples and the city of Latinus, and how he is to flee and bear each toil.)

'The practice of these warning agencies', as one scholar has noted, 'of applying the term *labor* to each fresh trial of Aeneas implies a perception of the similarity of the experience of Aeneas with the labours of Herakles on the part of those who presumably would have a clearer insight into the workings of destiny—Venus and the ghost of Anchises, for example.'[12] Aeneas himself, however, meanwhile expresses far more strikingly that he considers himself Herakles' heir. When he leaves Troy, he lifts his father on his shoulders, a scene which in both art and literature has been considered as the very incarnation of *pietas*. 'This labour will not weigh me down', Aeneas assures Anchises. For, as it turns out, around his shoulders he wears the lion's skin (2. 722). Besides Aeneas' being a saviour, σώτηρ, like Herakles, his immediate task—the pious rescue of his father—and the task for which he is setting out—*Romanam condere gentem*—have both the physical and the spiritual dimension which had characterized Herakles' labours since Pindar. The balance between the two aspects is exquisite; Vergil's Herakles ideal is a world apart from Apollonius'.

Aeneas' Herculean self-awareness is emphasized even more as the epic progresses. When he descends to the underworld he duplicates a feat of Herakles. It is by reference to Herakles that he tries to dispel the Sibyl's doubts. His justification begins on the note of his *labores* (6. 103–5):

> non ulla laborum,
> o virgo, nova mihi facies inopinave surgit:
> omnia praecepi[13] atque animo mecum ante peregi.

(For me, o prophetess, not one new or unexpected kind of labour rises up: I have foreseen them all and pondered them in my mind.)

The analogy is quite precise, for the fetching of Cerberus was Herakles' last and crowning labour. Aeneas then goes on to speak of his first Herculean labour, the rescue of his father (6. 110–11). All this builds up to the powerful conclusion of his speech (122–3):

> quid Thesea magnum,
> quid memorem Alciden?—et mi genus ab Iove summo.

(Why should I mention Theseus? why the great Herakles? I, too, have descent from Jove most high.)

The Sibyl fully understands the force of these arguments by acknowledging that Aeneas is god-born (125) and that he is engaged in a difficult labour: *hic labor est* (129). This labour is not, as Aristophanes' Dionysus believed, the descent to Hades, but the return to the world of reality, to the very *labores* with whose mention Anchises sends Aeneas back from Hades. As in Aeneas' departure from Troy, *labor* here stands for both the immediate—the actual retracing of the steps—and the more comprehensive, future task. One is again reminded of Euripides' Herakles whose real labours only began after he had successfully returned from the underworld. The terms in which the Sibyl describes the men who prevailed before Aeneas (129–31) clearly shows that she, too, considers Herakles as his chief model. Already Homer had stressed that Herakles was dearest of all to Zeus (*Il.* 18. 118), and in all of Greek and Roman mythology, he was the hero *par excellence* whose *virtus*, ἀρετή, was explicitly said to have raised him to heaven. Aeneas' claim to being Herakles' heir has prevailed, and the Sibyl will help him in his *insanus labor* (6. 135).

The Herculean reminiscences continue. When Aeneas sees various *monstra* (285), he acts like Herakles in Bacchylides' Meleager poem, draws his sword and tries to kill them before he learns that they are only shades.[14] Among the monsters are those against which Herakles fought —the centaurs, the Lernaean hydra, and Geryon. Another is the flame-spouting Chimaera which later appears on the helmet of Turnus. Aeneas' Herculean shadow-fight anticipates the real *labor* he faces after returning from the underworld.

When the Sibyl and Aeneas reach the river Styx, Charon explicitly refers to the precedent of Herakles and at first refuses to ferry Aeneas over. After the Sibyl reassures him that Aeneas is not a man of force, but *pietas*, Charon permits the 'gigantic Aeneas' (*ingentem Aenean* 413) to step into the boat. The result is almost the same as when Herakles came aboard the Argo (413–14): 'The sewn-leather boat groaned under his weight; marshy water seeped in through the rents he had made.' Somewhat later, Aeneas sees Dido as Lynceus in the *Argonautica* saw Herakles for the last time. From then on, Aeneas' way becomes a burden for him (*molitur . . . iter* 477), the kind of burden that Jupiter, implicitly likening Aeneas to Herakles, said Aeneas would have to shoulder (*molitur . . . laborem* 4. 233). Later in Book VI the shades of the deceased flee before Aeneas (489–93) as they had fled before Herakles in the *Odyssey* (11. 605–6). This Homeric adaptation is all the more remarkable as the literary model for Aeneas' descent into Hades was the Odysseus of the *Nekyia*. But while Vergil was strongly interested—mostly because of the popular *Odissia Latina*, Italy's national epic before the *Aeneid*—that Aeneas should supplant Odysseus, he was just as anxious to stress that Aeneas was Herakles' spiritual heir.

Finally, the Herakles theme in Book VI recurs in Anchises' ecstatic prophecy about Augustus' future greatness (6. 801–3). 'Not even Herakles', he exclaims, 'traversed so much of the earth, though he shot the bronze-footed deer, or brought peace to the woods of Erymanthus and made the Lernaean hydra tremble at his bow'—

> nec vero Alcides tantum telluris obivit,
> fixerit aeripedem cervam licet, aut Erymanthi
> pacarit nemora et Lernam tremefecerit arcu.

The passage is, to be sure, imperial panegyric, and Augustus' association with the Herakles theme needs some additional comment. Before discussing it, however, we should be aware that Vergil never stops at singing the praises of his emperor. The passage—and it is typical of virtually any passage in the *Aeneid*, even the most 'episodic' ones—is carefully integrated into the immediate and larger context. Throughout Book VI and even earlier Aeneas has been presented as a second Herakles; it is only natural that Augustus, who would bring to fruition the labours begun by Aeneas, should surpass Aeneas and his model, Herakles. The labours are purposely so chosen as to illustrate Augustus' particular achievement.[15] The poet is not really concerned to show that Augustus travelled more widely than Herakles, for of the three labours mentioned, only that of the Ceryneian hind, which Herakles pursued to the Hyperboreans, would have been suitable for that purpose. Rather, Herakles once more is depicted as the *sotēr* who brings peace (*pacarit*) as did Augustus who used the same word, *pacare*, three times in his autobiography. More specifically, Herakles pacifies Arcadia. Vergil had praised Augustus for this very achievement as early as the First *Eclogue*, and the implication is the same in the *Aeneid*. The fight of Herakles against Cacus also is placed into the bucolic setting of old Italy, which is ruled by Evander, king of the Arcadians.

Anchises follows up the Herakles *exempla* and the prophecy of Augustus' glory with a moral exhortation to Aeneas: he is to add to his *virtus*, the distinctive attribute of both Herakles and the Romans, by doing yet more (806)—

> et dubitamus adhuc virtutem extendere factis . . .?

Later in the epic, another father repeats almost the same exhortation to his son. This is in Book IX when Jupiter consoles Herakles, whom Pallas had invoked to grant him victory over Turnus (10. 468–9):

> sed famam extendere factis
> hoc virtutis opus.

This intentional echo reinterprets Anchises' admonition to Aeneas. Jupiter's and Anchises' advice is pragmatic in the best Roman tradition. What matters is the *res gestae*, the fulfilment of the task at hand. And, in the spiritual Herculean tradition, outward glory and outward success are minimized, if not eschewed entirely. Pallas fails in his combat with Turnus whereas Aeneas, though ostensibly victorious to the very end, is agonized by the conquests he must constantly make to bring the gods to Latium. The Augustan reign is in the too distant future, and the glories of Homeric carnage are in the too distant past for Aeneas joyfully to partake in either. He is the reluctant hero, somewhat like Jason—*Italiam non sponte sequor*—who is revolted by many things he must do, but accepts the demands of fate and the gods for the sake of a good that is greater than his personal interests. This is Vergil's god-fearing sublimation of Euripides' Herakles ideal. Nor was abhorrence of bloody deeds incompatible with Herakles' character by Vergil's time. The Greek historian Timaeus, who was one of the first to write on Rome and thus exerted a considerable influence over Roman historiography, had further expanded the notion of Herakles' unwillingness to engage in his bloody type of work. According to Timaeus, he did so only because of the orders of others, and when he had his own way, he instituted the Olympic games which featured contests that did not require the shedding of blood.[16] Likewise, Aeneas' ideal and, we might add, Vergil's, is that of *placida quies*, although the hero can achieve it only through bloody warfare with all its brutalizing effects.

So it is in the spirit of Herakles when, for the third time in the *Aeneid*, a father—Aeneas—addresses his son, Ascanius (12. 435–6):

> disce, puer, virtutem ex me verumque laborem,
> fortunam ex aliis.

(Learn, my son, *virtus* and true labour from me; fortune from others.)

Besides echoing the earlier father–son scenes, both of which involved Herakles, Aeneas' admonition recalls two other, earlier exhortations. In Book III Andromache, the wife of Troy's greatest warrior, ends her speech by exhorting Aeneas that he and the memory of Ascanius' uncle, Hector, should arouse in Ascanius the old-fashioned (*antiqua*) *virtus* and manly spirit (3. 342–3). It is the Homeric *aretē* of the warrior which Andromache, deprived of her own son, would like to see live on in her nephew. Similarly, in Book IX (641–2), where Ascanius has his glorious day in the field, Apollo—Augustus' favourite god—emerges as his divine cheer-leader and addresses the victorious Iulus: 'A blessing, boy, on your young *virtus*. That is the way to reach heaven, you offspring and father of gods'—

> macte nova virtute, puer, sic itur ad astra,
> dis genite et geniture deos.

But when Aeneas himself, who has just been wounded in battle, finally exhorts Ascanius, he reinterprets the martial *virtus*, to which Andromache and Apollo had appealed, as the Herculean *virtus* of endurance and toil. For a better Fortuna, or Tychē, Ascanius will have to look elsewhere. In the *Aeneid*, Fortuna is as closely associated with Juno as Tychē was with Hera in Euripides' *Herakles*. Herakles endured her bravely, and that is exactly the advice which old Nautes gives Aeneas and which Aeneas will follow in Book V after the Trojan women, instigated by Juno and Iris, have burned the ships (5. 709):

> quidquid erit, superanda omnis fortuna ferendo est.
>
> (Whatever will happen, all fortune is to be overcome by bearing.)

This is exactly what Aeneas will do, thus establishing himself as the true spiritual and heroic heir of Herakles. But what about Augustus? Or, more precisely, was Vergil motivated by an existing identification of Augustus with Herakles to cast his Aeneas in the image of Herakles also?

Vergil's intent in associating Augustus with Herakles was to hint at Augustus' deification. This is illustrated best by the several passages in which Horace mentions Augustus and Herakles in one breath. In the *Third Roman Ode*, for instance, Horace praises the just and steadfast man, and goes on to say that

hac arte Pollux et vagus Hercules
enisus arces attigit igneas,
quos inter Augustus recumbens
pupureo bibet ore nectar.

(By these merits Pollux and the far-wandering Herakles reached the citadels of heaven. Augustus will recline in their company and sip nectar with youthful lips.)

Because he has the same spiritual qualities as Herakles, Augustus will be deified also. At the beginning of his *Letter to Augustus* Horace established an even more explicit analogy between Herakles and the Roman emperor. The metaphor with which the poem begins, that of Augustus' lonely carrying of many burdens, at once recalls Herakles' endeavours. The three burdens which Horace enumerates in the next lines continue the analogy. They are protection with arms, civilizatory achievement, and correction with laws, the *νόμος*, as it were.[17] Then follows, as in other poems, the canon of god-born men who were deified, except that Herakles is accorded special mention:

diram qui contudit hydram
notaque fatali portenta labore subegit,
comperit invidiam supremo fine domari.

(He who crushed the frightful hydra and subdued the fabled monsters through the labour imposed on him by fate, he learned that envy could be overcome only by death that comes at last.)

Augustus' fight against the *Invidia*, Envy, of his enemies is a theme to which Vergil had alluded in the proem to the Third *Georgic* (37–9). It is as if Horace in this letter, which was written after the enthusiasm that had greeted the arrival of Augustus' reign had somewhat abated, was trying to console the princeps by reference to Herakles' lifelong frustrations. One is reminded of the furious disappointment of Milton's Samson Agonistes:

Made of my enemies' scorn and gaze
with his heaven-gifted strength.[18]

There is no indication that Augustus promoted his connection with Herakles. The Hercules cult at Tibur, today's Tivoli, apparently was linked to Augustus from his own time, but it is uncertain whether the initiative rested with him as he showed no special favour to the cult of Hercules in Rome or elsewhere. We need not see the heavy, helping hand of the emperor behind his association with Herakles in Horace's and Vergil's poetry because this association suggested itself readily and was not restricted to poetic allusiveness. When Augustus returned from warfare in Spain in 24 B.C. after an absence of almost three years, the Roman people greeted him joyously, for like Herakles he had risked his life to protect them from danger.[19] And the notion that a man might be deified for his service to mankind—and to the Romans in particular—was familiar in Rome. Cicero cites it repeatedly as the reason for Herakles' apotheosis; perhaps the passage most typical of both the sentiment and Cicero's style occurs in the First *Tusculan Disputation* (33): 'For what better nature is there among the human race than those men who believed they were born to aid, protect, and preserve mankind? Herakles went to the gods: he would never have gone unless he had undertaken that way for himself while he was among men.' Somewhat too late, Ovid chimed in and wrote from exile that like Herakles, Augustus had been raised to the stars because of his *virtus* (*Pont.* 4. 8. 63). Long before Cicero's time, the Romans had used the example of Herakles for deifying the founder of the city, Romulus. Ennius established it in literature 'giving approval to public opinion' (*famae adsentiens*), as Cicero puts it.[20] That the basis for it was popular rather than poetic can also be seen from some of the earliest Roman coins.[21] Their obverse shows the head of Herakles, their reverse the she-wolf suckling Romulus and Remus. Like Herakles, Romulus was the stronger of a set of twin brothers. With this connection in mind, Livy presents Romulus as adopting, of all foreign religious rites, only the cult of Hercules. 'For', Livy continues (1. 7. 15), 'by so doing he showed himself, even then, a favourer of that immortality which is the reward of *virtus*. His own destiny was already leading him to the same reward.' Augustus was the second Romulus, and the application of Romulus' Herculean associations to him was therefore entirely apposite.

All this sets Vergil's and Horace's endowment of Augustus with Herakles' aura quite apart from the tawdry servility which romantic prejudice often leads us to associate with court poetry and which in the decades after Augustus indeed came to pass in Rome. Other emperors craved association with Herakles, Caligula and Nero preferring, for good reasons, to play the role of the mad Herakles.[22] Herculean connections were almost forced on any emperor who was receptive as is shown by the example of Vespasian who, however, derided such attempts (Suet., *Vesp.* 12. 2). Whereas Martial's repeated praise of Domitian as 'the greater Herakles'[23] is nothing but the vilest flattery, Horace's and Vergil's comparison of Augustus to Herakles is free from any such cheapness. It is, as is especially evident from Horace's *Letter to Augustus*, an appeal to that 'moral energy' of which Herakles was the noblest embodiment in antiquity and in Elizabethan and Restoration drama.[24]

By linking Augustus to Herakles the Augustan poets may also have intended to detract from Pompey's and Antony's claims to be the successors of Herakles on earth. Although Antony looks like a good example on the stage of life of the braggart sham-Herakles of comedy, he apparently was quite serious about his presumed Herculean ancestry.[25] Appian (*B.C.* 3. 16) writes that Caesar reluctantly gave up his plan to adopt Antony because Antony was unwilling to exchange kinship with Herakles for the Julian descent from Aeneas. In view of all this it is hardly accidental that Octavian scheduled his great triple triumph, celebrating his victories over Antony and Cleopatra, on the day of the official, annual festival of Hercules at the Ara Maxima, August 13. It is exactly on this day that Vergil has his Aeneas arrive at the site of Rome and, on that occasion, he develops most extensively the analogies between his own hero and the greatest hero of the Greeks.

Aeneas comes to ask for Evander's help (8. 126ff.). The basis for this proposed alliance, Aeneas says, is his own *virtus* and their ancestral kinship. Consequently, so far from being an unwilling colonizer of Italy—*Italiam non sponte sequor*—Aeneas now willingly accepts the call of fate: *fatis egere volentem* (8. 133). The notion of Aeneas' spirit of endurance is continued by reference to the genealogies of both Aeneas and Evander. Both are ultimately descended from Atlas, and Atlas is therefore singled out twice—'mightiest Atlas, who on his shoulders sustains (*sustinet*) the heavenly spheres' (8. 13–6), and 'the same Atlas who uplifts the starry heavens' (141). In this capacity Vergil had mentioned Atlas in the Augustus panegyric in Book VI, where he was linked to Aeneas, while Horace in his *Letter to Augustus* hailed the princeps for sustaining (*sustineas*) his lonely burden like Herakles.

In his reply, Evander keeps up the Herculean allusions. He met Anchises, he says, when Anchises came to Arcadia during his voyage to the realm of Hesione (8. 157). This recalls Herakles' saving her from the sea monster, just as he would save primitive Rome from the monster Cacus. Evander bids Aeneas participate with him in the ritual and banquet at the Ara Maxima and places Aeneas on the seat of honour, which is cushioned with a lion's skin. After the completion of the meal, Evander tells Aeneas the story of Herakles and Cacus. The way in which this story has been prepared for and its length suggest that it is meant to be an integral part of the epic rather than aetiological appendage.[26]

To understand the poet's intent, it is again best to take as a starting point the unique features of his version. In contrast to the Cacus of Dionysius and Livy, Vergil's Cacus is not merely a thieving herdsman or a robber but a son of Vulcan and thus of divine origin. He is an infernal creature, a real *monstrum*, who belches forth smoke and fire and lives in a cave that the poet compares to the opening of hell itself:

> The court of Cacus stands revealed to sight;
> the cavern glares with new-admitted light.
> So the pent vapors, with a rumbling sound,
> Heave from below, and rend the hollow ground.
> A sounding flaw succeeds; and, from on high,
> The gods with hate behold the nether sky:
> The ghosts repine at violated night,
> And curse the invading sun, and sicken at the sight.
> The graceless monster, caught in open day,
> Enclosed, and in despair to fly away,
> Howls horrible from underneath and fills
> His hollow palace with unmanly yells.
>
> (Dryden's translation)

Accordingly, Vergil does not depict Cacus' theft of the cattle as a clever ruse, but as the act of a man who is possessed by the furies and who acts from sheer impiety and wickedness (8. 205–8):

at furiis Caci mens effera, ne quid inausum
aut intractatum scelerisve dolive fuisset,
quattuor a stabulis praestanti corpore tauros
avertit. . . .

(But Cacus, his wits wild with frenzy, lest he leave any crime or craft undared or unattempted, stole four beautiful bulls from their pastures. . . .)

Moreover, whereas all other writers—notably Dionysius, Livy, Propertius, and Ovid—describe the actual combat between Herakles and Cacus in a few words or, at most, ten lines, it is Vergil's central concern. Vergil spends almost fifty lines depicting Herakles' hard struggle and his conquest of the underworld monster. Lastly, Vergil added the hymn on Herakles which the Salian priests sing in commemoration of the event.

The contents of the hymn (8. 287–302) again are so chosen as to underscore the affinity between Aeneas and Herakles. Juno is singled out twice as persecuting Herakles. First, she sent *monstra* and snakes against him. In the epic she has already done the same, through Allecto, in Book VII. Then, more generally, the poet says that Herakles suffered countless, arduous *labores* because of *fatis Iunonis iniquae*. The poet used almost the same phrase when Venus explained to Cupid the reason for Aeneas' suffering: the hatred of unjust Juno (*odiis Iunonis iniquae* 1. 668). The phrase is, of course, reminiscent of the proem also. Herakles is further hailed as the destroyer of Troy, because Laomedon did not keep his promise. Similarly, Aeneas is about to conquer the city of the Latins because Turnus disputes his right to Lavinia, who had been promised to Aeneas. Freely adapting his mythological material, Vergil has Herakles fight against the 'cloud-born' centaurs Hylaeus and Pholus. Two of Aeneas' enemies had been compared, in the catalogue of warriors in Book VII, to such 'cloud-born centaurs' (7. 674–5).

Soon after, Vergil frankly identifies Aeneas with Herakles. When Evander bids Aeneas enter his domicile after the festival of Herakles, he tells him: 'Herakles, the victor, walked over this threshold. This house received him. Dare, my guest, to scorn riches; fashion yourself to be worthy also of the god, and come not disdainful of my humble household'—

> haec, inquit, limina victor
> Alcides subiit, haec illum regia cepit.
> aude, hospes, contemnere opes et te quoque dignum
> finge deo, rebusque veni non asper egenis. (8. 362–5)

So Aeneas is the measure of Herakles not only spiritually, but physically also: gigantic, *ingens*,[27] he enters into Evander's house as Herakles had done before him. The parallelism between Herakles and Aeneas is further enhanced as Evander describes them virtually as contemporaries. The next day, Aeneas turns out to be Herakles' follower indeed. After a sign from Venus confirms to him, beyond all doubt, that his task will be a bloody struggle against Turnus and the Latins, he immediately rises from the throne that, as we saw earlier, was covered with the lion's skin, kindles the fire on Herakles' altar, and joyously brings another sacrifice to Herakles, the household god of Evander (8. 541–4). Anticipating many good Romans, Aeneas himself now sacrifices to Herakles instead of being a mere spectator. And, to cap his association with the Greek hero, Aeneas, accompanied by Pallas, sets out for the war against Turnus on a horse that is caparisoned in a lion's skin (8. 552–3):

> A sprightly courser, fairer than the rest,
> The king himself presents his royal guest.
> A lion's hide his back and limbs infold,
> Precious with studded work, and paws of gold.
> (Dryden's translation)

The Herakles–Cacus episode, then, serves as a parable of Aeneas' struggle against Turnus. This is borne out by the many changes made by Vergil which are designed to liken Cacus to Turnus and by the numerous thematic and verbal parallels which underline the similarity of their behaviour.[28] The animal blood-thirstiness of Cacus, for instance, is paralleled by that of Turnus. Cacus' throat is drained of blood (*siccum sanguine guttur* 8. 261), and so are the jaws of the maddened wolf with whom Turnus is compared in Book IX (*siccae sanguine fauces* 9. 64). The blood-dripping heads that are nailed to the entrance of Cacus' cave (8. 195) anticipate the heads of Turnus' enemies which he attaches to his chariot (12. 511–12) before he does battle with Aeneas. All this indicates that the poet was anxious to impress on the reader the analogy between Herakles and Aeneas, and between Cacus and Turnus even at the risk of seeming tedious.

Great warriors and civilizers as they are, Herakles and Aeneas are not bent on bloodshed. They are goaded into a righteous rage by the deceitfulness and cruelty of their opponents. Vergil deliberately has the Salians hail Herakles as being 'not devoid of reason' (8. 299). Similarly, that heroic paragon of reason, Odysseus, is 'beside himself' with rage in the face of the crimes committed by the *monstrum* Polyphemus (3. 626–9). Polyphemus abides by divinely sanctioned conventions as little as does Cacus. Nor does Turnus, even though he is not a *monstrum*, but he breaks the sacred truce (*foedus*) and keeps the spoils of Pallas instead of giving them to the gods. Both these actions seal his doom. Forced by Turnus' treachery (*insidiisque subactus* 12. 494) as Herakles was by Cacus' crime and deceit (*scelerisve dolive* 8. 205), Aeneas overcomes and kills his opponent, whose tragedy is that he cannot live up to his own ideals, among them *virtus*. These themes reflect traditional concepts. Speaking of warfare, Livy (42. 47. 4) contrasts *dolus* and *insidiae* with *virtus*. To be sanctioned as holy and just, any war the Romans waged had to be defensive, at least in theory, and Herakles and Aeneas are involved in such a *bellum pium et iustum*. It is against this whole background also that the prayer of Pallas in Book X, who prays to Herakles as any Roman would, takes on its full significance.

Vergil's treatment of the Herakles–Cacus story is a genuine mythopoeic addition to the Herakles myth, and was recognized as such by Renaissance writers and artists. Ronsard, for instance, mentions the 'anger of Herakles killing Cacus' as one of his inspirational sources in the posthumous preface to the *Franciade*. This brings us to an important point. Whereas in the earlier books of the *Aeneid* Vergil had modelled Aeneas' *labores* on those of Herakles and even adapted Juno's opposition to Aeneas for that purpose, the roles are now reversed as a Herakles legend is adapted and, in large part, created to illustrate the nature of Aeneas' final struggle.[29] It is, above all, Vergil's concept of the heroism of both Aeneas and Herakles that made possible a symbiosis where there had been a seemingly unbridgeable gap in Apollonius. Aeneas' heroism is internal, and it is here that Vergil saw a strong similarity between his hero and Herakles as portrayed, for instance, by Euripides. Yet Vergil did not ignore the tradition of Herakles' warlike heroism especially as Aeneas had traditionally been known as a great warrior,[30] and the Romans, whom Aeneas typifies, had conquered Italy and the Mediterranean basin with arms rather than *pietas*. Like Pindar's Herakles, Aeneas must overcome force with force because Jupiter commands him 'to bring the whole world beneath his laws' (4. 231). This is the *nomos* idea as we know it from the Greek poet. At the same time, as Vergil had Aeneas reinterpret the warlike *virtus* of Ascanius as the Herculean *virtus* of endurance, so he now adapts the madness of Herakles as anticipating the warlike anger of Aeneas. Herakles fights *furens animis* (8. 228), *dentibus infrendens* and *fervidus ira* (8. 230). So will Aeneas, notwithstanding his compassion especially for his young opponents and his grief about the human sacrifice that is necessary for *Romanam condere gentem*.[31] Like Euripides or Theocritus, Vergil saw in his hero a human being rather than a superman. This is another reason why the emphasis in the Cacus story is not on Herakles' divine reward but on his struggle against the enemy. This also links this episode to Augustus' conquest of the hellish forces of the east at the end of Book VIII, and the note of Herakles as a model of the emperor's divinity is sounded only very discreetly, far more discreetly than in Horace's poems and incomparably more so than in Martial's and Statius' gross flattery of Domitian.

The important result for the literary tradition of Herakles is that Vergil harmonized what Euripides, for instance, had set off one against another: the internal and outward heroism of Herakles. Like Aeneas, he is still an epic hero whose great deeds are anything but belittled or considered anachronistic. And like Aeneas, he has ample spiritual strength, fortitude, and compassion.

This last quality, among others, indicates that Vergil's portrait of Herakles did not come straight from the Stoic textbook. For when Pallas prays to him, Herakles 'stifles a great sigh deep in his heart, and sheds tears in vain'—

magnumque sub imo
corde premit gemitum lacrimasque effundit inanes.
(10. 464–5)

This, once more, associates Herakles with Aeneas. When Anna was pleading with him on Dido's behalf, 'he felt anguish through and through in his heart; his mind remained unmoved, and his tears rolled in vain'—

> magno persentit pectore curas;
> mens immota manet, lacrimae volvuntur inanes.
> (4. 448–9)

Given, however, the varied strands of Vergil's inspiration and the innate Stoicism of the Romans, it is not surprising that Stoic concepts and terminology found their way into the *Aeneid*. This is a well-known phenomenon, although its relevance to Herakles and Aeneas is not that they were portrayed as Stoic sages. Both have pity and compassion, and both, as good Romans, have martial fervour and even fury, which does not agree with the Stoic ideal of imperturbability. But there were other qualities which Herakles exemplified to the Stoics and for which Vergil regarded the hero as a worthy model of Aeneas. The Stoics extolled the principle of *tonos*, 'strain' or 'effort':

> This term originally seems to have expressed muscular activity, and was next used by the Cynics to denote that active condition of the soul which is the true end of life; 'no labour', said Diogenes, 'is noble, unless its end is tone of soul.' . . . With Cleanthes the word becomes fairly common, first in the ethical application, in which 'tone' is a shock of fire, which if it be strong enough to stir the soul to fulfill its duties is called strength and force, and then in physics to explain the unceasing activity of the universe.[32]

In the Stoic allegories, Herakles personified this *élan vital*.[33] Unlike the Epicurean, the Stoic creed was not passive. Besides enduring adversity, the ideal Stoic would constantly and actively practise and exercise virtue, and even would look upon adversity as an opportunity for such exercise. Epictetus, who lived in the first century A.D., gives a spirited, popular illustration of Herakles' exemplary value in that respect (1. 6. 32–6):

> Or what do you think Herakles would have amounted to if there had not been a lion like the one he encountered, and a hydra, and a

> stag, and a boar, and unjust and monstrous men, whom he made his business to drive out and clear away? And what would he have been doing had nothing of this sort existed? Is it not clear that he would have rolled himself up in a blanket and slept? In the first place, then, he would never have become Herakles by slumbering away his whole life in such luxury and ease; but even if he had, what good would he have been? What would have been the use of those arms of his and of his prowess in general, and his steadfastness and nobility, had not such circumstances roused and exercised him? What then? Ought he to have prepared these for himself, and sought to bring a lion into his own country from somewhere or other, and a boar and a hydra? That would have been folly and madness. But since they did exist and were found in the world, they were useful as a means of revealing and exercising our Herakles.

The traditional necessity, *anankē*, of Herakles' labours now is literally turned into its opposite. The contrast, to which Epictetus returns in another discourse (2. 16.44), between sitting about at home in luxurious indolence and accepting the call to toil is, to cite only one example, the basis of Jupiter's appeal to Aeneas in *Aeneid* IV. That the sentiment voiced by Epictetus was current at Vergil's time is clear from Cicero's summation of it in a single, albeit Ciceronian, sentence (*Fin.* 2. 118).

Critical analysis, especially of a complex and sophisticated work of art such as the *Aeneid*, has the inevitable drawback of sorting out and fragmenting what the poet created as an organic whole. The various sources of inspiration for Vergil's Herakles—Roman cult and practice, Greek drama and epic, the Augustan aura of the deified man (θεῖος ἀνήρ), Stoic concepts, the popularity of the myth in Italy, the reaction against Apollonius and Lucretius, and some basic, initial similarity between Herakles and Aeneas which Vergil greatly refined—are not compartmentalized in the poem but complement one another and form an inseparable totality. The strongest reason, however, for Vergil's extensive mythopoeic adaptation of Herakles was, as we saw earlier, his role as the national hero of Greece. Herakles, in many ways, summed up the national experience of that country. His beginnings, like those of primitive Greece, were violent, and there were excesses with the concomitant anxiety to expiate them.[34] Then, at the time of Hesiod, there was growing concern for law; we need only think of lawgivers such as Lycurgus, Dracon, and Solon. Herakles came to personify the rudimentary civilizing efforts—he drains swamps, builds cities, and destroys wild beasts and tyrants. He, the supreme champion of justice and civilizer, precedes Greek colonists wherever they go. Herakles then became the supreme symbol of Greek individualism and humanism in the tragedies of Sophocles and Euripides. The sophists and philosophers finally accentuated his mental powers. Every age in Greece recast Herakles in its own image, and he thus became the incarnation of her history and aspirations. This is precisely the role which Vergil intended for Aeneas in Italy and Rome, and it is primarily for this reason that Herakles became an inspirational model for Aeneas. And, taking his inspiration from the Roman Hercules cult, Vergil doubtless hoped that his Italic readers would regard Aeneas with the same kind of personal intensity with which they worshiped Hercules.

NOTES TO CHAPTER VI

1. For detailed scholarly discussions of the cult of Hercules in Rome see J. G. Winter, 'The Myth of Hercules at Rome', *Roman History and Mythology*, ed. H. Sanders (*Univ. of Michigan Studies, Human. Series 4*, New York, 1910) 171–273, and Jean Bayet, *Les origines de l'Hercule romain* (Paris, 1925). More concise and up to date is K. Latte, *Römische Religionsgeschichte* (Munich, 1960) 213–21.
2. Winter (note 1, above) 173. Cf. R. Schottlaender, *Römisches Gesellschaftsdenken* (Weimar, 1969) 11ff.
3. The relevant passages have been collected by C. Knapp, *AJP* 40 (1919) 247–50, and are admirably discussed by W. Forehand, *The Literary Use of Metaphor in Plautus and Terence* (Ann Arbor, 1969; microfilmed Diss., Univ. of Texas, 1968).
4. For more detail see my discussion in *TAPA* 97 (1966) 203–35. My conclusions, of course, are only tentative.
5. The Latin church fathers seized upon Euhemerus' theory with glee; see Lactantius, *Div. Inst.* 1. 14ff. and Arnobius 1. 38 (imitating Lucretius), and pp. 188f. On the general subject see J. D. Cooke, 'Euhemerism: A Mediaeval Interpretation of Classical Paganism', *Speculum* 2 (1927) 396–410.
6. So, fittingly, Des Essarts 192.

7. Dio Chrysostom, answering as it were Lucretius and Tiberius, came to the hero's rescue by pointing out that the monsters Herakles overcame were not literally wild beasts, but desires and passions (5. 22ff.). Cf. the allegories of Herodorus cited on p. 56.
8. Varro as quoted by Servius, *Ad Aen.* 8. 564; Coluccio Salutati, *De laboribus Herculis* 3. 1. 6. For medieval representations of Herakles as a 'wild man' see R. Bernheimer, *Wild Men in the Middle Ages* (Cambridge, Mass., 1962) 101–2. Even Seneca echoed Lucretius' critique; see p. 174.
9. See, e.g. *Off.* 3. 25; *Nat. Deor.* 2. 62; *Leg.* 2. 19; *Sest.* 143; *Fin.* 3. 66; *Tusc.* 1. 28 and 4. 50, in addition to *Tusc.* 1. 32 and *Fin.* 2. 118, which are cited below. Cicero also admiringly translated Herakles' speech in Sophocles' *Trachiniae* 1046ff. (*Tusc.* 2. 20–2). This was the first translation of the passage into Latin and, as Huxley has noted (p. 23), Cicero emphasized Herakles' role as a victor, which is not found in Sophocles' play and is due to the Roman worship of *Hercules victor* and *invictus*.
10. So, e.g. H. Hill in *JRS* 51 (1961) 90. For the lack of the popularity of the Aeneas legend before Vergil see my *Aeneas, Sicily, and Rome* (Princeton, 1969).
11. There is nothing in the pre-Vergilian tradition of the Aeneas legend to suggest even remotely a similar role of Juno. For Ennius' view of her see Servius, *Ad Aen.* 1. 281 and 12. 841, and J. Vahlen, *Ennianae Poesis Reliquiae*, 2nd ed. (Leipzig, 1928) CLIX–CLX. It has long been recognized that Allecto is modelled on Euripides' Lyssa, and this is no accident because Vergil deliberately so characterized Juno as to recall the Hera—Tychē of Euripides' *Herakles*.
12. P. McGushin, 'Vergil and the Spirit of Endurance', *AJP* 85 (1964) 236. James Henry, *Aeneidea* 1 (London, 1873) 187–8 was the first to notice that *labor*, as applied to Aeneas, was meant to correspond to Herakles' ἄεθλος.
13. *Praecipere* is used here as a technical Stoic term, as is clear from Seneca's comment on this line in *Epist.* 76. 33. Stoicism was another, though not the overriding reason for the association of Aeneas and Herakles in the *Aeneid*; see below.
14. See p. 26. For the most recent view on a possible epic katabasis of Herakles, which was known to Bacchylides, Pindar, Aristophanes, and Vergil, see H. Lloyd-Jones, *Maia* 19 (1967) 221–9.
15. See E. Norden, *RhM* 54 (1899) 472–3.
16. *FGH* 566 F 22.
17. Compare Jupiter's command, which is defined as *labor* (233), To Aeneas in *Aen.* 4. 231: *ac totum sub leges mitteret orbem*, discussed below, p. 146.
18. Lines 32–3. *Invidia*, 'Envie', became a topos in the Renaissance; see, e.g. Veen, *Emblemata Horatiana* (Antwerp, 1607) 172–3. Thomas Drant, the first translator of Horace's *Epistles* into English, therefore translated the Horatian passage in a characteristically expansive way (*Horace His Arte of Poetrie, Epistles, and Satyrs Englished* . . . [London, 1567] sig. F. viii):

He that did crowse, and did culpon once
  Hydra of hellish spyte,
And monsters knowne with fatall toyle
  to fetters frusshed quyte,
Perceaved this by experience,
  the monsters all do fall
Through manliness: envie is tamed
  at death, or not at all.

For the use of the topos by Spenser see 211 and Dunseath 231–5.

19. See Horace, *Od.* 3. 14 with the excellent remarks of Kiessling-Heinze. Augustus came from Spain to Rome, as Herakles had done.—R. Schilling, 'L'Hercule romain en face de la reforme religieuse d'Auguste', *RPh* 68 (1942) 31–57 offers the most comprehensive discussion of the Hercules cult under Augustus, but misinterprets Augustus' indifference to it as Augustus' wish to de-emphasize the cult's significance.
20. *Tusc. Disp.* 1. 12. 28; cf. Tac., *Ann.* 4. 38. The identification of famous Romans with Herakles is well discussed by Anderson 29–45.
21. *BMC Rep.* 2. 124–5 nos. 28–33; E. A. Sydenham, *The Coinage of the Roman Republic* (London, 1952) 2 no. 6.
22. Caligula: Dio 59. 26; Nero: Suet., *Nero* 21 and 53.
23. *Maior Alcides*, as opposed to *minor Alcides*, i.e. Herakles himself: *Epigrams* 9. 101 and 64; cf. *Epigrams* 9. 65 and the sneer of Jean Lemaitre de Belges: 'le petit Hercule Grec', as cited on p. 223.
24. See Waith, *passim*, and esp. 16–18.
25. Shakespeare's very positive view of Antony's Herculean associations, which is discussed by Waith 113–21, thus has some historical justification.
26. I have discussed the Herakles–Cacus episode in more detail and from some other points of view in *AJP* 87 (1966) 18–51; see also V. Buchheit, *Vergil über die Sendung Roms* (Heidelberg, 1963) 116–33.
27. *Ingentem Aenean* (8. 367); cf. *ingentem Aenean*, also at the beginning of the line, in 6. 413 as discussed above on p. 135.
28. For details see the works cited in note 26, above.
29. This reinforces Aeneas' coming into his own in the second half of the epic. Another function of the Herakles–Cacus episode is that it provides a rejoinder to Lucretius' depreciation of Herakles' fight against *monstra*; yet another is Vergil's utilization of the technique of Greek tragedy to inform the reader in advance of what course the events will take (cf. Chapter III, note 5). This allows him to concentrate on their interpretation. Also, it was known in Rome that Herakles was connected with the beginnings of Carthage (Cic., *Nat. Deor.* 3. 42), and thus Vergil emphasized the god's connection with the beginnings of Rome.
30. For the considerable literary and artistic evidence see the first chapter of my *Aeneas, Sicily, and Rome* (note 10, above).

31. To regard *pietas* and martial fervour as mutually exclusive would be to confuse a modern attitude with an ancient one. Compare, in Renaissance literature, the rage of Ariosto's Orlando, comparable to the mad rage of Euripides' or Seneca's Herakles, and the warlike anger of Tasso's Rinaldo, which corresponds to that of Vergil's Herakles.
32. E. Vernon Arnold, *Roman Stoicism* (London, 1911) 160.
33. Cornutus, *Theol. Comp.* 31, *Stoicorum Veterum Fragmenta* 1 (von Arnim) fr. 514.
34. For a summary of the significance of the Greek Herakles in this and the next sentences see already Des Essarts 229–30; compare the poetic expression of a similar view by de Heredia as discussed on p. 269.

CHAPTER VII

Herakles in the Roman Elegiac and Epic Tradition

The importance Vergil accorded Herakles in the *Aeneid* was fully recognized by Vergil's contemporaries and followers. This, combined with the continued popularity of the Herakles cult and the Cynic/Stoic influence, accounts for much of the Silver Latin epic poets' compulsion to give Herakles a place in their works also. But Herakles' predominant part in the *Aeneid* had a further result. Although Augustus showed neither any special preference for the god's cult nor for being associated with him, Herakles, by virtue of his role as a prototype for Aeneas and thus also Augustus, came to be considered an Augustan symbol. Poets such as Propertius and Ovid, whose temperament and background were different from Vergil's, refused to take the Augustan symbols seriously. Their adaptation of the Herakles theme was no exception.

To make his aims clear enough, Propertius intended an outright comparison with Vergil in his treatment of the story of Herakles and Cacus (4. 9). The subject, to be sure, was more appropriate to epic than to elegy, but Propertius went beyond the simple exigencies of the genre in adapting Herakles for his purpose. The most significant change he made was to accord the episode only twenty lines and to make it into a mere prelude to a story which he invented for the occasion and described in far greater detail, nearly fifty lines: Herakles' adventure at the shrine of the Bona Dea. Besides minimizing Herakles' conquest of Cacus, 'Propertius suppresses certain elements of the story which might tend to enlarge its Roman and Augustan significance.'[1] In Propertius' elegy, Cacus is a clumsy chiseller rather than an infernal creature, and his monstrosity—'through his three mouths, share and share alike, he gave forth sounds' (line 9)—is more picturesque than terrifying. There is no mention of Evander and the inhabitants of proto-Rome, nor of their feelings at the death of Cacus. Besides, Propertius omits completely what had been the heart of Vergil's account, Herakles' fierce struggle. We are told that Herakles became furious when he discovered the theft (13–14) and in the next line, Cacus already lies on the ground, having been clubbed thrice on the head. So much for the heroics. The place of the melodious hymn by the Salian priests is taken by Herakles' command to his cattle to low so that he can name the Roman Forum after them. This, and not the Ara Maxima, will commemorate the conquest of Cacus. The foundation of the latter is pointedly postponed and presented as the result of Herakles' trivial and unheroic, but in Propertius' view, *maius opus*.

The link between the two stories is Herakles' sudden affliction with a terrible thirst. This alone is reminiscent of the comic and not the heroic Herakles. Perhaps Propertius insinuates that Herakles' thirst was the result of the grandiloquent effort to inaugurate the *nobile Forum*. At any rate, Herakles soon hears the giggle of some girls from a shaded shrine, whose extensive description by the poet is the elagiac counterpart to Vergil's epic account of Cacus' cave. The girls are shut in the shrine (*inclusas puellas* 23), the shrine of the women's goddess is closed (*loca clausa* 25), and Herakles pleads with them in front of the door (*ante fores* 32). With a few clever sketches, Propertius has cast Herakles in the role of a stock character of Roman elegy and comedy: the excluded lover (*exclusus amator*). Herakles' subsequent pleas and actions are also in the spirit of this convention. He recites a door-song, a *paraclausithyron*, to the inhabitants of the shrine who are called *puellae*—the standard term for girls in erotic elegy—rather than priestesses, and who play (*luditis* 33); *ludere* again is a common elegiac term. Like any elegiac lover in this situation, Herakles tries to impress the girls by bragging what a great fellow he is. The hero's voluntary depreciation of his deeds, as for instance in Euripides' *Herakles*, now is supplanted by their deflation in an elegiac context. Realizing that his arguments might not be impressive, after all, and that the girls might actually be scared of him, because he looks so shaggy and uncouth in his lion's skin, Herakles makes a pathetic attempt to identify with them. 'Once,' he says, referring to his stay at Omphale's court, 'I too was a serving girl, spinning with the distaff.' As if this touching picture of domestication were not enough, Herakles boasts that he even wore a bra (49–50): 'A soft band supported my shaggy chest, and even with my hard hands, I was a suitable girl.'

Patently ridiculous as this is, even without the background of the *paraclausithyron*, this characterization of Herakles could not fail to evoke special memories in Rome. In 55 B.C. Clodius had desecrated the rites of the Bona Dea by dressing like a woman, and the notoriety of the scandal, which led Caesar to divorce his wife on the famous grounds that she must be above suspicion, did not diminish with the passing of time. So Herakles is curtly refused by the priestess-duenna who keeps the gate. 'Go somewhere else,' she rasps, 'this cult and shrine are for women only.' Herakles' reaction is the mock-heroic repetition of his conquest of Cacus. As he angrily broke into the cave of the latter, so his rage now drives him to break down the door of the shrine.[2] He quenches his thirst, which is described as 'hot desire' (*aestus* 63), and thus Propertius hints once more at the true motive behind Herakles' passionate eagerness. As he had done after the conquest of Cacus, Herakles once more comments on his deed. 'Now', he grumbles, 'this corner of the earth is receiving me.' Although the primitive site of Rome was no more than that, *angulus mundi* still must have sounded unduly condescending to the Romans of the Augustan age, who saw even in the archaic city the incipient centre of all greatness. 'But I must believe', wrote Livy (1. 4. 1), 'it was already written in the book of fate that this great city of ours should arise, and the first steps be taken to the founding of the mightest empire the world has known—next to god's.' From the behaviour of god's son in Propertius' elegy one could hardly infer that.

It is only now, after all these antics, that Herakles founds the Ara Maxima. We learn that he had vowed it after recovering the cattle, but the potential heroic symbolism of the occasion is completely ignored. Instead, Herakles places all the emphasis on the ritual that is established for the altar. Filled with petty vengefulness, he declares that because the girls excluded him from their place of worship, he will bar women from his cult at the Ara Maxima. The punishment is more in the spirit of the rejected lover than that of the defender of justice and the *nomos*. In sum, we have witnessed a scene from the *Précieuses Ridicules* rather than the unravelling of yet another heroic chapter in the storied tradition of early Rome.

The genre of elegy, love elegy in particular, imposed its limitations on epic exploits although, as we have noted, this was not the only reason for Propertius' peculiar treatment of the theme. In the earliest Roman elegy, Catullus' poem addressed to Allius, the poet spoke flippantly of Herakles' admittance to Olympus 'so that the door of heaven would be ground down by more gods yet and Hebe would be spared a long virginity' (68. 115–16). More boldly, Propertius interpreted Herakles' self-immolation on Mount Oeta as his burning love for Hebe (1. 13. 23–4) and thus became the ironic and unwitting forerunner of the many neoplatonically inspired Renaissance poets, from Castiglione to du Bellay, who would rapturously and seriously sing of Herakles' '*incendio suave*'.[3] An episode that suggested itself more readily was Herakles' enslavement to Omphale. The romantic sentimentalization of this theme, which is also known from Pompeian painting of the period (Plate 11), became so well-worn that Ovid could mock its conventions,[4] and it was not until the late nineteenth century that it was rescued from its bathos by Rubén Darío, one of the modernist poets of Latin America. Primarily, however, Propertius, in this poem as elsewhere,[5] decided to use the resources of the genre to the fullest extent in order to demonstrate his inability to compose the sort of poetry which Vergil and Horace wrote more successfully. The result is the most comical and witty treatment of Herakles in Latin literature. Although Propertius at times felt and reacted against the pressure to write canonical, Augustan poetry, it would be a mistake to attribute to him political rather than literary motivations. Any serious subject, especially when it becomes a topos—and the Herakles–Cacus story was elaborately treated in the versions of four other Augustan writers which have survived and probably in some others which have disappeared—is bound to provoke parody. The overflow of *Hercules furentes* on the Elizabethan stage, for instance, caused—deservedly—the same satirical reaction.[6]

Ovid, the most prominent non-Augustan poet at Augustus' time, devotes two extensive treatments to Herakles. The first is the elegiac collection of fictitious letters from noble ladies to their famous, heroic paramours or vice versa. Unfortunately, Deianeira's letter to Herakles

(*Ep.* 9) is plagued by prolixity which is Ovid's fault more than Deianeira's. The situation, which is based on Sophocles' *Trachiniae*, is the Hellenistic-inspired translation of the stuff of drama—which was a reduction of the heroic aspects of Herakles already—into the bourgeois, everyday world.[7] Instead of a compassionate, sympathetic Deianeira, we now find a jealous shrew who rants for all of 143 lines before devoting another, highly rhetorical and rueful twenty-three lines to announcing her decision to die after she has been informed that she caused the hero's death. If there is any focus in this verbal rampage, it is not the events from the conquest of Oichalia to the death of Herakles nor is it Deianeira's psychological development.[8] All that matters is Deianeira's change of mood after *Fama*, the goddess of Rumour, has told her of Herakles' suffering. The other characters are eliminated; there is no Hyllus, and Herakles is degraded to a mere recipient of the letter. We may note in passing that whereas Sophocles expressly spurned the thought of giving anything but the briefest mention to Herakles' service to Omphale (*Trach.* 247–50), this story occupies more than one third of Ovid's poem, doubtless because of its topicality in elegiac poetry.

In the *Metamorphoses*, Ovid followed in Propertius' footsteps by deflating the heroism of Herakles not so much through bathetic domesticity as through sly humour. The account of Herakles' apotheosis serves to anticipate the deifications of Romulus, Aeneas, and Julius Caesar in the final books of the *Metamorphoses* in which Ovid seemingly conformed to Augustan themes. It is debatable whether the subject of apotheosis would have been a part of Ovid's book if it had not been an Augustan topos, as is quite evident from Horace's canon of deified men; at least its light-minded treatment by Ovid shows that he took it no more seriously than the other Augustan themes. Merely by seeing the true meaning of Herakles' deeds only in the metamorphoses they produced he could easily detract from their traditional significance. Ovid did not let it go at that but relished the occasion for parodying epic just as the last four books of the *Metamorphoses* are his mock-epic commentary on the *Aeneid*. So, at least in part, is the combat between Herakles and Achelous which Ovid describes before proceeding to the story of Nessus and the poisoned robe. 'It is a sad thing,' Achelous begins his account, 'to tell the story of one's own defeat, but at least the greatness of my conqueror is a great consolation' (*Met.* 9. 7). Aeneas had said the same to Lausus when he killed him (*Aen.* 10. 829–30). Herakles and Achelous lay claim to a *virgo* as beautiful as Lavinia,[9] and Herakles, like Aeneas, stresses his descent from Jupiter and the fame of his labours. Rebutting Herakles' arguments, Achelous goes on at length to emphasize that he will not be a son-in-law sent from foreign shores, but a native. Here again we find express verbal echoes from the *Aeneid*,[10] and Achelous continues in the same vein. 'It should not be held against me,' Achelous argues, 'if Juno does not hate me and has not inflicted any labours on me.' Herakles' reaction is to burst into anger (*accensae non fortiter imperat irae* 9. 28) as did Aeneas before killing Turnus (*furiis accensus et ira*; *Aen.* 12. 946). Naturally, Achelous tries to put off, in the narrative, the moment of his defeat as long as possible and boasts how he held his ground 'like a sea-wall against which the waves beat in vain'. This is the adaptation of the famous simile involving Latinus in *Aeneid* 7. 586–90. To bring out Ovid's intent even more, Achelous adapts yet another Vergilian simile for his comic braggadocio: he likens Herakles and himself to bulls as Aeneas and Turnus had been in *Aeneid* XII.[11] We saw earlier that Vergil had anticipated this simile in the Herakles–Cacus episode where Herakles was victorious in his fourth try and was praised for slaying the Lernaean hydra. Similarly, Ovid's Herakles does not get the better of Achelous until the fourth time around when the river-god metamorphoses himself into a snake whose size, as Herakles does not fail to tell him, does not compare to that of the Lernaean hydra.

As Herakles' apotheosis prefigures Aeneas', so the fight between Herakles and Achelous is Ovid's version of Aeneas' combat with Turnus. It is intentionally ludicrous and much of the effect comes from Vergil's noble lines being put in the mouth of a shaggy, grimy river deity. Yet there is nothing in this episode that would tend to ridicule Herakles himself. Although he is portrayed only as a brawny fighter, his apodictic terseness contrasts favourably with Achelous' boastful rhetoric (*Met.* 9. 29–30):

> melior mihi dextera lingua!
> dummodo pugnando superem, tu vince loquendo!

('I am a better talker with fists than tongue. Provided I win the fight, I'll let you win the debate.')

The next episode, that of Nessus, which Ovid rather jerkily conjoins with the preceding one, reinforces his light-hearted treatment of Herakles and his portrayal of the hero, along Apollonius' lines, as a strongman pure and simple. Whereas Deianeira is justly afraid of Nessus, who behaves like a Venetian gondolier,[12] Herakles is totally insensitive because he is too preoccupied with playing the role of the undaunted hero. The floods have challenged him and they must be overcome. And Herakles wants everybody to know that he is not choosing the way of least resistance: without looking for the smoothest current or some such, he dives right in (*Met.* 9. 115–17). This effort of the *kallinikos* is as brave as it is stupid, for it facilitates Nessus' wicked attempt.

The poison has been prepared, *Fama*—as in *Heroides* 9—has informed Deianeira of Herakles' affair with Iole, and the stage is set for his death. At first Herakles suppresses the pain by his *virtus*. Soon, however, the flames rack him, and Ovid's description of the hero's pain reads like the stage directions given by Artaud for the theatre of the cruel. The agony, however, fails to stir us because Herakles, at this point, gives a lengthy speech that is 'altogether too rhetorical'[13] for its setting and owes virtually nothing to the hero's credible outburst in the *Trachiniae.* And while the note on which the speech ends—'and there are people who think the gods exist'—echoes the cynical agnosticism of Euripides' Herakles, this impression is all too quickly obliterated by an elaborate description of Herakles' use of Lichas as a missile and Lichas' metamorphosis into a rock.

Nor is Herakles' end distinguished by metaphysical sublimation. When the flames shoot up on the pyre Ovid addresses him (9. 235–8):

> You cover the heap with your lion's
> skin and use your club as a pillow,
> and you are reclining with the countenance
> of a banqueter, crowned with garlands
> among the full cups of wine.

Herakles dies in the pose of a banqueter. The implication is clear: he of the big appetite, who spent all his life drinking and eating, should pass away accordingly. It is hardly surprising, then, that Jupiter, while Herakles' body is being devoured by the flames, takes a rather gay view of the proceedings. With joyful voice—*laeto ore*—Jupiter assures the gods that their fear (*timor*) for Herakles is his *voluptas*. Herakles will be quite all right; 'he who conquered all will conquer the fires you see'—

> omnia qui vincit, vincet quos cernitis ignes (*Met.* 9. 250).

The theodicean tag that Ovid appends to the whole story is reminiscent of the purpose of a Euripidean *deus ex machina*. It is deliberately unreal by contrast with the created reality. So Herakles sloughs off his mortal body and his 'better part' becomes venerable *augusta gravitate*—with august *gravitas*. We may not be guilty of overinterpreting if we see a mocking allusion to Augustus here, whose deification was modelled on Herakles', nor if we consider the recurrence of *gravitas*, a few lines later, where it refers to Alcmena's pregnancy (9. 287), as an intentional deflation of Herakles' newly acquired *gravitas* in death.

There is no trace of a direct, comic influence of Ovid and Propertius on the subsequent tradition. In fact, to cite only one example, the author of the medieval *Ovide moralisé*, blithely unaware of Ovid's humour as was his wont, interpreted the episode as another edifying lesson in Christian theology.[14] But while the halo of Cynic/Stoic idealization and Roman *virtus* and, alas, *gravitas* came to becloud the hero heavily, the versions of Ovid and Propertius kept alive, by way of literary parody, the theme of Herakles the unsophisticated amorist which became a favourite again in the Renaissance.

Such levity is not found in the post-Vergilian Latin epics which did much to strengthen Herakles' role as an exemplar of *virtus*. In his invocation to Nero in the *Pharsalia*, Lucan identifies the emperor with Herakles by imitating the Senecan account of Herakles' apotheosis.[15] This goes beyond mere flattery as Herakles, the eradicator of destructive evils, stands for a programme that led to the *pax Augusta*, which Nero is to continue. In the manner of Vergil, Lucan works through allusion rather than outright identification of the emperor with Herakles. By contrast, Silius Italicus was somewhat more explicit. As in the *Philoctetes*, Herakles is the model of the epic's protagonists, and Silius distinguished between the worthy and unworthy successors of the hero-god. But there is a nationalistic bias to it. True to the historical events, Hannibal appears earlier than Scipio and therefore is the earlier pretender to Herakles' fame. Hannibal's march from Spain to Italy and his scaling of the Alps place him in the succession of Herakles (*Pun.* 2. 356–7): 'Shameful it is to shun a path that Herakles trod and to shrink back from repeating his exploit.' After his conquest of Saguntum, Hannibal proceeds to sacrifice the spoils of that city on the altars of the famous Herakles temple at Gades. Carved on the doors of that temple are the hero's labours, and Hannibal 'sates his eyes with this *varia virtutis imago*' (*Pun.* 3. 45). The poet, however, has already hinted that Hannibal is not living up to this *virtus*, for he broke the faith, *fides*, and stormed the walls of 'chaste' Saguntum, and Jupiter frowned on it (*Pun.* 3. 1–2). Up to this point the situation of the lavishly sacrificing Hannibal parallels that of Herakles after the conquest of Oichalia, and Hannibal seems to emulate the transgressing rather than the virtuous Herakles. It turns out, however, that Hannibal is not emulating Herakles at all but in fact is working against him. For Herakles was the founder of Saguntum and had appealed to *Fides* to bring help to the Saguntines (*Pun.* 2. 475ff.). By destroying the city, Hannibal therefore allies himself with the powers that worked against *Fides* and Herakles, i.e. Juno and Tisiphone.

It is not surprising, then, that Hannibal's subsequent self-identification with Herakles when he crosses the Pyrenees (3. 420–41) and Alps reflects his wishful thinking rather than fact and that in this Roman epic it is the Roman generals who emerge as the true heirs of Herakles. The first mention of Herakles in the epic sets the tone. Mortally wounded, Murrus, the bravest of Saguntum's defenders, prays to Herakles for help (*Pun.* 1. 505–7). Before he ends, Hannibal already hovers over him for the kill and answers the pious prayer with scathing cynicism. 'Consider', he sneers, 'whether the hero of Tiryns will not far more justly assist us in our enterprise.' And, addressing Herakles: 'Unless my *virtus*, which is emulating yours, displeases you, give me the victory. As you destroyed Troy long ago, so let me destroy the Trojan offspring.' A propaganda poster could hardly be more effective as we are confronted with a drastic example of proverbial Punic cruelty compounded by hybris. Such is not the Herculean *virtus* of Regulus, whose fight against a huge serpent in Africa during the First Punic War is modelled on similar exploits of Herakles, including his fight against Cacus.[16] In Book 13, the fight of another Roman general, Fulvius, against three enemies is likened to

Herakles' against Geryon (*Pun.* 13. 191ff.). Most prominently, however, it is Scipio who supplants Hannibal, the Herakles *manqué*. Jupiter was Scipio's father (4. 475–6), and Jupiter's passion was aroused by Venus, who wanted to foil Juno's plea for a victorious Carthage (13. 620–5). This is told to Scipio by his mother Pomponia during Scipio's descent to the underworld which, like that of Aeneas, recalls Herakles' *katabasis*. To reinforce the similarity, Silius has Jupiter give Pomponia a place in Elysium next to Alcmena.

Above all, Scipio is another Herakles at the crossroads. After the poet has depicted the Carthaginians, including Hannibal, as being enslaved by *Voluptas* at Capua, Virtus and Voluptas appear before the young Scipio, and he has to make his choice between them. While Silius adheres to the outward scheme of Prodicus' version, he tailors the argumentation of the two ladies to the needs of the Roman setting. Voluptas from beginning to end criticizes the *furor* of exposing oneself to war and its dangers. But already Cicero, in his translation of Herakles' speech in the *Trachiniae*, had placed the emphasis on Herakles the victor[17] because he was worshipped as such in Roman cult. Voluptas' arguments therefore cannot impress the Roman successor of Herakles. Moreover, the reason proffered by Virtus reflects what to the Romans seemed the most significant aspect of the Herakles myth. The focus is throughout on the promise that a man who deserves well of the state will be deified. This was a Roman commonplace which, moreover, had been prominently associated with Scipio in Cicero's *Somnium Scipionis*. Even the metaphor which Silius uses for the apotheosis, the triumphal procession leading to heaven (*Pun.* 13. 98–100), is as Roman as can be. It anticipates the end of the epic where Scipio, in his triumph, is compared to Herakles and the other canonical demigods, and his divine parentage is emphasized once more (*Pun.* 17. 645–54). Virtus' final exhortation to Scipio is to overcome the Carthaginians. He readily assents and goes into battle like a second Herakles, just as Aeneas had done when he left the site of Rome for the war against Turnus. But whereas Vergil adapted Herakles for the national inspiration, he becomes a nationalistic figure in Silius.[18] As Herakles to many Greeks incarnated their own spiritual and cultural superiority over the *barbaroi*, so Silius' Herakles is an embodiment of that ideal *virtus* which, naturally, is found only among Romans.

Understandably enough, no such overtones are found in Valerius Flaccus' *Argonautica*. Retelling the story of the Argo for his Roman readers, Valerius rid Herakles of the ambiguities with which Apollonius had endowed him, and he and Vergil thus prepared the way for Herakles' unequivocally favourable portrayal in the Renaissance epopees. To move clumsily aboard a ship, to row like a madman, to take irrational revenge—all this would be incompatible with *dignitas*. But Valerius goes beyond portraying a stolid, pompous stereotype. He does not want us merely to look at the hero with awe, but we are meant to empathize with him. For instance, instead of bullying the innocent Mysians for hostages so he can assuage his grief for the lost Hylas, Herakles is compared to a lioness who has lost her cub (3. 737–40). He is the pious son of Jupiter, almost another Aeneas, and the argument about breaking off the search for him is prolonged so Jason can deliver a veritable *laudatio Herculis*. Valerius expressly condemns the plan to leave Herakles as frenzy (*furias* 3. 692), and Jason weeps and weeps again for Herakles, more profusely almost than Herakles' bereft family did in the dramas of Euripides and Seneca. But like Herakles' tears in the *Aeneid*, Jason's tears roll in vain.

In contrast to Apollonius, Valerius greatly expands the exploits of Herakles and even inserts two new ones. In Book II, he describes at length Hesione's rescue by the hero. The sentimental description of the maiden's desolate wails soon yields to an extended, most graphic picture of the onslaught of the monster, and Valerius is intent to impress upon the reader the threat which the beast poses to humanity. Herakles' gallantry is contrasted with Laomedon's unsavoury reaction —'treachery, subtle cunning and the plotting of a hateful crime'—but Valerius, in order to let his hero bask in a yet nobler light, only hints at the story of Herakles' revenge and does not make it part of the epic. After Herakles and the Argonauts are separated, both pursue their different ways but arrive at the shores of the Black Sea on the same day. The Argonauts' failure to be aware of Herakles' presence on that occasion is Valerius' way, which is rather more subtle than Apollonius', of underlining the disparate nature between their heroic world and Herakles'. Herakles is engaged in freeing Prometheus, an event of greater and more cosmic significance than Jason's fetching of the Golden Fleece, because Jupiter, as in Aeschylus' *Prometheus Unbound*, now shows the same compassion for Prometheus that led him earlier to interfere with Juno on Herakles' behalf. The Argonauts, ordinary mortals, cannot partake in such events; they can only see their manifestations without being able to interpret them (5. 171–6):

> But in their ignorance (for who could have believed that Alcides was on those hills, or ventured once more on hopes abandoned?) his comrades proceed upon their way; only they wonder from the deep at the wide-flung snow that strews the beaches, at the cloven crags and the huge shadow of a dying bird above them and the gory dew that drizzles through the air.

Their distance from Herakles is not only physical, but metaphysical. In contrast to Apollonius' epic, it is not the difference of age and time that separates the Argonauts from the hero. Instead, Herakles is the exalted benefactor of mankind who is superhuman rather than a superman.

The specific reason for Valerius' addition of these two episodes to the *Argonautica* emerges when we look at their symbolic associations in the early Empire. A painting with Herakles and Hesione was found in the Pythagorean Basilica at Rome's Porta Maggiore, where it signified the liberation of the souls of the faithful.[19] Similarly, the eagle that devoured Prometheus' liver was regarded, at latest since the first century A.D., as the infernal offspring of Typhoeus and Echidna (Apollod. 2. 5. 11). The emphasis, then, is on the mysterious and godlike aspects of Herakles, quite in contrast to the Herakles tradition which had emphasized what was humanly understandable in the hero. While Valerius may have been partially indebted to Seneca's *Hercules Oetaeus* for this concept of Herakles,[20] his characterization of Herakles, like Seneca's, is more directly an expression of the spiritual hopes and yearnings of their time. And Seneca's was to be of lasting importance.

NOTES TO CHAPTER VII

1. W. S. Anderson, '*Hercules Exclusus:* Propertius, IV, 9', *AJP* 85 (1964) 3. My interpretation of the elegy owes much, though not all, to Anderson's perceptive article (pp. 1–12). The convention of the excluded lover has been studied by F. O. Copley, *Exclusus Amator: a Study in Latin Love Poetry* (Baltimore, 1956). For Herakles as an excluded lover in comedy see p. 96 and Bieber 133, fig. 487, where he is represented standing in front of a shrine, just like in Propertius' elegy.
2. Compare *furis et implacidas diruit ira fores* (line 14) with *nec tulit iratam ianua clausa sitim* (line 62). Further parallels between the two episodes are pointed out by Anderson, p. 4.
3. See p. 221.
4. A.A. 2. 209–32, esp. 217–22; cf. Propertius 3. 11. 17–20. The topos is discussed by F. O. Copley, '*Servitium Amoris* in the Roman Elegists', *TAPA* 78 (1947) 285–300, esp. 286, 291–3. Catullus 55. 13 and Prop. 3. 23. 8 compare the labours of the lover to those of Herakles as Plautus had done in *Persa* 1–5; cf. Terence, *Eun.* 1026–7. Tibullus does not mention Herakles, whereas Ovid used his love for Deianeira and Iole as a mythological *exemplum* in *Amores* 3. 6. 35–8 and *A.A.* 3. 155–6.
5. Most prominently in his poem on the battle of Actium (4. 6); see my remarks in *WS* n.s. 3 (1969) 86–7 and J. P. Sullivan, *Arion* 5 (1966) 19.
6. See Chapter X, note 6.
7. Cf. the poem *Megara* referred to in Chapter V, note 34. It is a testimony to the unpredictability of poetic inspiration that *Ep.* 9 inspired such noble adaptations as Hölderlin's and Darío's.
8. Cf., with more detail, Stoessl 76.
9. *Pulcherrima virgo* (Met. 9. 9); cf. Vergil's description of Lavinia in *Aeneid* 7. 72; 11. 479–80; 12. 64–70, 605–6. For more detail on Ovid's version, see my article in *Wiener Studien* n.s. 6 (1972).
10. Cf. e.g. *nec gener externis hospes tibi missus ab oris* (*Met.* 9. 19) with *generos externis adfore ab oris* (*Aen.* 7. 270).
11. *Met.* 9. 46–9=*Aen.* 12. 715–24; noticed in the editions of Ehwald and van Proosdij.
12. As Stoessl, p. 80, puts it so well. But his criticism that Ovid never tells us how Deianeira finally got across the river is misguided.
13. B. Otis, *Ovid as an Epic Poet* (Cambridge, 1966) 200.
14. Its main points: Alcmena is the Virgin Mary, giving birth to Herakles—Christ '*sans charnel copulation*'; the fight of Herakles against Achelous is that of God against the devil; the two horns of Achelous are, respectively, the

symbol of sanctity and of pride; Deianeira is the soul which Herakles–Christ rescues from the machinations of Nessus, the devil. See Chrétien le Gouays, *Ovide Moralisé*, ed. De Boer, in *Verh. de Kon. Akad. van Vetenschapen* (Amsterdam, 1920), Book 9. 232–324, 453–86,

15. *Pharsalia* 1. 45–63, cf. Seneca, *H.O.* 1564–75, 1581, 1989–91. For details, see L. Thompson, *CP* 59 (1964) 147–53. Lucan's lengthy account of Herakles' fight against Antaeus (4. 593–660) illustrates once more that a Herakles episode was almost mandatory in Roman epic.
16. See esp. *Pun.* 6. 182–4. E. L. Bassett, *CP* 50 (1955) 1–20 discusses the episode in detail.
17. *Tusc.* 2. 9. 21–2. Sophocles' *ὦ χέρες, χέρες* (*Trach.* 1089) becomes *o ante victrices manus* and the concluding line: *multa alia victrix nostra lustravit manus* is Cicero's own addition; cf. Chapter VI, note 9.
18. Vergil made Herakles a model for Aeneas without taking him away from the Italians; e.g. Herakles' son Aventinus fights on the side of the Latins (*Aen.* 7. 655–69), and so does Gyas—with Herakles' arms—whose father Melampus was a companion of Herakles (*Aen.* 10. 317–22). By contrast, the association of the very beginnings of both Carthage (Cic., *N.D.* 3. 42) and Rome suggested to Silius the rivalry of Carthaginians and Romans for Herakles' succession, and the Herakles myth is turned into the vehicle for demonstrating Roman superiority. Still more chauvinistic are Statius' strictures of Hannibal—*semper atrox dextra periuroque ense superbus*—as the most unworthy follower of Herakles (*Silvae* 4. 6. 75–84). E. L. Bassett, 'Hercules and the Hero of the Punica', in L. Wallach, ed., *The Classical Tradition. Studies in Honor of Harry Caplan* (Ithaca, 1966) 262–4 regards Silius' Stoicism as another reason for his emphasis on Herakles and *virtus*.
19. See J. Carcopino, *La basilique pythagoricienne de la Porte Majeure* (Paris, 1927) 328–9.
20. Valerius' acquaintance with Seneca's play is suggested by several verbal echoes (e.g. *virtus in astra tendit, H.O.* 1991—*tendite in astra, viri, Arg.* 1. 563) and by the compositional technique Valerius uses for the Herakles episodes: like the scenes in Seneca's tragedies, they serve as self-contained tableaux rather than be closely connected with the narrative. For further references and discussions of authors and passages not considered here see the articles by Huxley and M. Piot, 'Hercule chez les poètes du 1er siècle après Jésus Christ', *REL* 43 (1965) 342–58. Statius, especially in the *Thebaid*, has the most frequent and most conventional references to Herakles as an exemplar. Ovid, *Pont.* 4. 13. 11–12 mentions a Herakles epic written by his friend Carus.

CHAPTER VIII

Seneca's Herakles

Seneca's portrait of Herakles is, above all, the result of the distinctive nature of Senecan drama.[1] Sophocles and Euripides had used the Herakles myth as a vehicle for expressing their attitudes to some ideas that were current at the time. They considered and reshaped the myth from a certain point of view, but, being literary artists rather than philosophers, their primary concern still was the myth, its individuals, and their characterization, and the myth did not provide merely the theatrical setting that was necessary for putting an abstract truth in dramatic form. That, however, was precisely the nature of Senecan drama. It has been said, quite justifiably, that unlike Greek tragedies Seneca's plays are not so much representations of people in action as they are representations of passion in people and things.[2] This is quite true of *Hercules Furens* and, somewhat less so, of *Hercules Oetaeus* which was probably not finished by Seneca in the form in which it has survived. To the devotee of Greek drama, the irrelevance of any analysis of Seneca's two Herakles plays in terms of 'plot' and 'character' may be disappointing, but any value judgement would only be an obstacle to an understanding of Herakles' role which, after all, is at least of great historical significance in the tradition.

This is not to say that there is nothing more to Seneca's dramas than their 'philosophical' content. As a dramatist, Seneca's interest was literary as well as philosophical. Here Seneca is a Mr. Facing-both-ways, a Janus-like figure in the Herakles tradition. There is enough evidence in Seneca's philosophical writings for his admiration for Herakles and his Stoic conception of the hero. Contemner of pleasures, Fortune, and circumstance, selfless benefactor *pro bono publico*, victor over all terrors, and exemplar of aspiration for the highest virtue—none of the important

Stoic qualities are missing.[3] Yet Seneca's aim as a dramatist was not just the *mise en scène* of Stoic precepts or heroes. The plays do embody principles and attitudes which are the natural product of Seneca's absorption in Stoicism,[4] but they are not Stoic drama pure and simple. Specifically, the theme of the two Herakles plays—death and man's right attitude towards it—was of considerable significance to a Stoic, but Seneca's extraordinary preoccupation with it was, at the same time, intensely personal and in many ways the result of the age in which he lived. Seneca's plays are, above all, literary creations even though many Stoic views appear in them. Thus, in spite of the almost complete absence of psychological character delineation, Seneca's Herakles is as much a literary figure as he is the incarnation of a philosophical and moral world view. In this instance again, the subsequent tradition tended to separate what a Greek or Roman writer still could see as an integrated whole. From the humanists of the German Renaissance to Thornton Wilder, we find a Herakles whose philosophical encumbrance not only becomes dominating but eventually submerges his individuality. This division between the literary and philosophical Herakles figure is one of the distinctive characteristics of his tradition. Unfortunately, the former—not in the least because of Seneca—could become as typological as the latter, and it is only where influences other than Seneca's prevailed that Herakles was able to assert a more individual *persona*.

In contrast to Euripides, Seneca de-emphasizes the externality of the hero's madness. In *Hercules Furens* there is no interlude with Lyssa and Iris. Instead, Juno vows in the prologue to inject madness into Herakles, although there is no hint of his innocence, let alone any anticipation of a more sublime assertion of his heroism. Why does Juno want to strike Herakles mad? In Euripides' *Herakles*, this was a senseless act for which no reason whatsoever was given except for the broad suggestion of the capriciousness of divine action. Seneca's Juno, by contrast, lists a whole series of motives in the prologue to the play. Mainly, she is disturbed about Herakles' ambition to gain acceptance into heaven, an ambition which she both belittles—by reference to her husband's sundry concubines who now grace the heaven as constellations—and deeply fears. At the base of this fear is the violence and destructiveness with which Herakles seeks to accomplish this goal—every goal, in fact.

Unlike Bacchus, who reached the stars in a measured, peaceful journey (*lenta via* 66), Herakles, the *violentus iuvenis* (43–4),[5] will do so by sheer muscle. 'He will seek a path through ruin and will desire to rule in an empty universe. He swells with his tested might and strength . . .' (67–8). Twice Juno singles out the most blatant example of Herakles' strong-man behaviour—his descent to hell. Herakles' original task, which Juno had imposed on him, was the conquest of Cerberus, but it is evident from Juno's remarks and the rest of the play that Herakles' journey signifies more than that. Far from considering Juno's order an imposition or an act of *anankē*, he fulfilled it gladly (*laetus* 42), and this is reflected in Herakles' own account of his exploit (600–15). For Herakles, the meaning of his descent to Hades is his claim to have overcome Death. 'If the regions of the third estate had pleased me,' he boasts, 'I might have reigned' (609–10). In other words, Herakles arrogates to himself the power over Death.

The choral ode that follows Juno's prologue suggests that, personal and biased as they may be, her objections to Herakles' *hybris* do not lack an objective justification. The critical comments of the chorus are an explicit, anticipatory corrective to Herakles' own claims. 'While the Fates permit,' the chorus advises, 'live happily. Men are driven to meet the speeding fates, each one uncertain of when he will meet his fate. Contrast this with Herakles. He thought he could force fate's hand and went to the Stygian waves of his own accord.' Addressing themselves to Herakles directly, the Theban elders continue: 'With too strong a heart, Alcides, are you hastening, before your time, to see the grieving ghosts; at the appointed time the Fates come.' Just as one may not linger and postpone the allotted day, so one must not anticipate or hurry it.

The exhortation to Herakles is purposely integrated into the larger framework of the ode which contrasts the life of tranquillity with that of ambition. The topos, which is more Epicurean than Stoic, is familiar enough from Horace's poetry, and Seneca reveals his true feelings about it in one of his *Letters to Lucilius* (39. 2–3):

> No man of exalted gifts is pleased with that which is low and mean; the vision of great achievement summons him and uplifts him. Just as the flame springs straight into the air and cannot be cabined or

> kept down any more than it can repose in quiet, so our soul is always in motion, and the more ardent it is, the greater its motion and activity.

True to the spirit of this exhortation, Seneca endows Herakles with the features of the Stoic *tonos* incarnate. Besides readily accepting his labours, he constantly asks for more than Juno can think up. Seneca does not allow us to lose sight of this theme. Amphitryon comments on Herakles' unceasing aspiration, and Megara, arguing with Lycus, emphasizes that Herakles' labours are essential to the manifestation of his heroic valour. The same point, as we saw in an earlier chapter, was also made by Epictetus in a very positive sense.[6] In *Hercules Furens*, however, Seneca depicts it as an obsession. Hardly has Herakles come on-stage when he blames Juno for letting his hands lie idle. After a few words with Amphitryon, he dashes off to take revenge on Lycus. When he returns, Amphitryon asks him to pray for an end to his labours and for some respite (*otium* 925), but Herakles will have none of that. Instead, he addresses a long prayer to Jupiter, which shows that his motives are disinterested but ends on the note of his desire for more labours yet: 'If the earth is still to produce any wickedness, let her make haste, and if she is preparing any monster, let it be mine.'

The monster that has been prepared for him turns out to be his madness. Its onset only reinforces Herakles' earlier attitude; he now raves that if the earth and underworld can provide no more antagonists, he will storm Olympus and try the heavens. Where Euripides had emphasized the jarring discrepancy between the sane Herakles, the loving father who saw his labours in perspective, and Herakles the madman, Seneca points out the continuity between the two by making Herakles consistently pursue the same goal. Herakles was something of a robot to start with; now he is a robot gone amuck. There definitely is the suggestion that the destruction he wreaks and his own destruction are the logical consequence of his will.[7]

No doubt many good Romans who looked on in horror would gnash their teeth at Herakles' misfortune and lend a kindlier ear to Herakles' profession of the selflessness of his motives than to Juno's incriminations. He had, after all, demonstrated his *virtus* and was fully deserving of heaven. Without questioning their assumption, even though Amphitryon tells his son that 'you look upon an unreal sky with troubled gaze' (954), let us return to Seneca's thirty-ninth *Letter*, where he pronounced unceasing activity a virtue, but not without attaching the following qualification: 'Happy is the man who uses this impulse for better things (*ad meliora*): because he will put himself outside of the law and power of Fortune.' That Herakles evidently is not able to do in *Hercules Furens*, and doubts about the use of his heroic *virtus ad meliora* recur throughout the play.[8] The chorus and Herakles claim that he sustained the world at peace—*orbis defensus* (883). He did so by his labours, which Amphitryon enumerates before concluding (249–53):

> But what do they all avail? He is absent from the world which he defended (*orbe defenso caret*). All the earth has felt that the giver of its peace is lost to it. Once again prosperous and successful crime goes by the name of *virtus*; good men obey the bad, might is right and fear oppresses law.

In order words, Herakles' journey to the underworld, which he regards as his greatest achievement, actually annulled his former services to mankind. While he spent his time exultantly parading Cerberus through the cities of Greece à la Ringling Brothers (58–9), political corruption sprang up everywhere, including his home. Herakles himself is brought face to face with this reality (631–3). His failure to bring an effective peace to the world is, in part, the ironic result of his desire to pacify the underworld (889–90). But were the dead not peaceful enough already? It becomes increasingly clear that Herakles lacks perspective and that his *virtus* is rather misguided.

Seneca continues to develop the equivocal implications of Herakles' descent to the underworld. What was its benefit? Juno says the road from the underworld has been opened, but only Herakles and Theseus were able to travel it. Later, immediately before Herakles appears, the chorus pointedly describes Orpheus' achieving the same goal by song and suppliant prayer rather than muscle. Megara, however, apodeictically asserts that Herakles 'reached the depths that he might gain the heights':

> inferna tetigit, posset ut supera assequi (423).

Her assertion is undercut by the ambiguity of the term *supera*, which she takes to mean 'heaven' whereas it frequently seems to mean 'earth' in this play.[9]

Belying his own opinion of it, then, the hero's descent into Hades lacks any real meaning. Herakles, who confronted death physically and thought he had overcome him, has to learn much more about death's power and significance before he can be accepted into heaven. So the inversion of the events takes its course, and Herakles experiences the real, metaphysical power of Death. The most extensive change Seneca made in the traditional story is designed to illustrate that Herakles' madness is interpreted *sub specie mortis*. 'So you think, in your pride, that you have escaped Styx and the cruel ghosts', Juno cries in the prologue. '*Here*, I will show you hell!' And she proceeds to summon the creatures of hell to take possession of the hero's mind. Above all, the unparalleled centre piece of the tragedy, Theseus' lengthy description of the desolation, horrors, dark caves and tortures of hell (662–827) is to reflect Herakles' state of mind.[10] It will be like the infernal wastelands where

> no meadows bud, joyous with verdant view, no ripened corn waves in the gentle breeze; not any grove has fruit-producing boughs; the barren desert of the abysmal fields lies all untilled, and the foul land lies torpid in endless sloth—sad end of things, the world's last estate. Their air hangs motionless and black night broods over a sluggish world. All things are with grief dishevelled, and worse than death itself is the abode of death.

We can see why the self-assertion of Euripides' hero would have been pointless in *Hercules Furens*. Herakles has to recognize Death's omnipotence; Death cannot be overcome by the methods he had used. After Theseus has finished, the chorus, sounding a distinctive Senecan theme, stresses that Death is what life is all about: 'For you, Death, all things are growing . . . for you, we all are preparing' (870–2). Death can be conquered only by an attitude akin to that of the chorus, and Seneca took his time to work out its implications in *Hercules Oetaeus*.

After the graphic power of the descriptions of hell and Herakles' madness, the play ends in low key. Herakles acknowledges the might of hell. He vows to build himself a pyre and to burn himself, 'spattered with impious gore', to death: 'To the nether gods I will give back Herakles'—*inferis reddam Herculem* (1218). Of course *Hercules Furens* does not so end, and this is one of the clearest examples that Seneca was not concerned to make his drama conform to Stoic doctrine in every detail. Besides being honourable, Herakles' suicide at this stage would have been entirely justifiable from the Stoic point of view.[11] Without claiming that the play is an harmonious creation—it is that as little as *Hercules Oetaeus* and the time in which Seneca lived—we can at least say that the end shows the hand of a skilful dramatist. Out of *pietas* for his father, Herakles does not follow through with his plan. This signals the return to his *pietas* for which the chorus had prayed while Herakles was resting in mad exhaustion (1093–4). In the same breath, the chorus had also begged for Herakles' *virtus* to return, and the return to his *pietas* suggests that his *virtus* will return also, and that it will not be his earlier uncontrolled, misguided *virtus* (*virtus indomita*; 39) which we have been witnessing. Moreover, Seneca so describes Herakles' pyre as to anticipate the pyre on which he will burn himself at the end of *Hercules Oetaeus* and to make obvious the difference in Herakles' attitude in the two plays. In *Hercules Furens*, Herakles wants to build the pyre so he can return to the underworld, whereas in *Hercules Oetaeus* the pyre becomes the symbol of his *virtus* that elevates him to heaven. In the later play Herakles will overcome death by his *virtus*, and not by purely physical valour, and Seneca hints at this change at the end of *Hercules Furens*.

In *Hercules Furens* Seneca leaves no doubt about Herakles' superiority over ordinary men such as Lycus. To that end he expands the debate between Amphitryon, Lycus, and also, Megara, and associates Herakles with the imagery of light throughout the play.[12] Herakles' first appearance, for instance, is marked by his prayer to Apollo, 'the lord of kindly light' (*o lucis almae rector* 592), and his seizure of madness takes on the appearance of darkness at noon (939–40): *mediam diem cinxere tenebrae*. In his two Herakles plays, then, Seneca dramatically expresses the evolution of Herakles. Already at the earliest beginnings of the tradition, Herakles had been an extraordinary and almost superhuman being who, however, was given more to an exercise of his physical than his spiritual strength. It was the latter to which he had to be converted. Unlike Euripides, Seneca wrote two plays to illustrate his conversion of the hero and, characteristically enough, he made death its touchstone.

Nor was his concern with Herakles' transformation the result merely of dramaturgic considerations. Already in his essay *On the Firmness of the Wise Man* (2. 1–2) Seneca pronounced Cato a truer exemplar of the wise man than the earlier ages had had in Herakles. For while Herakles despised pleasure and triumphed over all terrors, his achievements were mostly physical whereas Cato's valour was entirely spiritual:

> Cato did not grapple with wild beasts—the pursuit of these is for the huntsman and the peasant; he did not hunt down monsters with fire and sword, nor did he chance to live in the times when it was possible to believe that the heavens rested on one man's shoulders.

Cato, Seneca goes on to say, fought against the monsters of vanity and degeneracy. Lucretius' critique of the Herakles myth had made its mark, and much to his credit, Seneca provided an answer not by facile Stoic allegorizing,[13] but by dramas that are marked by an unparalleled intensity of tone.

By a deliberate coincidence of form and content, *Hercules Oetaeus* is every bit as colossal as Herakles himself. The poet's attempt to let Herakles' whole life pass in review accounts for those features of the play that have been much criticized, in particular its monstrous length and tiresome repetitions. Yet *Hercules Oetaeus* is not as unwieldy as it has been made out to be and 'succeeds in projecting a clearly defined interpretation of Hercules'.[14]

Some themes of *Hercules Furens* are continued and developed more fully in the second play and the prologue exemplifies their inversion. It now is Herakles who speaks it, and in many ways, it constitutes a direct answer to Juno's prologue to *Hercules Furens*, while also providing the first of several portraits that make up the total dramatic portrait of the hero in *Hercules Oetaeus*. Herakles wastes no time pronouncing himself to be the establisher of peace. His *virtus*, he says, rather than Juno urged him on (62–3), and this confirms our interpretation of the impulse to his labours in *Hercules Furens*. Because of his deeds, Herakles goes on to plead, Jupiter cannot deny him heaven any longer. In contrast to *Hercules Furens* there is not a shade of a doubt that his labours were those of a moral force and that Herakles has earned his acceptance into heaven. Conspicuously inverting Juno's description of the heavenly constellations as Jupiter's former paramours, Herakles points to the monsters which Juno sent to heaven after they had been conquered by him. By this the gods are threatened, and Herakles has to bring peace to them, a much more meaningful peace than the one he claimed to have brought to the underworld. Herakles' wish to be received into heaven will be fulfilled, though not in the way in which he expects his end to come about. His claim that 'Death has verily given me back to you' (13–14) thus is a consummately ironic introduction to the events of the play.

The chorus of the Oechalian captives immediately presents the other side of the coin. They dwell on Herakles' fierceness and towering rage, and their emotional outburst leads up to Deianeira's subjective and powerful portrait of the lustful Herakles. More importantly, the leitmotif of the play continues in the choral ode. It begins with a philosophical reflection (104–6): 'Mate of the gods is he whose life and fortune have gone side by side; but when it is slowly dragged out amidst lamentations, life has the lot of death.' This is the first and last time death is associated with something negative in this play, and it is the culmination of the view of death as harsh, oppressing, and undesirable as it was described throughout *Hercules Furens*. From now on, epitomizing the fundamental change that takes place in *Hercules Oetaeus*, death appears in an entirely different, positive light. 'Never is he unhappy,' the chorus goes on to say, 'for whom to die is easy' (111). And, somewhat later: 'Death, you pursue the happy and you flee the unfortunate'—

felices sequeris, mors, miseros fugis (122).

Herakles will be truly *felix* when he dies on Mount Oeta.

The lengthy scene with Deianeira and the Nurse need not detain us long. Seneca's Deianeira owes much to the carping Deianeira in Ovid's *Epistle* and hardly anything to Sophocles. As in Pound's adaptation of the *Trachiniae*, no sympathetic portrait of Deianeira is to detract from Herakles' stature even though Deianeira tries her best to do that, depicting all of Herakles' supposedly heroic achievements as arising from his sexual desires. The scene, like so many others in Seneca's plays, is designed for its own effect and has almost no influence on the subsequent action, but even here Seneca keeps her attention focused on the death theme. It is connected with the pivotal shift of Deianeira's mood in this scene: when she has finished ranting, she admits she still loves Herakles and plans to murder him out of love. Before her plan is inverted into its exact opposite—her resolve to commit suicide—the chorus of her friends sings an ode which expands on the theme of the first ode in *Hercules Furens* and provides another example of the continuing 'conversion'. The subject again is the contrast between the humble life and the life in high places, and it is amplified by the references to the power of Fortuna.[15] What Seneca wrote in his thirty-ninth *Letter* to Lucilius now is relevant to Deianeira. We have witnessed a graphic display of Deianeira's *animus* being vehemently *in motu*. But if Herakles in *Hercules Furens* did not turn his impetus *ad meliora*, Deianeira does even less so with the result that she becomes the victim of Fortune indeed. Before the chorus has ended, Deianeira rushes on-stage. 'What new reverse of Fortune whirls you about?' asks the chorus at the sight of her.

By contrast, Seneca uncompromisingly affirms Herakles' cosmic stature through Hyllus' words. As Herakles had invoked Apollo as 'the glory of heaven' (*caeli decus*; *HF* 592) so Hyllus now praises his father as 'that glory (*decus . . . orbis*) and sole guardian of the world, whom the fates had given to the lands in place of Jove' (749–50). The loss of Herakles is not a private loss: the whole world, the whole race, all men, all lands mourn him (758–62). So far, however, from seizing the opportunity to subdue Herakles for good, Death 'who once in his own realm was overcome', flees from Herakles (766–7). This sets the tone for the rest of the play. After the chorus had hinted at it earlier, death now is presented as deliverance, as a desirable good. Moreover, since Death is fleeing, the implication is that Herakles has to will his death and actively seek death. By so doing the hero will triumph over Death and, in contrast to *Hercules Furens*, truly conquer him.

Seneca gives additional emphasis to the theme by having Deianeira and Hyllus debate her decision to commit suicide. 'Death alone will be granted as a haven for my cares' (1021), she sums up her argument. For her as for Herakles, death is the ultimate wisdom.[16] Still, Herakles is unable to accept his death as readily as Deianeira so long as he must believe that Deianeira, and not he, caused it. This is too base a way to die and Herakles rebels against it with every fibre of his huge body. He is in no way resigned and muted as he was after the catastrophe in *Hercules Furens*. No: his opinion of himself and his achievements is as assertive as it was in the beginning. Almost like Prometheus he quarrels with Jupiter and insists that he is indispensable for the survival of heaven and Jupiter himself. Blind chaos will break loose again if he perishes. Grandiloquent as Herakles may seem, Seneca does not intend to undercut his hero now. Quite on the contrary, he does everything to affirm his cosmic role and, for that purpose, again inverts a motif from *Hercules Furens*. Before Herakles himself comes on the stage to deliver his truculent lament, the chorus has already anticipated him in predicting the downfall of the universe as a result of Herakles' utter defeat. 'Even death', prophesies the chorus, 'shall at last bring doom upon itself.' The source of the chorus' gloom is a prophecy of Orpheus, who was favourably contrasted with Herakles in the earlier play. 'The gods and even Jupiter', sang Orpheus, 'are under the law.' When Herakles, the incarnation of that *nomos*, is wronged and conquered, the whole world order will collapse.

The unheroic reason which Herakles thinks is responsible for his destruction causes him to yield unheroically to his excruciating pain. After the portrait of the lustful Herakles, Seneca now paints that of the suffering hero. Perhaps this stark depiction, more than anything else, indelibly fixed on the subsequent artistic tradition the impression of Herakles' heroic, corporal energy and his tremendous physique. It is under this aspect that Dürer, for instance, represented him even in the subject that was the hero's least physical exploit, his choice between virtue and pleasure (Plate 12). As he is being racked by the pain, Herakles moans about the decay of his *ingens corpus* (1230). He then addresses each of his limbs in turn, recalling the labours they helped him to accomplish, and his lament concludes with a graphic description of his face which is 'harder than rock, harder than steel and the wandering Symplegades' (1272–3). But now he sheds tears for the first time and even begs that the gods of the underworld might take him back. Alcmena has to exhort her son to assert his heroic self-mastery and 'to conquer the lords of Hell as he used to'.

In this manner, Seneca gradually prepares for the change in the hero's attitude to death. Ultimately, it must of course be motivated by Herakles' knowledge of its true cause. Before Hyllus apprises him of it, Alcmena expresses it more generally: 'Son, no woman's poison melts your limbs, but the hard round of your labours, your unceasing toil, perhaps have fed some deadly disease in you' (1396–8). This was the reason for Herakles' madness in *Hercules Furens*, but now it is restated under its positive aspect. Even more than his madness in *Hercules Furens* his destruction ultimately is willed by himself. The moment Herakles is told this by Hyllus he rises to a grandeur that overawes the onlookers and ends with his apotheosis. The gladiator's fight of life is over—*habet*, Herakles says (1472). His outcry is not one of woe, as in the *Trachiniae*, but of exultation. Seneca even reinterprets pointedly the exclamation of Sophocles' Herakles: 'No more for me the light of day!' (*Trach.* 1144). What is seemingly no more than a translation—*lux ista summa est* (*HO* 1473)—at once recalls the imagery of light with which Herakles was profusely associated in *Hercules Furens*. And whereas Sophocles, in order to make the hero's downfall appear all the more ignominious, stressed that the living Herakles has been overcome by a dweller of Hades, Seneca emphasizes the same point for entirely different purposes. Herakles takes heart because his death turns out to be the result, even if indirectly, of his own action and because no living enemy has conquered him. For that would have lessened his repute. Preparing for the complete and final reversal of the events in *Hercules Furens*, death, the apparent victor over Herakles, will in fact be conquered by him. 'Now let me choose a death glorious, renowned, illustrious, full worthy of myself. This day I will make famous' (1481–2). Seneca—again like Pound and for the same reasons—does not describe Hyllus' reaction to his father's last instructions but develops at length the next to the last portrait of Herakles: the model of Stoic endurance. Now it is he who exhorts Alcmena to cease wailing and, as she did in the preceding scene, he now anticipates what is to come: 'Your Alcides lives' (1498). Another reversal is added to this one. In the prologue to the first play, Juno had sneered that Herakles' deification would only make him share a place with Jupiter's concubines, whereas Herakles now proudly proclaims: 'By my *virtus* I have made my stepmother seem but the concubine' (1499–500). And then he sounds a note that was almost a commonplace in Stoic/Cynic writings:[17] 'I have deserved to be Jupiter's son.' His kinship with Jupiter was not a godsend but the result of a moral effort, his *virtus.*

This valour also helps him overcome the one thing he had not yet vanquished on earth: the flames. 'Fire has taken its place among the labours of Hercules,' says Philoctetes in his long description of the hero's fiery burial, which 'is a *locus classicus* of Stoic fortitude.'[18] He joyfully mounts the funeral pyre and, completing the series of reversals from *Hercules Furens*, his triumphant posture is likened to that which he assumed when he was parading Cerberus through the Greek towns. His endurance, the Stoic kind, is as active as the courage he has shown in his heroic labours (1740–6):

> Midst scorching heat and threat'ning flames, unmoved, unshaken, to neither side turning his tortured limbs, he encourages, advises, is active still, though all aflame. In his attendants he inspires fortitude, you would think that he is on fire because he is burning from within. The whole crowd stands in speechless wonder and the flames have scarce belief, so calm his brow, the hero so majestic.

Eugene Waith has ably summed up the scene as follows:[19]

> The flame of his valour faces the flames of the poison and the funeral pyre, so that the hero rather burns than is burned. The suggestion is given in three words, '*urere ardentem putes*' (1744). Not only concurring in his fate, he seems to will it from the moment he recognizes the fatal bequest of Nessus as the fulfilment of the prophecy. He identifies his will with cosmic order—again flame with flame, the primal element in nature—and thus transcends his mere humanity.

The tableau of the trinity of the *mater dolorosa*, the father in heaven invoked by Herakles, and the divine son, which was to be eminently suggestive in the Christianized Herakles tradition,[20] is soon replaced by another, the manifestation of the god Herakles. The concluding portrait is designed for the greatest possible audio-visual impact.[21] At first we hear only Herakles' voice from above, telling his mother to cease mourning. The theatre reverberates with Herakles' exultant announcement: 'My *virtus* has borne me to the stars and to the gods themselves':

iam virtus mihi
in astra et ipsos fecit ad superos iter (1942–3).

This is the final rejoinder to Juno who had claimed that Herakles *iter ruina quaeret* (*HF* 67).[22] Concluding the ambiguity that Seneca had established about the hero's final destination,[23] Alcmena thinks once again that Herakles returned to Tartarus and overcame him for a second time. Through this contrast, his apotheosis therefore is all the more magnificent and, by reference to Herakles' flawed underworld adventure in the earlier play, all the more meaningful. When he finally is seen appearing as a god, he ends his speech on the note that he has again conquered hell. The *virtus indomita* of the strong-man has given way to true heroic and Stoic *virtus*. This '*virtus* fares to the stars, fear is doomed to death'—

virtus in astra tendit, in mortem timor (1971).

After Herakles' epiphany is over, the chorus restates this theme: 'Never to Stygian shades is glorious valour borne. The brave live on. . . .'

numquam Stygias fertur ad umbras
inclita virtus. vivunt fortes (1983–4).

Hercules Oetaeus ends with a ringing affirmation of Herakles' godhead when the chorus invokes him as the guarantor of world peace and a protector mightier yet than Jupiter himself.

Seneca's preoccupation with the theme of death, as Otto Regenbogen has demonstrated in a masterly essay,[24] must be viewed against the background of his time. The horrors and persecutions during the reigns of Caligula and Nero daily confronted especially courtiers such as Seneca with the ever-present reality of death. Together with the Stoic ethics and the traditional, soldierly Roman pathos of the readiness for death this contemporary experience led Seneca to shape his very own philosophy of death which permeates his writings. Its basic idea is that life is a preparation for death. 'It takes a whole life to learn how to die,' Seneca wrote in *De Brevitate Vitae* (7. 4) and Herakles is the dramatic illustration of this. The ability to die well is the criterion for the quality of one's life: *male vivet quisquis nesciet bene mori* (*Tranq.* 11. 4). Seneca's definition of what it means to live well is equally relevant to his Herakles. 'The wise man must withstand toil and danger and want and all the threatening ills that clamour about the life of man. He must endure the sight of death, of grief, of the crashes of the universe and all the fierce foes that confront him' (*Vit. Beat.* 11. 1). Frequently, Seneca compares this life to that of the gladiators, and the metaphor appears in the description of the deaths of both Deianeira and Herakles.[25] All this was no macabre exercise by Seneca; Tacitus concludes his stirring description of Seneca's suicide by noting that 'even in the height of his wealth and power he was thinking of his life's close' (*Ann.* 15. 64). In sum, more than any other classical author, even Pindar, Seneca projected his own aspirations, anguish, hopes, and philosophy of life and death into Herakles. His Herakles, like Hölderlin's and Browning's, is an intensely personal adaptation. It is this purpose, and not literary mythopoeia, that absorbed Seneca's tremendous, raw, dramatic power, a *virtus indomita* itself.

We have already mentioned the typological consequences of Seneca's characterization of Herakles for the subsequent tradition, Elizabethan drama in particular. It remains to single out another of its results. Seneca's portrait of Herakles, especially in *Hercules Oetaeus*, completely reversed the humanizing direction his depiction had taken for the last five hundred years. As in the original myth, Seneca emphasized what was god-like and mysterious in the hero. Since Seneca was known as the only model of classical drama before the rediscovery of the Greek playwrights and since he maintained his influence even after that, he determined, more than anyone else, the form the myth took in later European literature until the nineteenth century. Herakles' divinity, conjoined with philosophical and moral idealization, was to weigh on him heavily. 'Hercule se feit Dieu par la seule vertu', wrote Joachim du Bellay[26] and he had read his Seneca well.

Yet Seneca, in a work that unfortunately was not very influential, was able to treat Herakles in a lighter vein. His comic portrait of Herakles in the *Apocolocyntosis*, the 'Gourdification' of the Emperor Claudius, bears out the view that comedy often is a release from the things we have to take most seriously.[27] Seneca himself had lived in terror of Claudius, who had exiled him, and the satire breathes the spirit of nasty exhilaration. When Claudius knocks on the doors of heaven, Herakles—because 'he had travelled all over the world'—is summoned to look him over. Even he is shaken by the monstrous sight of the emperor and thinks his thirteenth labour has arrived. Since Claudius wants to be deified he lays great stress on his presumed Trojan-Julian descent. He almost fools Herakles who, in Seneca's words, is pretty gullible, perhaps because he was inclined to sympathize with Claudius since he himself had been deified and provided a precedent for Augustus' deification. At any rate, when he is told that Claudius is lying, Herakles once more plays the role of the strong-man. He bullies him with threats, and delivers a dramatic speech—*tragicus fit*—to make himself all the more terrifying. This is the sort of mock-tragic bombast that Shakespeare's Nick Bottom recites in 'Ercles' vein'. Even so, Herakles is still scared of the weird Claudius who goes on to beg him that Herakles be his advocate in the divine senate. There they encounter considerable hostility. Taking his Stoicism lightly, Seneca exploits the occasion for a persiflage even of the Stoic concept of god:

> He (Claudius) cannot be an Epicurean god: they are 'untroubled and troubling none'. A Stoic god? How can he be 'globular, with no head, no foreskin', as Varro says? There *is* something about him of the Stoic god, I now see. He's got neither a heart nor a head.

And the speaker confirms his assertion by swearing 'By Hercules!' right to Herakles' face.

The last glimpse we catch of Herakles reveals him as a shrewd wheeling and dealing floor manager of Claudius' cause, reminding the gods of past favours, promising them more, and reminding them again of the cardinal rule of all political transactions: 'One hand washes the other'—*manus manum lavat* (9. 6). This is, of course, not the first time Herakles was associated with persuasive abilities. Pindar had faintly hinted at them, Sophocles had derided them, Apollonius had given a splendid example of them, and in the century after Seneca, Lucian, even if ironically, depicted the Gallic Herakles as the exemplar of inspired eloquence, a notion that was idealized in the Renaissance.[28] In the *Apocolocyntosis* Herakles' verbal labour is almost crowned with success. He wins over a clear majority until Augustus gives his maiden speech, an impassioned indictment of Claudius' misdemeanours. Accordingly, Claudius goes where, in Seneca's opinion, he belongs: to hell.

Defending Bacchus and Herakles, Amphitryon told Lycus in *Hercules Furens* that 'after much toil, *virtus* is used to unbend' (476). Such was Euripides' view in the *Alcestis* and Seneca's in the *Apocolocyntosis*, and happily, it was not forgotten entirely by their literary successors.

NOTES TO CHAPTER VIII

1. For good, general characterizations of Senecan tragedy see Otto Regenbogen, 'Schmerz und Tod in den Tragödien Senecas', *Vorträge der Bibliothek Warburg* 7 (1927–8) 167–218, now available as a separate reprint (Darmstadt, 1963); C. J. Herington, 'Senecan Tragedy', *Arion* 5 (1966) 422–71; and W. H. Owen, 'Commonplace and Dramatic Symbol in Seneca's Tragedies', *TAPA* 99 (1968) 291–313. Owen's article reached me only after this chapter had been written, and his interpretation of *Hercules Furens* (pp. 302–6) supports mine in all essential aspects. See also Waith 30–8 and Stoessl 88–126.
2. So Herington 456; he does not, however, consider *Herakles Oetaeus* an authentic work of Seneca's (467 n. 61). Waith 204 n. 28, has compiled the most important studies of the authenticity question in a lengthy note; to these should be added B. Axelson, *Korruptelenkult. Studien zur unechten Seneca Tragödie Hercules Oetaeus* (Lund, 1967). I would assume that Seneca, for one reason or another, failed to revise the play, but all this is not crucial for the Herakles tradition because *Hercules Oetaeus* was thought to be Senecan until the early part of this century.
3. See *Ben.* 1. 13. 3; 4. 8. 1; *Tranq.* 16. 4; *Const.* 2. 1; and the often overlooked *laus Herculis* of the chorus in *Agam.* 825–67.
4. So N. T. Pratt, *TAPA* 79 (1948) 7, modifying the views of B. Marti, *TAPA* 76 (1945) 216–45.
5. Cf. *Agam.* 825: *violentus ille.*
6. See pp. 147f.
7. Cf. Waith 33.
8. I am much indebted here to the stimulating article by D. Henry and B. Walker, 'The Futility of Action: A Study of Seneca's *Hercules Furens*', *CP* 60 (1965) 11–21, esp. 15–17, although I cannot agree with many points of detail and with their conclusion.
9. E.g., *opima victi regis ad superos refert* (48); 275–7; 317–18; 566–8. See also note 22, below.
10. Herington (note 1, above) 452; cf. Regenbogen (note 1, above) 201. The passage has met with a mixed reception in literary criticism; it was praised by Lessing and has been ridiculed by T. S. Eliot, among others (*Selected Essays* [London, 1966] 69).
11. See the discussion by Arnold (Chapter VI n. 32) 309–11; cf. the view of the later Cynics, contemporary with Seneca, who regarded Herakles' death as suicide because he had succumbed to physical and spiritual corruption (Höistad 54–6).

12. For more detail see Waith 32 and N. T. Pratt, *TAPA* 94 (1963) 208–9 with note 19.
13. Which reached new heights in the writings of Seneca's contemporary Heracleitus who interpreted the three-headed Cerberus, e.g. whom Herakles dragged into the light of the day, as philosophy and its three parts (*Alleg. Hom.* 33).
14. Waith 35.
15. It is of more than historical interest that Queen Elizabeth took it upon herself to translate this choral passage into English blank verse.
16. Stoessl 89.
17. Dio Chrys., *Or.* 2. 78 and 69. 1: Herakles is the son of Zeus because of his *aretē*; Epict. 2. 16. 44.
18. Waith 37.
19. Waith, loc. cit. *Ben.* 4. 8. 1 is the clearest expression of Seneca's belief that Herakles was to return into primal fire.
20. Compare also, e.g. Aelius Aristides' (second century A.D.) praise of Alcmena almost in terms of the mother of the Messiah in his *Discourse on Herakles* (*Or.* 5. 31).
21. The terminology seems justified because Seneca's technique is quite cinematic.
22. It also dissolves the ambiguity of the expression *ad astra* and *ad superos* that had been connected with Herakles' seeking, finding, or opening a way (*viam petere*, *invenire*, *patefacere*) from hell in *Hercules Furens*; see the line references in note 9, above.
23. According to Herakles and the chorus, he will return to Tartarus (1514, 1525–7). The chorus then reverses itself and says Herakles will be elevated to the stars (1570–1, 1581 [where Herakles is invoked as 'comrade of Apollo'; cf. *HF* 592–6]). Herakles finally asks Jupiter to admit him to the stars (1703–4) because he is ashamed, though not afraid, to go back to the shades (1706–7).
24. Regenbogen (note 1, above) esp. 210–18.
25. *HO* 1457, and 1472 (as pointed out above, p. 178); cf. *Const.* 16. 2; *Tranq.* 11. 5; *Prov.* 2. 115.
26. *Les Regrets*, Sonnet 172. The terminology used by Boethius at the end of the fourth book of his *Consolation of Philosophy* also suggests Seneca's influence. After a (non-canonical) enumeration of the twelve labours Boethius urges the reader to follow Herakles' example:

    Ite nunc fortes, ubi celsa magni
    ducit exempli via: cur inertes
    terga nudatis? superata tellus
    sidera donat.

27. See pp. 97f. I follow the Budé edition of the *Apocolocyntosis* by René Waltz (Paris 1966).
28. See pp. 222ff.

CHAPTER IX
Exemplar Virtutis

The portraits of Herakles in the Greek and Roman authors that we have discussed so far make it abundantly clear that he was indeed a hero of many faces. The classical foundations of the myth were broad enough to provide subsequent writers with a great variety of choices. But here we come upon a paradox. It is undeniable that these choices were realized, but it is due, at least in part, to their already great number that little was added to Herakles' personality. A fundamental addition to the myth, such as Dante wrought for the myth of Odysseus, thus inspiring a whole new tradition, is lacking unless we choose to consider the Christianization of Herakles as such a change.

We might ask at this point whether additions or elaborations of this kind are necessary for the successful survival of a myth. The answer is that they are not, unless they are the outgrowth of a reinterpretation of the myth in contemporary terms. It is a commonplace in the study of mythological figures that in order to be kept alive, they must be constantly reinterpreted, and this was certainly true of the Herakles myth in classical literature. But how much reinterpretation really was necessary for Herakles after the end of the classical period? After all, to a greater extent perhaps than other myths, his myth had been interpreted under the aspect of timeless relevance already in antiquity. Man choosing between good and bad, man struggling for a decent fate in a hostile universe, man fighting for justice, order, and peace, man succumbing to the power of love and death, to name only a few examples—all these are themes that have occupied men's minds and fired their imagination throughout history. The implications of the Herakles myth were, and are, anything but anachronistic.

By contrast, the figure of the hero himself could easily be so considered and has proved a principal stumbling block for vernacular adaptations. The medieval and many Renaissance writers solved the problem much as the author of the *Shield of Herakles* had done: they simply draped Herakles into the contemporary garb of a knight or nobleman and brought the external features of his exploits up to date so that he could credibly appear as the ideal *cortiere* or *preux* Herakles. In this milieu even Herakles' vaunted club was stolen easily and replaced, depending on the circumstances, by a lance, a rapier, or a scimitar. The modern reader may regard this as a naïve exercise but carried to its logical, albeit multivestite, extension, it does put into focus a central problem in the adaptation of any mythological figures. A contemporary Herakles could not possibly be represented as going out to fight a hydra, a boar, or a lion, just as a modern Ulysses would not be the hero who is braving the perils of the sea, outsmarting a one-eyed cannibal, or being trapped in the palace of a witch. The modern adaptor will abstract the meaning of such episodes and proceed to put them in contemporary terms, recreating situations that are today's equivalent to the classical, mythological events. If adapted in such a way, an ancient hero or myth might be barely recognizable in their modern dress and, as T. S. Eliot's *Cocktail Party* has shown, often they are not unless the name tag gives away the author's intent. The critics of Pound's and Joyce's literary heart transplants thus may contend that not all of the ancient trappings can be sacrificed if the modern version is to bear more than a nominal resemblance to the original one. In other words, they may argue, with some justification, that the ancient setting is not totally dispensable and in fact is instrumental in establishing a hero's identity.

Regardless of how one may feel about this question, the salient fact in this survey of Herakles' post-classical life is that whereas Ulysses found his Joyce and Kazantzakis, Herakles did not. Instead of inventing modern adventures for antiquity's most versatile and many-faceted hero and putting him into modern costume, writers from Marlowe to Eliot have preferred to do without the physical appearance of Herakles and instead transfer some of his spiritual qualities to some other hero, whether it be Tamburlaine, Antony, or Harcourt-Reilly, who in that sense are Herakles' successors. And Herakles could fare worse. One can almost feel the discomfiture of other writers, such as Shelley, d'Annunzio, Rilke, and Gide, about what to do with the hero, and more often than not, they resolved the problem by eliminating him completely.[1] A study of the particular reasons why Herakles becomes a casualty in the versions of these writers and others would be quite fascinating and revealing, but here we can be concerned only with the basic reasons and with attempting to put them in their historical perspective.

The biggest obstacles to Herakles' adaptation in contemporary terms after the Renaissance were twofold. One was the emphasis, pronounced with indelible fervour by Seneca, on his being a god. The other was the very extensiveness of his myth that tied him inextricably to the ancient world in virtually every imaginable detail. It left little room for inventive additions and discouraged even partial modernization because the bulk of Herakles' unreconstructed ancient associations would still loom oppressively large. The attempts to resolve the dilemma were as varied as the writers who undertook them. They could be intensely personal, as in the case of Browning and even more so, Hölderlin, with very little relevance for anyone but the poets themselves. Or they would provide, as Archibald MacLeish has, a contemporary setting into which the ancient myth, temples and all, could be inserted and linked with a present-day action that would underline the myth's modern relevance. Other writers, such as the French Parnassians, the Swiss Carl Spitteler, and the American Theodore Morrison, left the ancient setting intact and merely added their own interpretive touches to it.

It is this readaptation of the hero, and the difficulty writers encountered in effecting it, that is of primary interest in the tradition. Again a comparison with Ulysses is illuminating. Unlike that of the crafty Greek, the literary tradition of Herakles is not marked by the interplay of hostility and admiration which, in Stanford's well-put phrase, 'tossed his reputation up and down like a cork on the tideway'.[2] Nor was he linked nearly as closely to any particular classical author as Ulysses was to Homer and accordingly, he did not have to suffer from the philosophical and literary controversies about the merits of his creator. Vilifications of him are far and few between and in this respect postclassical tradition followed the pattern of the classical. Near the end of the latter, for instance, Lucian did not except Herakles from his satirical mockery of the gods, but at the same time we owe him one of the most inspired praises of Herakles, which he put in the mouth of a

Cynic philosopher.[3] Similarly, Sophocles had mitigated his attack on Herakles—and it should be stressed that others have read the *Trachiniae* differently—by Herakles' portrayal in the *Philoctetes*, and later onslaughts on the hero were restricted to the fathers of the church, Tertullian in particular. The vigour of the patristic attack had its peculiar reasons. Herakles was a pagan god and his patronage by Commodus and Maximian, among others, had to be taken seriously.[4] Once the religious threat he posed had vanished, Herakles, along with other pagan deities, conveniently entered into the realm of allegory and under the aspect of the supreme exemplar of virtue and justice was eventually even identified with Christ.

The following chapters, then, are intended as a survey of the vernacular adaptations of the Herakles theme. The medieval and Renaissance tradition can properly be said to be centring on the typological use of the hero and a brief sketch of the patristic background will help us to understand it better. Nonetheless, because of the variety of roles in which Herakles continues to appear simultaneously it would not be wise to write separate chapters on Herakles the philosopher, Herakles the virtuous ideal, Herakles the lover, and so on. Such characterization will be subsumed in this and the following chapters, whose organization is mostly chronological although not strictly so. Let us therefore return to Herakles' fortune in the Middle Ages and the Renaissance, where his role as the exemplar of virtue predominated though it by no means ended there. We will then proceed to his reappearance on the tragic stage, and to some reinterpretations of his character especially in the nineteenth and twentieth centuries.

The Christian fathers continued where Lucretius and the Euhemerists had left off. Whereas the philosopher Cornutus, in the first century after Christ, still had stressed that the strength of certain men in *both* body *and* mind had led to their heroization (*Compend. Theol.* 31), Lactantius and Saint Augustine were emphatic in denying Herakles every mental ability. Once more he is only the strong-man who clubs the lion, Cacus, and Cerberus, but who is outshone by Agnes, a thirteen-year-old Christian martyr who conquered the devil. 'Him that girl conquered,' adds Saint Augustine, 'who deceived many about Herakles.' Lactantius links Herakles less with the devil but is even more explicit about the hero's metaphysical limitations. 'All these works', he proclaims, 'are those of a strong man (*fortis viri*), but of a human nonetheless. For the things he overcame were fragile and mortal.' Herakles has *fortitudo*, physical strength, but he forfeits any claim to virtue by his outrageous conduct of life. Lactantius excoriates him as a lecher, libertine, and adulterer, thoroughly unfit to share in any Christian notions of divinity. But what could one expect? Herakles, after all, was a product of adultery and the depravity was congenital. Tertullian's sarcasms on Herakles' ungodly conduct are, if anything, more biting yet. Noting the curious bisexuality of Herakles' relationship to Omphale he sneers: 'So much was secret Lydia at liberty that Herakles was prostituted in Omphale and Omphale in Herakles.'[5]

The basic theme of these interpretations, it should be stressed once more, is, like so much else in patristic writings, a continuation of classical thought. Even Seneca, as we have seen, had been plagued by some doubts about Herakles' metaphysics and a pagan contemporary of Tertullian, Apuleius, offered his variation of Lucretius' comparison between Epicurus and Herakles, Seneca's between Herakles and Cato, and Saint Augustine's between Agnes and the pagan hero–god. After an Epicurean, a Stoic, and later, a Christian, a Cynic now is compared to Herakles, yet the moral of the story is the same: 'As poets tell, Herakles once subdued by his courage those frightful human and bestial monsters and cleansed the world. Similarly that philosopher was a Herakles against wrath, envy, avarice, lust, and other monsters and shameful acts of the human mind; he drove out all these diseases from the minds of men, rid families of them, and overcome malice.'[6] The only new element in the church fathers' denigration of the hero was their belief that Herakles, like the other Olympian deities, was a devilish creation. Herakles bore the brunt of their attack because, for a long time, he appeared as paganism's direct rival of Christ who was, in spite of the many similarities between the two life stories, the exact opposite of Christ: the man who became god, in contrast to the god who became man. The Christian belief was that instead of *virtus*, god's saving grace opened the doors of heaven to mankind. This is the particular reason for the shrillness of the patristic denial of Herakles' *virtus* and the pagan *dea virtus* in general. Although the odium in which the pagan gods were held abated with the official abolition of the pagan state religion, the reconciliation between the Christian dogma and the ancient concept of *virtus* as a state of perfection did not come about until the fifteenth century; even Petrarch was extremely circumspect in alluding to the story of Herakles' choice between Virtue and Vice.[7]

Through the din of the church fathers' denunciations the voice of those who saw in Herakles a paragon of spiritual rather than corporal prowess is heard only feebly. Plutarch, whose writings did much to reinforce the idealization of Herakles as a protagonist for justice and *aretē*, plays down the uniqueness of Herakles' physical strength by writing that this quality was common among the men of the age in which Herakles lived. It was his regard for justice, equity, and humanity that set him apart and made young Theseus emulate him,[8] just as Spenser's Artegall was to emulate Herakles. Plutarch also pronounced Herakles as 'most skilled in logic' and in a similar vein, Servius considered Herakles *mente magis quam corpore fortis* and explained the hero's conquest of Cerberus allegorically as his victory over all earthly lusts and vices.[9] Heracleitus the allegorist (first century A.D.) denied even more emphatically that Herakles was a champion of physical strength and insisted that he was a wise man, a philosopher, and an initiate of 'the celestial science' (*Alleg. Hom.* 33). But it was left to Fulgentius at the beginning of the sixth century to create the kind of Herakles allegory in which the Renaissance would revel. In his *Mythologiae*, Antaeus is lust, Cacus—along the lines of etymology which Hecataeus had already emphasized—evil incarnate, while the Hesperides represent the power of learning and study of which man must avail himself. Herakles is *virtus* throughout, but a *virtus* devoid of heavenly aspirations. This entirely mundane *virtus* is very akin to the Homeric *klea andrōn*; Fulgentius in fact defines Herakles as ἡρώωον κλέος—*virorum fortium fama* (2. 5). Therefore it can be overcome by libido, symbolized by Omphale, a story which Fulgentius presents very sympathetically and without the heavy-handed or sarcastic moralizing that became characteristic of it later.

Under this aspect, it was possible even for bona fide Christian writers to perpetuate Herakles' memory. In the ninth century, the bishop Theodulph of Orleans interpreted Herakles as virtue and so did Albericus of London in more detail in the twelfth.[10] Another tradition that contributed to the survival of the pagan gods during the Middle Ages was the euhemeristic tradition. Far from using Euhemerism for detraction, Isidore of Seville held that as a benefactor of humanity, Herakles had every right to be remembered with gratitude. Since he and other ancient heroes were historical figures, he assigned them a place and date in history and thus they acquired new prestige. A little more than a century later Rémy of Auxerre discarded the notion that the gods of Olympus were nothing but diabolical creatures. When Herakles fully emerged in the thirteenth century, the mantle of respectability had been draped tightly around his formerly bare shoulders, and the modes of respectability were both courtly and Christian.

What is more remarkable than the survival of the hero himself is that of his imaginative qualities. To this the renewed emphasis on Herakles as a god in the waning days of the Roman empire had been anything but conducive. Reinforcing the Roman propensity, which only Vergil and Seneca had been able to transform into literary expression, of seeing in Herakles primarily a figure of cult and religion, it threatened to undo the Greeks' emancipation of the god from the realm of religion into that of literary imagination. It was all very well for Fulgentius and others to preserve Herakles by way of allegory, but allegory has no life of its own. Thus it is delightful to see Herakles' fortunes as a medieval knight culminate in a work whose cheerful liveliness and narrative aplomb contributed much to the continued readability of the hero's exploits.

This work was the *Recueil des hystoires de Troyes* (1464) by Raoul Le Fèvre which William Caxton published in England ten years later. Caxton's version was immensely popular, with more than twenty editions of it appearing over the next two and a half centuries, and much the same was true of Le Fèvre's work in France.[11] Thus the medieval Herakles enjoyed the popularity and large reading public of a Prince Valiant and the chivalrous note was sounded again in Elizabethan verse when the spirit of the times was congenial. Le Fèvre's choice of Herakles as the hero of the first two books—the third, and least original, only was his version of Guido delle Colonne's Latin paraphrase of Benoît de Sainte Maure's *Roman de Troie*—is explained by the claim of the court of Burgundy to Herculean descent. This was a widespread phenomenon, ranging from Castile and Navarre to the Hapsburgs and spreading across the Channel even to England. What accounts for the literary interest of Le Fèvre's work, however, is his obeying Philip the Good's order to make some original additions rather than merely compiling, in the manner of Boccaccio and later, Heywood, all the ancient sources and versions. So we find a few touches here of a medieval Kazantzakis and Le Fèvre develops a sympathetic, integrated portrait of the hero from which only the starkly humorous tones are missing. The whole is a shrewd blend between keeping a semblance of the ancient flavour and transposing the rest into the medieval milieu. For instance, although ostensibly conforming to the law of Lycurgus, Herakles' education—supervised by Eurystheus, who now is appointed Herakles' foster father—is essentially that of a medieval knight. The first Olympian Games are part athletic competition and part medieval tournament. On that occasion we also catch the first glimpse of the courtly adaptation of Herakles the amorist. Gone are the days of unrestrained, exuberant passion, let alone brute animalism. At the sight of a 'right fayr damoysell Named megere' Herakles is

> sore abasshid and shamed/The damoysell
> on that other syde was also shamfaste . . .
> For as she had seen hercules wrastle, she
> had sette alle her love on hym. And they wiste
> not/none of hem bothe what to saye . . .

After a long, muted courtship and many adventures on his part he finally reveals his passion to her; they are married and he is knighted at a great tournament. Courtly etiquette and refinement led Le Fèvre to make even more thorough-going adaptations. The story of Herakles' madness, for instance, is transformed into romantic tragedy: the hero listens to Linceus' (Lycus') false accusations of adultery and kills both him and the innocent Megara. In a similar fashion, so far from being portrayed as a scruffy fellow, as he had been in the versions of Sophocles and Ovid, the river god Achelous now appears as a malignant knight to whose castle Herakles has to lay siege, and Le Fèvre dismisses Achelous' various metamorphoses as simple allegories.

Throughout this successful adaptation of Herakles into the world of the medieval romance Le Fèvre does not forget the hero's spiritual qualities. We need not dwell on the emphasis on Herakles' selfless quest for justice and his liberation of others from oppression because this manifestation of the *alexikakos* was very much akin to the chivalrous ideal and provided the most natural basis for his adaptation as a knight. Nor need we be particularly surprised at the re-emergence of Herakles' persuasive abilities, although this was only a minor trait in the Latin tradition which Le Fèvre utilized. More startling are his academic pursuits that far exceed any intellectual efforts with which he was credited in the classical tradition. He goes to Atlas, the king of Libya, whose principal possession is not the sky, but a bulk of books. In a total reversal from the boorish nature boy who slew Linus because he worked him too hard, Herakles now smites Atlas when Atlas at first is reluctant to teach him. Ruefully, Atlas loads all his books on a camel —or, in one manuscript, a mule (Plate 13)—and follows Herakles to the court of Affer, the king of Egypt. As soon as he hears, however, that Herakles was 'the moste noble and vertuous man that ever had been' he teaches him all his sciences and his pupil turns out to be an academic prodigy: 'he lerned and prouffited by quyk and sharp engyne in suche wise that he comprised all/And that afterward he became the beste philosopher and the most parfyt astronomyen of all the world'.

Atlas thereupon joins Herakles' entourage for the hero's next few adventures which tax his mind as well as his body. The Lernaean hydra, for instance, is as formidable for her Sphinx-like, sophistic riddles as for her fierceness in battle. The story of her seven heads, Le Fèvre explains, really refers to her disputative powers: when Herakles had answered one of her questions, 'the monstre replyed by seven argumentes'. But 'all way hercules was full of philosophie and expert in all scyence', and therefore he succeeds in defeating the monster. More peacefully, the hero proceeds with Atlas to Athens to teach philosophy and astronomy, and again Le Fèvre metamorphoses one of Herakles' physical feats into an academic one. Because he was such an authority on astronomy, the students said 'that he susteyned and bare the heven on his sholders'. Herakles' intellectual curiosity never leaves him, pragmatically linked as it is with his exploits. For example, he turns many a page trying to solve the mystery of the smoke that envelops Cacus and he again summons Atlas as a scientific adviser. In his endeavour to bring some learning to the natives of Spain, he founds a 'study' at Salamanca, but the local students 'were so rude and dulle that their wyttes coude not compryse any connyng of scyence'. Faced with this rather common dilemma and not wanting to see his educational dreams shattered, Herakles hits upon a device for which many a modern professor might secretly envy him: he creates a life-like statue of himself which teaches and answers questions as he would, while he goes on an indefinite leave of absence. And it is he, and not Athens, that is the school of Greece and noblemen flock to him to 'proufitte in vertue, in noblesse, in honour, in armes, in phylosophye, in astronomye, and in alle other perfeccion, etc.' This enumeration—it does not include Herakles' amorous adventures to which Le Fèvre, catering to the spirit of the age, added a few—is a good summary of the author's concept of the hero.

One might think at first that Le Fèvre fleshed out the simple portrait of Herakles as a knight by adding the emphasis on his intellectual pursuits because of the influences of the Renaissance. But the curious fact is that the Renaissance took a far more one-sided view of the hero which is quite removed from the *homo universalis* of the *Recuyell.* Aside from the bulky moral tradition, to which we shall turn soon, comparison is especially instructive with a work that was written under much the same circumstances as Le Fèvre's and appeared in print almost in the same year (1475). That was *Le fatiche d'Ercole* by Pietro Andrea de Bassi, a courtier of Niccolo d'Este.[12] Like Le Fèvre, de Bassi was urged by his prince to write on Herakles for reasons of dynastic genealogy; Ercole I d'Este, Niccolo's son, was born in 1433 and it is to him that we owe the magnificently printed first edition. De Bassi, like Le Fèvre, knows how to tell a good story, although in a more prolix, long-winded, and, eventually, somewhat repetitious manner as the work is organized around the twenty-three labours that the author counted up in his sources. Herakles' mores again are adapted to those of the court, especially in regard to his exploits as a ladies' man, but any intellectual effort yields to exultant corporality from the outset. Herakles is well educated all right, as any Italian prince would by the age of fifteen, and he knows his grammar, philosophy, and astronomy. But enough is enough: '*Piaceva ad Hercule la scientia, ma di longo più li piaceva adoperare le corporale forze ale quali li pari non trovava.*' The views of an Italian Renaissance prince would be no different. Accordingly, Herakles has no academic avocations nor does he find his intellectual mettle tested by sophism-spouting hydras. In contrast to Le Fèvre, who even interpreted such labours as supporting the heavens and slaying the hydra in intellectual terms, the exploits of de Bassi's hero are entirely physical.

There were, to be sure, intimations of Herakles' intellectual prowess in Petrarch's unfinished sketch of Herakles' life, and in Boccaccio whose *Genealogiae* were utilized both by Le Fèvre and de Bassi. In Heracleitus' vein Petrarch speaks of Herakles as '*famosior philosophus*' and defines him further as a prototype of 'those who earned equally outstanding fame in martial exploits and natural capacities,'[13] the latter perhaps referring to the talents of the mind. Yet the most significant reason for his achievement and fame remained his corporal strength.[14] Boccaccio, who discusses and approves many of the allegorical interpretations, mentions the view, which can be traced as far back as Plato, that the Hydra symbolized a sophist, and he emphatically agrees with the view that Atlas in reality was an astronomer.[15] By and large, however, Herakles' labours are still those of *virtù*, not of *virtus*, the same *virtù* with all its corporal associations that found its most splendid artistic expression in the works of Pollaiouolo.

In sum, Le Fèvre's Herakles stands out as one of the few great vernacular portraits of the hero. Amidst his medieval accoutrements, Herakles' outlook is curiously turned towards the original Greek conception of him. He is not the Thunderer's son, as in Seneca's plays, who overawes ordinary mortals, but once more he is totally human, beset by human weaknesses like each one of us, and the 'good comrade' with whom the simple denizen of the Greek world had felt comfortable. He is not a man like Euripides' hero, who truculently wrestles with the harsh decrees of Fortune, but he is a human being who through his extraordinary talents, his own means and *aretē* overcomes all obstacles—monsters, tyrants, and temptation.[16] By a spark of imaginative sympathy Le Fèvre evoked the authentic Herakles and the hope and dream he incarnated. For Le Fèvre, the most common kind of Herakles literature of his day, the allegories, was only a starting point and he deprived them of their aridity by transforming them into splendid and engaging narrative.

Such, however, unfortunately was not the general fate of Herakles during the Renaissance. While Le Fèvre still had the talent and the imagination to make the story of the myth live on—and that is the primary reason for the immense success of the *Recuyell*—most other authors, to use a distinction made by Benedetto Croce,[17] were preoccupied with the myth's interpretation. Simply placing the story into the contemporary milieu would not do; it was far more important to ask what Herakles stood for and what his myth was really all about. And this interpretation of the myth, in contrast to Euripides or Vergil or post-Renaissance authors such as Browning or Pound, did not take place within the framework of literary creation, but it mostly was exegesis pure and simple. It was not until Spenser's *Faerie Queene* that the two would coalesce again.

The earliest and most comprehensive works of the kind were written both in Italy and Spain. Characteristically enough, the starting point of Coluccio Salutati's *De laboribus Herculis* (*ca.* 1406) was the request of a friend to interpret for him Seneca's *Hercules Furens*.[18] After the friend's death, however, the Florentine chancellor and humanist broadened the scope of the undertaking and his unfinished work, interspersed with many digressions, is a methodological compendium of the various interpretations that had come to be proposed for each episode. Diligent categorization now takes creativity's place: the hero's labours can be understood either *ad litteram*, or *moraliter*, or *naturaliter*, and allegory asserts itself as the dominant mode of interpretation. Salutati does not deny the historical existence of Herakles and most of his opponents, and his documentation from the ancient authors is impressive for this and any other views. Still, for him all this is only a convenient starting point for establishing abstractions. To the diversity of Herakles' traits and exploits, which had accumulated in antiquity, now is added the systematic and massive diversity of their interpretation. This put an organic and coherent *vita* of the hero beyond reach, and rather than look at Herakles as the amalgam of compartmentalized and rather schematic *modi interpretandi*, Salutati shifted the emphasis to the view of the hero as a symbol of an abstract idea. He is not only *homo virtuosus*, *virtuosissimus* Herakles, *homo virtuosus in fortitudine atque constantia*, but he is virtue itself, 'a higher state of virtue', 'reason', and 'both virtue and reason'; he is not only a concrete *vir contemplativus*, but he is the 'light of explored truth'.[19] What is important is not so much that Salutati cites the poets' view of Herakles as a *vir perfectissimus*, which struck a responsive chord in the Renaissance, but that Herakles ceases to live as such a man and becomes the incarnation of an abstract idea instead. He symbolizes virtue in all its aspects—physical, moral, spiritual, and even intellectual—and this virtue is active, as is indicated by Salutati's etymology for 'Herakles': *heris kleos* in Greek, *gloria litis* in Latin, or 'glorious in strife' (3. 9. 5). Yet we do not any longer have a living, breathing Herakles before us, but a type.

Although devoid of Salutati's massive erudition, Enrique de Villena's *Los doze trabajos de Hercules* (1417) essentially follows the same method as the *De laboribus Herculis*.[20] The accents may be somewhat more concrete here and there, but the analytic scheme for each episode is followed more rigorously yet. Writing for his peers who could not read Latin, the Spanish aristocrat follows Boethius' canon of the twelve labours—the researches of Salutati, by comparison, had turned up thirty-one—and subdivides each episode into the account according to the poets (*istoria nuda*), an allegorical interpretation (*declaración*), followed by the historical or euhemeristic 'truth' (*verdad*) and finally, the moral and practical application (*aplicación*) with reference to the twelve estates of Spanish society. For example, Antaeus symbolizes the desires of the flesh, fostered constantly by contact with carnality, i.e. the earth. The historical truth is that Antaeus was a king in Libya; he was called a giant because he was taller than anyone else, and he was cruel and given to 'las terrenales e carnales cosas.' The moral, addressed to the professors and academics, is to check all carnal inclinations because they are the worst enemy of scholarship and virtue.

Besides the schematization of Herakles' role, then, the greatest stress is laid on Herakles as a moral force. The facile help of allegory was enlisted to rid the hero of any objectionable inconsistencies of character. Herakles' madness is the most revealing case in point. We have already seen that Le Fèvre changed the story significantly so it would not inject a jarring note into Herakles' chivalresque adventures. Salutati was even more radical: according to him, the slaying of Megara is a triumph of the soul over the flesh. And as Megara's three sons are symbols of irascibility, sensuality, and concupiscence, Herakles has every good reason for murdering them.[21] Not since Pindar had Herakles been justified so abruptly and the literary potential with which the story had provided Euripides and Seneca now is eliminated virtually over night.

We will see, however, that this does not apply to the treatment of Herakles on the tragic stage which followed its own laws and therefore will be discussed separately.

The concept—and we cannot speak of portrait any more—of Herakles, which Salutati and Villena had anticipated, dominates the sixteenth-century view of the hero. He is no longer only the magnanimous hero who reaches 'to the toppe of . . . glory', as Castiglione had regarded him, as did Dante and Abraham Fraunce,[22] but there is an unremitting stream of writings that extol his moral value. So far from being inventive, the two great compendia of classical mythology, Natale Conti's *Mythologiae libri decem* (1551) and Vicenzo Cartari's *Images of the Gods* (1556), are a solid and influential reflection of the interpretation of classical mythology at the time.[23] Proceeding from the etymology of Herakles' name, Conti declares that for him it is a symbol of 'honour, courage, and virtuous excellence of mind and body alike' (p. 708). Conti, Cartari and, somewhat later, Piero Valeriano[24] hold that Herakles' victories over monsters and tyrants represent the triumphs of the virtuous mind over all sorts of vice. Cartari further stresses Herakles' strength of mind ('fortitudinem in animo'), his suppression of *indomitas animi cupiditates*, and his tranquillity of mind amid turbulence. While these handbooks at least mentioned some other interpretations of the Herakles myth, the contemporary emblem books were even more one-sided in their emphasis on Herakles representing virtue. In Cesare Ripa's *Iconologia* (1593) Herakles comes to mean 'Valore', both physical and of the mind: 'Valour being a joining of the virtue of the body with that of the entire soul.' He is the emblem of heroic virtue, which has three constituent parts: 'First, the moderation of anger, second, the tempering of greed, and last, the general contempt for strife, for pleasure, and thus for talking.'[25] In another emblem he is shown slaying a dragon, which Ripa explains as the subduing of concupiscence by virtue. Herakles' traditional garb, the lion's skin, symbolizes generosity and strength of mind and the club represents reason. Both Ripa and Andrea Alciati in his *Emblematum liber* (1531) dwell on Herakles' choice of virtue over vice. So, in even more detail, does Geoffrey Whitney in his *Choice of Emblems* that is based on Alciati. After listening to the two ladies at length, Herakles states his choice in these words:[26]

Oh pleasure, thoughe thie waie bee smoothe, and faire,
And sweete delightes in all thy courtes abounde:
Yet can I heare, of none that haue bene there,
That after life, with fame haue been renoumde:
  For honor hates, with pleasure to remaine,
  Then houlde thy peace, thow wastes thie winde in vaine.
But heare, I yeelde oh vertue to thie will,
And vowe my selfe, all labour to indure,
For to ascende the steepe, and craggie hill,
The toppe whereof, whoe so attaines, is sure
  For his rewarde, to haue a crowne of fame
  Thus HERCULES obey'd this sacred dame.

Whitney describes Herakles as a man who will struggle all his life against pleasure and vice. His good qualities will be exemplary and his turbulent and complex temper is ignored.

The revival of Hercules Prodicius in Italy and England had been preceded by the reappearance of this theme in German humanism at the end of the fifteenth century. The fable had been dormant during the Middle Ages, but Sebastian Brant, in his *Ship of Fools* (1494), used the version of the church father Basilius.[27] Though Brant mentioned the parable only in passing, the immense popularity of his work doubtless helped to engender that of the fable. Already in 1490, a dramatization of it had figured in the entry of Charles VIII in Vienne, and it was followed by a host of others on the stage of the early sixteenth century. Jacob Locher, drawing heavily on Silius Italicus, expanded it into a *Concertatio Virtutis cum Voluptate* and Brant himself, in Strasburg in 1512, staged a play that dealt exclusively with Herakles' choice. Underscoring the moral relevance of the play, many other adaptors replaced Herakles with their ruling monarchs—Maximilian, Charles V, Francois I and Henry II of France, and others. Latin and vernacular translations of Xenophon's version were finally made, that by Budé perhaps being the most famous.

The importance of these plays and the many poems that were written on the same subject does not lie in their literary merits but in the almost axiomatic association they were able to inflict on our hero (cf. Plate 14).

Certainly, the transformation of a philosophical parable into something more than drama of recitation—a task at which only few authors succeeded—is interesting to study, but the dramaturgical problems were not insoluble and an old hand like Metastasio, for instance, could easily inject some suspense and emotion into the story by making Virtue appear as a *dea ex machina* just when vicious catastrophe was about to strike.[28] More importantly, Herakles' role now was narrowed down drastically. Instead of being the best of men, he became merely the most virtuous of men, and instead of the multiple interpretations that had characterized the work even of an unimaginative writer like de Villena, moral interpretation pure and simple prevailed. Episodes from Herakles' life could of course always be moralized easily and were; in his earliest appearance in English literature, to name but one example, the Monk's Tale in Chaucer's *Canterbury Tales*, Herakles' fatal love for Deianeira is used as an example of a worthy, mighty man being overthrown by the caprice of Fortune. But this was only *en passant* and did not compare to the moral intensity with which our hero came to be regarded now. The result for the literary tradition was that Herakles attracted many writers who, *a priori*, considered the utility of literature in moral terms and therefore were looking for a moral hero.

A programmatic example of this attitude is found in the middle of the sixteenth century when Giovambattista Giraldi Cintio, a friend of the d'Este family, published his epopee, *Dell'Ercole canti ventisei* (1557). Giraldi clarified his intent in a letter to Bernardo Tasso.[29] To him, 'poetry is nothing else but a first philosophy which, like a schoolmistress of life working secretly, proposes to us under poetic covering the image of a civilized and praiseworthy life drawn from the fountain of that philosophy'. The poet, according to him, must seek to represent conduct that is appropriate to 'honest and honourable living, to praiseworthy actions' and he has attended to morality throughout 'by praising the virtues, condemning the vices, and giving wherever necessary the rewards to the former and the punishments to the latter, in order to instruct persons of various ranks, according to their station, in the praiseworthy life'. This is not to say that Giraldi's *Ercole* is a monotonous sermon in epic verse. There are entertaining digressions, many invented by the author himself. But while there is a vestige of inventiveness, there is no genuine creativeness, and even the devices for the *delectare*

are ancillary to the wish to instruct. Giraldi's epic cannot rank with Ariosto's or Torquato Tasso's, and this is not Herakles' fault. With much the same principles in mind as Giraldi, the humanist and Sevillan poet Juan de Mal Lara (1523–71) wrote a lengthy poem on Herakles' seventeen labours, which has not been preserved[30] whereas Lilio Gregorio Giraldi's *Vita Herculis*, a prose work (1539), is squarely in the tradition of Salutati. Literary inventiveness and the desire to entertain are forsaken completely, and both Herakles' moral monstrosity and the author's monotonously monumental erudition smother whatever *vita* there was left in Herakles by that time.

So Herakles *moralizatus* was, if not reborn, at least created in large part in the Renaissance and was to hold his sway well into the eighteenth century. Prodicus, for one, certainly would have been surprised at the moralistic fortunes of his hero because such had not been the primary intent of his parable. But there was a cross-current which channelled Herakles' energies in a more active and less priggish direction. It appeared almost simultaneously both in France at the end of the Middle Ages and in early Florentine humanism and shows once more that Herakles could be many individual things to many individual men. At the beginning of the fifteenth century, we find the poetess Christine de Pisan urging the noblemen in her manual of the perfect knight to aspire to Herakles' *vertus nobles et fortes*.[31] These virtues, which imply strength both of the body and the mind, are not meant to be passive; the knight can do on earth what Herakles accomplished by descending to hell:

> Assez trouveras guerre en terre
> Sans que l'ailles en enfer querre.

This view of Herakles as representing the life of action replaced its opposite that had been prevalent in the Middle Ages. A medieval commentary, for instance, which was attributed falsely to Saint Thomas, glossed the exhortation that Boethius had appended to his list of Herakles' twelve labours—*ite nunc fortes*—as meaning that the virtuous should overcome the desires of the flesh through a life of contemplation.[32] By so doing they would be received into the Christian heaven. Similarly, although without any Christian overtones, the author of the *Integumenta Ovidii* interprets Herakles as representing the *virtus* of reflection, which is under attack from Juno, the active life.[33]

The Florentine humanists, however, voiced exactly the same view as Christine de Pisan did at that very time. They were attracted to Herakles because he was a natural symbol of the active life. Even if the surprising preference of these men for the active life can be explained by contemporary circumstances—Florence was fighting for her life against Milan; Herakles, who had been placed on the Florentine seal at the end of the thirteenth century, was a slayer of tyrants as well as monsters—their outlook did live on. Some fifty years later, Marsilio Ficino used Herakles to illustrate the superiority of fortitude over temperance: while temperance keeps us from becoming beasts, fortitude may transport us to the estate of the all-conquering gods. In this way the *fortitudo*, to which the church fathers had limited Herakles, is sublimated without any loss of its physical connotations. Ficino's teacher, Cristoforo Landino, had considered Herakles as the supreme example of the active and, at the same time, wise life: 'Hercules was wise. But not wise for himself; rather, his wisdom served almost all men. For in his wanderings over the greater part of the world, he destroyed horrendous wild beasts, vanquished pernicious and savage monsters, chastised the most cruel tyrants.'[34] In England, William Fulbecke, the author of *A Booke on Christian Ethics* (1587), cited the glory of Herakles' choice to illustrate that one cannot be Herakles without being active and a few years later, Grimaldus Goslicius used the Herakles story to make the point that the contemplative life cannot be virtuous.[35]

Occasionally, as Fulbecke's remark shows, the impulse for a moral interpretation of Herakles in terms of the active life could come from the conception of Herakles as Christ. More often than not, however, the identification of Herakles with Christ, just like the Herakles Prodicius, would freeze into the rigid pose of typology. What we may call, for lack of a better term, Herakles' Christian fortune began in literature in the early fourteenth century. We have already mentioned the scriptural allegory of the *Ovide Moralisé* by Chrétien le Gouays. Where Fulgentius and Salutati had merely allegorized, Chrétien le Gouays uses anagogic allegory with the same uncompromising zeal. Herakles' conquests, for instance, of Busiris, Diomedes, the Hydra, Geryon, the Amazons and Achelous represent the victorious battles of Christ, the Saviour, who

Toute pechié vainquit et toute vice,
toute errour et toute malice
et pour le peuple delivrer
volt son cors à paine livrer
et mort reçut joieusement
en la crois pour le sauvement
et pour l'amour de ses amis.[36]

At about the same time, Dante compared Herakles' descent into hell with Christ's and in a *canzone* that is commonly attributed to him, invoked Herakles to return to earth once more to do his work of righting all wrongs and purifying the lands.[37] While ostensibly addressing Herakles, Dante here doubtless thinks of Christ. He invokes Herakles with '*O di Iddio vero erede, che vivi in fama e sarai in sempiterno*.' The poem ends with a Herculean paraphrase of the *Salve Regina*:

E poi in luogo del gran Atalante
Le stelle e'l ciel' rotante
Sostenne in questa dolorosa valle:
Cosi sostenga il mondo con le spalle.

The *canzone* that follows makes the parallelism even clearer as it is addressed to Mary whom Dante invokes in similar terms and in a similar capacity as he does Herakles.

In spite of all superficial similarities, Chrétien le Gouays' and Dante's Christianizations of Herakles are a world apart. Dante was no simplistic zealot who interpreted pagan myths in terms of a Christian *philosophia moralis*. But what are we to make of his identification of the two saviours? Is it a clever literary exercise or a deliberate resurrection of a pagan mystery? Neither explanation would do justice to Dante's thought. His Christian Herakles is characteristic of Dante's work in that it shows the convergence and interpretation of the classical and the Christian traditions. The second merely continued the first; even before the arrival of Christendom the classical Herakles had had an *anima naturaliter Christiana*. The fusion of the classical with the Christian imagination is entirely natural.

Such harmony is lacking in Ronsard's *Hymne de l'Hercule Chrestien*, the most programmatic and also, most controversial proclamation of

Herakles as another Christ.[38] Ronsard proceeds from the view which had gained much acceptance in the preceding centuries, in England notably through John Ridewall, that the Greek myths were prophetic just like the Hebraic. The pagans, however, deaf to the revelation as the Jews had been,

> ont converty les paroles predittes
> Que pour toy seul la Sybille avoit dittes
> A leurs faux dieux, contre toute raison,
> Attribuant maintenant à Jason,
> et maintenant à un Hercule estrange
> Ce qui estoit de propre à ta loüenge.

Still, the poet continues, even the most perverted mind cannot fail to see

> Que la plupart des choses qu'on escrit
> D'Hercule est deüe à Jesus Christ.

And Ronsard goes on to list eighteen parallels between Jesus and Herakles—far fewer, incidentally, than scholars in our century have found in support of their theories[39]—from their birth, threatened by the serpents and Herod's soldiers, to their death on Calvary/Oeta.

Ronsard's hymn met with heavy criticism from the Huguenots and a mixed response from the Catholics. Because of his positive connotations as the defender of truth, justice, and the divine law, Herakles' name could not escape being injected into the struggle of the reformers; Luther, for example, was cast as the German Alcides, slaying the hydra of Papism, as was Henry VIII in England and Zwingli as *Hercules Helveticus* by his Swiss compatriots. Nor was Herakles absent from the discussions of the reformers and their sympathizers. Erasmus, in his customary, enlightened way, held that one could learn more from the labours of Herakles than from a sacred work or superficial reading of the Bible, whereas Reuchlin echoed the church fathers' strictures about Herakles' morals.[40] It is a commentary on the times that flawed as it is, Ronsard's hymn stands out as a literary creation. It is a *tour de force* that has no real connection with any earlier or later Christianizing views of Herakles and it did not take a stand on the question that had interested the Middle Ages and the Florentine humanists most, i.e.

whether Herakles stood for the active or the contemplative life. But against the background which we have just traced it is also clear that Ronsard at least transposed Herakles from the realm of moral exhortation and propagandistic squabbles into that of literary exercise. Neither the Herakles *moralisé* nor Herakles as a typological symbol may strike us as particularly satisfying. But at least the latter, because it was inherently a more literary creation, could be given genuine poetic expression and power by a great poet, and in England, John Milton did what Dante had done in Italy.

'Throughout his life', as Merritt Y. Hughes has written, 'Milton instinctively thought of Herakles as symbolically related to Christ.'[41] In one of his earliest poems, *On the Morning of Christ's Nativity* (1629), the image of Herakles/Christ strangling the snakes is the culmination of the review of the pagan deities. In the poem on *The Passion*, which was written one year later, Milton again described Christ in Herculean terms:

> Most perfect hero, tried in heaviest plight
> of labours huge and hard, too hard for human wight.

The most famous instance of Milton's identification of Christ with Herakles occurs at the climax of *Paradise Regained*. There the fall of Satan is compared to the conquering of Antaeus by Herakles (4. 562–71):

> But Satan smitten with amazement fell
> As when Earth's son Antaeus (to compare
> Small things with greatest) in Irassa strove
> With Jove's Alcides, and oft foil's still rose,
> Receiving from his mother Earth new strength,
> Fresh from his fall, and fiercer grapple join'd
> Throttl'd at length in th'Air, expir'd and fell;
> So after many a foil the Tempter proud,
> Renewing fresh assaults, amidst his pride
> Fell whence he stood to see his victor fall.

In contrast to Ronsard's lengthy and forced parallels, Milton reserved the use of Herakles as a suggestive symbol of Christ for a few, but extremely significant occasions and integrated it harmoniously into the context of his poems.

Aside from Browning, Edmund Spenser in his *Faerie Queene* is the major English poet who made the most extensive use of Herakles. Much of his preference for Herakles has been attributed, with some justification, to the conventions of Renaissance epic especially as defined by Torquato Tasso.[42] The heroic poem was, ideally, to present a solution to the problem of the relationship between the active and the contemplative life. By that time, the view prevailed that the virtuous life was one of action, and we have already seen that Herakles had come to exemplify it. The action, however, could not be so represented as to make it appear that it was of value *per se*, but it was always meant only to reflect the virtue that guided it. To make this meaning explicit, the heroic poet used allegory, and for that purpose Herakles, with his long tradition of allegorical interpretation, again suggested himself readily.

Why, then, did Spenser not write a *Herculeid* outright? The subject had been on his mind, as is evident from the words he puts in the mouth of Calliope, the epic Muse, in *The Teares of the Muses*. Epic heroes, she laments, who were once 'wont the world with famous acts to fill', are now 'corrupted through the rust of time'. That, however, applies only to the externals of their 'famous acts'. As inspirational examples of virtue these heroes have lost none of their validity:

> Therefore the nurse of vertue I am hight,
> And golden Trompet of eternitie,
> That lowly thoughts life up to heavens hight,
> And mortall men have powre to deifie:
> Bacchus and Hercules I raised to heaven,
> And Charlemaine, amongst the Starris seaven.

In other words, one might think that Spenser was bothered by certain anachronisms as far as the externals of the 'famous acts' of Herakles were concerned, although he considered their moral meaning, as is very clear from the *Faerie Queene*, completely valid. But this is hardly true. For the literal monsters against whom the knights of the *Faerie Queene* fight are every bit as fantastic as those overcome by Herakles; it suffices to mention Orgoglio and his Beast, Geryoneo, and the Blatant Beast.

What is more, some are deliberately modelled on Herakles' antagonists. We must look elsewhere for the reasons Spenser made Arthur and his knights, rather than Herakles, the actual heroes of his epic.

Ultimately, these reasons—patriotic and genealogical—are not too different from Vergil's and even Ronsard's, who ignored the urging of Jacques Peletier du Mans[43] and wrote a *Franciade* instead of an *Herculeid*. It is especially the comparison between Spenser's and Vergil's use of Herakles that reveals profound similarities and suggests that in his adaptation of Herakles, some general, poetic reasons were at work along with the specific, contemporary theories of genre. Herakles was connected with the beginnings of England—at Spenser's time notably by William Warner[44]—because of his conquest of the tyrant Albion much as he had been with the beginnings of Rome through his conquest of Cacus. Unlike Livy and Dionysius, Sir Walter Raleigh even held that the legends of Herakles were 'truly written, without adition of Poeticall vanitie'.[45] Arthur's credentials, however, as a vernacular hero and a Christian were still more impeccable than Herakles' and recommended him better as the hero of an English epic. But once more it is, as in the *Aeneid* and, more remotely, in the *Philoctetes*, the ideal presence of Herakles that permeates the *Faerie Queene*. The only difference is that in keeping with the literary taste of the times, this presence—when explicitly stated—takes the form of allegories. Like Aeneas, Arthur and Artegall are not compared exclusively with Herakles, and a recent writer has aptly observed that 'references to Herakles in the *Faerie Queene* are persistent but intermittent, often dimly felt rather than explicitly stated'.[46] Superior poet that he was, Spenser, like Vergil, did not use the Herculean analogies to set up a schematic, controlling structure, but as in Milton and Vergil, they are an integral part, above all, of the poetry and the poetic contexts of the *Faerie Queene*.

It is mainly Arthur to whom the Herculean analogies are applied, but through deliberate contextual associations—again very much in the manner of Vergil—they are linked to the principal adventures of the individual knights. In the First Book, for instance, the Red Cross Knight's fight with the Dragon anticipates Arthur's with Orgoglio's beast. Both monsters are reminiscent of the Hydra—and Orgoglio's beast is explicitly compared to her (I. vii. 17. 1–5). In the battle with the Dragon, Spenser suggests a more general parallel between the labours of Herakles and Red Cross' works. The latter's sufferings are greater than Herakles' final agony (I. xi. 27):

> Not that great Champion of the antique world,
> Whom famous Poetes verse so much doth vaunt,
> And hath for twelve huge labours high extold,
> So many furies and sharpe fits did haunt,
> When him the poysoned garment did enchaunt,
> When Centaures bloud and bloudy verses charm'd;
> As did this knight twelve thousand dolours daunt,
> Whom fyrie steele now burnt, that erst him arm'd;
> That erst him goodly arm'd, now most of all him harm'd.

Of course these episodes have allegorical meanings as the monsters define the vices—sophistry, tyranny, and ignorance—that oppose holiness, and Spenser's comparison of Red Cross with Herakles takes on its full significance in the light of the Renaissance commonplace that Christ was a more perfect Herakles. Yet their expression is anything but hackneyed, and these meanings do not heavily interpose themselves between Spenser's poetry and its appreciation by the reader.

We may leave aside other well-known Herakles analogies in the *Faerie Queene*—the most famous perhaps is Arthur's fight against Maleger, which is modelled on Herakles' against Antaeus (Libido)—and instead concentrate on Book V, in which the Herculean reminiscences are most pervasive. Nor is this an accident. The subject of the book is Justice, and Herakles' most prominent role in the tradition had been that of a bringer and establisher of justice. Therefore Spenser associates Artegall, the book's champion, with Herakles at the outset even more obviously than Vergil had connected Aeneas and Herakles at the beginning of the *Aeneid* (V. i. 2–3. 2):

> Such first was Bacchus, that with furious might
> All th'East, before untam'd, did over-ronne,
> And wrong repressed, and establisht right,
> Which lawlesse men had formerly fordonne:
> There Justice first her princely rule begonne.
> Next Hercules his like ensample shewed,
> Who all the West with equall conquest wonne,

And monstrous tyrants with his club subdewed:
The club of Justice dread with kingly powre endewed.
And such was he of whom he I have to tell,
The Champion of true Justice, Artegall.

This initial parallel with Herakles sets the tone for the entire Book. Spenser's use of Herakles here goes well beyond establishing allegorical equations. At the beginning, it serves to point up the universal implications of his subject. Spenser goes on to eschew any simple analogies that might have suggested themselves to a lesser poet; the details of Artegall's battle, for instance, against Grantorto owe nothing to the Herakles myth. The analogies Spenser draws are more subtle and significant. Artegall's character from youth to maturity is so described as to suggest Herakles', 'compounded of the same faults, promising the same virtues'.[47] Like Herakles' problems, those of Artegall are more internal than external. Before he can restore justice in lawless Fairy Land, Spenser's hero has to come to grips with his own discordant nature.

Artegall's companion is Talus 'who in his hand an yron flale did hould/With which he thresht out falsehood, and did truth unfould' (V. i. 12. 8–9). The club of Herakles, an emblem of prudence and wisdom, thus belongs to Artegall's arsenal, since Talus is to 'doe whatever thing he (Artegall) did intend' (V. i. 12. 5). With this weapon Talus overcomes Braggadocchio, who at a crucial moment is called Sanglier and thus is compared to the Erymanthian Boar (V. i. 20. 7), whereas Talus, like the conqueror of the Nemean lion, is 'strong as Lyon in his lordly might' (V. i. 20. 5). The most common allegorical interpretation of Herakles' conquest of the boar was the quelling of intemperance, and Spenser's handling of this theme provides one of the clearest examples of his meaningful use of the Herakles myth. Not content with showing that Intemperance, as personified by Sir Sanglier, has been overcome, he proceeds to develop the relevance of the episode to Artegall himself. Spenser's method is not unlike Euripides' as he splits up his Herakles type into two different characters. Talus takes care of the externals of the fight: it is he rather than Artegall who bodily overcomes the opponent. But then Spenser makes us look into Artegall's soul and shows that his hero yet has to overcome the far more important *sanglier* within. In the next canto, we see him lacking self-control: he creates havoc at the tournament of Virtue, lets Braggadocchio reassert himself so he can discomfit Florimell, and finally throws such a temper tantrum that he himself, the appointed bringer of peace, has to be 'pacified' (V. iii. 36. 5). In the preceding Book, he was defeated by Britomart because he fell to pride, wrath, and desire, and the pattern is repeated in the fifth canto of Book V when he succumbs to Radigund, the queen of Amazons. Whereas Herakles overcame Hippolyte, Artegall is a Herakles *manqué* who, however, comes to share another fate with his model (V. v. 24):

> Who had him seene, imagine mote thereby,
> That whylome hath of Hercules bene told,
> How for fair Iolas sake he did apply
> His mightie hands, the distaffe vile to hold,
> For his huge club, which had subdew'd of old
> So many monsters, which the world annoyed;
> His Lyons skin chaunged to a pall of gold,
> In which, forgetting warres, he only joyed
> In combats of sweet love, and with his mistresse toyed.

In adapting this episode, Spenser again went beyond the limitations of the tradition. While the Latin poets had treated the theme with romantic sentimentalization, the moralistic tradition, retaining some of Tertullian's bite, used it for the purpose of ironic instruction. At Spenser's time, for instance, Sir Philip Sidney had this comment:[48]

> So in Hercules, painted with his great beard, and furious countenauance, in a womans attyre, spinning, at Omphales commaundement: for the representing of so straunge a power in Love, procures delight, and the scornefulnesse of the action, stirreth laughter.

By contrast, Spenser makes this often ridiculed episode the turning point of Artegall's adventures. Deprived of all his external and physical glory as Herakles was after his madness in Euripides' play, Artegall falls back on his inner resources. He accepts his state (V. v. 26. 1–6):

> Thus there long while continu'd Artegall,
> Serving proud Radigund with true subjection,

> How ever it his noble heart did gall
> T'obay a womans tyrannous direction,
> That might have had of life or death election:
> But, having chosen, now he might not chaunge.

Or, as Andrew Marvell put it, Artegall makes destiny his choice, and the same was true of Euripides' hero. He resists any further temptations of his pride, redeems his past failings, and gradually grows into wisdom. It is now that he can begin his true quest for justice. And Spenser, like Euripides, purposely inverts Artegall's exploits: 'In the following cantos, Spenser has presented his hero with situations deliberately analogous to those that revealed his past failings but which now demonstrate his commitment and capabilities.'[49]

For the performance of these labours, Artegall is joined by Arthur. Artegall's development has shown what it takes to be a knight in the manner of Herakles and we now can fully understand the implications of Arthur's role. By becoming a Herakles primarily of inner strength, Artegall now is truly what his name signifies—Art-e-gal, Arthur's peer. Arthur then overcomes the Soldan, another Diomedes (V. viii. 31). Later, both Artegall and Arthur defeat Malengin/Cacus and Arthur continues the Herakles pattern by defeating Geryon's son, Geryoneo. Finally, the end of the Book once more sets into relief Artegall's spiritual progress. He frees Irena in a similar way to Herakles' rescue of Hesione and this is the moment of his greatest triumph—he has established peace. But like Horace's Herakles, Artegall has to confront a final enemy: *Invidia*, Envie. Writing with Augustus in mind, Horace remarked that only death could set an end to the struggle against envy.[50] Spenser adapted the theme freely and made the assault of Envy, Detraction, and the Blatant Beast the last, but limited test of Artegall (V. xii. 42):

> And still among most bitter wordes they spake,
> Most shamefull, most unrighteous, most untrew,
> That they the mildest man alive would make
> Forget his patience, and yeeld vengeaunce dew
> To her, that so false sclaunders at him threw:

> And more, to make them pierce and wound more deepe,
> She with the sting, which in her vile tongue grew,
> Did sharpen them, and in fresh poyson steepe:
> Yet he past on, and seem'd of them to take no keepe.

Artegall's stoic resolve and inner peace can be shaken as little as Herakles'.[51]

It is more than probable that Spenser made use of the Herakles myth in the subsequent books of the *Faerie Queene*. Much likelihood speaks for an Arthurian analogue to the Prometheus episode, but we can leave such speculations to those who are better equipped to engage in them. Spenser's adaptation suggests other considerations that are of greater relevance for the literary tradition of the myth.

There is, above all, the striking similarity between his associative, allusive technique and that of Vergil and, even more importantly, the equally striking similarity between Spenser's and Euripides' view of Herakles. Direct imitation of Euripides can be safely excluded, nor did Spenser learn—in the strict sense of the word—his technique from Vergil. Rather, his adaptation points to the creative life that is immanent in any myth and can be evoked by individual poets at different times, without the direct kind of debt which we are often too prone to see at work. In Spenser's *Faerie Queene*, the life of the myth itself and that of its interpretation, which had been separated throughout the Middle Ages and much of the Renaissance, coalesce once more. And while Herbert Read's observation that a myth 'persists by virtue of its imagery'[52] is true in many, minor ornamental uses of the Herakles myth, with which we are not concerned here, it is only poetic intuition that can flesh out this imagery, give it a profound meaning again, and save it from becoming a conceit or mere convention.

We said earlier that the two greatest obstacles to a successful adaptation of Herakles were the external anachronism of many of his exploits, and his divinity. The first, as we have seen, was no problem in Elizabethan England. Fantastic exploits still caused delight in their own right, even without the necessity of allegorical glosses. As for the second, Spenser's view of Arthur, as set forth in the author's Letter to Sir Walter Raleigh, easily allowed for accommodating the emphasis on the hero's divine nature. Arthur personifies 'magnificence', magnanimity, which is the sum total of all other virtues. As a symbol of the magnanimous human spirit attaining immortality Arthur is not too far removed, for instance, from Cicero's concept of Herakles. More specifically, Spenser thought of magnanimity in Aristotle's terms, and Aristotle had opposed the 'heroic and divine kind of nature' to brutishness.[53]

Whereas Milton, in the seventeenth century, took his Herakles seriously, Ben Jonson offered a lighter view of the time-honoured theme of Herakles at the crossroads. In his masque *Pleasure reconciled to Virtue* (1619) the gluttonous Herakles reappears, even if only indirectly, after many lean centuries of oblivion. A chorister parades around at the beginning of the play, worshipping the god of the belly with Herakles' bowl, a descendant of the bowl with which Herakles once sailed over the ocean. So Herakles is characterized from the outset as not being averse to the finer things in life, even though when he comes on stage himself, he describes himself as a friend of Virtue. Mercury intervenes and amid much dancing and singing, the two traditional opponents are reconciled—'Pleasure the servant, Virtue looking on'. Virtue and Pleasure cease to exist as ethical polarities but are elegantly transformed into two different ways of life, the life of pleasure merely enhancing what virtue has to offer. In that respect, Jonson was the forerunner of Metastasio and Goethe.

In Augustan eighteenth-century England, however, the more stately and frozen 'classical' version of Prodicus' parable returned to the fore, mostly under the influence of Shaftesbury's aesthetic treatise *Notion of the Historical Draught of Hercules* (1713). Two years earlier, *The Spectator* (No. 183) had painted the edifying picture of Prodicus' travel through Greece 'by vertue of his Fable, which procured him a kind Reception in all the Market Towns, where he never failed telling it as soon as he had gathered an Audience about him'. Within less than thirty years around the middle of that century, the fable was treated in poetry at least four times, notably by William Shenstone.[54] Like Giraldi Cintio, Shenstone held that 'the most important end of all poetry is to encourage virtue' (*Essay on Elegy*), and if he had not said so one could certainly infer it from the poem. Dr. Johnson, who ordinarily—and rightly—was critical of Shenstone's poetical efforts, commented very favourably on *The Judgment of Hercules* (1741): 'The numbers are smooth, the diction elegant, and the thought just.' Still, its poetic merits are as slight as could be expected from a sermon put in verse. Whether these poems—and Shenstone's exemplifies their tone though, happily, not their length—sent a stir through their readers' hearts we do not know. In Germany, however, the mortification of Herakles into a monstrous moral prig stirred a temperamental reaction from a young man named Goethe.

The occasion was Wieland's operetta *Alceste* (1773) and the author's fulsome praise of it in several letters to the editor of the *Teutscher Merkur*.[55] Wieland's point of departure was hardly objectionable; he tried only what many adaptors of classical themes, including Goethe in his *Iphigenia*, would do, that is to adapt them to the tastes and sensibilities of his own time. The result was a mixture of the daintiness of German rococo and the pale, plaster-cast like classicism of Winckelmann's 'noble simplicity and quiet grandeur'. To Wieland, it was unthinkable that Admetus would knowingly accept Alcestis' sacrifice, and 'burlesque scenes' such as the quarrel between father and son, Admetus' promise to take a statue of Alcestis with him to bed and, above all, Herakles' drunken ranting in a house of mourning simply were unacceptable at the court of Saxe-Weimar. Accordingly, there is hardly a moment when the protagonists do not lengthily pronounce their virtuous conduct and noble motives. Herakles, for one, appears and, set against a Winckelmannian backdrop of laurel trees and Doric columns, immediately soliloquizes on virtue's being the be-all and end-all of his life (III. 1):

O du, für die ich weicher Ruh
Und Amors süssem Schmerz entsage,
Du, deren Namen ich an meiner Stirne trage,
Für die ich alles thu',
Für die ich alles wage,
O Tugend!

(O you, for whom I renounce soft rest and Amor's gay sport, you whose name I am bearing on my forehead, for whom I do everything, for whom I dare everything, O virtue!)

It is because of Alcestis' virtue that Herakles decides to bring her back: 'And shall an urn enclose so much virtue?—No! So long as I am truly the Thunderer's son, it shall not be!' Herakles' friendship for Admetus, so far from being simple *xenia*, takes on the grandeur of *Nibelungentreue*. The hero fairly spouts sententious maxims and, his eyes shining like a boy scout's who has done his good deed of the day, he brings back the veiled Alcestis. Where there was urbane irony in Euripides, bombast rules in Wieland's final scene. But, of course, keeping Admetus on tenterhooks was only a game, however moral its implications; like a good courtier, Herakles apologizes for it and Admetus' reply perhaps sums up best the refined milieu into which our hero has been transposed: 'Untender (*unzärtlich*), Herakles, was thine behaviour!'

It was the bloodlessness of Wieland's adaptation, which Wieland complacently judged superior to the original, that prompted Goethe to rebel. Under Herder's influence and, even more so, under that of a bottle of Burgundy, he opposed to the fashionable prettifications of Rococo Hellenism a Herakles who possessed boundless physical energies and a superhuman *élan vital*. In his farce *Gods, Heroes and Wieland*, Wieland dodders on the stage in a night cap and gown, and is shocked to find, instead of his own well-proportioned Herakles 'of middle height', a veritable colossus, a giant, a monstrous *braver Kerl*. This Herakles is the true superman who, like Nietzsche's, takes the right to hurt and destroy, as well as to build and order.[56] So far from being the exemplar of virtue, this Herakles boasts of forcing his will on women 'even against their will'. 'But don't you know virtue', exclaims Wieland, 'for whom my Herakles does everything, for whom he dares everything?' The answer is a long, merciless derision by Herakles/Goethe of Wieland's small-minded concept of the virtuous Herakles. 'Prodicus' Herakles,' sneers Herakles at the end, 'that's your man. A schoolmaster's Herakles. If I had really met those two ladies, you see, I would have grabbed one under this arm, the other under that arm, and forced both of them to come along.' So much for blasphemy and for the fact that there are indeed many things between heaven and earth of which a schoolmaster is not cognizant.

Physical as Goethe's Herakles is, he bears only superficial resemblance to Apollonius' or Shelley's, who saw in Herakles merely a symbol of strength.[57] For Herakles was the incarnation of what Goethe, at this stage of his life, saw in the Greeks and his Herakles also expresses a spiritual dimension. Herakles represented naturalness, without any inhibitions or shackles imposed by convention. In his own rather uncritical way, Goethe recaptured the spirit of Herakles in the Euripidean *Alcestis*, who had also been intended as the 'natural' antithesis of over-civilization. For Goethe, the Herakles theme was no mere literary exercise but a way of self-expression. Herakles was one aspect of the dynamic, daemonic force of genius which Goethe was trying to control all his life. The bookish, pallid classicism of Winckelmann and Wieland did not offer any answers here, nor did the simplistic moralizations of Herakles' life. In the light of the latter's massive and virtually unbroken tradition in Germany from the Renaissance throughout the Baroque to Goethe's own time—a few weeks before the *Alceste*, Wieland had produced another lyric drama, *Herakles at the Crossroads*, for the explicit instruction of the seventeen-year-old prince of Saxe-Weimar—Goethe's break with it is a considerable achievement.[58]

Nor did his preoccupation with Herakles end here. Fourteen years later, we find him in Rome modelling a head of Herakles. His reading of the *Odyssey* and first-hand observation of the Greek monuments in Sicily had confirmed once more his admiration of the Greeks regardless of the contemporary interpretations that were trying to mould them in the image of the eighteenth century. Goethe's endeavour now was more philosophical and aesthetic: he was searching for an expression of the *Urmensch*, God's idea of man. The statues of the Greek gods represented, in perfection, the different individual qualities which made up this idea, and Goethe probably realized that it was nearly impossible to create an artistic expression in which all these qualities would be caught up. Evidently, however, Goethe must have thought that a representation of Herakles approximated this idea most closely because of the breadth of characteristics with which Herakles had traditionally been endowed. The raptures of Faust and Chiron in the second part of *Faust* seem to be Goethe's comment on his earlier and unsuccessful attempt (lines 7381–97):

Faust: I beg, of Herakles I would be learning!
Chiron: Oh woe! Awaken not my yearning!
Phoebus I never had seen, nor yet
Seen Ares, Hermes, as they're called in fine,
When my enraptured vision met

A form that all men call divine
A king by birth as was no other,
A youth most glorious to view,
A subject to his elder brother [Eurystheus]
And to the loveliest women too.
His like will Gaea bring forth never
Nor Hebe lead to Heaven again . . .

And then:

Songs struggle in a vain endeavour,
men torture marble all in vain.
Faust: Though men may strive in stone and story
Never has he appeared in all his glory.
You have now spoken of the fairest man . . .

In their poignancy, these last lines are unrivalled in the entire Herakles tradition. They express Goethe's deeply felt realization of the hero's immense complexity. Presumably, many of the writers who adapted him were aware that their treatment was only partial and they chose that aspect of Herakles which to them seemed most significant or simply suited their purposes best. The Herakles of Pindar, Sophocles, or Seneca tells us as much or even more about the author's aims than about the hero himself. These writers were not insensitive, but they did not share Goethe's thoroughly modern sensibilities and consequently were not pained by the realization that no single artistic or literary treatment of Herakles could do justice to the many facets of his character. Nor did Goethe simply identify with Herakles as he had in his Storm and Stress days. His own versatility, however, the complexity and contradictions of his character, and the rich variety of his own development led him to a rare, sympathetic understanding of Herakles' same qualities.

Goethe's attack signalled the impending end of the dominance of the moralistic interpretations of Herakles. The conflagration that gutted the palace in Weimar in 1774 thus is almost symbolical. The nineteenth century, with its flourishing of classical scholarship, helped further to discard the simplistic role which the Renaissance and Baroque versions of Prodicus' fable had imposed on the hero. Yet even so he was not completely reborn as a literary hero. The conception that he stood for a moral or philosophical principle persisted and two American writers tried to give expression to it in this century.

On the surface the first of them, George Cabot Lodge, looks like a mixture of Giovambattista Giraldi and Winckelmann on the rather refined New England scene around the turn of the century. Certainly, Herakles' adoption by a Boston Brahmin of impeccable educational and social credentials gives the final lie to Lucretius' and Tertullian's slanders about his being a primitive brute, devoid of any spiritual capacities. In many ways, Lodge continued where Goethe—wisely—had left off. Goethe resigned himself to the impossibility of Herakles' finding an adequate expression in either art or literature, because the hero's qualities were more encompassing and universal—Herakles as the *Urmensch*—than those of any other man or god. Lodge started from the other end: to his mind, the final, deepest questions about man's existence and fate could be expressed most worthily by being attached to Herakles. In his dramatic poem *Herakles*, which rolls on over 270 pages, the internalization of the hero is total.[59] Herakles is the timeless, universal symbol of the soul's or will's pilgrim's progress toward the final vision of the truth. Lodge resolves the problem of anachronism by not fleshing out his Herakles, but he does so at tremendous cost. In the Boston poet's latter-day *gnosis* Herakles loses his personality, not because he is reduced to an allegory as he had been in the Renaissance, but to a spiritual and ethical principle pure and simple. An abstraction thus takes the place of a figure that Hesiod and Pindar, for instance, had been able to see in both moral and concrete terms. The elevated moral tone of the *Herakles* abounds with repetitious sententiousness and turgidity. We might echo Dr. Johnson by saying that 'the thought is just' but as a poem Lodge's *Herakles* is, and perhaps had to be, a colossal failure.

Almost fifty years later, Thornton Wilder, in his *Alcestiad*, made an equally pronounced attempt to express through Herakles some of the ultimate philosophical or religious questions about man's fate. Wilder started from a far more defined philosophical system than Lodge had, that of Soren Kierkegaard. Like Julius Caesar in *The Ides of March*, Wilder's hero again is attempting to ascertain whether his role is of his own making or whether he is a divine agent. His labour of killing the

Hydra, which he has just completed before arriving at Admetus' court, gives rise to his doubts:[60]

> He doubts his descent from Zeus; he doubts that the god has any part in his achievement. The doubt creates within him two contradictory feelings. One, he is proud and concludes that he must be a 'good man' to have accomplished so great a task. Two, he is reduced to Kierkegaard's fear and trembling, for if the god has no part in his work, then it is meaningless and he can comprehend nothing. His concern is that 'someone will come to me and ask me . . . descend into the Underworld, into Hell . . . and bring back someone who has died'. He has come to seek the answer from Alcestis.

Herakles offered himself ideally for the role that Wilder has given him. At least in the classical tradition he was characterized by the ambiguity between his human and divine aspects. The Homeric and Euripidean defier of the gods had been their pious instrument in Pindar and Vergil. In the *Alcestiad*, Herakles is frightened by his relationship with the infinite, although it is only this relationship that can give his actions meaning. Wilder bravely tried to dramatize Herakles' shift from doubt to faith as much as could be done, even though he realized that in Kierkegaard's own opinion it defied dramatization because the decision is lonely and inexplicable. As in Lodge's *Herakles*, then, our hero once more is in search of his identity. After he finds out that Alcestis' death has been concealed from him, he shouts in terrible anger:

> I am not a man, since my best friend Admetus will not treat me as a man . . . if I am not fit to share the grief of my friends. . . . For you, I am an animal, a stupid animal who goes about killing animals! You think I have no mind or heart or soul!

It is as if Herakles were defending himself against his ancient detractors. At the same time, Herakles is a modern character whose latent doubts about his humanity come into view here. He desperately wants to become himself, refusing as he still does his relationship with the infinite, the God. It is an expression of Kierkegaard's idea of despair:[61]

> To become oneself is to become concrete. But to become concrete means neither to become finite nor infinite, for that which is to

> become concrete is a synthesis. Accordingly, the development consists in moving away from oneself infinitely by the process of finitizing oneself, and in returning to oneself infinitely by the process of finitizing. If, on the contrary, the self does not become itself, it is in despair, whether it knows it or not. . . . Not to become one's own self is despair.

Herakles' fears are confirmed: he is asked to go to the underworld and bring back Alcestis who has died. His descent to Hades is the dramatization of Kierkegaard's idea of fear and trembling. So 'Herakles risks all that is dear in the world—life itself—for an ideal, his platonic love for Alcestis; but in the same act he regains all that is dear—life—made dearer and provided with meaning by his recognition of his relationship with the god.'[62]

Because he is metaphysically overworked, Wilder's Herakles is as little a dramatic success as Lodge's, for the same reason, had been a poetic one. This does not reflect on Wilder's abilities as a playwright; he never allowed the *Alcestiad* to be published in English and now would like to disown the play completely, 'if that were possible',[63] and we might have been unfair to him still to discuss it. Yet these relative failures are more meaningful and instructive than the successes, for instance, of the operatic Herakles. From the hero who was endowed with unlimited physical strength Herakles, through the mediation of Euripides in particular, was transformed into a metaphysical protagonist. For too long a time perhaps, his energies of that nature were guided into the well-defined channels of morality, and the straightlaced do-gooder, created in the image of the age, superseded the metaphysical struggler. But could there really be a successful representation of the latter? Our modern *Weltbild*, as exemplified by Kierkegaard's philosophy, is considerably more complex than that of fifth-century Athens and Euripides' antithesis between divine fate and human greatness is too simple to be entirely satisfying today. Besides, there is a limit to which one can burden the hero of a poem or a play with metaphysical complications and the proper medium for their exploration, short of an outright philosophical treatise, would be the novel. And this is the genre from which Herakles has been excluded so far.

It was, then, as in the Greek and Roman authors, the fragmented

Herakles who continued in the literary tradition. His aspects other than the ethic-moralistic one were not forgotten entirely in the non-dramatic literature even of the Renaissance and the sixteenth, seventeenth, and eighteenth centuries, even though they could not equal the attention which the *Hercule moralisé* commanded. Ronsard's poetry provides perhaps the most encyclopaedic example of the survival of Herakles' most important characterizations from Greek and Roman literature. Ronsard could view Herakles both as a paragon of physical force and in a more meaningful spiritual role,[64] and his diverse applications of the myth range from the sublime—Herakles as the model of various princes and statesmen—to the banal. Herakles' reappearance as a lover mostly belongs to the latter category. The medieval tradition had discarded the view of Herakles as the proud, conquering womanizer and emphasized his victimization by love instead, and the Renaissance continued in that vein. In the humanistic theatre of Ravisius Textor, for instance, we find a startling recurrence of Propertius' view of Herakles' death: a woman made him burn.[65] In the mainstream of this tradition, Ronsard defends the social unacceptability of his love for a chambermaid with Herakles' *amour* for Iole:[66]

> Si j'aime depuis naguère
> Une belle chambrière,
> Hé, qui m'oseroit blasmer
> De si bassement aimer?
>
> . . . .
>
> Hercules, dont l'honneur vole
> Au ciel, aima bien Iole,
> Qui prisonnière dontoit
> Celuy qui son maistre estoit.

This, it should be remembered, is the same poet who sang the praises of Herakles as another Christ! At least in his tendency not to be concerned about contradictory portraits of the hero Ronsard was a true disciple of the Greek and Roman classics.

The same can be said generally of the adaptations of Herakles the amorist. True enough, what Propertius had casually tossed off as a snickering depreciation now has its serious, neo-Platonic revival, but soon becomes the kind of cliché which the comparison between Herakles and the lover had been in Latin literature. Du Bellay finally is the Renaissance Ovid who mocks the well-worn conventions of this conceit along with the Promethean one:[67]

L'autre qui paist un aigle devorant
S'accoustre en Promethée,
Mais cestui-là, par un plus chaste voeu,
En se bruslant veult Hercule estre veu.

The number of sixteenth-century poets who burned like Herakles was legion, but in contrast to our hero, very few achieved immortality in the process. We reach the nadir of originality in the seventeenth century when Phillip Ayres *Compares the Troubles which he has undergone for Cynthia's love to the Labours of Hercules* in a poem that is not much longer than its title and, to cap it all, turns out to be a translation from Battista Guarini.[68]

In France, however, the unique emphasis on one particular aspect of Herakles created the closest thing to an inventive addition to the myth. At the beginning of this survey, we described the conflict between *virtus* and *fortitudo* and we have seen that it was resolved in favour of *virtus*. Still, a good part of the tradition escaped this narrow antinomy, which was spawned by the patristic attack and subsequently led to the hero's virtuous overcompensations, and it revived the notion of Herakles' intellectual rather than moral or physical achievements. We saw a good example of this in Le Fèvre's *Recueil*, but more was to come. The Renaissance humanists rediscovered Lucian's description of a curious picture of Herakles which he claimed to have seen in Gaul. In it, the god, besides wearing his customary insignia, was portrayed as aged and wizened, and dragging his followers joyously after him by delicate chains of gold and amber, which were fastened to their ears and the god's pierced tongue. Lucian's Gallic mentor explained the symbolism of the figure as follows (*Herakles* 4. 6):

> We do not agree with you Greeks in thinking that Hermes is Eloquence. We identify Herakles with it, because he is far more powerful than Hermes. . . . In general, we consider that the real Herakles was a wise man who achieved everything by eloquence and applied

persuasion as his principal force. His arrows represent words, I suppose, keen, sure, and swift, which make their wounds in souls.

It is not surprising to find Herakles representing eloquence although the theme had not been given great emphasis in antiquity. All this changed in the Renaissance under the influence of the Gallic national pride in Herculean origin. The earliest translation of Lucian's story into French was that of Geofroy Tory in *Champfleury* (1529) and inspired a vogue of further poetic and prosaic elaborations. After translating Lucian's Greek text into Latin, Budé did the myth the rare honour of retelling it in French in his *Institution du Prince* (1547), the only work the 'prince of French humanists' ever wrote in the vernacular. Erasmus, in his *Adagia*, 'saw in it a timely device for reviving the ancient ideal of eloquence'.[69] The increasing popularity of this Herakles was well taken into account by the popularizing mythological handbooks; each new edition of Conti's *Mythologiae*, for instance, contained more material on him. Alciati's *Emblems* depict Herakles as the sheer *Typus Eloquentiae* and illustrate him on a woodcut with the title: *Eloquentia fortitudine praestantior* (Plate 15). On the other hand, parodies—more in the spirit of Lucian—such as that by Dürer (Plate 12) were not lacking either.[70] The French, however, considered him with complete seriousness. Besides the Gallic Herakles, the Greek one, 'le petit Hercule Grec', as Jean Lemaitre de Belges called him, progressively paled into insignificance. Tory and Jean le Blond argued, speciously of course, that the ancients acknowledged the Gallic language by making Herakles Gallic and thus the superiority of French over their own languages. Rabelais asked his patron to protect him like a second Gallic Herakles 'en scavoir, prudence, et eloquence'.[71] And the myth powerfully sums up Joachim du Bellay's plea for the use of French as a literary language in his *Defence and Ennoblement of the French Language* (1549): 'Vous souvienne . . . de votre Hercule Gallique, tirant les peuples après luy par leurs oreilles avecque une chesne attachée à sa langue.'

Although this interpretation of Herakles did not influence, let alone inspire, any portraits of him after the Renaissance, it would be rash to dismiss it as a sideshow that has merely curiosity value. For it provides another excellent example of Herakles' representing the aspirations of an age. As Pindar, Euripides, and Isocrates had refined the national hero of Greece by projecting their values into him, so the humanists, the French humanists in particular, used the Gallic Herakles as a personification of the ideas with which they were most concerned. And like in Greece, the political and potentially chauvinistic interpretation of the hero yielded to the cultural. In the Renaissance, 'eloquence' had a wider meaning than it has today. It connoted not merely verbal dexterity but cultural aspirations at large. A man like Budé went even further and held that a man could not be eloquent unless he was *vir bonus*. The idea is related to the Greek one of the *kaloskagathos*, which Herakles had represented to an outstanding degree. In the eyes of the humanists, the triumph of Herakles had been brought about by knowledge and justice, and Barthélemy Aneau, a commentator on Alciati, put it most concisely:[72]

> Armes font place aux lettres. Car des cœurs
> (Tant soient ils durs) Eloquens sont vainqeurs.

And these scholars hoped that their princes would triumph in the same manner. This was idealistic, to be sure, but it was an eloquent testimony to the enduring value of Herakles as an ideal.

NOTES TO CHAPTER IX

1. Shelley assigned Herakles a minimal role in the *Prometheus Unbound*; see below, n. 57. In Calderon's *Estatua de Prometeo* Apollo, and not Herakles, announces that Prometheus will be spared, but Calderon may not have known Aeschylus' play. Gide, in *Le Prométhée mal enchaîné* dispenses with Herakles because of his emphasis on human action and decisions, although a shade of Herakles' liberating function is discernible in Damocles (see H. Watson-Williams, *André Gide and the Greek Myth* [Oxford, 1967] 46–7). Similarly, Rilke (*Alkestis* in *Der neuen Gedichte erster Teil* 1907) does away with Herakles, because Alcestis is reborn. In d'Annunzio's Hylas poem, as in Leconte de Lisle's, the hero is mentioned only by name. Herder, Goethe's revered teacher, banished Herakles in favour of Apollo in his *Admetus' Haus, der Tausch des Schicksals* (1803). Herculean characters replace Herakles, as is shown by E. W. Waith's study.
2. Stanford 119.
3. Lucian, *The Cynic* 13.

4. For the imperial patronage of the cult of Herakles see, most recently, F. Taeger, *Charisma. Studien zur Geschichte des antiken Herrscherkults* 2 (Stuttgart, 1960) 394ff. For Herakles as the rival of Christ see Simon 125–66. Not surprisingly, Julian the Apostate warmly espoused Herakles' cause; see esp. *Or.* 7. 219C–220A; *The Caesars* 319D, 325A, 335D; *Letter to Themistius* 253C and 264A. Making a passing sneer at the Gospel, Julian claims in *Or.* 7. 219D that Herakles did not travel in the Sun's cup but walked over the water like on dry land.
5. *De Pallio* 4 (*P.L.* 2. 1095). St. Augustine is quoted from *Sermones* 273. 6 (*P.L.* 38. 1250), Lactantius from *Div. Inst.* 1. 9. Cf. St. Augustine, *Sermones* 24. 6 (*P.L.* 38. 166) and 273. 3 (*P.L.* 38. 1249), and Lactantius, *Div. Inst.* 1. 18. Much additional material can be found in the article by Gaeta, who discusses the tradition from the end of the classical period to the beginning of Renaissance humanism.
6. *Florida* 4. 22. It is typical of the elasticity of the tradition that in *Apol.* 22 the same author takes an entirely favourable view of Herakles as the Cynic model of virtue, who deserves heaven as his reward.
7. In *De vita solitaria* (1. 4. 2; 2. 9. 4); he did not, however, mention it in his 'Life of Herakles' in *De viris illustribus.* See T. E. Mommsen, *JWI* 16 (1953) 178–92. In his *Trionfo della fama* (1. 93) Petrarch offers the traditional praise of Herakles as a bringer of justice.
8. *Theseus* 6. 4–5; cf. *Moralia* 90 D.
9. Plutarch, *Mor.* 387D; Servius *ad Aen.* 6. 123, 395. Plutarch also wrote a *Life of Herakles*, which has not been preserved.
10. Theodulph: *P.L.* 115. 331; Albericus, the third of the Mythographi Vaticani, is cited from the edition by A. Mai (Rome, 1831) 269–74.
11. Twelve editions between 1476 and 1544 alone, along with twenty manuscripts, attest its popularity there. The first two books also were published separately from the third as *L'hystoire de Hercules* or *Les proesses et vaillances du preux Hercules* (eight editions) and translated into Flemish (*Die hystorie van den stercken Hercules* 1556) and Irish (*Stair Ercuil ocus a bas* [last quarter of the fifteenth century; see the edition by Gordon Quin; Dublin, 1939]). Caxton's *Recuyell* is cited from the two-volume edition by H. O. Sommer (London, 1894). More material on the courtly Herakles, including in the French entries and dumb shows, has been collected by Jung 13–16 and 30–40. A medieval poem of about two thousand lines (published by W. Meyer, *Zeitschr. roman. Philologie* 10 [1886] 363–410) is remarkable for describing Hector's David-like conquest of Herakles, but this particular portrait of Herakles as a bully left no marks on the tradition, except that one might compare his characterization in the dramas of Rotrou and La Tuillerie (pp. 233f.). Conversely, Dante compared Herakles' fight against Antaeus to David's against Goliath (*De Mon.* 2. 9).
12. The work probably was composed in the 1420s; my citation is from the Ferrara edition. No further details are known about de Bassi's identity.

13. P. de Nolhac, 'Le "De viris illustribus" de Pétrarque. Notices sur les manuscripts originaux suivies de fragments inédits', *Notices et extraits des manuscrits de la Bibliothèque Nationale et autres bibliothèques* 34 (Paris, 1891) 134.
14. See Petrarch, ibid.: *vires vero corporee monstruorum omnium domitorem, sospitatorem gentium multarum ac velut commune orbis auxilium, usque ad opinionem divinitatis per cuiusdam singularis fame preconium extulerunt.*
15. G. Boccaccio, *Genealogie deorum gentilium libri*, ed. Vincenzo Romano (Bari, 1951), Book 13, chapter 1, 131d–134b. The Platonic reference occurs in *Euthydemus* 297c.
16. Cf. Jung 30.
17. In his critique of Seznec's methodology, 'Gli dei antichi nella tradizione mitologica del Medioevo e del Rinascimento', in *Varietà di storia letteraria e civile* 2 (Bari, 1949) 50–65.
18. Coluccio Salutati, *De laboribus Herculis*, ed. B. L. Ullman, 2 vols. (Zurich, 1951); see also Ullman, *The Humanism of Coluccio Salutati* (Padua, 1963) 19ff. It should be stressed that Salutati's work is important not because it reached a wide circle of readers, as is often implicitly assumed—there were only two manuscripts, a trifle compared to the more than twenty of Le Fèvre's *Recueil*—but because it is the most characteristic expression of the tendencies of the age.
19. Salutati 3. 27. 13; 3. 26. 6; 3. 28. 13; 3. 36. 5; 3. 33. 11; 3. 33. 12; 3. 16. 12; 3. 15. 8.
20. Edited by Margherita Morreale (Madrid, 1958). There is a somewhat tendentious article by the same editor, 'Coluccio Salutati's *De laboribus Herculis* (1406) and Enrique de Villena's *Los doze trabajos de Hercules* (1417)', *SP* 51 (1954) 95–106, extolling Villena's strengths and damning Salutati's faults.
21. Salutati in the first edition of *De laboribus Herculis*, as cited by Ullman, *Humanism* 24.
22. B. Castiglione, *The Courtier*, trans. Sir Thomas Hoby (1561), in *Three Renaissance Classics*, ed. B. A. Milligan (New York, 1953) 576; Dante Alighieri, *Epistolae*, ed. Paget Toynbee (London, 1920), *Epist.* 7, pp. 95–6; Abraham Fraunce, *The Countess of Pembrokes Yuychurch* (1591) 47.
23. References are to the Venice edition of 1581 of Conti's work and to the Venice edition of 1556 of Cartari's.
24. *Hieroglyphica, sive de sacris Aegyptiorum* (Basel, 1575) f. 23 verso.
25. Reference is to the Siena edition of 1613; the quotations in the text occur on pp. 635 and 673. The flexibility of the hero is again underscored by Alciati's praise of him, at the very same time, as the paragon of eloquence; see below, pp. 223f.
26. G. Whitney, *Choice of Emblemes* (1586), ed. Henry Green (London, 1866) 40. To get an idea of the fantastic influence of emblem books like Alciati's we must realize that Alciati's alone had appeared in 127 editions by 1600!
27. See the excellent discussion of Panofsky 52ff. For detailed discussions of the representations of Herakles on the humanistic stage consult the valuable

surveys given by Panofsky 83ff. and D. Wuttke, *Die Histori Herculis des Nürnberger Humanisten und Freundes der Gebrüder Vischer, Pangratz Bernhaubt gen. Schwenter* (Cologne and Graz, 1964), esp. 200ff.; cf. Jung 132–6.

28. Metastasio, *Alcide al bivio* (Vienna, 1760), music by Johann Adolph Hasse.

29. In *Lettere Di XIII Huomini Illustri* (Venice, 1565), Book 17, pp. 867–900; the quotations are from pages 871, 868, and 881. See B. Weinberg, *A History of Literary Criticism in the Italian Renaissance* 1 (1961) 140–2. Camillo Guerrieri-Crocetti, *G. B. Giraldi ed il pensiero critico nel secolo XVI* (Milan, 1932) 543–641, judges Giraldi's work more kindly.

30. De Mal Lara's references to his work have been collected by F. Sánchez y Escribano, *Juan de Mal Lara. Su vida y sus obras* (New York, 1941) 170–2; from them it is clear that the purpose was moral (*Philosophía Vulgar*, f. 184 recto) and a massive compilation of the ancient accounts of the hero (*Recibimiento* f. 54 recto). For further literary treatments of Herakles in Spain see José Maria de Cossio, *Fábulas mítologicas en España* (Madrid, 1952) 200, 515 (a *Herculeidas* of Antonio Gomez de Oliveira, early seventeenth century), 753, 802–3 (the last two are burlesques). Robert B. Tate, 'Mythology in Spanish Historiography of the Middle Ages and the Renaissance', *Hisp. Review* 22 (1954) 1–18 has admirably discussed the background of Herakles' adoption into Spanish history. For Camões references to Herakles, all of them rather conventional, see Mary L. Trowbridge in *Classical Studies in honor of William Abbott Oldfather* (Urbana, 1943) 200 n. 37.—Lilio Gregorio Giraldi's *Vita* can be found in his *Opera* 1 (Leyden 1696). Spenser, for one, was familiar with Giraldi's work through Bryskett's translation.

31. Christine de Pisan, *Epitre d'Othéa* 3 in *Les cent hystoires de Troyes* (Paris, 1522).

32. Cited by Jung 113. Of the ancient writers, Plotinus differentiates most clearly between Herakles' active and contemplative *aretē* (*Enneads* 1. 1. 12).

33. Probably Giovanni di Garlandia; see the edition by F. Ghisalberti (Milan, 1933). The passage referred to is *Integumenta* 347–8.

34. E. Garin, ed., *Testi inediti e rari di Christoforo Landino e Francesco Filelfo* (Florence, 1949) 31. The speaker is Lorenzo de Medici. Ficino's comment on Herakles is found in Plato, *Opera*, Latin trans. by Janus Cornarius, with argumenta and commentaria by Marsilio Ficino (Basle, 1561) 387. For more detail, see Waith 42–3.

35. W. Fulbecke, *A Booke of Christian Ethics* (1587), sigs. D8 verso–E recto; Grimaldus Goslicius, *The Counsellor* (1598), sig. M recto.

36. C. de Boer, ed., *Ovide Moralisé* (Amsterdam 1931) 9. 989–95.

37. *Inferno* 8. 109ff. and 9. 97ff. The *canzone* has been published in *Deutsches Dante Jahrbuch* 12 n.s. 3 (Weimar, 1930) 133ff.; see Simon 177–9 to whose discussion this paragraph and the next are much indebted. Dante's other references to Herakles are conventional, although Herakles may be portrayed as using needless force in the slaying of Cacus (*Inf.* 25. 32–3). But cf. note 11, above.

38. Paul Laumonier, ed., Pierre de Ronsard, *Œuvres complètes* 4 (Paris, 1914–19) 268–76.
39. See, e.g. F. Pfister, 'Herakles und Christus', *ARW* 35 (1937) 42–60, who concludes that the author of the *Urevangelium*, the source of the three synoptic Gospels, modelled his work on a Cynic/Stoic biography of Herakles; and A. J. Toynbee, *A Study of History* 6 (Oxford, 1939) 465.
40. Erasmus, *Enchiridion militis Christiani* (Basle, 1518) 63; J. Reuchlin, *De arte cabalistica* (Haguenau, 1517) Book 2, f. 30ff. In *A Dialogue betwixt Hercules and the two Ladies, Voluptuous, and Vertuous*, which is a part of *The Shepherds starre* (1591), Thomas Bradshaw cast Herakles as the Protestant champion, and the two ways are the old and the reformed religion.
41. In his edition of John Milton, *Paradise Regained, The Minor Poems, and Samson Agonistes* (Garden City, 1937) 408.
42. See Hallett Smith, *Elizabethan Poetry* (Cambridge, Mass., 1952) 301–2. The works of Dunseath and Wolk have been most helpful for my discussion of Spenser as has M. Y. Hughes, 'The Arthurs of the *Faerie Queene*', *Etud. Angl.* 6 (1953) 193–213. Spenser is cited from Edwin Greenlaw and others, *The Works of Edmund Spenser: A Variorum Edition* (Baltimore, 1947).
43. Who held in his *L'Art Poétique* (1555) that the loftiest work that can be written 'is a Heracleid, with the loftiest and most heroic title, which has yet to be announced in the Royalty of the Muses' (pp. 86–7 in the edition of A. Boulanger; Paris, 1930). He tried his hand at such an epic, but abandoned the effort. Aristotle, who had rejected a Herakles epic on the grounds that 'unity of plot does not . . . consist in the unity of the hero' (*Poetics* 1451a), was rebutted by Giovambattista Giraldi (*Discorsi intorno al comporre dei Romanzi, delle Comedie, delle Tragedie* [Venice, 1554] 14–15). Ariosto also discarded the Aristotelian principle and one of his recent editors, L. Caretti (*La letteratura italiana, storia e testi* 20 [Milan and Naples, 1954] 843) suggests that the poem's title may have derived from Seneca's *Hercules Furens*, especially as Ariosto's first apostrophe to his patron, Ippolito d'Este, names him as 'generose Erculea prole' (I. 3). But there is no Herculean imagery to speak of in the poem; similarly, Tasso's references to Herakles are purely conventional.
44. William Warner, *Albion's England* (1586); also, William Harrison, *Description of England* in *Holinshed's Chronicle* (1596) fol. 4a. Spenser mentions the story in *Faerie Queene* II. x. 11. 5–10; IV. xi. 16.
45. *The History of the World* (London, 1652) 402.
46. Donald Cheney, *Spenser's Image of Nature: Wild Man and Shepherd in 'The Faerie Queene'* (New Haven, 1966) 173.
47. Dunseath 51.
48. *Defense of Poesie*, in A. Feuilleret, ed., *The Complete Works of Sir Philip Sidney* 3 (Cambridge, 1912) 40; cf. *The Countess of Pembrokes Arcadia*, ibid., vol. 1. 75–6. On Spenser's 'mistake' of Iole for Omphale see the *Variorum* edition, vol. 5. 203–4.
49. Dunseath 184.

50. See p. 139 with note 18.
51. Dunseath 234 aptly compares this passage with Plutarch's Herakles, 'who took less heed of grievous words and slanders than he did of flies' (*Moralia* 90D); cf. note 8, above.
52. *Collected Essays in Literary Criticism* (London, 1938) 103.
53. Cicero as cited in Chapter 6, note 9, esp. *Nat. Deor.* 2. 62 and *Tusc.* 1. 28, 32; Arist., *Nic. Eth.* 1. 1145a; see Hughes (note 42, above) 211.
54. Besides Shenstone, by Robert Lowth (in Spence's *Polymethis* 1747, pp. 155ff.); an anonymous poet (1752), and William Dunkin (1769). For some other references to Herakles, see Bush, *Mythology and the Renaissance Tradition* 189, 200, 278. A few decades earlier, Fénelon continued the moralizing tradition in France by making Herakles accept the burning of Nessus' robe as a just punishment for his marital infidelity (*Télémaque* 12. 96).
55. *Teutscher Merkur*, January to March 1773. R. Müller-Hartmann, *JWI* 2 (1938–9) has shown that Gluck's opera *Alceste* (1767) incited Wieland to write his *Alceste*. Gluck had eliminated Herakles from the story. For the background, see Humphry Trevelyan, *Goethe and the Greeks* (Cambridge, 1941) 68ff., 169ff. The passage from *Faust* on pp. 216f. is quoted from the translation of G. M. Priest (1941) by permission of Alfred A. Knopf, Inc.
56. Trevelyan, op. cit., 75.
57. In *Prometheus Unbound* III. 3, Herakles unbinds Prometheus with these words: 'Most glorious among spirits, thus doth strength/To wisdom, courage, and long-suffering love,/And thee, who art the form they animate/Minister like a slave.' This is the extent of his role in Shelley, certainly a drastic diminution of his role in Aeschylus' play. A survey of critical opinions is listed by L. J. Zillman, ed., *Shelley's Prometheus Unbound. A Variorum Edition* (Seattle, 1959) 521–3. To them should be added Neville Rogers, *Shelley at Work*[2] (Oxford, 1966) 166: '. . . he awkwardly introduces yet another character, Hercules, to perform the unbinding: in this perhaps he was anxious to show symbolically the power of love to command even the personification of strength.' One can generalize and say that Herakles did not hold much fascination for the romantic writers, Browning being the proverbial exception to the rule. For an earlier, very allusive self-identification of Shelley with Herakles see Rogers 19–20.
58. For the Baroque adaptations of Herakles see Will Tissot, *Simson und Herkules in den Gestaltungen des Barock* (Stratoda, 1932) 94–113, 122–8 (from 1593 to 1799). Herakles' positive and moral aspects were stressed even in the puppet theatre. I am certain that Wieland's *Die Wahl des Herkules* was on Goethe's mind also when he wrote his farce, although I have not found this suggestion in any of the pertinent secondary works.
59. *Poems and Dramas of George Cabot Lodge* 2 (Boston and New York, 1911) 185–454. Henry Adams found much to praise in the *Herakles*; see *The Life of George Cabot Lodge* (Boston and New York, 1911) 162–82.

60. Donald Haberman, *The Plays of Thornton Wilder. A Critical Study* (Middletown, 1967) 42. My description of Wilder's play owes much to Haberman's detailed discussion on pp. 39–53, especially as Haberman was able to consult the typescript of the *Alcestiad*. There are no English editions although I have consulted the German translation by Herbert E. Herlitschka, *Die Alkestiade* (Frankfurt and Hamburg, 1960).
61. S. Kierkegaard, *The Sickness unto Death*, trans. Walter Lowrie, (Princeton, 1941) 44.
62. Haberman, op. cit., 43.
63. Letter to the author, 22 May, 1969. Wilder was aghast at the shallowness of von Hofmannsthal's and also, Browning's treatment (on which see below pp. 235f. and pp. 261f.); perhaps this led him to overcompensate. At the same time, Wilder is keenly aware of the diversity of Herakles' traits. Herakles in the *Alcestiad* at first is depicted in a mildly comical way, but this portrayal and the philosophical one never coalesce.
64. For the former view see, e.g. the Hylas story (discussed on pp. 120–1) and the monotonous cataloguing of Herakles' exploits in the *Elegy to Muret*; for the latter, Herakles' shouldering the heavens as a symbol of the statesman (*Sonnets divers*, Laumonier ed. vol. 2. 339, and *Premier livre des Elegies*, ibid., vol. 5. 15) and Herakles being credited with the cultural achievements of Prometheus in the *Hylas*, Laumonier ed. vol. 4. 265. R. Trousson, 'Ronsard et la légende d'Hercule', *Bibliothèque d'humanisme et de Renaissance* 24 (1962) 77–87 offers a fairly full discussion of Ronsard's uses of Herakles.
65. Ravisius Textor, *Dialogi* (Paris, 1530) f. 226 verso. For Propertius see p. 156. Jung 137–57 gives a well documented survey of the theme of Herakles the lover in the Middle Ages and the Renaissance.
66. *Œuvres complètes*, Laumonier ed., vol. 3. 128.
67. *Œuvres*, ed. Chamard (Paris, 1931), vol. 4. 210, lines 107–10. On the other hand, the same poet took the conceit perfectly seriously in the conclusion of the tenth of his *Sonnets de l'honneste amour* (Chamard ed., 1. 146). Castiglione, *The Courtier* (4. 49) provides another good example of the neo-Platonic attitude.
68. George Saintsbury, ed., *Minor Caroline Poets* 2 (Oxford, 1921) 341.
69. R. E. Hallowell, 'Ronsard and the Gallic Hercules Myth', *Studies in the Renaissance* 9 (1962) 247, with reference to Erasmus, *Adagia*, s.v. 'Herculei labores'. Hallowell's article (pp. 242–55) contains further material on the Gallic Herakles, as does Jung 73–92.
70. See E. Wind, 'Hercules' and 'Orpheus': two mock-heroic designs by Dürer, *JWI* 2 (1939) 206ff. Wind argues that since Herakles has a cockscomb, he must be *Hercules Gallicus*.
71. Dedicatory letter prefacing the *Quart Livre* (Paris, 1552).
72. André Alciat, *Emblèmes*, trans. and comm. by B. Aneau (Lyons [G. Rouille], 1549) 222.

CHAPTER X

The Tragic Herakles Revisited

The Greek tragedians, who valued inner qualities more than external events or manners, had enriched Herakles' personality fundamentally by adapting him for their genre. So had Seneca, even if in an entirely different way. When Herakles reappeared, however, on the stage of Elizabethan England and seventeenth-century France, neither literary imagination nor a playwright's forceful projection of his own heartfelt view of life were present to give substance to his role. By and large, the adaptations of this period and the eighteenth and nineteenth centuries are purely external and exemplify that little did it profit the hero to become well-adjusted to the spirit of the times if he lost his soul in the process. It we still delay over these plays, it is only for the sake of giving a reasonably complete survey of Herakles' fortune in the vernacular literatures and of putting the dramas of Wilder, Wedekind, Pound, and MacLeish into a better perspective.

Of Shakespeare's contemporaries and near-contemporaries, only Thomas Heywood made the attempt to put Herakles on the stage as Herakles. Whereas the Greek tragedians and Seneca wisely confined themselves to dramatizing one or the other episode from the hero's life, Heywood tries to present many and, as a result, dramatizes none. In the *Silver Age* (1613), a massive cast and Herakles' fustian heroism are the props that have supplanted any real drama. Within the confines of this mythological 'show', Herakles can do little else but stalk from scene to scene, overcoming ever new opponents in ever bigger brawls. It all culminates in his conquest of the powers of hell which are the bathetic counterpart to Dante's mixture of Christian and pagan mythology. The stage directions alone are revealing in the extreme:[1]

> Hercules sinkes himselfe: Flashes of fire; the Divels appeare at every corner of the stage with severall fire-workes. The Iudges of Hell, and the three sisters run over the stage, Hercules after them: fire-works all over the house.

The same sound and fury along with, appropriately enough, the brassy note, continue in the sequel, *The Brazen Age*. It contains many of Herakles' labours and his death and is, like the earlier play, in all essentials the dramatization of a mythological comic strip. The characterization of the hero is not even flat: rather, it is the purely accidental result of dramatic non-technique. Because of the externalization of his exploits, Herakles can do little but brag about them, which he does amply. For once, the pained spectator can sympathize with the objections of Seneca's Juno to sharing heaven with this pompous, uncouth robot.

While Heywood's dramas may be said to be the nadir of the Herakles tradition in literature, they were not too far below the Elizabethan dramatists' standard conception of the hero. That was the cliché of the mad Herakles, but a mad Herakles quite different from Euripides' or Seneca's. For one thing, Herakles' madness was considered as referring to his slaying of Lichas. Aside from the *Brazen Age*, this view is found in Heywood's *Apology for Actors* and, about two decades later, in the *Hercules furente y Oeta* of the Spaniard Francisco Lopez de Zarate.[2] Even more than this shifting of the madness to a lesser event, it was the conventional explanation for it that diminished the literary and psychological interest which Herakles' madness had held. This explanation was physiological and medical: the hero was said to have suffered from epilepsy.[3] In antiquity, the medical view of Herakles as a 'melancholy' hero is found as early as in the *Problems* ascribed to Aristotle, a work that enjoyed great popularity under his name in the Renaissance. But whereas the author of the *Problems* still emphasized that the disease was the result of a man's excellence 'in philosophy, poetry, or the arts' (*Problems* 30. 953a), this view was largely ignored in the Renaissance. Besides the entries in the Latin dictionaries and standard reference works[4] under 'Herculanus morbus' the comments of Seneca's first English editor, Thomas Farnaby, are rather typical. Farnaby describes in detail the physiological processes leading to the hero's frenzy and its abating; Herakles' sensation of darkness is caused by excretion of black bile rising from the stomach to the brain. He then must fall asleep and exhale the dark and bitter humour before his frenzy can ebb away completely.[5] Thus the mad Herakles ceased to excite the literary imagination and became a mere convention and, all too often, a gimmick instead. As such, he served as an analogue for the deranged heroes notably in Robert Greene's *Orlando Furioso* (1594) and John Marston's *Antonio and Mellida* and *Antonio's Revenge* (1602). His treatment in these plays invited and received its satirical reaction.[6] In contrast to Spenser, who was able to transform the allegorical conventions of Herakles once more into epic poetry, no Elizabethan, Jacobean or, for that matter, eighteenth-century dramatist attempted to restore any meaning to the *Hercules furens* convention. The theatre public of these times therefore could hardly help but regard Herakles as a bombastic poltroon. It may well be that Shakespeare had the *Hercules furens* tradition in mind when he dramatized the madness of Othello, Antony, and Julius Caesar[7] and he restored dignity to a convention that had become an absurdity. Still, this was a far cry from seeing a tragic, inner motivation or ulterior meaning in the madness of Herakles himself.

In the France of Louis XIV, ranting and raving alone were not enough to keep the courtiers in the theatre. Amorous intrigues, however, were, and Herakles was to serve his new masters as handily as he had Omphale. Adaptations of this kind have slight literary merit, but they did develop two portraits of Herakles which determined his reputation on the stage for two centuries and ultimately, the reaction against it of Wieland, Alfieri, and others. The first cast Herakles in the image of the insensate lover, who is as unconcerned about the feelings of his amorata as he is ready to use force to get his way. This characterization can be traced back to Sophocles *Trachiniae*, where Herakles cared not about Deianeira's feelings nor, implicitly, those of Iole. Playwrights such as Rotrou and La Tuillerie took it upon themselves to dramatize especially the latter story explicitly enough. For that purpose, Iole is given another lover—Arcas in Rotrou's *Hercule mourant* (1632), and the hapless Philoctetes in La Tuillerie's *Hercule* (1682)—whom she loves in return. In both plays Herakles is the callous bully who pulls his semi-divine rank and still loses out to the human rival in the end because, alas, true love and woman's heart cannot be forced, not even by the hero who conquered the whole world.

Philoctetes' description of Herakles in La Tuillerie's play will exemplify the prevailing tone and characterization (I. 5):

> Et tu ne connois pas Hercule comme moi.
> Il est dans ses fureurs, comme dans ses faiblesses,
> Barbare à ses rivaux, injuste à ses maitresses,
> Inexorable amant, implacable ennemi,
> Enfin jamais jaloux, ni cruel à demi.

Even the melodramatic ending of Rotrou's tragedy, where Herakles after his apotheosis desists from wanting Arcas sacrificed—his thirst, he says, quenched by ambrosia, needs blood no more—is not apt to undo the hideous impression that has been built up of him throughout the play.

By contrast, Herakles emerged as an entirely different kind of lover in the adaptations of the Alcestis theme especially for the opera.[8] In Quinault's drama, which served as the libretto for Lully's opera (1674), we encounter him as a Don Juanesque gallant who rescues Alcestis not in the least because he loves her, whereas Aurelio Aureli in his *L'Antigone delusa d'Alceste* (1664) depicted him as a ladies' man who succumbs only too willingly to Alcestis' charms. This sugary work became the basis for Handel's *Admeto* (1727) and the *Alcestis* of Johann Ulrich König. Handel's oratorio *Hercules* (1744) occupies the middle ground between these two views of the hero. Herakles is the great lover of Iole, who spurns him, but instead of trying to force her, he sings of love's taking the place of his armed exploits:

> Now farewell, arms! from hence the tide of time
> Shall bear me gently down to mellow age;
> From wars to live I fly, my cares to lose
> In gentle Dejanira's fond embrace.

Handel continues to dwell on the antithesis between the amorous and the moral calling of Herakles, but in keeping with the genre, the theme is simply sounded over and over again rather than dramatically developed. Handel took pains to dissociate his hero from any trace of crudely selfish love and therefore even transformed Herakles' hideous final command in the *Trachiniae* into a happy end: Jove ordains that Iole should marry Hyllus.

This melodramatic tradition of Herakles the lover constitutes the mitigating circumstances for adaptations such as Wieland's. Wieland had originally planned to yield to its force by letting Herakles fall in love with Alcestis' sister, but he abandoned the idea because it smacked too much of the hero's operatic excesses and too little 'of the noble simplicity of the whole'. And the sublimation of the hero continued even after the simplistic Hercules Prodicius had faded away. In Italy, Latin chivalry began to steal a march on Nordic virtue and it consummated its triumph in Vittorio Alfieri's *Alceste seconda* (1799). Here, Herakles fairly oozes with magnanimity and still is hard put to outdo the magnanimous feelings of the other protagonists. He is told about Alcestis' death from the outset; there is no drunken misbehaviour, but an immediate, resounding declaration to rescue the *ver sublime unica moglie* of *miserissimo Admeto*. This is the Italian offspring of Hesiod's and Le Fèvre's shining white knight, a hero whose most attractive *raison d'être* is that he can strike a grand pose. Within a century and a half, the callous monster thus had been transformed into the epitome of generosity and noble humanity. Understandably enough, Admetus wants to kneel down before this *semidio*, but Herakles bids him to rise with the most august understatement of the tradition:

Sorgi: altro non sono
Io, ch'un mortal; ma non discaro ai Numi.

Nor can he refrain from moistening his noble brow with 'sweet unusual tears' at the sight of Alcestis' and Admetus' conjugal bliss and fidelity. Truly, as the chorus exclaims in the last line of the play, the two have become worthy of the 'sublime Alcides'.[9]

Exaltation, of course, means different things to different writers in different locales. When Alcestis retreated over the Alps to Vienna, Herakles took on the form of the *philosophe* of a Grinzing tavern or Viennese coffee-house who sombrely meditates on the mysteries of life. This happened, as we saw earlier, in Hugo von Hofmannsthal's (*Alkestis* written in 1893). The play is another case in point of an honestly attempted adaptation of a classical theme to the sensibilities and taste prevailing at a writer's time and habitat. Breathing as it does the melancholy and the shallowness of the *fin de siècle* and the waning days of the Hapsburg empire, the play is more interesting as an historical document than as a creative reinterpretation of the myth. Hofmannsthal's aim was to follow Euripides' text as closely as he could, but to ennoble the sentiments of the protagonists and to give some mystic-symbolic significance to the whole.[10] In keeping with his ultimate role as the Redeemer (*Heiland*) in this play, Herakles is treated with utter seriousness from beginning to end. Instead of letting Herakles' simply burst on the stage, Hofmannsthal carefully builds up the impression of Herakles' grandeur by describing the effect of his approach on a representative sample of Greek men. This *parodos* culminates with the exclamation of the oldest man who counts himself lucky to have seen Herakles before his death. *Vedere Ercole e poi morire!* It is a time-honoured sentiment, as old as Odysseus' faithful dog, and with its mixture of dignity, schmaltz, and sadness it sets the appropriate tone for Herakles' further role in the drama. The drunken scene, as we have seen, yields to melancholy reflections on death, and there is no banter in the final scene which ends with the hero's leaving as slowly as he had come on the stage. Once more, everybody's attention is focused on him, and there is the intimation that he, who has thought so deeply about death, might not return from his next exploit.

By 1917, however, the impact of the work of scholars like Gilbert Murray, Wilamowitz, and Verrall with their detailed editions and discussions of Euripides' plays could not be ignored any longer.[11] The result was a return to the Euripidean concept of the hero and the demise of the pasteboard and tinsel world in which Herakles had lived for more than two centuries. The turning point came with the *Herakles* of Frank Wedekind, and the plays of Ezra Pound and Archibald MacLeish reveal a continuing creative preoccupation with the meaning of the Herakles myth.

Even more elaborately than Euripides, Wedekind explored the contrast between the divine, conventionally heroic and the human Herakles. Instead of concentrating, like the Greek tragedians, on a single, focal event of the hero's life, Wedekind strings together eleven scenes which formally are even less related to one another than the tableaux of Seneca's dramas. The ultimate model for this kind of station drama was the mystery plays dealing with the passion and resurrection of Christ, and Wedekind deliberately chose this form to underline its inverted content. For Herakles has no Christlike ambitions: he desperately seeks domestic, human happiness rather than try to save the world. In spite of the Euripidean inspiration, then, Wedekind sets his accents differently. Whereas Euripides' hero accepts human heroism in the face of divine, random necessity and cruelty, Wedekind's struggles for his humanity. Basically, this Herakles—similar to some scholars' view of Sophocles' portrait of him in the *Trachiniae*—is a superhuman misfit who really belongs on Olympus rather than on the earth.

In many respects Wedekind's *Herakles* is the dramatization of the early Goethe's concept of the hero as a superman, who builds up as well as he destroys—the Nietzschean *Lust am Vernichten*—and whose excessive sensual desires, so far from arising from human baseness, are the true characteristic of his superhuman, even Dionysiac nature, which is too great for ordinary mortals to comprehend. A number of Wedekind's earlier plays reflect Nietzsche's philosophy of life and dramatic theories, and *Herakles* is their culmination rather than the exception.[12] Herakles exemplifies the titanic, barbaric nature of the Dionysiac which Nietzsche thought characteristic of Greek tragedy, and it is coupled with a ruthless will to power. Against this background we can read Herakles' fight with Apollo in symbolic terms. Like a good Stoic or Cynic, the Pythia urges Herakles to use his head and to let it control his limbs, and like Seneca's Amphitryon, she admonishes him to rest after each of his violent exploits. These themes bespeak Wedekind's good acquaintance with the literary tradition. But Herakles refuses and Wedekind makes explicit what Seneca had only suggested—that Herakles' fury and madness are in many ways only the result of his constant exertions. This becomes one of the leitmotifs of the play; Herakles uses the argument, for instance, to justify his actions to Eurytus:

Eur. You could recuperate at home with your loved ones. But you pounced on them like a murderer.

Her. The fury, unleashed in Herakles by always greater monsters, kept on raging.

Herakles' motivation is not the result of divine caprice, nor is it controllable like that of the ordinary mortal. When Apollo reminds Herakles that it is a god-given grace to be a man, Herakles can only reply: 'One has got to be able to be a man. I'm not successful at it.'

Amid an imagery of light and dark, which is quite reversed from that of Seneca, Apollo tries forcibly to confine Herakles to the boundaries of ordinary human behaviour. In vain. The superman, alienated from both gods and men, cannot be so overcome:

> Zwischen Gottheit und Menschheit im Ehbruch gezeugt,
> Von den Göttern verhöhnt, von den Menschen verhasst,
> Schaff ich neu mir Bahn,
> Überrennend, was breit in die Quere sich stellt!

Of all the writers in the tradition, Wedekind is the one who emphasizes perhaps most acutely the isolation and loneliness of the hero. Not since Homer depicted Herakles in a similar limbo between the heavenly and human realms had he appeared in such awesome solitude. Euripides' hero had his Theseus, Seneca's, his father and mother, and Sophocles' was lonely because any dying man is lonely in his last hour. For Wedekind's Herakles, however, this is the unalterable condition of his life.

One result of this condition is that Herakles' heroism cannot transcend its subjectivity and that his labours have no meaning for mankind. In this regard Wedekind goes beyond both Seneca, who had called into doubt only the utility of the hero's descent to Hades, and even Sophocles. Wedekind chooses Herakles' liberation of Prometheus as the prime example of his attitude to the hero's achievement.[13] The feat has no meaning except for Herakles' satisfaction to have accomplished it voluntarily. The whole theme is developed gradually and with much skill. At Omphale's court Herakles professes his concern for the 'whining human race' which is helpless while Prometheus is chained to the rock. The mere setting, however, of this utterance undercuts any solemnity: we find a Herakles, like the one Propertius had described with so much glee, dressed up as a girl and surrounded by his dancing playmates. At his wedding banquet, Herakles reiterates his resolve to free Prometheus and finally sets out for the task. His motivations are entirely self-centred: he wants to get away from the lures of Iole and Deianeira because they drain his energies. Nor does Wedekind stop here to put the deed into its proper perspective. He makes Herakles depart with the realization that the strength he needs for this, his greatest achievement, is nothing compared to the strength he would need to achieve 'the humble dignity of man'. And before he frees the Titan, Herakles is characterized once more as a man who is better with his muscles than his head: he himself praises Lichas for relieving him of 'the wretched strain of thinking'. Thus the liberation of Prometheus is merely the hero's greatest physical achievement. Nothing is said, in spite of Prometheus' prodding questions, about the universal implications with which the event had been endowed since Aeschylus and, even more, Calderon, Goethe, and Byron.

As for Seneca's hero, although for different reasons, death is the salvation for Wedekind's Herakles. It means the end of being torn between two worlds and belonging to neither; only in death can 'Herakles feel entirely like Herakles'. Herakles' final prayer is not for world peace or his acceptance into heaven, but a thanksgiving to Zeus that he, the superman, is the master of his own destruction. His last words, in their pessimism, are reminiscent of Ajax's good-bye to his son in Sophocles' *Ajax*, as Herakles now wishes that Prometheus, the bearer of his arms, may be luckier than Herakles had been.

The play ends with an epilogue in heaven. Herakles confronts Hera who, like Seneca's Juno, admits to her fear of his untamed, divine force. Herakles replies by reiterating the basic themes of the play: endowed with divine talents and yet mortal, he had more difficulty than anyone else in fitting 'into the yoke of man'. Everything was easier to gain, he continues, than the domestic hearth. And of the countless women he possessed, there was none whose heart he was able to win. Thus even Hebe's hedonistic promises elicit only his doubts, although the end of the play suggests that he will avail himself of them in order to assert his divinity.

Wedekind's unique contribution to the tradition is his profoundly pessimistic characterization of the hero. Little would be gained by measuring it in terms of the classical tradition which Wedekind used freely and with which it sharply contrasts. Perhaps the modern, as opposed to the classical, definition of the 'tragic' may account for this basic theme, for Euripides' 'tragedy' ends on the positive note of human, heroic greatness and Seneca's is pervaded by the essentially joyful anticipation of the liberating power of death. Nor it is improbable that Wedekind was profoundly affected by the maniac horrors and the concomitant dehumanization caused by the First World War and by his country's impending doom.[14] But whatever the internal or external motives, his interpretation of the myth is in no way incongruent with the myth itself. We are not entirely judging by hindsight when we argue that Wedekind dramatized an aspect of the myth that had been inherent in it. The religiously faithful and the philosophers had harmonized and rationalized Herakles' intermediate position between gods and men as that of the mediator. The inspiration behind this view was essentially moral. To an author, however, who was interested primarily in exploring dramatic conflict, the myth took on an entirely different but no less true meaning. Even if there are affinities with some of Nietzsche's writings that can be classed as philosophical, Wedekind's aims were essentially literary.

This is not to say that *Herakles* is a great play, because it most emphatically is not. In its worst aspects, it outdoes Seneca—one tableau follows another and the monumental phrases especially of Herakles defy any acting of a part like this. Besides, there are too many loose thematic ends. The most prominent example is found in the Prologue where Wedekind announces the universal implications of the play: Herakles will exemplify the fate of man or a man's fate (*ein Menschenschicksal*). The meaning seems to be that being the slave of one's own instincts and drives—a favourite theme in Wedekind's previous plays—is actually a manifestation of the divine spark within. Yet the thought remains muddled and the *Herakles* is the tragedy of superman and not, like Euripides' *Herakles*, that of man. The task was too much for Wedekind's dramaturgic and poetic abilities, as it had been for Lodge's a few years earlier, but—to echo Dr. Johnson—'the thought is just', more just, at any rate, than that of many of his predecessors.

In Ezra Pound's *Women of Trachis* (1954) we enter into an entirely different world. There is not a trace of the flatness or bombast under which virtually all post-classical Herakles dramas had laboured in the giant shadow cast by both Seneca and the moralistic transfiguration of Prodicus. Like no other dramatic poet, Pound has recaptured the vitality that Herakles possessed on the Attic stage. In keeping with Sophocles' inspirational original, the number of pages on which Pound's Herakles appears is small, but they are a landmark. H. A. Mason has summed this up perfectly by saying that 'Pound's figure is credible and self-consistent; it takes hold of us and forces us to live through something.'[15] Indeed Pound's adaptation provides one of the best examples in the tradition that Herakles could become a figure of such absorbing interest to a poet as to make him indifferent to the other characters and aspects of the story.

In so doing, Pound proceeds far more deliberately than he has been given credit for. He minimizes Deianeira's role purposely and not, as has been alleged, because of ignorance or misunderstanding of the Greek play. Sophocles' intent, so far as we have understood it, was to create a very sympathetic characterization of the heroine so that it might contrast all the more strongly with his portrait of Herakles. Pound's aim is quite different. His sympathies lie with Herakles and he diminishes everything that would tend to run counter to this impression.[16] He is not a Pindar who is concerned with justifying his hero, because to Pound Herakles' greatness needs no justification, but he takes all nobility away from Deianeira since it would put his hero into an unfavourable light. Instead of playing a forceful part as in Sophocles' drama, Deianeira is relegated to a wishy-washy role in Pound's.

One or two examples may stand for many. One of Deianeira's greatest moments in the *Trachiniae*, as we saw earlier, is the Oedipus-like, resolute manner in which she tries to pry the truth from Lichas. At the same time, her speech on that occasion is of considerable psychological interest as she attempts by indirect means to convince Lichas that she is not going to take tragically what he has hitherto kept back from her.[17] Pound trivializes both these aspects. Deianeira starts by imploring Zeus on Oeta, Daysair, with a blasphemy. Sophocles' 'Do not cheat me of the truth' is powerful in its simplicity; Pound's 'Don't weasel to me' makes Deianeira sound like a fishwife. So does much of the often artificial slang that follows here and characterizes her earlier and later utterances. The positive idea which Sophocles put at the heart of Deianeira's speech and which is as much intellectual as it is aesthetic and moral, becomes vapid and trivial in Pound's version:

BUT . . .
if he taught you to lie,
the lesson you learned is
not
a nice one.

Equally symptomatic is Pound's change of Sophocles' description of Deianeira's first encounter with Iole. Sophocles dwells on it for some time (lines 307–32) and gives much prominence to Deianeira's genuine compassion. Pound shortens this scene drastically. All that remains of Deianeira's sympathy is two arid sentences: 'I'm sorrier for her than for the rest of them' and 'I don't want to add to her troubles, she's had enough.' As if this vestigial show of emotion were too much already, Daysair at once begins to cluck like a busy-body housekeeper: 'Everybody in! Have to hurry to get things in order!' In sum, Pound deliberately banalizes Deianeira which was the only way to give Herakles positive prominence within the framework of Sophocles' play.

There is another fundamental change which Pound made for the same purpose. The relationship between Herakles and Zeus is one of the recurrent themes in the *Trachiniae* and both explicitly (lines 274–9) and by suggestion, Sophocles is at pains to show that Zeus disapproves of Herakles' conduct and finally even has a hand in bringing about his son's death. Pound couches his reduced version of the former passage in the most harmless terms—'Zeus wouldn't stand it'—and accordingly, omits Deianeira's subsequent prayer to Zeus (303–6) which Sophocles intended for contrast. Similarly, in the final scene Pound systematically omits many lines which show the conflict between father and son and Hyllus' abhorrence of Herakles' inhuman commands.

Instead, one of the stage directions even suggests Herakles' apotheosis, an ending which Sophocles had so zealously denied to the hero. After coming to the realization of the meaning of his life, Herakles 'turns his face from the audience, facing them without the mask of agony; the revealed make-up is that of solar serenity. The hair golden and as electrified as possible.' Even when Herakles came first on stage, he appeared in 'the mask of *divine* agony'. This is not gimmickry, but Pound's ingenious and profoundly meaningful solution to the obstacle that Herakles' divinity had presented for all modern adaptors. We might say that Pound deifies Herakles in secular terms. His hero is not a god of extraneous grandeur nor is he simply a great man. There is something divine in him from the very start and it comes forward fully when Herakles gains insight into the workings of his life and is brought to the realization—and Pound considered this the key phrase of the play—that his seemingly disjointed life has formed an unbelievably coherent pattern: 'SPLENDOUR, IT ALL COHERES.' Apotheosis in our secular world is not transference to a far-away, mythological Mount Olympus but the perception of the meaning of one's life. The idea was suggested by the role of the oracles in Sophocles' play but Pound, perhaps inspired by Sophocles' *Oedipus at Colonus* where this idea is developed in full, suggests that anyone who has insight into the oracles and his life is more than mortal. So Pound's Herakles recaptures, in modern terms, the Greek concept of Herakles as a hero: a man who is neither totally human, nor totally divine, but partaking of each.

These few, central examples suffice to demonstrate that Pound has made considerable changes in adapting Sophocles' drama. Whether his version should be considered a 'translation' is largely a matter of nomenclature and we may beg the question by calling it a creative translation.[18] More important for our purposes is the question why Pound decided to cast his Herakles as he did. We can only speculate on the reasons, but some suggestions may be offered. First, to him the vital Herakles, brimming with masculine strength, may have seemed more authentic than the other, more spiritual manifestations of the hero. This is a Herakles who is full of life and vigour and is not just an egomaniac monster. We should note that Pound identifies him with the 'solar vitality'[19] and forcefully makes him come on the stage *in medias res*, with none of Sophocles'—or, for that matter, Hofmannsthal's—preliminaries of whispering attendants, the moans of Hyllus, or the hero's gradual, bewildered return to consciousness to soften the impact. Pound sees Herakles in all his archaic, heroic ferocity, with simple metaphysics. Secondly and related to this, this kind of hero, exalted in his physical power, defeated by a woman, and headed for self-extinction is a known figure on the twentieth-century American stage especially from the plays of Eugene O'Neill.[20] This is not to suggest anything such as direct influence or to press for minute similarities, but this concept of the hero was 'in the air', and, in his treatment of the conflict between Deianeira and Herakles, Pound is much more akin to O'Neill than to Ibsen. Most importantly, however, and as in the case of Pindar, Hölderlin, or Browning, it is once more the personal experience which seems to have led Pound to Herakles. Pound's many years of enforced seclusion and isolation, of living in this world and not really being a part of it, suggested the similar fate of the Greek hero. In Euripides' *Herakles*, Herakles is at last reconciled with this world; in the *Trachiniae*, he is not, and only the personal experience of alienation explains Pound's arbitrary assertion that 'the *Trachiniae* presents the highest peak of Greek sensibility registered in any of the plays that have come down to us'. The mask of agony worn by Herakles also is Pound's. But it is significant, and further testimony to Pound's profound understanding of the spirit of the Herakles myth, that he, like Euripides and Spitteler, did not endow his Herakles with the Sophoclean aura of grim pessimism. The mask of agony yields to the real visage of serenity, a serenity which is not placid in the manner of Winckelmann but which, one feels, has to be fought for every day anew.

The remarkable feature of Pound's play, then, is that without any elaborate, ambitious modernization of a mythological hero *à la* Joyce he shows us a Herakles who is as Greek as he is modern. *The Women of Trachis* is, to be sure, dealing with only one aspect of the hero, but so were the Greek dramas and Pound's version, not in the least because of his personal, absorbing involvement with Herakles, has a sense of immediacy that is hard to get from the conventional translations.

The most recent play about Herakles, Archibald MacLeish's verse drama of the same name (1967), is also the most deliberate attempt to point out the relevance of the myth to modern times. In MacLeish's own words: 'What started me off was the realization, more or less out of the blue, that the great modern myth is not Jesus but Herakles—not God become man but man become God . . . it is still true that man-become-God is the great contemporary tragedy—dead sons and ruined faith.'[21] The play has two acts; the short first act centres on Professor Hoadley, a physicist who has just come to Greece after receiving the Nobel Prize, whereas the second act, which is three times as long, is about Herakles' homecoming after his labours, with Hoadley's family—though not Hoadley himself—as the spectators and even participants. The re-enactment of the Herakles myth in our own time, with Herakles taking the place of Hoadley, suggests its continued, timeless validity and serves as a corrective for Hoadley's limited understanding of both the myth and his own achievements.

Hoadley, who, stricken as he is in his wheel-chair, is made to resemble Herakles physically[22] as well as spiritually, has come to Greece at the pinnacle of his success because this our century is 'a fabulous century, worthy of the Greeks'. His own generation, he claims, has achieved greatness and labours which can be expressed most fittingly by the greatest myth of the Greek imagination, that of Herakles. This Herakles, as seen and described enthusiastically by Hoadley, is the defiant fighter against the universe, against the horrors of suffering, and against the terrible that is in God. He is the hero who daringly overcomes death itself, 'to master everything on earth and under it'. Such is the world that Hoadley, the world's greatest physicist, envisages and is about to create, essentially a world of frightful, Orwellian happiness. And Hoadley sees a Herculean analogue in all this. After mastering everything, Herakles asked the oracle what would happen to him then. The oracle refused to answer and Herakles therefore gave the answer himself. That is where, according to Hoadley, the Herakles myth ends. 'What more could any living, breathing creature do?' he asks.

His wife, 'a handsome, haunted woman in her thirties', such as one would imagine Megara and Deianeira to be, is not satisfied with this explication of the myth's meaning. 'Oh no,' she answers, 'not *more*. Not *do*. There must be something else beyond the *doing*.' She insists that the story does not end with Herakles' giving the oracle himself, just Hoadley gave his oracular peroration in Stockholm:

> No, no. That's not the end that ends things.
> Let's go tomorrow. Let's find out.

She, the sensitive, humane woman, is rebelling against Hoadley's brave, new world much as Juno, for different reasons, was rebelling against Herakles' insensate dispensing of blessings in Seneca's play:

> To want the world without suffering is madness!
> What would we be or know or bear
> or love without the suffering to love for?

The second act is set, implicitly, at Delphi, but MacLeish, anxious not to burden the modern validity of the myth by massive, external, ancient paraphernalia, limits the stage props to the sparest minimum—a huge closed door, the slabs of two columns, a few marble drums in the grass. At this site arrive Mrs. Hoadley, her daughter, and her English governess, Miss Parfit, joined soon enough by one of the ubiquitous Greek guides. The argument of the previous day is resumed. Miss Parfit, a bookish creature of limited perception, denies that there is any truth to the myth, whereas Mrs. Hoadley asserts that its truth is timeless. They recall the story of Herakles and at the very moment the guide claims the myth has ended once and for all, Megara appears. In many ways, she resembles Deianeira of Sophocles' *Trachiniae*—the lonely, frightened, frustrated wife who has long been waiting for the return of her husband. Primarily, however, MacLeish uses her for scrutinizing the meaning of Herakles' labours. Like Wedekind, he extends the doubts Seneca had had about Herakles' descent to Hades to the hero's labours in general. Why did he do it, engaging in archaic savagery that negates his every claim to being 'a grown, intelligent, sensible, thinking man?' The guide gives the Pindaric, textbook answer: 'Because he does.' Yet, as Mrs. Hoadley had said on the previous day, 'there must be something else beyond the doing'. Therefore Megara goes on to say that she realizes Herakles had to do it all because he has been promised that he will be a god, a notion which she bitterly ridicules. For—and the parallel to Hoadley becomes increasingly clear—instead of the mad search for a presumably better, nobler life, she affirms that '*this* one might be good enough to live'.

The stage is set for Herakles who returns triumphantly after all his labours to receive the final answer from Apollo's priestess. Hybris is written all over him. He brags about his accomplishments, acts out his great exploit in Hades, throws his weight around, sends the guide sprawling, tosses the Hoadley girl up and down as he did Cerberus, brags that he has overcome death, and makes everybody cower. Yet MacLeish contrasts this first impression of Herakles with the moving welcoming scene between him and Megara—much as in Euripides' play—in order to point out that the hero is not devoid of tender sensibilities. Soon enough, however, the question of the motive for his labours is sounded again. Herakles pleads the classical argument—the act of god, *anankē*. Megara disagrees. 'We go ourselves,' she replies, 'Destiny waits for us.' Herakles becomes irritated because he knows full well he has only begged the question. This is the reason he desperately wants the ultimate answer from the priestess. There is no deed that he, like Hoadley, has not done, but in contrast to his modern counterpart, he is searching for the meaning behind it all. 'A life', he exclaims as he strikes the closed doors of the temple, 'is inconceivable without the silence/answering somehow!' In much simpler terms than the Herakles of Lodge or Wilder, MacLeish's hero tries to satisfy his Faustian urge to learn the ultimate meaning of life. 'I've done my part, God Apollo!' he yells frenziedly

> Persist against impossible, unequal odds,
> set the world straight, staunch the horror,
> slaughter the enemies and then? . . . and then?

At last the priestess replies. In her response, the myth becomes apocalyptic as well as symbolic. Herakles has blood on his hands, she says, his own blood. The hero at first is incapable of seeing what she means. He goes on to boast of his fearlessness, but firmly and inexorably, Xenoclea brings back the memory of his sons. Their murder was the price for his becoming a god. Herakles' divinity is nothing transcendental, but it is the mundane, overbearing, and successful will to power. It is the power that was given to a man like Hoadley, a power that is murderous and destructive rather than creative and beautiful. Megara's long reply to Herakles at the end of the play centres on this theme and echoes the fears Mrs. Hoadley had expressed at the end of the first act:

> Nothing, neither love nor trust
> nor happiness matters to the will of god:
> it *can* and down the city tumbles . . .
> down the children in bloody dust.
> Nothing is as terrible as the will of god
> that can and can and can . . .

Megara pleads with Herakles to relinquish conquering the world, to give up his godhead and to return to his humanity. But all in vain. As the first act ended with Hoadley's pronouncement that Herakles would answer the oracle, with his violently twisting his wife and the wine shining on his face, so the second concludes with Herakles shouting 'violently: his face blazing in the sun'—

> By god, I'll give the oracles myself.
> I'll see and say and say and say . . .
> I'll answer it!

In the brief epilogue, Mrs. Hoadley, her hopes shattered, begs to be released from 'this broken story'. It is a release that will never come because, as she has emphasized throughout the play, the myth continues to be valid and will never end.

Permeated as it is with reminiscences from the Greek tragedians, Seneca, and even Pound, MacLeish's treatment of the myth is imaginative and original. In his headstrong defiance, Herakles is a Promethean figure rather than the noble, humbled hero of Euripides or Seneca. Primarily, however, MacLeish's interpretation amounts to an inversion of the Herakles myth not unlike Sophocles' *Trachiniae*, although the emphasis is different. The beneficent *alexikakos*, who achieves supreme accomplishments for the good of mankind, confuses the means with the end and his deeds become a menace rather than a blessing. Sophocles had shown what happens when Herakles used all his powers and labours for his own good. By adapting this theme for dramatizing the uses and abuses of modern technology and science and their destructive and dehumanizing potential, MacLeish has given it a dimension that is both relevant to our time and timeless. And whereas Pound has been eminently successful in evoking the raw power of Greeek drama, MacLeish, in all the simplicity of his verse, recalls the poetic, lyric, and imagistic qualities that figured so prominently in Attic tragedy.

It may be objected that our discussion has heaped undue praise on twentieth-century playwrights and that this indicates modern bias rather than balanced, historical perspective. Yet it is undeniable that their plays go far beyond the superficial kind of originality that was applied in the neoclassical period to the death of Herakles or his rescue of Alcestis. Plays of the latter kind merely underscore Herakles' traditional adaptability, whereas the moderns are attempting to search for the meaning of the myth in creative and not, as in the Renaissance, exegetical terms. That, after all, was also the objective of the ancient playwrights. Comparison with the Greek dramatists, however, also sets in relief the relative failure of the moderns to write plays about Herakles that are effective on the stage. Just because their energies are almost totally absorbed in bringing out the reflective qualities of the myth, the moderns relegate dramaturgical considerations to second place at best. Wilder withdrew his play, Wedekind's is impossible to stage, MacLeish laments that 'I failed to make my point on the stage',[23]

Dürrenmatt wrote his Herakles play for the radio and not for the theatre, and even Pound's version was first heard on the radio rather than performed on the stage. The plays make for fine reading and recitation but, with the possible exception of Pound's, not for powerful staging. Many reasons can be suggested for this, the most important perhaps being the general emphasis on Herakles as an idea rather than a person or dramatic character since the Middle Ages, if not earlier, and the poor quality of Herakles' dramatic adaptations in the post-classical period. Today's playwrights face a similar problem to that of Aeschylus, Sophocles, and Euripides, i.e. to adapt the myth to the exigencies of the theatre. For the ancients, as we have seen, this was more of a spiritual problem than a technical one, whereas today it seems to be the other way around and hence, a lesser difficulty. What matters most, however, is that initial as it is and holding out the promise of further adaptations, the rediscovery in our century of Herakles as a dramatic hero is not simply derivative, but authentic and original.

NOTES TO CHAPTER X

1. Act Three; cited from *Heywood's Dramatic Works* 3 (London, 1874) 159. For the popular response to the *Silver Age* and especially the *Brazen Age* see E. K. Chambers, *The Elizabethan Stage* 3 (Oxford, 1923) 345. For other plays connected with the Herakles theme between 1566 and 1597 see Chambers, vols. 2. 90 and 143–4, 3. 477–8, and 4. 4 and 381.
2. Zarate's play—available in the edition of J. S. Diaz, *Obras varias de Francisco Lopez de Zarate* 2 (Madrid, 1947) 279–462—is of slight literary merit. Although Heinemann 1. 7 mistakenly labels it a combination of Seneca's two Herakles plays, it owes little to Seneca and much to its author's rather tedious fantasy.
3. For a more detailed discussion, see the article by Soellner.
4. Including Erasmus' *Adagia* (Cologne, 1612) fol. 511; others are listed by Soellner 314 n. 15.
5. Seneca, *Tragoediae* (London, 1613) 24–39.
6. Soellner 318–19, singles out James Shirley's *Love's Tricks or the School of Complement* (printed in 1631) and the academic play *Lingua* (printed in 1607).
7. As is suggested by Soellner 321–4 and, with particular reference to Antony, by Waith 116–21.
8. In her stimulating article on 'Alkestis in Modern Dress', *JWI* 1 (1937–8) 46–60 E. M. Butler discusses the spirit of these operas in some detail. For other

plays about Herakles in seventeenth- and eighteenth-century French drama see H. C. Lancaster's standard surveys.

9. In the nineteenth century, the note of Herakles' magnanimity was also sounded in Lord de Tabley's *Philoctetes* where Herakles, among other things, admonishes Philoctetes to 'learn to forgive, tho' these deserve it not' (John Drinkwater, ed., *Select Poems of Lord de Tabley* [London, 1924] 188).
10. Cf. von Fritz 284, and Walter Jens, *Hofmannsthal und die Griechen* (Tübingen, 1955) 30–44.
11. The most obvious example of Verrall's influence is Theodore Morrison's treatment of the Alcestis story; see von Fritz 293–5 and below, pp. 285f. Wilamowitz' influence manifested itself most clearly in Rilke's concept of Alcestis; see E. Zinn, 'Rainer Maria Rilke und die Antike', *Antike und Abendland* 3 (1948) 201–10, 241ff.
12. F. Rothe, *Frank Wedekinds Dramen. Jugendstil und Lebensphilosophie* (Stuttgart, 1968) has demonstrated Wedekind's debt to Nietzsche's conceptions, but overstates Wedekind's departure in this respect in *Herakles* from his earlier plays (p. 138). *Herakles* is cited from the edition of A. Kutscher and R. Friedenthal, *Frank Wedekind. Prosa, Dramen, Verse* 2 (Munich/Vienna, 1964) 597–663.
13. Cf. Rothe 140–1.
14. Certainly the contrast with Spitteler's optimistic view of Herakles is very striking. Spitteler (see pp. 279ff.) composed his work at about the same time in a Switzerland free from any troubles.
15. 'The Women of Trachis', *Arion* 2 (1963) 119. *The Women of Trachis* first appeared in the *Hudson Review* 6 no. 4 (1954); I have used the edition of Denis Goacher (London, 1957).
16. In this respect, Pound's play can be compared with Seneca's *Hercules Oetaeus* although style and execution are, of course, as different as can be.
17. Cf. Mason 114, and pp. 48f., above.
18. On Pound's technique as a translator see especially J. P. Sullivan, *Ezra Pound and Sextus Propertius* (Austin, 1964) 17–23.
19. For the solar interpretation of the Herakles myth in antiquity see especially Macrob., *Sat.* 1. 20. 6; cf. our remarks on Mallarmé and De Heredia on pp. 266 and 270f. Pound's merit is to have used this interpretation inspirationally rather than literally.
20. *The Hairy Ape* in particular. Yank's metaphysic also is simple and perfect, and he is the central link of a chain of cause and effect, which finally leads to his immolation. His brutality, power, and ferocity starkly contrast with Mildred's qualities.
21. Letter to the author (18 March 1970).
22. MacLeish describes him as 'a huge bulk of a man, strong hands straining at the flanges of the wheels'. *Herakles* is cited, by permission of Houghton Mifflin Company, Boston, from the 1967 edition, copyright by Archibald MacLeish.
23. MacLeish, letter to the author (18 March 1970).

CHAPTER XI

Herakles Redivivus

Such were some of Herakles' post-classical adventures on the dramatic stage. It remains to describe his creative readaptations in genres other than the theatre. Happily, outside of the latter genre this process began long before our century and, for the most part, was the outgrowth of personal and literary imagination rather than based on a system for reinterpreting Greek myth. Yet such systems did exist and we must turn briefly to two of the major ones to determine their place in the tradition.

Allegorical interpretation did not end with the Renaissance. It reared its head again in the works of Giambattista Vico in the early eighteenth century, notably in his *New Science* (1725). But whereas humanists like Salutati and de Villena had puzzled over the various implications of the stories, Vico reduced their significance in accordance with his view that all the ancient myths were symbolical representations of historical forces and movements. Whereas the Renaissance allegories had retained at least a trace of Herakles' literary personality, his dehumanization now is complete as he serves the one and only purpose of illustrating an abstract theory of political science. In the *New Science*, Herakles stands for the early, aristocratic form of society and government which is gradually replaced by that of the plebeians. It is in this light, for instance, that Vico expounds Herakles' struggle with Antaeus:

> Finally Hercules (a character of the Heraclids or nobles of the heroic cities) struggles with Antaeus (a character of the mutinous *famuli*) and, by lifting him into the air (leading the *famuli* back into the first cities on the heights), conquers him and binds him to the earth. From

> this came a Greek game called the knot, after the Herculean knot by which Hercules founded the heroic nations and by reason of which the plebeians paid to the nobles the tithe of Hercules, which . . . was the basic institution of the aristocratic commonwealths.

Compared with Vico's tedious, technical exegesis, the Renaissance view of the same episode as man's struggle against libido is positively delightful.

Similarly, Vico's chilling scientific approach manages to take all the sex out of Herakles' dalliance with Iole and Omphale: 'But Hercules in his old age becomes effeminate and spins at the behest of Iole and Omphale; that is, the heroic right to the fields falls to the plebs.' There is, in sum, little one can add to the succinct conclusion which W. B. Stanford has reached in his discussion of Vico's treatment of Odysseus. Arguing that Vico had no axe to grind against the literary tradition of Odysseus or Odysseus personally, Stanford states that Vico's 'attitude is more radically destructive: it is anti-humanistic. . . . Clearly, it was not a congenial climate for mythopoeic imagination.'[1] Still, the Hellenic soul of Friedrich Hölderlin was to work out an intensely personal and comprehensive interpretation of Herakles later in the same century.

Before turning to Hölderlin, we may give a passing glance to another, more recent mythological system into which Herakles was fitted. This is the Jungian theory of archetypes in which Herakles plays only a minor role, hardly comparable to the frequency with which Vico, for better or worse, had cited him. Jung classes Herakles among the archetypes as 'the slayer of dragons',[2] which is to overlook the majority of Herakles' roles, to say the least. Goethe did more justice to the myth when he considered Herakles the closest approximation to the 'primal man', because Herakles stood not only for one potentiality of the human psyche, but for more than did any other archetypal figure.[3] Elsewhere, Jung interprets Herakles' nocturnal journey in the bowl of the Sun as the return or 'rebirth' of consciousness.[4] Such interpretations are mechanistic and their significance is marginal; the renewed vitality of the Herakles myth had to come from a different kind of inspiration.

In its most sublime form, the myth was recreated in the poetry of Hölderlin.[5] Here it regains the function which it had had in all of Greek literature: it mirrors the development of the poet's attitudes and world view just as it had summed up the progressive experience and changing attitudes of the Greeks. As it had in ancient Greece, the Herakles myth grew with Hölderlin, and Hölderlin, perhaps like no other post-classical author, had both the scholarly knowledge and the intuition to grasp the myth's essence, and he had the ability to express it poetically. There is little that Hölderlin added factually to the myth and he would have been scandalized at making any radical or innovative changes. To him, the Greek form of myth was modern enough because it corresponded perfectly to the world which he created for himself and in which he lived. This world, however, was not the 'real' world of his contemporaries, from whom he lived quite apart. Hölderlin holds a unique place in the tradition because, unlike almost all other writers, he had no inclination to adapt the myth to the tastes and sensibilities of his time. Instead, he breathed life into the traditional form of the myth by letting the myth express his personal experience. By a rare coincidence this form—and the spirit behind it—were as traditionally Hellenic as they were subjective and Hölderlinesque. The reason is that Hölderlin was the most consummately Hellenic of all latter-day Hellenists.

Hölderlin's progressive treatment of Herakles' first labour, the conquest of the Nemean lion, epitomizes the early stages of his own development and of his use of the Herakles myth. Its beginning, traceable in a draft of the *Hymn to Truth*, is conventional. Hölderlin says he will rejoice over his goal in this poem as Herakles rejoiced after overcoming the lion. Soon, however, the event takes on greater profundity. In the *Hymn to Mankind*—again in a prior draft—Hölderlin views Herakles' deed as a symbol of man's conflict with the world around him. By engaging in this conflict, man becomes aware of his own power and of his divine nature:

> Wie sich im ungeheuren Kriege
> Mit der Natur der küne Riese misst!
> Der Löwe fällt! sie fühlt im wilden Siege,
> Des Helden Seele, dass sie göttlich ist. . . .

(How the bold giant copes with nature in immense war! The lion falls! In this wild victory the hero's soul feels that it is divine.)

In regarding the first labour of Herakles as the primal step of man's development Hölderlin is not unique; in his specific treatment of the event he is. Vico, in coldly analytic terms, had argued that 'the lion is here found to have been the great ancient forest of the earth, burned down and brought under cultivation by Herakles, whom we find to have been the type of political heroes who had to precede the military heroes. This sign also represents the beginning of time-reckonings, which among the Greeks began with the Olympiads. . . . They must have begun with the Nemean games of which we are told that Hercules was the founder.'[6] Later, de Heredia also saw in this labour the essential first step in Greek and western history, though he was particularly fascinated with Herakles' taking over some of the animal nature of the slain beast. By contrast, Hölderlin returned to the idealized meaning that had been characteristic of Herakles in Greek religion.

A few years later, Hölderlin perfected this idea further in another hymn, *To the Genius of Daring*. The poem builds on the original stanzas of the *Hymn to Mankind*. Hölderlin is not content any longer just to affirm the awareness of Herakles' or man's soul of its divinity, but Herakles, the prototype of mankind, actively asserts himself over the unordered state of nature. Here, in striking contrast to Wedekind's Herakles, for example, Herakles becomes a veritable Apollonian protagonist, who rises above the mad destructiveness of the primal state of being which Hölderlin associates with Dionysus. Herakles' conquest of the Nemean lion symbolizes the overcoming of this primitive state by man's discovery of the mind. This is the heroic ideal —rather than a process of historical evolution—through which the genius of daring comes to the awareness of his nature and of his freedom to act. Hölderlin here took the traditional idea of Herakles, the liberator, integrated it into the complex of his own ideas, and by so doing, gave a renewed spiritual dimension to it. In a far more meaningful way than in Jung's or Vico's systems, Herakles here is the archetype of human existence, much as he had been in Prodicus' fable. Hölderlin further saved this concept from becoming trite and conventional by setting his own experience and existence deliberately in relation to those of Herakles:

> Einst war, wie mir, der stille Funken
> Zu freier heitrer Flamme dir erwacht. . . . .

Oft hör' ich deine Wehre rauschen,
Du Genius der Kühnen! und die Lust,
Den Wundern deines Heldenvolks zu lauschen,
Sie stärket mir oft die lebensmüde Brust . . .

(Once there awakened, for you as it had for me, the quiet spark, to a freer, clearer flame. . . . Often I hear your arms sounding, you genius of the bold! and the desire to listen to the wondrous deeds of your heroic race often strengthens my heart, which is tired of life.)

Even at this early stage—Hölderlin was barely twenty-three years old—Herakles for him served the purpose of self-expression and not of literary exercise. This development continued in the hymn *Destiny* (*Das Schicksal*), where, for the first time, the emphasis is not on Herakles' first labour, but on all of his struggle. Hölderlin equates Herakles' life-long fight against destiny, *anankē*, with both his own and, more generally, man's actively striving for ethical freedom. Once more Herakles' *virtus* is not contemplative, but active, as it had been in antiquity and in Renaissance Florence. There is no question that Hölderlin was thoroughly familiar with the classical tradition, although the impetus for this particular characterization of Herakles came from the poet's preoccupation with Kant's philosophy at the time.[7] The Herakles myth needed no adaptation for this purpose; it was ideally suited for illustrating Kant's teaching that a combination of virtue and happiness could be realized in the infinite progress of practical action. The discovery of Herakles' *anima naturaliter Kantiana* was more natural and, at the same time, more poetic, than that of his Christian soul had been.

Hölderlin did not stop at this stage. In his *Hymn to Herakles*, which was written somewhat later, his earlier emphasis on the struggle for perfection yielded to his exuberant feeling of having achieved perfection and complete confidence in his powers. Oddly enough, the external impulse for writing the hymn came from Hölderlin's effort to translate Ovid's *Heroides* IX. The result certainly would have bemused the Latin poet as Hölderlin's hymn owes nothing to Ovid and everything to his own spiritual growth. The poet has reached the kind of maturity that makes him a worthy companion of Herakles in Olympus. Immortality, exults Hölderlin, is only a matter of the will, the same will that made him and Herakles persist through the existential struggle in the *Hymn to Destiny*. It is on this note that the *Hymn to Herakles* ends:[8]

> Son of Kronion! On your side
> I am now stepping, blushingly,
> Olympus is your reward:
> Come, and share it with me!
> I was born mortal, I admit,
> but immortality
> is what my soul has won for itself,
> and my soul keeps the promise it has given.

In his famous poem, *The Only One*, in which he summed up the conflict between Greece and Christ in his mind, Hölderlin went on to refer to himself as 'Herakles' brother'.

It remained to explore the implications of this kinship with Herakles, and this Hölderlin did in his most Pindaric effort, *The Rhine*. From this point on, we find him concerned with using the myth less for expressing the condition of mankind in general than his own condition or merely Herakles', but Herakles was Hölderlin and Hölderlin was Herakles. Preparing to be the herald of the return of the Greek gods—an undertaking that ended in his madness—Hölderlin became even more Greek in his thought than he had been earlier. *The Rhine* is primarily about the interrelation between fate and freedom and between divine infinity and human limitation. Herakles, who is half god and half man, personifies the conflict between these opposites as well as the ensuing compromise. Hölderlin first presents the hero in the exuberance of his divine powers—analogous to the young river Rhine, who makes a mockery of all obstacles and order and floods his banks. If Herakles had his way, he would return at once to Olympus, leaving chaos behind him; this is the sublime forerunner of Verhaeren's and Wedekind's Olympian misfit. Therefore, Hölderlin continues, Herakles has to be tamed by a 'greater one' and be confined to the fate of his human existence. Herakles' madness thus is interpreted as the gods' just punishment of overweening, human autarchy, but there is a conciliatory aspect to it also: the gods need heroes and men to complement them (105–13). When Herakles appears for the final time in the poem he is bearing 'the burden of joy with loving arms'. Fulfilling his last labour, the bearing of heaven, the half-god acquiesces in his human state of dependence and therefore will be rewarded with immortality. The very sky which Herakles is bearing is a symbol of the divine fullness in which Herakles shares by being a half-god. It is remarkable that the train of thought in this poem, so far as it concerns Herakles, is closer to Seneca than to any of the Greek adaptors of the myth. As we saw in Spenser's case, it is the inherent dynamic life of the myth rather than direct imitation which again accounts for this phenomenon.

So, of course, does the creative imagination of the poet. For Hölderlin, though he has been said to have been a better scholar and worse poet than Keats, with whom he has often been compared, did not merely restore the Greek myth as an archaeologist would try to restore a piece of Greek statuary in its literal, original form. Even where Hölderlin is inspired by Pindar, his own qualities of imagination take over and save him from becoming an uninspirational imitator. In two poems on the Titans and the gods, for instance, which were left incomplete, Herakles appears, as he had in Pindar, as sent out by the father to establish *nomos*.[9] Once more, Herakles is the purifier (*Reiniger*), but it is profoundly characteristic of Hölderlin that he spiritualizes and even etherealizes the whole idea. We are not startled any longer by graphic descriptions of mares devouring humans and the like, but Herakles is the agent of the 'reflecting god' (*der sinnende Gott*) and the antinomies are 'the rough and the raw' and 'the pure'. Hölderlin tempers and sublimates Pindar's Herakles with Winckelmann's concepts, but the result is far removed from the pallid languor of Winckelmann's plaster-cast Greeks. Quite on the contrary, in his hymn on *The Ister* Hölderlin contrasts the fiery, Dionysiac temperament of the Greeks, which is prone to chaos, with the cool sobriety of Herakles that complements it. Herakles, however, is not simply an 'Apollonian' figure of placid serenity, but he is an active, dynamic life force. A reminiscence from Pindar's *Third Olympian* provided the starting point—and it is no more than that—for Hölderlin's thought. Pindar told of Herakles' journey to the shady springs of Ister so that he could fetch the laurel from the Hyperboreans 'to be the fairest memorial of the Olympic contest' (*Ol.* 3. 14–15). Hölderlin expands this idea into the contrast between the cooling shade of the olive tree, a symbol of calm and restraint, and the dangerous and devouring fire of the Greek mind:

> So I am not astonished that he
> invited Herakles to be his guest,
> shining afar, down there at Mount Olympus,
> when Herakles in order to seek shade
> came from the hot Isthmus,
> for they were full of spirit there,
> but it calls, for the sake of the minds,
> also for cooling. Therefore he preferred
> to go to the springs of water here . . .[10]

Instead of *nomos*, Herakles brings back to the Greeks the spirit of temperance, calm, and restraint, the spirit of the proverbial 'nothing in excess'.

Aside from Hölderlin's Hellenic/Germanic temperament, it was the idea around which his thinking revolved in the final years before his madness that determined his peculiar view of Herakles. That idea was the return of the Greek gods after the imminent end of the present age. Herakles is their herald. At the beginning of the Greek existence, as spelled out in *The Ister*, the hero imparted to the Greek people the temperance of the occident as the necessary counterweight to their chaotic, fiery temper. Conversely, he now, as he prepares Hesperia for the return of the gods, guides 'us (of the occident) who are born sluggish' through the fateful event to their new existence because he is an active, fiery, and stimulating force who creates order out of the cataclysm of the new world day. That also is Hölderlin's vision of Herakles in a fragment entitled *Once I Asked the Muse*. Herakles is the bringer of both coolness and fire and the polarity of the Greek soul is caught up in his person. Once more Hölderlin was true to the spirit of the Greek myth by regarding Herakles not as one-sided, but as the most perfect incarnation of the Greek character. At the same time, the myth takes on a very distinct and individual form at Hölderlin's hands because he interprets it eschatalogically.

Hölderlin's late poem *Chiron* (1801) represents the culmination of his views of Herakles and combines, in utmost density, all the themes with which the poet had associated the hero. Chiron's dual shape becomes for Hölderlin the symbol of an unbalanced existence whose harmony will be restored by Herakles. Chiron, as Apollodorus tells us,[11] was hit accidentally by one of Herakles' poisoned arrows. Since he was immortal, he spent many years suffering in his cave until Herakles returned and announced that Zeus would take Chiron's life for that of Prometheus. Hölderlin, in his typical fashion, interprets the whole story in spiritual terms. Chiron's early life was one-sided in its naturalness, but one day

> disenchanting the wild field, the sorrowful one, there came
> to me the demigod, Zeus' servant, the balanced man (*der gerade Mann*).

Herakles brought Chiron the sober, clear-headed thinking of the mind. It gradually 'poisons' Chiron because he now succumbs to that extreme which is the opposite of his earlier, unbridled, natural fierceness. Chiron now surrounds himself with a world of reason and its products, but he is painfully aware of his new imbalance. Therefore he longs for the coming of 'a friendly saviour'. This saviour is Herakles, who will appear amid the apocalypse:

> Then I hear the saviour in the night, I hear
> him killing, the liberator, and down there
> full of lush herbs, like in visions
> I see the earth, an immense fire.

Like Seneca, Hölderlin/Chiron views death as the moment of fulfilment. For this death signals the return of the light, which is nothing else than the return of the gods to Hesperia. As in *Once I Asked the Muse*, Herakles will restore to Chiron the vital fire and, for a moment at least, restore the harmony which Chiron had been lacking and which Herakles personifies. Herakles' role is active; as in Greek myth, though on a much more sublime level, he is the 'purifier' whereas in *The Rhine*, he had been only the 'pure-born' (*Reinentsprungener*). Chiron and Herakles thus become the principal figures of Hölderlin's myth-historical eschatology.

Hölderlin is as difficult a poet to appreciate as his poems are difficult to translate into English. The latter fact seems to have contributed to the relative ignorance of him among the English-speaking peoples. There is in him much of a modern-day Heracleitus, whom the Greeks called 'The Obscure'. And yet, in the expert words of Miss Butler, 'Hölderlin is probably the greatest poet even the German race, so prodigal of great poets, has produced. He is certainly one of the supreme poets of the world.'[12] Besides the complexity of his thought and expression, there is an unearthly quality about him and an intense spirituality that made him unfit for this world. All his life, Hölderlin wanted to be a Greek and this is why he identified with Herakles, because Herakles was the incarnation of the Greek spirit and experience. Still, this traditional aspect of Herakles was only the point of departure. Primarily, Herakles' portrait by Hölderlin is the product of the most remarkable and, by all standards, most consummately ethereal symbiosis of a poet and a mythological figure. In this mutually energizing process Herakles once more becomes what he had not been for many centuries: an actual person, even if a very refined one.[13] Hölderlin enriched Herakles' character by adapting him to his own mentality. This is, of course, what the ancient poets, from Pindar onwards, had done, even if sometimes in a less personal way, and Hölderlin was their direct heir. Aeschylus, Euripides, and the Cynic and Stoic philosophers had spiritualized the hero progressively. This development reached its organic culmination in Hölderlin's poetry. In the end, it was impossible to sublimate Herakles any further without making him into an abstraction, and Hölderlin, 'Herakles' brother', went mad—as Euripides' Herakles did after he had achieved all that was humanly possible.

In contrast to Hölderlin, Robert Browning let Herakles enter into his life not until late. Ten years after Elizabeth Barrett's death Browning retold the story of Alcestis in the form of a recital by a young Greek poetess named Balaustion. The memory of his wife determined Browning's intensely personal involvement with the story. Euripides had been her favourite classical author and much has been made of Browning's role as a latter-day Euripides.[14] Elizabeth Barrett, in fact, is Balaustion as well as Alcestis; a quatrain of her poetry appears as the epigraph for *Balaustion's Adventure* (1871) and Robert Browning, who once had rescued his wife from the grave, certainly identified with Herakles. Besides, his friend Frederick Leighton had treated the theme in art and Browning even refers to Leighton's painting in lines 2672–5 of *Balaustion's Adventure*. Whereas William Morris, only three years earlier, had followed the prevailing trend of the post-classical tradition by eliminating Herakles from the story,[15] Browning grandly restored the hero and gave him more eminence than he had had even in Euripides' play. The 'contagion of magnanimity', to use Douglas Bush's well-turned phrase,[16] with which Herakles imbues all those around him, may be reminiscent of Alfieri, but the resemblances are no more than superficial. Naïvely romantic and one-sided as Browning's portrait of Herakles is, the exuberant enthusiasm that gave rise to this particular characterization is far from being mired in the cliché. The fervour with which Browning espoused and ennobled him is comparable to Pindar's; like Pindar, Browning rid his hero of all excesses that he thought objectionable and once more Herakles becomes a simple and uncomplicated figure. We may regret the lack of psychological subtlety, but Browning's portrait, even with all of its Victorian and romantic externals, evokes the authentic, pre-fifth-century hero.

Very straightforwardly, then, Herakles is cast once more as the liberating *alexikakos*. The poet uses the hero's specific deed in Euripides' play only as a point of departure for singing the general praises of Herakles, the divine helper of mankind. Whereas Euripides hinted at the serious underlying themes, but still was able to look at the entire action in amusement, Browning universalizes, suppresses anything that might be comic, and tries to project all of Herakles' nobility and cosmic significance into the one episode of Alcestis' rescue. We have discussed this aspect of Browning's adaptation earlier[17] and need not elaborate it. It remains to note, however, that in accordance with this fundamental change of conception, Herakles' motivation for helping Admetus changes also. He does not act from hospitality, let alone from the desire to point out to his host, successfully or not, the limitations of over-civilization. Instead, the simple, almost congenital desire to help a friend is the sole motive. This, in turn, led to another significant change. Browning transformed the satyric gaiety which, in spite of all serious overtones, was peculiar to Herakles in the *Alcestis*, into joyous, noble exuberance; Herakles is, as Dowden put it, 'a very saint of joyous effort'.[18] That this was indeed the aspect Browning wished to emphasize is clear from his introduction of Herakles, which sets the tone for the hero's role. Unlike the Herakles of Sophocles or Hofmannsthal, Browning's hero inspires joy and not awe (1044–51):

Even so,
Sudden into the midst of sorrow, leapt
Along with the gay cheer of that great voice,
Hope, joy, salvation: Herakles was here!
Himself, o' the threshold, sent his voice on first
To herald all that human and divine
I' the weary happy face of him,—half God,
Half man, which made the god-part God the more.

The next three lines are all that Browning owes Euripides in this passage. The rest (1055–78) once more is Browning's own invention and one of the most inspired paeans in the whole tradition on Herakles' gift to bring 'hope, joy, salvation'. 'I think', Browning concludes on a characteristically personal note, 'that Herakles, who held his life/Out on his hand, for any man to take—/I think his laugh had marred their threnody.'

This Herakles, then, is essentially a projection of Browning's own temperament. Browning's hero is as optimistic as Spitteler's was to be and even more exuberant, and his characterization is about as opposite from Wedekind's and Verhaeren's as could be. In spite of all the differences from Euripides' play, it was the spirit of *Alcestis* that provided a congenial basis for Browning's adaptation and view of Herakles; when the poet, buoyed by the success of *Balaustion's Adventure*, turned his attention to adapting Euripides' *Herakles* in *Aristophanes' Apology* (1875), he wrote a translation with a commentary worked in, and the result is rather uneven.[19]

Part of the reason may be the difference in emphasis in the two works. In *Balaustion's Adventure*, the *Alcestis* paraphrase is the dominating part of the poem and a parade piece in its own right. By contrast, the reading of the *Herakles* occupies only a little more than one fourth of *Aristophanes' Apology* where it serves to illustrate the points Browning has made in Euripides' defence. Yet this fact alone is interesting enough and we may linger over it briefly. In Browning's opinion, the *Herakles* was Euripides' 'consummate tragedy' (3526). This judgement, of course, is subjective and explained by Browning's predilection for Herakles.

After *Balaustion's Adventure*, Browning—almost like Euripides—saw in Herakles the hero who 'height over height ever surmounting' (*AA* 515–16) had overcome one obstacle after another and whose indomitable spirit was exemplary even in defeat. Here again, Browning's attitude to Herakles, as his attitude to antiquity in general, was intensely personal as is shown by Mrs. Orr's testimony: '. . . when Mr. Browning . . . translated the great tragedian's words, his own eyes were dimmed. Large tears fell from them, and emotion choked his voice, when he first read aloud the transcript of the *Herakles* to a friend, who was often privileged to hear him.'[20] The external link between the two poems—Euripides has presented his *Herakles* to Balaustion after hearing of her recital of the *Alcestis* in Syracuse—is merely the expression of the inner connection that Browning perceived between the two Euripidean plays. Browning intuitively recognized that the *Herakles* in many ways is a true continuation of the *Alcestis*. Furthermore, the aspects of the *Herakles* which Browning singles out as central to his defence of Euripides are indeed the salient themes of the play. It is generally believed that Browning reacted against the criticism of Euripides by August Wilhelm Schlegel, a criticism which Browning puts in the mouth of his Aristophanes. Schlegel and his followers accused Euripides, among other things, of treating the gods in too familiar a way, of opposing belief in the gods with philosophical doctrines, of debasing the idea of Destiny, and of painting heroic characters in degrading colours by reducing them to the condition of beggars.[21] Browning/Balaustion, by contrast, regards these changes as Euripides' most remarkable, positive achievement. Far from elevating Herakles into a demigod as he had done in *Balaustion's Adventure*, Browning therefore retained the Euripidean emphasis on Herakles' humanity and acceptance of *anankē* as well as Euripides' debunking of the gods. The Euripidean *Herakles* needed no elaborating here and this is why Browning contented himself with a more conventional translation.

At first sight, it may seem paradoxical that in the *Herakles* Browning's contribution to the tradition is precisely that he refrained from adapting and, thus, tampering with Euripides' portrait of the hero. At a time when Matthew Arnold used classical themes for escapism, when Swinburne dismissed Euripides as a 'botcher' and a 'scenic sophist', and when Wilamowitz pronounced Herakles' madness to be the result of his megalomania, Browning sounded the true and authentic Euripidean note by helping the poet speak for himself. *Balaustion's Adventure* and the *Herakles* of *Aristophanes' Apology* are two very different contributions to the tradition, but the spirit behind them, that of a sincere enthusiast, is the same.

While Browning was singing Herakles' praise out of the fullness of his poetic heart, the hero's re-emergence in France was a more intellectual affair. This is not to detract from Browning's great erudition; on the contrary, the prevailing view is that he displayed too much of it in *Aristophanes' Apology* and that it tends to smother all poetry except in the translation of *Herakles*. French rationalism, however, was more than just pure learning. Poets like Leconte de Lisle and José Maria de Heredia fitted Herakles into an ideology of antiquity that was based on a fresh scrutiny of the pagan myths and Christianity. The bias in favour of the former was pronounced most clearly by Leconte de Lisle's friend Louis Ménard. Especially in his *Hellenistic Polytheism*, Ménard held that Greek religion presented a truer philosophical picture of the universe and both he and Leconte postulated a return not to the Greece of classical times, but the primitive Greece.[22] And the hero-god *par excellence* of that era had been Herakles. Along with the 'scientific' preoccupation with myth went the Parnassian emphasis on poetry as a science. At first sight, then, this new Gallic Herakles may be expected to be less full-blooded and more cerebral than his Browningesque counterpart and certainly, it is stunning to see the hero, in Sully Prudhomme's poem on the Stables of Augias for instance, walk off as a lover of the arts rather than anything else. Yet this rationalism was not cold, but permeated by romantic and even mystic elements. One of the best and most influential examples in this respect is the treatment of Herakles by the historian Jules Michelet.

Michelet, famous chiefly for his inspired histories of the French Revolution and of France, had started out as a translator of Vico's *New Science* (1827), but he did not stop there. The animated picture he develops of Herakles in his *Bible d'Humanité* (1864) is far removed from the scientific chill of his Italian mentor.[23] The only point on which the two agree is the origin of the legend, but Michelet's subsequent discussion epitomizes his fundamental difference of attitude. Both contend, with much justification, that the Herakles legend in the beginning was the legend of the lower classes, the populus. Whereas Vico, however, went on to socio-political interpretations, Michelet rehumanizes Herakles and that is his distinctive contribution to the tradition. His discussion of Herakles is encyclopaedic in the best French tradition: he is not content with a dreary enumeration of the various facts and versions, but he is concerned to have Herakles emerge from all this as a hero who has *bonté*, even to an excess, and *humanité*. That, according to Michelet, was the original and essential element of the myth:

> Hercule, qui montre cet excès de bonté, cela est neuf, original. C'est le ciel même du génie grec. Le ciel du cœur détruit le ciel de fantaisie et d'imagination.

Time and time again, Michelet demonstrates that Herakles has, to use modern parlance, 'soul', which makes him vastly superior to the classical heaven of the Olympian gods. Herakles is as impetuous as Achilles, but he has more *bonté*. Odysseus is far from having the great heart of Herakles; 'Odysseus seeks his small fatherland, Herakles his great one.' Herakles is touched by Alcestis' plight, as well as by that of men in general; therefore he becomes the great civilizer and bringer of peace. He is more compassionate—the terms actually used by Michelet are *doux* and *douceur de l'âme*—and magnanimous than the gods whose existence becomes meaningless because of Herakles' very existence. For the same reason—and this was written at the heyday of the German scholarly theory that Herakles was essentially a Dorian—Michelet affirmed that Herakles 'is justly the opposite of the Spartan spirit. He is the man of humanity outside the exclusive egoism of a city so absorbed in itself'.

The same almost empathetic involvement with the hero made Michelet the last apologist of the tradition. Herakles' slaying of Iphitus, his most hideous and inexcusable crime since Homer and Sophocles, is justified by Michelet. Herakles, begins Michelet, was deeply afflicted by the loss of his brother whom he loved, and 'les forts sont très faibles au chagrin'. Add to this the strain of his labours, especially the descent to Hell. So far from making him into a megalomaniac robot as in the plays of Seneca and Wedekind, Michelet uses these events for pointing out how they have shaken the hero. Thus Herakles 'invoque le médecin dangereux qui se moque de nos maux', Love. Iole spurns him; Iphitus, her brother, beats back 'the bastard, the servant of Eurystheus'. Herakles kills him out of impulsive, grievous irritation; he at once is inconsolable about his action and willingly seeks and accepts punishment. The incident is another example of Herakles' humanity and not of his *hybris*.

Michelet's portrait of Herakles is one of the few that does justice to the complexity of the hero's character. Within the framework of Herakles' humanism Michelet makes mention of all the salient, traditional characteristics of Herakles. This does not amount to a dreary catalogue, quite unlike the Renaissance compilations from Salutati onwards, but Michelet writes with gusto, is evidently engaged in his subject, and looks at the myth from a fresh point of view. Curiously anticipating Nietzsche's emphasis on the contrast between the Apolloian and the Dionysiac, Michelet opposes Herakles to Bacchus and depicts him in terms of *alter* Apollo. Like Apollo, Herakles sums up the serenity and strength of the Greek character, but he has what Apollo is lacking: labour, suffering, and death. Again, these are human afflictions and in spite of all its romantic overtones, Michelet's characterization of the hero is thoroughly Euripidean: Herakles is great because of his humanity.

That, however, was not the universally accepted view of Herakles in France during the second half of the nineteenth century. We do not have to concern ourselves with Stéphane Mallarmé's revival of the one-sided interpretation, which tends to be more allegorical than symbolistic, of Herakles as a solar deity,[24] except that this view may have influenced Pound *en passant*. More original is Leconte de Lisle's view of Herakles.

Like Michelet, Leconte cherished a return to the early Greek religion, but it led him to view Herakles as a god rather than a man. *Khirôn* (1852) is his most programmatic poem in this respect. The poem, almost an epyllion, is an attempt to describe the state of mind of early Greek civilization. Chiron primarily is the incarnation of the godfearing, primitive dweller of early Greece. The gods are his friends and companions, and he unquestioningly accepts their superiority. But later, after the invasion of the Pelasgians and Hellenes, there takes place the battle between the gods and the giants. By placing this mythological event after the establishment of the Hellenes in Greece, the poet clearly intended it as a symbol of the first uprising against the old religious ideas.[25] The subsequent account of Chiron makes this very explicit: the gods' vulnerability instills grave doubts about their power in Chiron's mind. It is for these doubts that the gods proceed to punish Chiron, depriving him of his immortality:

> J'osais délibérer sur le Destin des Dieux!
> Ils m'ont puni. Bientôt les Kères indignées
> Trencheront le tissu de mes longues années;
> La flèche d'Héraklès finira mes remords . . .

The characterization of Herakles is contingent on this context. Instead of striking Chiron accidentally, as he had in the ancient myth, Herakles becomes the instrument of divine justice even in this version. Accordingly, even while merely describing the setting of the poem—Orpheus' visit with Chiron during the voyage of the Argo—Leconte de Lisle had earlier introduced Herakles unmistakably in his superhuman aspect. He is the foremost of the Argonauts and described more elaborately than the others:

> Le puissant Héraklès, fils de Zeus et d'Alkmène,
> Qui deploie en tous lieux sa force surhumaine,
> Et qui nâquit dans Thèbes alors que le soleil
> Cacha durant trois jours son éclat sans pareil.

Later, Chiron conveys to Herakles the willing acceptance of his fate:

> Porte au grand Héraklès suprêmes adieux:
> Dis-lui que, résigné, soumis à des lois justes,
> Je vois errer ma mort entre ses mains augustes,
> Et que nulle colère, en mon coeur paternel,
> Ne brûle contre lui pour ce jour solennel.

A des lois justes—Herakles once more is the executor of the *nomos*. Leconte's attitude is reminiscent of Pindar's: *Khirôn* is the swan-song about the archaic world and its values and Herakles, in this unique adaptation of the Chiron story, appears as their preserver.

Like Browning in *Balaustion's Adventure*, Leconte de Lisle thus became the herald of Herakles' divinity. His hymn on the solar Herakles (*Héraklès Solaire*) is one single exclamation on this theme, massing together ever new superlatives in praise of the god:

Le plus beau, le meilleur, l'aîné des Dieux propices!

The poetic fervour of this hymn—a genre the poet chose probably because of its early association with Herakles—more than makes up for the learned equations of Herakles' various labours with the course of the sun. Similarly, Leconte begins *La Robe du Centaure* by addressing Herakles under the archaic aspect of his divinity:

Antique Justicier, o divin Sagittaire.

Herakles the archer had preceded his more familiar representation with the club and the lion's skin. In twentieth-century sculpture his representation under the former aspect again came to express best the hero's dynamism and vitality (Plate 15).

The poem, however, is much more than an exercise in learned archaism. Leconte gives the event meaning by allegorizing it: the robe of Deianeira is Herakles' indomitable desire, and not at all in the carnal sense, that consumes him. Allegory, as we saw earlier, had been a traditional *modus interpretandi* of Herakles especially in the Renaissance and had become well-worn. This should not prejudice us against allegorical interpretations *per se*[26] because Leconte's interpretation is fresh and imaginative. Unlike Du Bellay, for instance, who echoed the traditional cliché that Herakles' *virtus* had made him a god, Leconte de Lisle evokes the notion, inherent in the myth, that Herakles' insatiable desire and spiritual ambition were not stilled by the twelve labours, literally burned him to death, and thus made his substance become divine:

Vos suprêmes soupirs [i.e. of the desires], avant-coureurs sublimes,
Guident aux cieux ouverts les âmes magnanimes;
Et sur la hauteur sainte, où brûle votre feu,
Vous consumez un homme et vous faites un Dieu!

Leconte thus imaginatively broadened and revitalized a notion that had become a conceit as early as in Propertius' poetry and had reached its heyday in the Renaissance. In *Little Gidding*, T. S. Eliot later combined the original concept of Herakles' burning love with the loftiness with which Leconte, but only by eliminating the notion of love, had endowed the subject. Eliot's mode of expression, however, is symbol, and not allegory:

The only hope, or else despair
Lies in the choice of pyre or pyre
To be redeemed from fire by fire.
Who then devised the torment? Love.
Love is the unfamiliar Name
Behind the hands that wove
The intolerable shirt of flame
Which human power cannot remove.
  We only live, only suspire
  Consumed by either fire or fire.

The Herakles poems of Leconte de Lisle's favourite pupil, José Maria de Heredia, are marked even more strongly by the tendency to cut out the inessential and to get, as succinctly as possible, at the true character of the hero. In *The Trophies* (1893), whose aim has been well summarized by Gilbert Highet,[27] Leconte's influence is evident because this poetic survey of European history begins with six sonnets on Herakles, who thus stands for the earliest history of Greece. Much has been made of de Heredia's cult of beauty, but he himself wanted these poems to have more than a purely aesthetic dimension. 'The artist', he proclaimed, 'must have in himself the feeling of life at all epochs.'[28] Therefore the poet's imaginative task was to become a contemporary of the characters he was describing—not exactly an easy task—and no false note could be tolerated. To that end, the poet had to immerse himself in a study of the myths, legends, and historical details. This kind of study alone, which took de Heredia some thirty years, was apt to do away with the clichés that uninspired Renaissance compilers had heaped on Herakles and that had been echoed by the subsequent tradition. For the poet, however, the 'scientific', methodical study of the data was only the preparatory step. It led to new insights, but these could be expressed only poetically to let their suggestive power have its full effect.

Already the first poem of the cycle, *Némée*, shows de Heredia's originality.[29] We have good reasons to suppose that he chose the theme because it had been identified, since Vico, with the advent of civilization in Greece, but where Vico elaborates at length, de Heredia works by implicit suggestion. Nor does he see in Herakles the paragon of divinity or humanity, as Leconte de Lisle and Michelet had. There is a brief description of the sunset, suggesting the end of an epoch (and perhaps even the end of the solar Herakles), and then, in the twilight, of the terrified reaction of the shepherd who sees the lion. De Heredia wastes no time on describing the slaying of the lion and, consequently, omits any mention of the beneficent aspects of the *alexikakos*. The next vignette, with which the poem ends, shows a Herakles who ominously grows out of the dusk and almost has taken on the aspects of the lion:

> Car l'ombre grandissante avec le crépuscule
> Fait, sous l'horrible peau qui flotte autour d'Hercule,
> Mêlant l'homme à la bête, un monstrueux héros.[30]

It would be wrong to over-interpret the poet's omission of Herakles' beneficence as a deliberate detraction, for he was far more captivated by the visual result of Herakles' labour, which to him reflected the spirit of the hero's effort. Already Hesiod and Pindar had emphasized that Herakles could overcome force only by force, and Seneca, followed by Wedekind and MacLeish, had warned of the effects this was to have for the hero's soul. De Heredia goes to no such length, but the last line, in all its Parnassian density, contains the powerful suggestion that Herakles could overcome the animal only by becoming a monstrous beast himself. A drawing by Antoine Bourdelle ('Héraklès Néméen', 1913) seems to mirror the same concept. De Heredia does not say whether the hero's raw, animal force is a positive quality, for much of the peculiar brilliance of the sonnet consists in its open end.

This ambivalence continues in the next poems. In *Stymphale*, de Heredia chose a labour which, so far as we can tell, had provoked hardly any poetic treatment in the tradition. Besides being remarkable for breaking new ground, the poem again reveals de Heredia's careful study of the myth. According to the story, Herakles scared the birds out of their hiding places with a bronze rattle and this might have been enough to drive them out permanently. But Herakles did not stop at that. He went on to shoot all the birds, much to the puzzlement of the ancient writers who tried to find some reason for his action.[31] Of all the labours, then, this particular one perhaps least lent itself for any great paeans on Herakles' beneficent help to mankind, and de Heredia does not sing one. He elegantly hints at the solar interpretation of the myth—the birds are the clouds dispersed by the sun's rays—but he is even more intent to impress upon the reader Herakles' thirst for blood. Like murderous lightning does he strike into the thick clouds of birds, causing the dead animals to rain down upon him. The final picture is that of Herakles standing beneath the sun and the blue sky, while dripping with blood and smiling. Again, de Heredia does not praise Herakles nor does he condemn him, but the graphic description of the carnage wreaked by the hero reminds one of the senseless slaughter perpetrated by Sophocles' mad Ajax on a flock of innocent sheep.

Herakles is mentioned only in passing in the next poem, *Nessus*, and not at all in *The Centauress*. When he reappears, however, in *Centaurs and Lapiths* as driving out the lascivious crowd of centaurs, it is implied that by so doing, he has outgrown his own, earlier animal nature. Nessus wildly desires Deianeira and curses 'l'amour qui dompte l'homme', and the Centauress, considering even this love too civilized, wishes for the centaurs' return to their female counterparts. When the poet, in *Centaurs and Lapiths*, describes the centaurs' attack on Hippodameia, he leaves no doubt about their animalism and it is significant that Herakles who, analogously to the centaurs, had been characterized as part hero, part beast in the first two poems, now beats back their uncivilized forces. The poet goes to some length about this to make his intent clear. There is not a word about Theseus, who figures prominently in the tradition as sharing in this role, the lion's skin has lost its animalistic associations, the centaurs are tamed (*dompté*) by Herakles' angry glances just as Nessus was tamed (*dompté*) by his love, and they, the centaurs, now are called 'monstrous', the very word on which de Heredia ended his description of Herakles in the first poem. It is as if Herakles/Odysseus, such as Homer envisaged him, had come alive again, casting a pall over the banquet room merely by revealing his true identity:

> Alors celui pour qui le plus grand est un nain,
> Se lève. Sur son crâne, un mufle léonin
> Se fronce, hérissé de crins d'or. C'est Hercule.
>
> Et d'un bout de la salle immense à l'autre bout,
> Dompté par l'oeil terrible où la colère bout,
> Le troupeau monstrueux en renâclant recule.

De Heredia continues this theme in the final poem of the cycle, *The Flight of the Centaurs*, in the most elaborate way yet. At the outset he characterizes the centaurs as the destructive, drunken forces of murder and rebellion. They have no place in a civilized cosmos and are driven back to the wasteland they came from. The lion image of the first poem now takes on completely positive connotations: its smell instills the fear of death in the centaurs' hearts. Once more it is the centaurs who are beastly (*bétail*) and not Herakles, and the poem ends with the splendid scene, for which de Heredia may have been remotely indebted to Apollonius, of the centaurs' flight from the pursuing, gigantic shade of Herakles under the pale light of the moon. Chaos, crudeness, and brutishness yield to civilization. Herakles' achievement is heightened by the absence of any bloodshed, in contrast to *Stymphale*; the mere sight of him is enough to pacify the world. This further underscores the hero's progress from the use of brutal, bestial force to sublimity and authority.

In the literary tradition of Herakles, de Heredia's sonnets are, without overstatement, the most stellar example of the inverse proportion between bulk and declarative power. In spite of the poems' utter economy and de Heredia's preoccupation with the brilliance of the visual moment, Herakles is not crystallized into a symbol but reacquires an awesome, dazzling personality. This small cycle of poems is a happy example that thorough and even scholarly study of a myth need not stifle the imagination; in fact, it is only the *poeta doctus* who can elicit more original and, at the same time, authentic features from the myth and thus insure its creative survival.

Sully Prudhomme was a lesser poet than de Heredia and in his one poem on an Herculean theme, *The Stables of Augias* (1867), he is more effusive than de Heredia in all his six poems taken together. Still, one is hard put to determine what is more surprising: the choice of the topic in the first place or the originality of its treatment, involving as it does a characterization of Herakles that is refreshingly free from clichés. We saw earlier that only a follower of Theocritus had made an attempt at writing about this particular labour, which was hardly apt to inspire great flights of poetic imagination, and he solved the dilemma by substituting for the Augias story that of the conquest of the Nemean lion. Prudhomme, in an epyllion that would have delighted the Alexandrians, proceeds not quite so drastically. The grimy aspects of the labour are not ignored, but sublimated. Says Herakles:

> Qui n'ose pas lutter avec le degoût meme
> Connaît encore la crainte et n'est pas vraiment fort . . .

The exploit in the stables anticipates the descent to Hades, but Prudhomme's description of Herakles' attitude to Augias and his four sons is even more original. They all have different excuses for not performing the task themselves. Herakles accepts only the reasons of the fourth son, who is an artist. After emphatically stating, beginning with the lines that we have just quoted, that his own mentality is different, Herakles sympathetically accepts the artist's ethos as complementing his own:

> Et toi surtout demeure, ami des beaux contours,
> Enfant qu'un peu de glaise amuse, aime toujours!
> Dans le temps de rapine et de meurtre où nous sommes,
> Il en faut comme toi pour adoucir les hommes.

In turn, it is only Phyleus, the artist,[32] who sympathizes with Herakles to the point of tears while the others are deriding the hero's task. They continue to do so even after Herakles returns, and he slays them and their treacherous father. The youngest son, however, he crowns, for the justiciar of the world full well recognizes the value of the sensitive soul 'possessed by the sacred art'.

This view of Herakles is not due to arbitrary poetic fancy but once more evokes an authentic facet of the tradition. Already on Hesiod's *Shield of Herakles* Muses had found their place and some early lyric poets, as well as the Athenian Ephebes, had recognized Herakles as their patron god. In Hellenistic and Roman times the memory of this Herakles had been kept alive in the form of the Herakles Musagetes, whereas whenever the Middle Ages—Le Fèvre's *Recueil* is the best example—or Renaissance came close to this aspect of the hero, he emerged either as a Faustian polymath or as the paragon of eloquence, which, even in the wide meaning that it had at the time, did not necessarily imply a high degree of sensibility. So Prudhomme's characterization of the hero, in a very surprising context, is a welcome return to one of his original and much forgotten aspects.

This was not the end of the transformation of those labours of Herakles that had been treated poorly by the tradition. What de Heredia had done in *Stymphale* and Prudhomme in *The Stables of Augias*, Rubén Darío, a representative of Latin American *modernistas*, continued in his *To a Poet* (1886).[33] Darío tried in the poem to sum up the character of the poetry of a contemporary whom he much admired, Sálvador Díaz Mirón (1853–1923), and to address himself to his ideal of a poet in general. Earlier in the same year another poet, Gutiérrez Najéra, had said of Mirón's verse[34] that, being the opposite of effeminacy, 'vigorous like the youth Herakles, it assails, and conquers, and destroys'—

> vigoroso come Hércules mancebo,
> acomete, conquista y estermina.

These lines became the inspirational leitmotif of Darío's poem and his adaptation of the story of Herakles and Omphale. The mythological event serves to point up the contrast between what the poet should be and what he should not be. In Darío's view, the poet must be a toiling fighter, capable of the great efforts which have their most fitting mythological analogue in the labours of Herakles. It is the startling discrepancy between great potential and its utter waste that attracted Darío to the myth of Herakles and Omphale and led him to use it as a universal symbol of the poet's task:

> Hércules loco que a los pies de Onfalia
> la clava deja y el luchar rehusa,
> héroe que calza femenil sandalia,
> vate que olvida la vibrante musa.
>
> ¡ Quién desquijara los robustos leones,
> hilando, esclavo, con débil rueca;
> sin labor, sin empuje, sin acciones:
> puños de fierro y áspera muñeca!
>
> No es tal poeta para hollar alfombras
> por donde triunfan femeniles danzas:
> que vibre rayos para herir las sombras,
> que escriba versos que parezcan lanzas.

(Herakles, crazy, who at the feet of Omphale/drops his club and refuses to fight,/hero who wears feminine sandals/poet who forgets the vibrant muse.//Who would break the jaws of robust lions/ spinning, slave, with a weak distaff/without toil, without thrust, without actions/fists of iron and rough wrists!//Such is not the poet to trample on rugs/whereon feminine dances triumph/who throws thunderbolts to pierce the shadows/who writes verses that seem like spears.)

There can be no mediocrity for the poet. He must be a Titan. Darío begins his poem with the splendid metaphor of there being 'nothing more sad than a Titan who is sobbing/mountainous man enslaved by a lily'. Poetry has to be masculine, proud, self-assured, sustained by a sublime *machismo* whose greatest incarnation was Herakles, and it must be free from the false note of effeteness:

Relampagueando la soberbia estrofa,
su surco deje de esplendente lumbre,
y el pantano de escándalo y de mofa
que no lo vea el águila en su cumbre.

(Let the proud stanza, flashing, / leave a furrow of shining light, And the swamp of scandal and mockery/should not be seen by the eagle from his eyrie.)

So it happened that after centuries of cheap sentimentalization and sarcastic didacticism this particular myth was given a new and startlingly meaningful application in Latin America. Darío was greatly influenced by the Parnassians, such as Leconte de Lisle, and this certainly accounts for his refusal to echo the traditional clichés of the myth. From there, however, it is still a bold, imaginative step to freeing the myth from all triteness, to readapting its meaning and creatively universalizing it. This particular treatment of myth is not unparalleled in Latin American poetry of the period, though it is the only example involving Herakles, and Darío's procedure, despite the thousands of years and miles that separate them, has some touches of Pindar: he rid the myth of implications that were damaging to the hero and then proceeded to use it as a general paradigm. But unlike Pindar, Darío did not alter myth to suit his purpose; instead, he merely looked at it differently. The aspect of the myth that he chose to express was both in the eye of the beholder and, genuinely meaningful as it is, innate in the myth itself.

Whereas Darío was concerned only with one aspect of Herakles' life, Emile Verhaeren, the last of the Parnassus-inspired poets who figures prominently in the Herakles tradition, returned to a comprehensive view of the meaning of the hero's life and death. It is not in Renaissance drama but in Verhaeren's poem *Hercule*, which was published in the collection *Les Rhythmes Souverains* (1910), that we find a revival of the true Senecan note. Verhaeren begins his poem (see Appendix)[35] with the central question that Seneca had developed in his two plays: what more could Herakles do to raise himself? This is the Herakles who has reached the end of his life and who is tired and worn down. His exploits have gone on for so long that they have become monotonous; the repetitious phrase *depuis quels temps* in the first stanza suggests the monotony. What was the result of all his labours? A lot of noise. And now the hero is beset by fears that younger heroes might literally outshine him. The contrast between the old heroism and the new reaches as far back in literature as Apollonius' *Argonautica*. Verhaeren connects it with the mention of Herakles' burning torso and his illuminating the night, which ominously anticipates what is to come: his fiery death. Concluding this survey of dense and utterly effective characterizations of Herakles is the mention of his loneliness, a motif which many moderns, especially Wedekind, Pound, and Wilder, chose to emphasize because they saw in this trait the strongest indication of the ancient hero's modernity. Verhaeren, with apodictic conciseness, sets in relief the paradox of Herakles' progressive loneliness as his works encompass more and more of the world:

> Et jour à jour, ses pas sonnaient plus solitaires
> Même en retentissant jusqu'au bout de la terre.

For the first time we then see Herakles in action. He ascends Mount Oeta, and his anger and impatience drive him to uproot all the trees. Verhaeren goes to great lengths to stress that this action is devoid of any rational reflections or high purpose. Herakles acts impulsively and he himself does not understand the reasons. Finally, his rage subsides. He reflects on his deed and becomes painfully aware that he is only reiterating what he did in his childhood. There is no admiration for his actions, nor is there any meaning to them. Instead, Herakles feels that he is persecuted by mocking voices.

As if this were not enough to emphasize the senselessness of the hero's behaviour, Verhaeren proceeds to paint yet another picture of Herakles in action. This Herakles is nothing more than a masochist. He wants to insult himself and act like a child, and so he tears up all the trees in sight. Verhaeren dwells on describing incisively the scene of devastation. The bleeding tree stumps are left behind and the birds, crying forlornly in the night, are deprived of their nests. The description may have been inspired by de Heredia's *Stymphale*, but instead of a suggestive vignette we now have a tableau of utter senselessness and devastation.

As in Seneca's plays, this tableau is soon followed by another one. Dark, peaceful night has settled down, which serves Verhaeren once more to exploit the discordance between the peace and harmony of nature and Herakles' persistent mania.[36] So long as this hero is alive, he cannot be at peace with the world in which he lives. Hence, as Verhaeren said at the beginning of the poem, relentless noise is the only result of his labours. For Herakles' violent nature, and not beneficence or love or justice, is the motive for his exploits. The peace of the night fails to calm his rage. He looks up to heaven and, as Seneca's Juno had feared, wishes to rival it out of sheer, foolish jealousy. He starts setting on fire all the logs and tree trunks to tell heaven, as Verhaeren puts it, that he has created a star on earth. Then, ostensibly by accident and not as the result of lifelong planning, Herakles decides to immolate himself to conquer death. Here Verhaeren departs decisively from the Senecan precedent and the tradition in general. Herakles stands by the fire, the flames graze him, and on the spur of the moment he decides to immerse himself in the fire. The impression is that he embarks on his final labour in the same haphazard, impulsive way as he had on all earlier ones. The theme of the conquest of death is Senecan, as is the graphic description of the hero's burning and his Stoic defiance of pain. Even the catalogue of labours was inspired by Seneca, but Verhaeren's treatment of it is deliberately more monotonous and builds up to their disparagement by Herakles himself, who speaks of 'the mad rhythm of my exploits'. This is completely consistent with the poet's attitude to Herakles' labours throughout *Hercule*: they are the meaningless consequence of mania.

Yet in the end, Verhaeren somehow seems to qualify his earlier view. Herakles' life may have been madness by ordinary human standards because Herakles was able to take his fill of life much more than the ordinary mortal:

> . . . ma force inassouvie
> A si bien dévoré et absorbé la vie
> Qu'à cette heur de feu je suis tout ce qui est . . .
>
> Jamais le sort mortel ne me dompta le coeur.

Verhaeren's view of Herakles anticipates that of Wedekind. The hero was a superhuman misfit on earth and therefore he is joyous in death because only death can liberate him from the earthly constraints that had been imposed upon him. The event inspired Verhaeren to one of the finest, epigrammatic characterizations of Herakles in the tradition: 'Je suis heureux,' he exclaims, 'sauvage, immense, et rayonnant.'

We noted earlier that one of the chief obstacles to any successful vernacular adaptation of Herakles was the emphasis on his divinity. The manner in which Verhaeren solved the problem is of more than peculiar significance. There has not been even a hint earlier in the poem that Herakles undertook his labours in order to be deified. Therefore the episode that had traditionally epitomized Herakles' arrival at his divine aspirations, his burning on Mount Oeta, could be viewed in entirely secular terms also. Verhaeren was no Sophocles who had an axe to grind and deprived Herakles' death of its associations with apotheosis because he wanted to show the hero in an unfavourable light. Rather, in the twentieth century and modern times in general, divinity and deification simply could not evoke the meaning which they had had in antiquity, and accordingly, every writer in this century has played down, if not outright eliminated, these aspects of the hero. In Verhaeren's poem, Herakles' death has no great cosmic or religious significance. It has meaning only for Herakles himself, in a purely personal way. Within this context, Herakles' former cosmic role is also reduced appropriately to something more personal. He, 'who is everything there is' and thus 'a part of the universe' will return his body to the cosmos—the lands, fields, mountains, and oceans. This is as much of cosmic symbolism as the poem would admit, and its scale is less than grand. *Hercule* ends on the note of the hero's singing joyously into the beginning of the new day that is dawning for him on Mount Oeta. The poem has moved from twilight to daybreak and the day that rises (*grandit*) answers Herakles' initial question—*que faire désormais pour se grandir encore*—because it has liberated him from his earthly existence.

It may strike us as ironic that Herakles, the boon companion and friend of mankind in ancient Greece, should have been metamorphosed, more than twenty-seven centuries later, into a loner—strikingly similar to so many modern heroes—alienated from man and his world. Or we may view this as another testimony to his astonishing adaptability. But again, there is no linear, consistent line of development. In the very same year in which Verhaeren published his poem Herakles reappeared as the dauntless mediator between gods and men in the poetry of Carl Spitteler. Forty years later, we encounter him as man's jolly, folksy, even if not too bright companion in Theodore Morrison's *The Dream of Alcestis* and a few years thereafter, Friedrich Dürrenmatt finally dared to present the most difficult Herakles of them all in our time, the comic one, in *Herakles and the Stables of Augias*.

Of these three writers, the Swiss Nobel Prize winner Spitteler doubtless merits the greatest attention because he courageously revived the epic genre in modern times.[37] In 1866, upon reading Ariosto under the guidance of Jacob Burckhardt, he decided to dedicate most of his life to writing an epic on Herakles. In view of the peculiar qualities especially of his main work, *Olympian Spring* (1900–6, revised in 1910), it is all the more regrettable that he failed to abide by his original purpose. This regret was shared by him in his later life when he spoke of his Herakles epic, though he never wrote one line of it, as being more perfect, richer, and more unified than *Olympian Spring*. For by temperament and aesthetic predilection, Spitteler would have been a matchless master of breathing real and vivid life into Herakles on the grandest scale since antiquity. The Renaissance epics, such as Giraldi Cintio's, had been massive but devoid of inspiration, whereas each of the more creative adaptations of the hero has tended to concentrate on one or two salient aspects of his character. Perhaps it was once more the very fullness and complexity which had accrued to Herakles' character in the course of time that prompted Spitteler to change his mind. There is no doubt, however, that the main characteristics of Spitteler's epic style, as evident in *Olympian Spring*, would have been singularly suitable for a Herakles epic: the plasticity of both descriptions and language, the realism of the characters and episodes—Spitteler at various times inveighed against the appropriateness of *Tiefsinn*, all too great profundity of thought, for epic subjects[38]—and his penchant for the droll, the graphically comic, and even the burlesque. Spitteler might have given us a Herakles with his full, traditional range from the realistic to the ideal, from the burlesque to the sublime, a Herakles who would have been both spiritualized, as in Lodge's or Wilder's works, and full-blooded. As things stand, we can be grateful to him for giving Herakles an eminently meaningful and suggestive role at the end of *Olympian Spring*, which is more of a new beginning than an end. This short epilogue is symptomatic of what Spitteler might have been able to do on a larger scale; it is, purposely and for all of the poet's denials, fraught with *Tiefsinn*, but as in Spenser's *Faerie Queene*, the meaning does not impinge upon the vivid, narrative qualities of the story.

Whether the epilogue about Herakles is a satisfactory conclusion to the entire epic is disputable, but it is equally doubtful that there could be a perfectly compelling end to a work as complex and expansive as *Olympian Spring*.[39] The epic begins with the establishment of a new dynasty of gods after Kronos' fall by Ananke, the masculine, automaton-like power in Spitteler's cosmogony. The gods ascend to Mount Olympus and compete for Hera, who through Ananke's machinations becomes the wife of the pragmatic, imperious Zeus rather than the highminded, spiritual Apollo. The third and central book shows the gods exercising their individual powers to the fullest. Finally, Ananke decrees that their time of play must end. Zeus takes cognizance of the world of men and because they are so base and unthinking he wants to destroy them. He reconsiders, however, and sends down Herakles, his ideal of man, so that Herakles might salvage whatever good there is to be found in the human world and regenerate mankind.

The final version of the epic's end with Herakles' mission was the product of several years of arduous labouring, writing, and rewriting.[40] The finale of *Olympian Spring*, Herakles' *Erdenfahrt* (voyage to earth), thus is one of the most deliberate works in the tradition. Spitteler's first version of the ending was fraught with grim pessimism and accordingly, so was Herakles' role. In that version, Zeus was resigned that in this world dominated by Ananke nothing constructive could be done about the human race. He still sent out Herakles, but his mission, especially after Hera robbed him of all his divine talents, was doomed to humiliation and defeat. The desperation of the whole episode culminated in the following verse:

> Nachdem das Menschenvolk den Herakles empfing
> Geschah ihm wie geschah, und ging ihm wie ihm ging.

(After the race of men had received Herakles, it happened to him as it happened, and it turned out for him as it turned out.)

In one of the most pessimistic adaptations of the Homeric theme of the easy-living gods Zeus wilfully shut himself off from this world to devote himself to a life which, day in, day out, was to consist of dance and amusement.

Such gloominess would have been entirely consonant with other twentieth-century views of Herakles from Verhaeren to MacLeish. Yet it is perhaps a reflection as much on the hero and his myth as on Spitteler's own temperament that the positive, heroic, and hopeful aspect prevailed. The classical author whose concept of Herakles Spitteler's resembles most again turns out to be Euripides. It is likely that Spitteler was familiar with Wilamowitz' edition of Euripides' *Herakles* (1895) who had stressed Euripides' innovation of emphasizing Herakles' purely human heroism in defeat at the play's end.[41] At any rate, by choosing this Euripidean theme for the open end of his epic, Spitteler greatly enhanced its dimension of eternal validity.

There are traces of the *kallinikos* in Herakles before he sets out for his mission but Spitteler, far more directly than Euripides, fixes the readers' eyes on the eventual outcome. As a result, he stresses Herakles' human nature from the very start. He purposely uses the first mention of Herakles as the culmination of Song Three, entitled 'Men'. To emphasize Herakles' human origin, Spitteler boldly dispenses with the story of Zeus and Alkmena. Instead, Zeus goes to the tree nursery of the goddess Genesis and asks for a 'half-way decent human soul'. The human souls are seen floating on a lake. Zeus gives them orders and they all obey without hesitation except for one uncooperative soul in the last row. 'Why don't you do as I say?' asks Zeus. 'Because there is no sensible reason for it.' 'But the others do it.' 'I don't care; I'm not in their service and under their yoke.' So Herakles, in this typical example of Spitteler's inventive and graphically symbolic treatment of myth, is at once classed with the human race and set apart from it by virtue of his mentality rather than descent. This is the kind of independent soul that Zeus has been searching for and the whole rigorous education which he subsequently affords Herakles has only one objecttive: to strive for and respect the truth.

Thus Herakles, at the beginning of Song Five, emerges physically and by blood as a mere man, or actually 'manikin' (*Zwar an Geblüt und Leibestracht ein Menschlein bloss*), as a 'tributary to the earth', but in will and motivation far superior to the grovelling, ignominious *hoi polloi*. This notion of the aristocratic, valuable individual in contrast to the masses is one of the central ideas Spitteler was trying to express in the final part of his epic. As an incarnation of everything noble Spitteler's Herakles is every bit as aristocratic as Pindar's, without sharing in the emphasis Pindar had put on Herakles' divinity, just as Spitteler's thought is more akin to Ortega y Gasset's scorn of the mass psyche than to Nietzsche's praise of the superman. Spitteler's Herakles is a return to the Greek ideal of Herakles—constantly to better oneself—but Herakles selflessly espouses this ideal for its own sake and not because of some ultimate reward. Zeus explicitly denies to him the possibility of Olympus, popular favour, worldly power, or an honourable reward. Instead

Gleich jedem andern wartet sein das Tränenbrot,
Und seiner tausend Mühen Endziel ist der Tod.

(The bread of tears awaits him as it does everybody else, and the ultimate end of his thousand labours is death.)

Herakles, in other words, is a humanistic ideal and not an otherworldly one. By adapting the myth in this manner, Spitteler rid it of the problematic implications of Herakles' divinity which had beset and obstructed the vernacular adaptations for centuries.

Only one thing Zeus asks for Herakles: that he be not humiliated by men and that he earn fame because men respect him. After Zeus has made him drink from the fount of truth, the other Olympians come and endow Herakles with their attributes such as courage, unerring intellect, beauty, and good cheer. This is the passage most reminiscent of Herakles *kallinikos*. In high spirits he therefore begins his journey to earth and triumphantly avows his high purpose, to the accompaniment of heavenly choruses and melodies of harps singing in exultation.

It is, not surprisingly, at this point that the peripety occurs. Hera, who in keeping with Spitteler's inspiration is described more in terms of an Alpine witch than the Thunderer's white-armed sister, hatefully blocks Herakles' way, tears up Moira's letter, deprives him of his divine attributes, and sends the 'Powerful One' with Herakles, just as Aeschylus' Prometheus was manacled by Kratos and Bia. Nor is this all. Frothing at the mouth, Hera yells after him that his whole life will be lacking fulfilment, that there will be no glory and no respect for him, no rewards, just endless frustration and finally, death. In the face of these taunts, Herakles' human heroism asserts itself. He prefaces his reply by saying that he does not even care to hear the reasons that impelled Hera to her ghastly action. They are too emotive to be discussed or commented upon. Where Vergil spent many lines condemning the irrationality of Hera's behaviour, Spitteler's Herakles damns her by ignoring her, but like Vergil's Herculean hero, he is thus established as superior to his divine antagonist. He accepts his human condition, Herakles continues, even though he is embittered. For there is one thing of which Hera cannot deprive him: his labours and his soul will be one, and there will be no discrepancy between his task and his will. With one bold stroke, then, Spitteler removed the two main obstacles to an entirely positive view of the hero's labours: their external motivation and Herakles' ultimately selfish aims. Even in the oldest myths, Herakles undertook his labours as the atonement for a transgression, whereas in *Olympian Spring*, they are the outgrowth of his great soul. Nor will they serve for his own aggrandizement. The function which Spitteler had intended for his Herakles—to be the great, hopeful finale of his epic—determined his view of Herakles' labours and unlike Sophocles or MacLeish, he was not concerned with exploiting the hero's traditionally problematic attitude to his labours for dramatic purposes. Hence he changed the tradition.

Angered as she is by Herakles' unhuman refusal to accept utter defeat, Hera plays one final trump card: she summons Malice, 'who created the universe', to make Herakles subservient to woman. Instead of going to great lengths telling the stories of Omphale or Iole, Spitteler subsumes their general implications in Hera's threat. Knowing that he is virtually defenceless against this affliction, Herakles begs Hera to indulge in her cruel hatred, but to spare him utter shame and humiliation. Hera does not promise to do so; gloating over the hero's agony, she departs from the scene and the epic.

All Herakles can do now is address a humble prayer to Zeus, asking him for forgiveness if he cannot carry out his tasks as well as he had intended, because Hera has weakened him. His prayer is such that it moves even his companion; one is reminded of Lyssa being moved by Herakles' plight in Euripides' drama. His prayer is heard and through all of nature, Zeus beckons encouragingly to his son. Thus strengthened, Herakles ends the epic on a soaring note of optimistic defiance: 'Let courage be my motto so long as I live! My heart says: "Nevertheless!" . . . Ignorance, I provoke you! Malice, I dare you! Let us see who will tame the one whom Zeus ordained!' This is the voice of a Promethean Herakles such as Aeschylus, two thousand and five hundred years before Spitteler, had envisaged the hero.[42] Obedient to the gods and acquiescing in his lot to the point that Ananke is not even mentioned any longer, he will try to regenerate a base human race not by impressive physical achievements, but by setting a superior spiritual example to follow.

Spitteler duly received the Nobel Prize for *Olympian Spring*, but his work is even less well known among the English-speaking peoples than Hölderlin's.[43] Again there is no suitable translation and the modern prejudice against an epic in rhyme is well-nigh insurmountable, in spite of Dryden's polished translations. And yet this detracts in no way from Spitteler's importance. For Spitteler reintroduced mythopoeia into the Greek legends in general and the myth of Herakles in particular. Hölderlin's adaptation had been intensely personal, Browning's romantically exuberant, whereas the Parnassians had crystallized Herakles into a brilliant and grandiose, but somewhat evanescent moment. By contrast Spitteler re-created myth. For the first time in non-dramatic literature since Le Fèvre and, to a lesser degree, Spenser, a remarkably complete Herakles lives and breathes again unencumbered by heavy symbolism or anaemic spiritualization. Indeed, the few pages that Spitteler finally devoted to Herakles bear testimony to his lifelong preoccupation with the hero. While not being overly complex, this Herakles shares in all the significant traits of the tradition except for the grossly burlesque one. He is, as he always has been, a meaningful figure, incarnating both humanity and the aspirations for a better humanity. At the same time, he talks, walks and acts as he had done in ancient Greece and his vivid and graphic presence once more coalesces with his ideal timelessness.

Theodore Morrison's characterization of Herakles in *The Dream of Alcestis* (1950)[44] is of a different kind, though it is no less lively and realistic. Morrison's poem is quite unique in the tradition because it is based on the interpretation proposed by a modern scholar, A. W. Verrall. In *Euripides the Rationalist* (1885) Verrall had reacted sharply against the ennobling of Admetus and Herakles by many adaptors of the play, Browning in particular. Verrall rejected the explanation that the end of the play was brought about by Admetus' hospitality and asserted that Euripides did not want us to take the return of *Alcestis* seriously. In the *Alcestis*, Verrall continued, Euripides obviously had the heroine buried in excessive haste and hence we could infer that she had not really died but was in a state of suspended animation. Herakles therefore did not have to engage in a heroic fight with Death, but he merely went to the grave and finding his suspicions confirmed, he brought Alcestis back home and used the opportunity for playing a hoax on Admetus.

All this would not be inconsistent with writing an even more sophisticated comedy of manners than Euripides had written, but besides his acceptance of Verrall's over-reaction against the adaptors' idealization of Herakles, Morrison's decision to have Alcestis after her 'rescue' choose between being the wife of Admetus or Herakles led him to simplify Herakles' character. It is, to be sure, a simplification in the opposite direction from the *Weltschmerz* of Hofmannsthal or the romantic cosmocrator of Browning, and while this Herakles strikes a genuine note because his role is a return to that which he held in Greek comedy, the Herakles of Euripides' *Alcestis* was richer because the *Alcestis* was more than an ordinary comedy. Necessary as these reservations are in the context of the tradition, they do not lessen the delight of seeing, after many decades and centuries of profound, highly spiritual, and even sublime adaptations, Herakles in that role in which the Greek people loved him most of all: the jovial and good-hearted Ralph Royster Doyster who has got more strength than brains and always needs an outlet for it.

Another aspect of the *Dream of Alcestis* is that it goes beyond Euripides' original in that Morrison answers at length the question which Euripides had left open, i.e. the relationship between husband and wife after they have been reunited. Thus Herakles, with a slight assist from the operatic tradition, serves as a foil in a different way than he had in Euripides' play. For kindly-hearted as he is, Herakles has 'too much force, turbulent, and blind' that would have crushed Alcestis as it crushed Deianeira. Therefore Alcestis finds her way back to Admetus who, in spite of his imperfections, is a more balanced and humane person. Still, it is entirely consonant with the comic tradition that even so, there is no denigration of the hero. Morrison even takes care to eliminate the two comic traits that had been construed unfavourably in the tradition: Herakles the amorist and Herakles the braggart. The hero is modest and relaxed about his achievements even when he is prodded by flatterers. But personable as he is, the lasting impression one has of Herakles in this poem is that, high jinks, rollicking fun and all, he is indeed a world apart from men. Doubtless we would be guilty of arguing too much under the influence especially of other contemporary adaptations, including Dürrenmatt's, if we persistently saw Herakles' lonely pathos lurking ominously underneath the comedy. But we might ask ourselves whether his assumption of the comic role was not traditionally an attempt to bridge the gulf that had to exist between a superhuman hero-god and the ordinary mortal, and an attempt to assure the Greek citizen that in spite of all the differences, Herakles could be just one of the boys. As such he could jovially entertain the wedding guests of Ceyx; in Aristophanes' plays, however, he felt more comfortable with his own kind and ventured only as far as Cloudcuckooland before retreating to Olympus.

And when Herakles had to deal with mankind, frustration was apt to be his sole reward. In a comic vein Friedrich Dürrenmatt took the same view which his compatriot Spitteler had adumbrated earlier. In his radio play *Herakles and the Stables of Augias* (1954)[45] Herakles' physical violence is pushed to the point of caricature as it had been in Greek comedy; at regular intervals the enraged hero breaks the arm, the leg and finally, the skull of his amanuensis Polybios who somehow manages to survive. Far more essential to the comic mood of the play is Dürrenmatt's use of anachronism. Homer had made Herakles a contemporary of Odysseus to castigate him all the more harshly for his archaic manners.[46] Dürrenmatt writes as if the story was taking place in our days, but it is Herakles who is ahead of his contemporaries.

The plot is as simple as it is innovative. Since Herakles refuses to be unionized by the organization of professional Hellenic heroes he has to pay taxes and is debt-ridden. Unintellectual and uncomplicated as he is, he resents, for instance, having to pay great sums for a few lines to poets such as 'Komer' (Homer) so that they do public relations work for him. As bankruptcy is near once again, Herakles stoops to contract with the government of Elis to clear the place of the manure that has accumulated there for generations. He arrives at the scene, greeted by high school bands, officialdom, and fan clubs. The traditional 'Purifier's' task takes on very literal dimensions as he surveys the scene and recommends the use of the rivers. Further action is denied to him. As he uneasily camps outside the city, paying a muscular native to play, in his place, the ladies' man whom the poets have falsely built him up to be, a plethora of committees studies the implications of Herakles' proposal. The Elians begin to fear that the truth of many of their cherished assumptions might be put to the test if Herakles went ahead; specifically the great architectural treasures that are believed to be buried beneath the manure might turn out to be non-existent and the resultant effect on the people's morale could be disastrous. The changes would also uproot the economy and, much more importantly, lead to an abandonment of the traditional way of life. The real obstacle that Herakles is facing is people's inability to accept a drastic departure from tradition and convention, as Phyleus points out to Deianeira:[47]

> Look, Deianeira, this is what I fear: that everything will start all over again, that the manure will come back, that Herakles' whole labour will be in vain because we don't know how to live without manure because nobody will show us the opportunity of man, his potential

to do great, beautiful, true, and bold things, because the manure is only the symbol of our folly and ignorance. I am afraid of the future, Deianeira.

For good reasons, then, and quite in contrast to the writer of Theocritus' *Idyll* 25 who had nicely perfumed the story, Dürrenmatt is most intent to have both Herakles and the listener wallow in the manure from the outset and thus to stress its ubiquitous, all-pervasive presence. Naturally, the task of clearing it away is beyond the powers of Herakles and any man and, one suspects, any god. Boars, monsters, and highwaymen can be conquered; attitudes, prejudice, and entrenched ways of thinking and living cannot. Herakles cannot make Elis a 'land worthy of man' as Phyleus continues to hope. The Elians refused to let Herakles help them, says Augias in the end, 'because they were afraid of what they wanted and of which they knew that it was rational'. Herakles cannot prevail and departs for yet baser work in Stymphalia where, for all we know, the story might repeat itself.

So the play becomes a parable for a good many things. With its combination of brilliant sophistication, humour both subtle and broad, and a serious, underlying theme it catches best, of all post-classical plays, the spirit in which Euripides had written his *Alcestis*. Herakles' labours are to no avail in an over-structured and convention-minded world. In Euripides' play, Herakles had had no trouble defeating Death, but Euripides had given no encouraging hint that he would be able to overcome Admetus' way of thinking. As in the *Alcestis*, Herakles stands in Dürrenmatt's play for an unspoiled, simple kind of humanity which, however naïve, uncomplicated, and archaic, is essential for 'a life worthy of man'.

But Dürrenmatt develops two more facets of this picture. In the first place, he presents us with the waste of Herakles' potential: while the bickering goes on in Elis and his plan is ground from one level of the bureaucracy to the next, the hero has to work in a circus to make a living. Instead of being given the opportunity to use his strength for the common good, he is allowed only to use it for show, while being defrauded of half of his fee every night by the clever circus director, a 'man of this world'. Secondly, and serving as a fitting end for this chapter and the whole survey of the tradition: there is the realization that the grace and the good, for which Herakles has stood since his early beginnings in Greece, cannot be forced on mankind. He is not an external agent from whom man can expect miracles that will change the world, but every man must become Herculean in working for the good and the humane himself. This is what Augias tells his despairing son in the play's tag, which may seem heavy-handed but is entirely congruent with a powerful component of the tradition: the moralistic one. When Herakles has left, Augias leads Phyleus into a garden which he has secretly cultivated over the years. Out of the manure and the dung he has made fertile vegetable soil and he has transformed the misshapen environment into blossoms, flowers, and fruit trees. It is, as Augias says, the garden of his resignation. His ambitions, like Herakles', have been frustrated and mankind does not want to accept the Herculean ideal of constantly trying to rise above its limitations. But it is entirely consonant with the myth and the tradition that Augias does not end on a note of despair, but on a confident call to ever new efforts:[48]

> These are difficult times in which one can do but so little for the world, but at least we shall do whatever little we can do: that is, our own. . . . So let this garden be yours. . . . Dare now to live and to live here, amidst this shapeless wasteland: this is the heroic labour that I impose upon you, son, this is the labour of Herakles that I am laying on your shoulders.

NOTES TO CHAPTER XI

1. Stanford 186. Vico is cited from the translation of *The New Science* by T. G. Bergin and M. H. Fisch (Ithaca, N.Y., 1968). The passages quoted are §618 and §657.
2. See J. Jacobi, *The Psychology of C. G. Jung*[5] (London, 1952) 62.
3. Cf. also the comment of Maud Bodkin, *Archetypal Patterns in Poetry* (London, 1934) 245: 'The archetypal hero-figure stands poised between height and depth, between the Divine and the Devilish, swung forward and upward in reflection of imagination's universal range, hurled backward and downward in expression of individual limitation and the restraining censure of the whole upon the part.' Herakles' various roles in the tradition more than live up to this characterization.

4. See J. Jacobi, *Complex, Archetype, and Symbol in the Psychology of C. G. Jung* (New York, 1969) 183–4; cf. 152.
5. My discussion of Herakles in Hölderlin's poetry is much indebted to Hötzer's thorough and sensitive study, which has an extensive bibliography. Also valuable, though less detailed, is Kurt Berger, *Menschenbild und Heldenmythos in der Dichtung des deutschen Idealismus* (Berlin, 1940), esp. 247–52. For the general background see Butler, *Tyranny* 203–40 and Highet 377–9.
6. Vico (note 1, above) §3; cf. §540.
7. Hötzer 40 and W. Böhm, *Hölderlin* 1 (Halle, 1928) 96.
8.

> Sohn Kronions! an die Seite
> Tret'ich nun erröthend dir,
> Der Olymp ist deine Beute;
> Komm und theile sie mit mir!
> Sterblich bin ich zwar geboren,
> Dennoch hat Unsterblichkeit
> Mein Seele sich geschworen
> Und sie hält, was sie gebäut.

9. *Die Titanen* and *Wem aber die Himmlischen*, in *Hölderlin: Sämtliche Werke*. Grosse Stuttgarter Ausgabe, ed. by Fr. Beissner, vol. 2 (Stuttgart, 1951) 217ff.; discussed at length by Hötzer 106–18.
10. Lines 26–35:

> . . . So wundert
> Mich nicht, dass er
> Den Herkules zu Gaste geladen,
> Fernglänzend, am Olympus drunten,
> Da der, sich Schatten zu suchen
> Vom heissen Isthmus kam,
> Denn voll des Muthes waren
> Daselbst sie, es bedarf aber, der Geister wegen,
> Der Kühlung auch. Darum zog jener lieber
> An die Wasserquellen hieher.

11. Apollodorus 2. 5. 4; cf. p. 45 with note 11.
12. Butler, *Tyranny* 205.
13. By contrast, Hölderlin's contemporary Friedrich Schiller, for instance, eloquently repeated the traditional concept of Herakles as the hero who accepted punishment for his transgressions and thereafter was received into Olympus; see especially his poem *Ideals and Life*. But for him the Greek gods were dead whereas Hölderlin fervently believed in their return.
14. See, for instance, the typical comment of W. C. DeVane, *A Browning Handbook*[2] (New York, 1955) 351: 'There was a genuine kinship between Euripides and himself'; cf. R. A. King, *The Focusing Artifice* (Athens, Ohio, 1968) 201. Major discussions of *Balaustion's Adventure* are DeVane 349–59; F. M.

Tisdel, '*Balaustion's Adventure* as an Interpretation of the *Alcestis* of Euripides', *PMLA* 32 (1917) 519–46; Bush, *Mythology and the Romantic Tradition* 364–73; von Fritz 273–80 and most comprehensively, R. Spindler, *Robert Browning und die Antike* 1 (Leipzig, 1930) 17–85 and 2. 278–93, 353–61.

15. William Morris, *The Love of Alcestis* in *Earthly Paradise* (1868). Bush, 372 n. 18, also mentions *Alcestis*, a dramatic poem by John Todhunter (1879) and the *Admetus* (1871) of Emma Lazarus. Herakles is completely turgid in W. S. Landor's Dramatic Scene *Heracles, Pluto, Alcestis, Admetus* (1859) (in Stephen Wheeler, ed., *The Complete Works of Walter Savage Landor* 14 [London, 1933] 233–7) and so are Landor's other references to him, notably in *Birth of Poesy, Canto* 2 (Wheeler edition, vol. 16. 241–3) and *Canto* 3 (Wheeler ed., vol. 16. 258). Nor did Herakles fare much better in Book Three of William Morris' *The Life and Death of Jason* (1866)—a work that was highly praised by Swinburne, among others—although Morris is one of the many writers who minimizes Herakles' role in the Hylas story (Book Four).
16. *Mythology and the Romantic Tradition* 369.
17. See pp. 73ff.
18. Dowden as quoted by Bush, *Mythology and the Romantic Tradition* 371.
19. Most criticism of *Aristophanes' Apology* centres on its being tediously learned and saturated with recondite allusions, see, e.g. Bush 373–5; DeVane 375–84; and the survey of opinions by Spindler 2. 358–69. C. N. Jackson has meticulously studied the 'Classical Elements in Browning's *Aristophanes' Apology*', in *HSCP* 20 (1909) 15–74, and another tabulation of Browning's classical sources is T. L. Hood's article in *HSCP* 33 (1922) 79–180. For a more perceptive analysis of Browning's aims see F. M. Tisdel, *Browning's Aristophanes' Apology, Univ. of Missouri Studies* 2. 4 (1927); cf. Donald Smalley, 'A Parleying with Aristophanes', *PMLA* 55 (1940) 823–38. Spindler 2. 296–349 offers much valuable detail on Browning's translation of the *Herakles*.
20. Mrs. Sutherland Orr, *Life and Letters of Robert Browning*, rev. ed. by F. G. Kenyon (Boston and New York, 1908) 294.
21. Spindler 2. 334.
22. See Henri Peyre, *Louis Ménard* (Yale, 1932) 490–7 and Highet 456–7.
23. *Bible d'humanité* is cited from *Œuvres complètes de Jules Michelet* 35 (Paris, 1899); the chapter on Herakles is found on pp. 173–91. For a good discussion on Michelet see G. P. Gooch, *History and Historians in the Nineteenth Century* (New York, 1949) 175–85.
24. See *L'Héraclès Grec ou L'Hercule Latin* in *Les Dieux Antiques* (1880), on pp. 1213–18 in the Pléiade edition of his *Œuvres Complètes* by H. Mondor and G. Jean Aubry (1945). Cf. Chapter 10, note 19.
25. Cf. J. Vianey, *Les Sources de Leconte de Lisle* (Montpellier, 1907) 364–5.
26. Cf. C. B. Wheeler, *The Design of Poetry* (New York, 1966) 144ff.
27. *The Classical Tradition* 442: 'Beginning with the earliest legends of Greece, and passing through Rome to the Middle Ages and the Renaissance, it freezes the whole of western European history in a series of vividly coloured

and dazzlingly bright crystals, each of exactly the same form and each showing some heroic enterprise or moment of beauty at its highest intensity.'

28. In his article on Daniel Vierge in *Revue Illustrée*, 1 July 1894, as cited by M. Ibrovac, *José-Maria de Heredia. Sa vie—son œuvre* (Paris, 1923) 219 n. 1.
29. M. Ibrovac, *José-Maria de Heredia. Les sources des Trophées* (Paris, 1923) 4–11 refers to other French authors who adapted some of the episodes from Herakles' life.
30. The inspiration for this last line came from Théodore de Banville's poem *Némée* (1874):

    Ils étaient à la fois deux heros et deux bêtes,
    Mêlant leurs durs cheveux, entre-chôquant leurs têtes.

    By condensing these two lines, de Heredia achieved a greater sense of identification of hero and beast. More importantly, whereas de Banville began his poem by suggesting the similarity between Herakles and the lion only to proceed more conventionally by describing the hero's superiority over the beast, de Heredia ended his *Némée* on the note of the identification of the two. Another poem by de Banville on Herakles, *Tueur de Monstres* (1873), is entirely conventional.
31. See H. J. Rose's summary in his *Handbook of Greek Mythology* (New York, 1959) 213.
32. This particular role of Phyleus is original with Sully Prudhomme. The ancient tradition knows of his quarrel with his father Augias, because Phyleus objected to Herakles' being wronged; see Pausanias 5. 1. 10; Diodorus 4. 33. 4; Apollodorus 2. 5. 3, and 3. 10. 8, and Callimachus frs. 198 and 383 (Pfeiffer). But there is not a word of Phyleus' being an artist.
33. *A un Poeta* appeared in the collection entitled *Azul*, which was published first in 1888. Ernesto Mejía-Sánchez, *Hércules y Onfalia. Motivo modernista* (Mexico City, 1964) surveys the occurrences of the theme especially in nineteenth-century French, Spanish, and Latin American literature; best known perhaps is Victor Hugo's *Le rouet d'Omphale* (1856) on which see Leo Spitzer in his *Romanische Literaturstudien* (Tübingen, 1959) 277–85. Before writing *A un Poeta* Darío had studied Ovid's Ninth *Letter*, and this effort had the same unexpected result as it did in Hölderlin's case (see above, p. 255). It also inspired Darío to write an article on 'Hércules y Don Quichote' in which he mainly contrasted the former's lasciviousness with the latter's chastity; see R. Darío, *Letras*, ed. Librairie Garnier (Paris, 1911), esp. 143–4.
34. In his poem *A Sálvador Díaz Mirón*, whereas the title alone of Darío's poem indicates that the ideas set forth in the poem are meant to be more widely applicable than being only a tribute to Díaz Mirón.
35. Because editions of *Les rythmes souverains* are not easily available, the poem is reprinted *in toto* in the Appendix; the edition used is that of Mercure de France (Paris, 1913) 25–31.
36. Cf. our discussion of Theocritus' *Hylas* on p. 118.

37. On Spitteler see primarily R. Faesi, *Spittelers Weg und Werk* (Frauenfeld, 1933) and O. Rommel, *Spittelers 'Olympischer Frühling' und seine Epische Form* (Berne and Munich, 1965); also, K. Messleny, *Karl Spitteler und das Neudeutsche Epos* (Halle, 1918) and the various books and articles listed by Highet 703 n. 20, to which should be added Butler, *Tyranny* 316–22. I have benefited most from the studies of Faesi and Rommel, whereas W. Adrian, *Die Mythologie in Spittelers Olympischem Frühling* (Berne, 1922) has next to nothing to say on Herakles. *Olympian Spring* is cited from the edition by G. Bohnenblust (Zurich, 1945).
38. Spitteler as quoted by Faesi 233 and 237.
39. One can usefully compare this to the dispute about the end of the *Odyssey*.
40. On this see especially Rommel (note 37, above) 106–24.
41. Wilamowitz, Herakles 129–30. There is a startling coincidence between Wilamowitz' summary of Herakles' attitude—*ich trag es dennoch* (p. 130)—and that of Spitteler's Herakles: 'Mein Herz heisst: Dennoch!' (p. 609 in the edition cited in note 37, above). Messleny 194–5 states unequivocally that Spitteler must have been acquainted with the *Herakles* of Euripides.
42. See pp. 42ff. Herakles' resemblance to Prometheus has been noted by A. H. J. Knight, *MLR* 27 (1932) 443 n. 2. Conversely, the Prometheus of Spitteler's earlier long poem *Prometheus and Epimetheus* (1881) was modelled in many ways on Herakles; see Messleny 191–5 for a detailed discussion.
43. J. G. Robertson praised it to the sky in his *Essays and Addresses on Literature* (London, 1935) 102. Against Miss Butler's critique that, although it is a 'remarkable work of genius', *Olympian Spring* is flawed because mythology cannot express reality (*Tyranny* 322) see, e.g. Mircea Eliade, op. cit. (Introduction, n. 3) *passim*, and Philip Wheelwright, *Metaphor and Reality* (Bloomington, 1962) 130–4, 172–3.
44. Cited from the edition of the Viking Press (New York, 1950). Von Fritz discusses Morrison's poems on pp 293–5.
45. F. Dürrenmatt, *Herkules und der Stall des Augias*, Komödie © Copyright 1963 by Peter Schifferli, Verlags A. G. 'Die Arche', Zurich. The quotations on pages 287, 288, and 289 are quoted by permission of the publisher; the translations are my own.
46. See p. 12.
47. Dürrenmatt 40–1.
48. Dürrenmatt 66.

CHAPTER XII

Epilogue: Herakles as a Literary Character and an Idea

Lilio Gregorio Giraldi prefaced his brave attempt at a *Herculis Vita* with the remark: '*Herculis est labor omnem de Hercule historiam contexere.*'[1] If we shall not now try to *contexere* all of the vagaries of Herakles' literary fortune during the twenty-seven centuries from Homeric Greece to our present time it is not for fear of *Herculis labor*, but, as suggested in the Introduction, because the variety of Herakles' roles defies any systematization in the form of thesis or all-embracing exegesis. Myth is kept alive through the ages by constantly being reinterpreted and this reinterpretation most often takes the form of adaptation to the prevailing sensibilities of a given age. It is problematic to call this process of assimilation merely an external influence because we must differentiate reinterpretations of timeless validity, even though they may have been occasioned by the *Zeitgeist* of a specific period, from the more extraneous, time-honoured tendency to fit any traditional legacy into the contemporary mould. Good examples of the former kind of adaptation are the uses of the myth by Euripides, Seneca, Darío, Wedekind, and Spitteler, and of the latter, the versions of Rotrou and Wieland, and the Christian Herakles of Ronsard. Genre, of course, is another determining factor in the tradition. The exigencies of the genre could reduce Herakles to an archaic stereotype, as seen in Apollonius' *Argonautica* and, to a lesser extent, Theocritus' Hylas *Idyll*, but they could also open up a new spiritual dimension for Herakles as in Greek tragedy and the epics of Vergil and Spenser, thus effecting more than merely external changes in the hero's characterization. A writer's personal reaction, ranging from utter repugnance to self-identification, was one of the strongest elements in the literary perpetuation of the myth and was greatly responsible for the vicissitudes of the characterization of Herakles. Herakles' literary fortune starts with Homer's condemnation and had it not been for the personal interest of Bacchylides and Pindar in the hero, he might have become, in serious literature, an archaic relic by the beginning of the fifth century B.C. Writers such as Sophocles, Seneca, and de Heredia viewed Herakles with mixed feelings and enriched the tradition by bringing into conflict the various aspects of his character. On the other hand, positive personal interaction between author and hero ranges from Aristophanes' brief identification with Herakles in his fight against the monster Cleon to Hölderlin's lifelong projection of himself into his 'brother Herakles' and his self-realization as something of Herakles' strength and spirit entered into him.

What attracted all writers—serious, comic, Christian, and moralistic alike—to Herakles was his traditional, pre-Homeric quality of being superhuman. We have discussed in detail this aspect and the various factors determining a writer's response in the Introduction and the previous chapters and there is no need for repetition here. Pre-Homeric as it is, the literary genesis of Herakles is shrouded from our sight, but we must dwell for one moment on one of its aspects that had profound implications for Herakles' fate in the tradition. That was his transition from the hero of the folktale to the hero of myth and legend. The development is not peculiar to Herakles because, as Bruno Snell has observed, 'it is a characteristic trait of Greek mythology that the motifs of *Märchen* are always remoulded into the forms of saga. Saga differs from empirical reality in that it furnishes, along with the facts, also the deeper meaning. The later enlightenment argued that the meaning which emerges from an event is a matter of human interpretation; but in the saga this meaning asserts itself as a valid, divine component of the tale.'[2]

In Herakles' case this divine component was, of course, greatly intensified by his divine aspirations as a hero and his actual divinity in cult. This, in turn, deepened once again the meaning of the myth. And it is precisely this meaning, the idea and ideas which Herakles could stand for, that constantly threatened to get the better of Herakles the person and literary character. The tension between these two concepts shaped much of Herakles' literary fortune. The earliest of the authors whom we have surveyed, Homer, regards Herakles as a real person, a contemporary of Ulysses in fact, and his own reaction to our hero is quite personal. Under a positive aspect, we find an even more intense attitude on the part of Pindar. But Pindar also accentuated the idea for which Herakles stood, and this tendency accelerated in authors later in the fifth century. In Sophocles' *Philoctetes* Herakles' *persona* is minimized and it is the Herakles ideal, and the imperfect attempts of his would-be followers to live up to it, that dominate the action of the play. Prodicus' parable is an early culmination of the same tendency. Prodicus chose Herakles as the protagonist not out of any particular concern for Herakles, but because Herakles was the most suitable mythological personification of the point Prodicus wished to make, i.e. man's progress from *physis* to *nomos* by means of voluntary deliberation. The view of Herakles as an exemplar rather than a *persona* found a resounding echo in the tradition based on Prodicus' parable, even if this tradition changed its focus. To the Stoics and Cynics, Herakles could easily become an example of general morality rather than of personal behaviour and in antiquity it is only Seneca's Herakles who is as much of a literary as a philosophical hero. Vergil's and Spenser's Herakles is saved from being an abstraction mostly by his evocative, suggestive powers, whereas authors such as Salutati, Giraldi Cintio, and Lodge, and the moralistic tradition in general viewed him merely as an idea without fleshing him out. We can say, with some justification, that the hostility of the early Christian tradition to taking Herakles 'for real' denied him both his personality as a man and his idealistic value of man becoming god.[3] The idea for which Herakles stood recovered from this faster than did his literary personality, but the import of the idea was changed significantly as Herakles was regarded merely as a virtuous man, and the emphasis was on the virtuous and not, as in the ancient secularizations of the theme, on the man. It is, as we have seen, not true that the tradition of Herakles as an exemplar of virtue obliterated all his earlier appearances and characteristics. Still, to revive him as a literary figure in the Middle Ages and the Renaissance it took a drastic step, such as Philip the Good's exhortation to Le Fèvre to have the courage to write 'more than their books mention', in short, to be original.

One factor which seems to have obstructed such originality and encouraged the tendency to transpose Herakles into the realm of ideas is, as we have seen, the massive range of his manifestations in the tradition even in antiquity. The mythological tradition and the ancient literary tradition endowed Herakles more richly than any other ancient hero. If this testified to his unparalleled versatility it also confronted the later adaptors with a bewildering too much. Already in the fourth century B.C., an author like Isocrates remarked on this, even if rhetorically. But in Goethe's comment on Herakles, and in Spitteler's and perhaps even Ronsard's failure to write epics on Herakles we find the clearest expression of a writer's frustration with the magnitude of the task, which deterred him from undertaking it. Magnitude of that kind attracts the scholarly rather than the poetic temperament and the assiduous researches of Salutati, de Villena, and Lilio Gregorio Giraldi kept the baffling array of Herakles' works and details of his life from being unknown. But ignorance, as Stanford has remarked in discussing Dante's adaptation of Ulysses, can be the mother of mythopoeia.[4]

All this, however, did not preclude originality and true creativity of adaptation. Many of the most significant treatments of the myth come precisely from writers who had studied and read both the Greek and the Roman originals intensively. We need to think only of Hölderlin, Browning, the Parnassians, Verhaeren, and Pound. Here study of the myth becomes not an impediment but an inspiration. This was largely possible only after the extant remains especially of Greek literature became generally available and an author in search for Herakles could go back directly to the Greek originals instead of having to rely, for example, on emblem books or summary compilations. Nor were these adaptors troubled by taking a fresh look at only one or two aspects of the hero's character for this had been the procedure of most of their ancient predecessors also. It is the quality of Herakles' experience, and not its quantity that accounts both for the timelessness of many roles in which he was rediscovered and for the originality of their treatment. Instead of merely echoing and adapting traditional aspects of the myth, some authors were able to elicit some heretofore latent aspect of it. Wedekind's characterization of the hero as a profoundly lonely figure between the worlds of gods and men is one example, in spite of the many flaws of his play, and Darío's evocation of Herakles at Omphale's court as an example of suppressed creativity is another.

As is clear from these last examples and many others surveyed in the earlier chapters, it would be wrong to postulate a dichotomy between meaning and idea on the one hand, and Herakles' literary personality on the other. Adaptors of the theme from Hesiod and Euripides to Dürrenmatt and MacLeish were attracted to Herakles precisely because he was a meaningful figure besides being a character in his own right for a good and even dramatic story. If the meaning or the idea impinges constantly on the narrative and literary qualities of the work of art we will have philosophy or exegesis rather than literature;[5] the skill of authors such as Seneca, Spenser, and Spitteler can be gauged exactly by their ability to avoid this pitfall. On the other hand, to make Herakles simply the character of a well-told story would be to relegate him to the *Märchen* world from which he was emancipated long ago. To find an equilibrium between these two aspects was difficult and challenging, but it was achieved gratifyingly often. It was *Herculis labor* and not the impossible, frustrating task of Sisyphus.

NOTES TO CHAPTER XII

1. See p. 201 with n. 30.
2. B. Snell, *The Discovery of the Mind*, trans. by T. G. Rosenmeyer (New York, 1960) 207.
3. Cf. our remarks on Petrarch on pp. 189f. with n. 7.
4. Stanford 3.
5. Cf. Benedetto Croce's distinction between the life of the myth and that of its interpretation, as mentioned on p. 196 with n. 17.

APPENDIX

Emile Verhaeren

HERCULE (1910)

Que faire désormais pour se grandir encore?

    Hélas! depuis quels temps
Avait-il fatigué les soirs et les aurores.
    Hélas! depuis quels temps,
Depuis quels temps de tumulte et d'effroi
Avait-il fatigué les marais et les bois,
Les monts silencieux et les grèves sonores
Du bruit terrible et persistant
        De ses exploits?

Bien que son cœur brûlât comme autrefois son torse,
Parfois il lui semblait qu s'éteignait sa force;
Tant de héros plus prompts et plus jeunes que lui
Avaient de leurs travaux illuminé la nuit.

Et jour à jour, ses pas sonnaient plus solitaires
Même en retentissant jusqu'au bout de la terre.

Lentement le soleil vers le Zénith monta,
Et, depuis cet instant jusques au crépuscule,
            L'Œta
Put voir, marcher et s'arrêter sans but, Hercule.
            Il hésitait
            Devant les routes,

Allait et revenait et s'emportait
Pour tout à coup se recueillir comme aux écoutes;
Son esprit s'embrouillait à voir trop de chemins
Trouer les bois, couper les plaines;
La colère mauvaise enflamma son haleine,
L'impatience entra dans ses doigts et ses mains,
Et, brusquement, courant vers la forêt prochaine,
Avec des rauquements sauvages dans la voix,
Il renversa comme autrefois
Les chênes.
Son geste fut si prompt qu'il ne le comprit pas.

Mais quand sa rage, enfin calmée et assouvie,
Lui permit de revoir en un éclair sa vie
Et sa terrible enfance et ses puissants ébats,
Alors qu'il arrachait, par simple jeu, des arbres,
Ses bras devinrent lourds comme des bras de marbre
Tandis qu'il lui semblait
Entendre autour de lui mille rires bruire
Et les échos cruels et saccadés lui dire
Qu'il se recommençait.

Une sueur de honte inonda son front blême
Et le désir lui vint de s'outrager soi-même
En s'entêtant,
Stupidement,
Comme un enfant,
Dans sa folie;
Et devant le soleil dont la gloire accomplie
De cime en cime, à cette heure, se retirait,
On vit le large Hercule envahir les forêts,
En saccager le sol, en arracher les chênes
Et les rouler et les jeter du haut des monts
Dans un fracas confus et de heurts et de bonds
Jusques aux plaines.

L'amas des arbres morts emplit tout le vallon;

Hercule en regardait les fûts saignants et sombres
Faire à leur tour comme une montagne dans l'ombre.
Et les oiseaux dont il avait broyé les nids
Voler éperdûment en criant dans la nuit.

L'heure de cendre et d'or ou l'immensité noire
Allume au firmament ses astres et ses gloires
  Survint tranquillement
Sans que sa large paix calmât l'esprit dément
  Et les rages d'Hercule;
Ses yeux restaient hagards et ses pas somnambules.

Soudain il jalousa le ciel et ses flambeaux;
L'extravagance folle entra dans sa pensée,
Si bien qu'il s'arrêta à cette œuvre insensée
D'allumer troncs, écorce, aubier, feuilles, rameaux
Dont l'énorme splendeur trouant la nuit stellaire
    Irait dire là-haut
Qu'Hercule avait créé un astre sur la terre.

      Rapidement
    Sur l'innombrable entassement
Comme un vol sur la mer d'écumes et de lames
      Passent les flammes;
Une lourde fumée enfle ses noirs remous;
    Et les moussces et les écorces
Et l'emmêlement noir des brindilles retorses
  Craquent ici, là-bas, plus loin, partout.
Le feu monte, grandit, se déchevèle, ondule,
Rugit et se propage et s'étire si fort
  Qu'il frôle, avec ses langues d'or,
      Hercule.
Le héros se raidit, sentant sa chair brûler.
Il se vainc, se retrouve et ne veut reculer;
Même pour étouffer la bête dans son antre,
Comme au temps qu'il était l'âpre justicier,
    Il s'enfonce dans le brasier

Jusques au centre.
Son cœur est ferme et clair et ses pas sont légers;
D'un bond, il est là-haut et domine les flammes.
Il est rapide et fort: il confronte son âme
Avec le plus urgent et le plus fol danger
Et tandis que les feux battent à grands coups d'aile
Autour de son torse velu
Lui, le héros, comprend qu'il ne lui reste plus,
Pour entreprendre enfin une lutte nouvelle,
Qu'à conquérir sur un bûcher brassillant d'or
Sa mort.

Et sa voix chante:
'Vent rapide, nuit étoilée, ombre penchante,
Moment qui vole et fuit, heure qui va venir,
Souvenez-vous, attardez-vous,
Hercule est là qui vous célèbre et va mourir.

La gloire autour de moi vibra comme enflammée:
J'ai, dans mon sang, le sang du Lion de Némée;
L'Hydre, fléau d'Argos que Typhon engendra,
A laissé sa souplesse et sa rage en mes bras;
Je cours de plaine en grève à larges pas sonores
Ayant rythmé mes sauts sur les bonds des centaures;
J'ai déplacé des monts et changé les contours
Que les fleuves d'Ellis traçaient avec leur cours;
A coups de front bruté contre sa large tête
Un taureau recula devant ma force, en Crète;
Stymphale a vu ma flèche ensanglanter ses eaux
Du trépas noir et monstrueux de ses oiseaux;
J'ai ramené vivant du fond des forêts mornes
Le cerf dont l'or et dont l'airain formaient les cornes;
Pour lui voler ses bœufs et tuer Géryon
J'ai battu les pays jusqu'au Septentrion;
J'assujettis sous les coups sourds de mon poing raide
Les chevaux carnassiers du sombre Diomède;

Pendant qu'Atlas s'en fut voler les fruits divins
Le monde entier, sans les ployer, chargea mes reins,
Ceinture ardente et plus belle qu'une couronne,
Je t'ai conquise aux flancs guerriers de l'Amazone
Et j'ai forcé Cerbère et ses têtes en feu
A lever les regards vers l'azur nu des Dieux.'

Soudain un bref sursaut de feux rampants et blêmes
Jaillit du bois tassé sous les pieds du héros
        Et le brûla jusqu'en ses os,
    Mais Hercule chantait quand même:
    'Je sens mes bras, mes mains, mes doigts,
    Mon dos compact, mon col musclé
        Encor peuplés
    Du rythme fou de mes exploits.
Au long des ans nombreux, ma force inassouvie
A si bien dévoré et absorbé la vie
Qu'à cette heure de feu je suis tout ce qui est:
Et l'orage des monts et le vent des forêts
Et le rugissement des bêtes dans les plaines.
J'ai versé dans mon cœur les passions humaines
Comme autant de torrents aux souterrains remous.
Joie et deuil, maux et biens, je vous ai connus tous.
Iole et Mégara, Déjanire et Omphale,
Mon martyre a fleuri sur vos chairs triomphales,
Mais si longue que fut mon errante douleur,
Jamais le sort mortel ne me dompta le cœur.
Je souffre en cet instant et chante dans les flammes;
L'allégresse bondit au tremplin de mon âme;
Je suis heureux, suavage, immense et rayonnant,
            Et maintenant,
Grâce à ce brasier d'or qui m'exalte et me tue,
        Joyeusement je restitue
Aux bois, aux champs, aux flots, aux montagnes, aux mers,
Ce corps en qui s'écroule un morceau d'univers.'

Le bûcher tout entier brûla jusqu'à l'aurore;

Des pans de feux tombaient et montaient tour à tour,
A l'orient du large Œta grandit le jour
Et le héros chantait toujours,
Chantait encore.

Books and Articles Cited by Authors' Names

Alpers, J., *Hercules in bivio* (Göttingen 1912)

Anderson, A. R., 'Heracles and his Successors', *HSCP* 39 (1928) 7–58

Bieber, M., *The History of the Greek and Roman Theater*, 2nd ed., (Princeton, 1961)

Biehlolavek, K., 'Zu den ethischen Werten in Idealtypen der griechischen Heldensage (Herakles und Achilles)', *WS* 70 (1957) 22–43

Brommer, F., *Herakles. Die zwölf Taten des Helden in antiker Kunst und Literatur* (Münster and Cologne, 1953)

—— *Satyrspiele. Bilder griechischer Vasen*, 2nd ed., (Berlin, 1959)

Bush, D., *Mythology and the Renaissance Tradition in English Poetry* (Minneapolis and London, 1932)

—— *Mythology and the Romantic Tradition in English Poetry* (Cambridge, Mass., 1937)

Butler, E. M., *The Tyranny of Greece over Germany* (Cambridge, 1935)

Conradie, P. J. *Herakles in die Griekse Tragedie* (Groningen, 1958)

Des Essarts, E., *Du type d'Hercule dans la littérature grecque depuis les origines jusqu'au siècle des Antonins* (Thèse, Paris, 1871)

Dunseath, T. K., *Spenser's Allegory of Justice in Book Five of the Faerie Queene* (Princeton, 1968)

Ehrenberg, V., 'Tragic Herakles', *Aspects of the Ancient World* (Oxford, 1946) 144–57

Farnell, L. R., *Greek Hero Cults and Ideas of Immortality* (Oxford, 1921)

Flacelière, R., and Devambez, F., *Héraclès. Images et récits* (Paris, 1966)

Fritz, Kurt von, 'Euripides' Alkestis und ihre modernen Nachahmer und Kritiker', *Antike und Moderne Tragödie* (Berlin, 1962) 256–321

Gaeta, F., 'L'avventura di Ercole', *Rinascimento* 5 (1954) 227–60

Gruppe, O., 'Herakles', *RE Suppl.* 3 (1918) 910–1121

Heinemann, K., *Die tragischen Gestalten der Griechen in der Weltliteratur* (Leipzig, 1920)

Highet, G., *The Classical Tradition* (New York, 1957)

Höistad, R., *Cynic Hero and Cynic King* (Lund, 1948)

Hötzer, U., *Die Gestalt des Herakles in Hölderlins Dichtung. Freiheit und Bindung* (Stuttgart, 1962)

Huxley, H. H., 'The Labours of Hercules', *Proceedings of the Leeds Liter. and Philosoph. Society, Liter. and Philosoph. Section* 7. 1 (1952) 20–30

Jung, M.-R., *Hercule dans la littérature française du XVIe siècle. De l'Hercule courtois à l'Hercule baroque* (Geneva, 1966)

Panofsky, E., *Hercules am Scheidewege*. Studien der Bibliothek Warburg 18 (Leipzig, 1930)

Pohlenz, M., *Die griechische Tragödie* (Berlin, 1954)

Preller-Robert, *Die griechische Heldensage* 2. 2 (Dublin and Zurich, 1967) 422–675

Schmid, W., and Stählin, O., *Geschichte der griechischen Literatur* (Munich, various dates)

Schweitzer, B., *Herakles* (Tübingen, 1922)

Seznec, J., *The Survival of the Pagan Gods*, trans. by B. F. Sessions (New York, 1953)

Simon, M., *Hercule et le Christianisme* (Paris, 1955)

Soellner, R., 'The Madness of Herakles and the Elizabethans', *Comp. Lit.* 10 (1958) 309–24

Stanford, W. B., *The Ulysses Theme*, 2nd ed. (Oxford and Ann Arbor, 1968)

Stoessl, F., *Der Tod des Herakles* (Zurich, 1945)

Waith, E. M. *The Herculean Hero in Marlowe, Chapman, Shakespeare, and Dryden* (New York, 1962)

Wilamowitz-Möllendorff, U. von, *Euripides. Herakles*, 2nd ed. (Berlin, 1895)

Wolk, A. W., *Hercules and the Faerie Queene* (Univ. Microfilms, Ann Arbor, 1966 = Univ. Nebraska Diss., 1965)

General Index

General Index

(Less important references are not cited. Roman numerals followed by arabic figures refer to chapters and footnotes)